Thank you!

KOYOHARU GOTOUGE

I'm Gotouge. Here's volume 10. Thank you very much to everyone who cheers for me and helps out. I'm grateful from the bottom of my heart for the many letters and presents. You should absolutely be proud to say, "I'm the one who helped this artist rise up!" It might be fun to snort triumphantly and thrust out your chest too. For the readers, I will continue to raise my combat abilities to attack and defend at will, and work hard!

DEMON SLAYER:
KIMETSU NO YAIBA
VOLUME 10
Shonen Jump Edition

Story and Art by
KOYOHARU GOTOUGE

TRANSLATION John Werry
ENGLISH ADAPTATION Stan!
TOUCH-UP ART & LETTERING John Hunt
DESIGN Jimmy Presler
EDITOR Mike Montesa

Printed in Italy

Published by VIZ Media, LLC
P.O. Box 77010
San Francisco, CA 94107

10 9
First printing, January 2020
Ninth printing, February 2022

ratings.viz.com
RATED T TEEN

PARENTAL ADVISORY
DEMON SLAYER: KIMETSU NO YAIBA is rated T for Teen and recommended for ages 13 and up. This volume contains realistic and fantasy violence.

VIZ MEDIA
viz.com

SHONEN JUMP

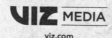

DEMON SLAYER
KIMETSU NO YAIBA

10

HUMAN
AND DEMON

KOYOHARU
GOTOUGE

CHARACTERS

TANJIRO KAMADO

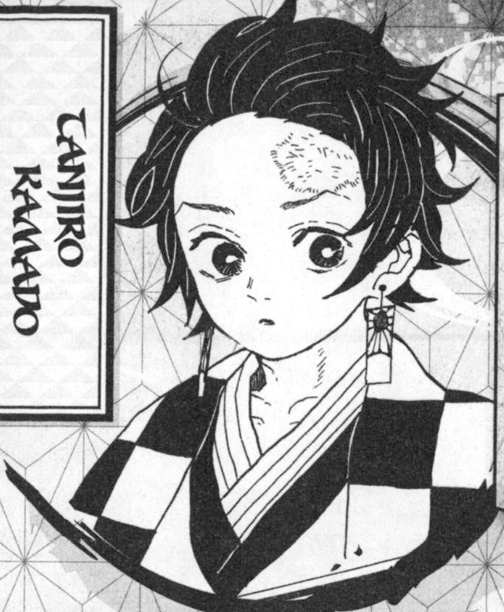

A kind boy who saved his sister and now aims to avenge his family. He can smell the scent of demons and an opponent's weakness.

NEZUKO KAMADO

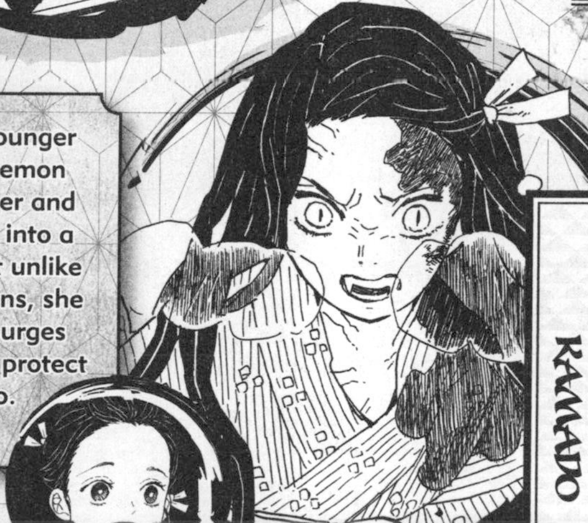

Tanjiro's younger sister. A demon attacked her and turned her into a demon. But unlike other demons, she fights her urges and tries to protect Tanjiro.

STORY

In Taisho-era Japan, young Tanjiro makes a living selling charcoal. One day, demons kill his family and turn his younger sister Nezuko into a demon. Tanjiro and Nezuko set out to find a way to return Nezuko to human form and defeat Kibutsuji, the demon who killed their family!

After joining the Demon Slayer Corps, Tanjiro meets Tamayo and Yushiro—demons who oppose Kibutsuji—who provide a clue to how Nezuko may be turned back into a human. On a new mission, Tanjiro boards a steam train and joins up with Rengoku, the Flame Hashira. A lower-rank demon attacks the train, but they are able to protect the passengers and defeat the demon, but Rengoku is killed in the process.
To overcome Rengoku's death, Tanjiro and others take on a new mission to investigate reports of a demon in the Hanamachi entertainment district in town.

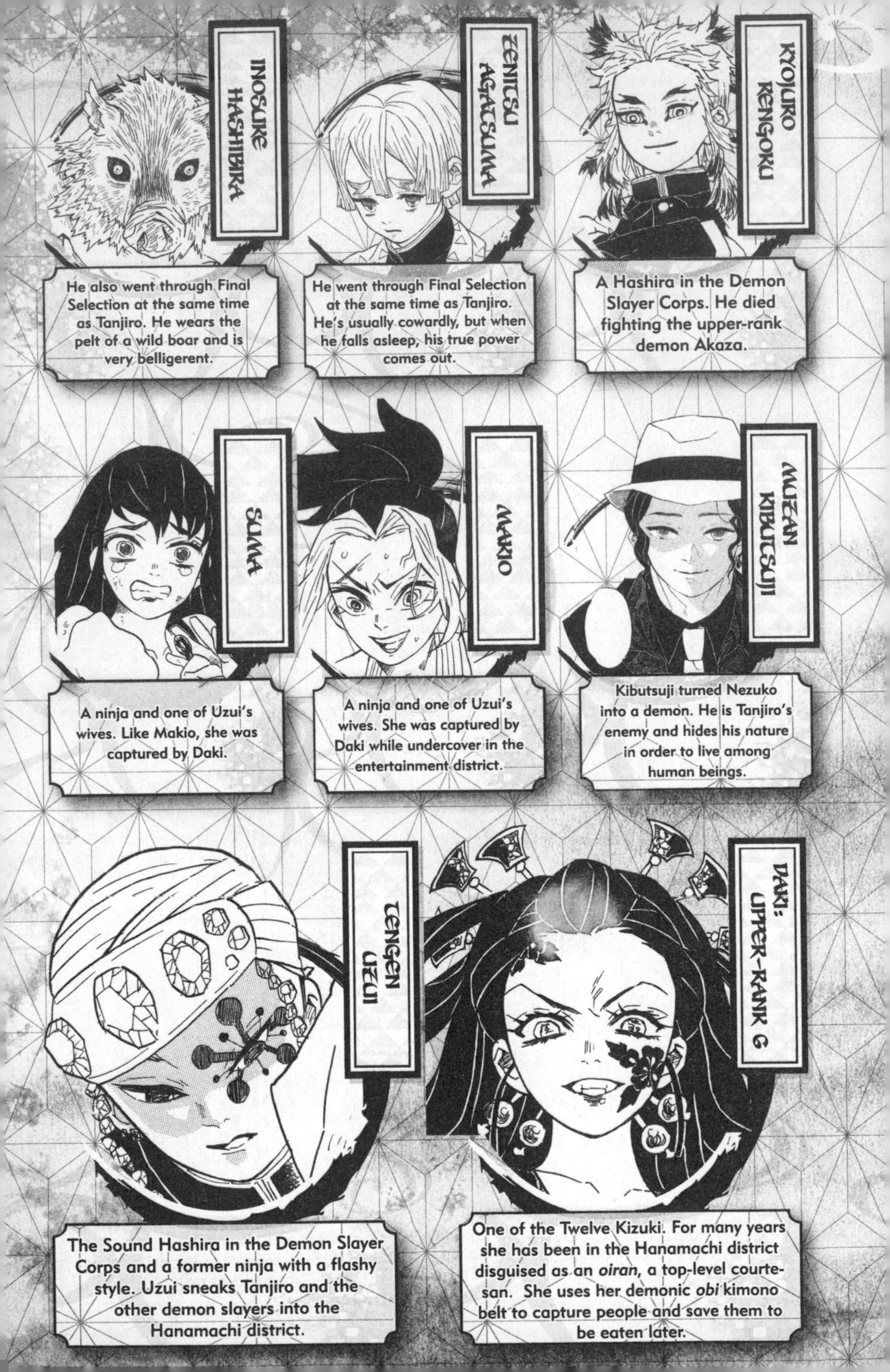
KYOJURO RENGOKU
A Hashira in the Demon Slayer Corps. He died fighting the upper-rank demon Akaza.
ZENITSU AGATSUMA
He went through Final Selection at the same time as Tanjiro. He's usually cowardly, but when he falls asleep, his true power comes out.
INOSUKE HASHIBIRA
He also went through Final Selection at the same time as Tanjiro. He wears the pelt of a wild boar and is very belligerent.
MUZAN KIBUTSUJI
Kibutsuji turned Nezuko into a demon. He is Tanjiro's enemy and hides his nature in order to live among human beings.
MAKIO
A ninja and one of Uzui's wives. She was captured by Daki while undercover in the entertainment district.
SUMA
A ninja and one of Uzui's wives. Like Makio, she was captured by Daki.
DAKI: UPPER-RANK 6
One of the Twelve Kizuki. For many years she has been in the Hanamachi district disguised as an *oiran*, a top-level courtesan. She uses her demonic *obi* kimono belt to capture people and save them to be eaten later.
TENGEN UZUI
The Sound Hashira in the Demon Slayer Corps and a former ninja with a flashy style. Uzui sneaks Tanjiro and the other demon slayers into the Hanamachi district.

CONTENTS

DEMON SLAYER
KIMETSU NO YAIBA

10

HUMAN
AND
DEMON

CHAPTER 80: VALUE

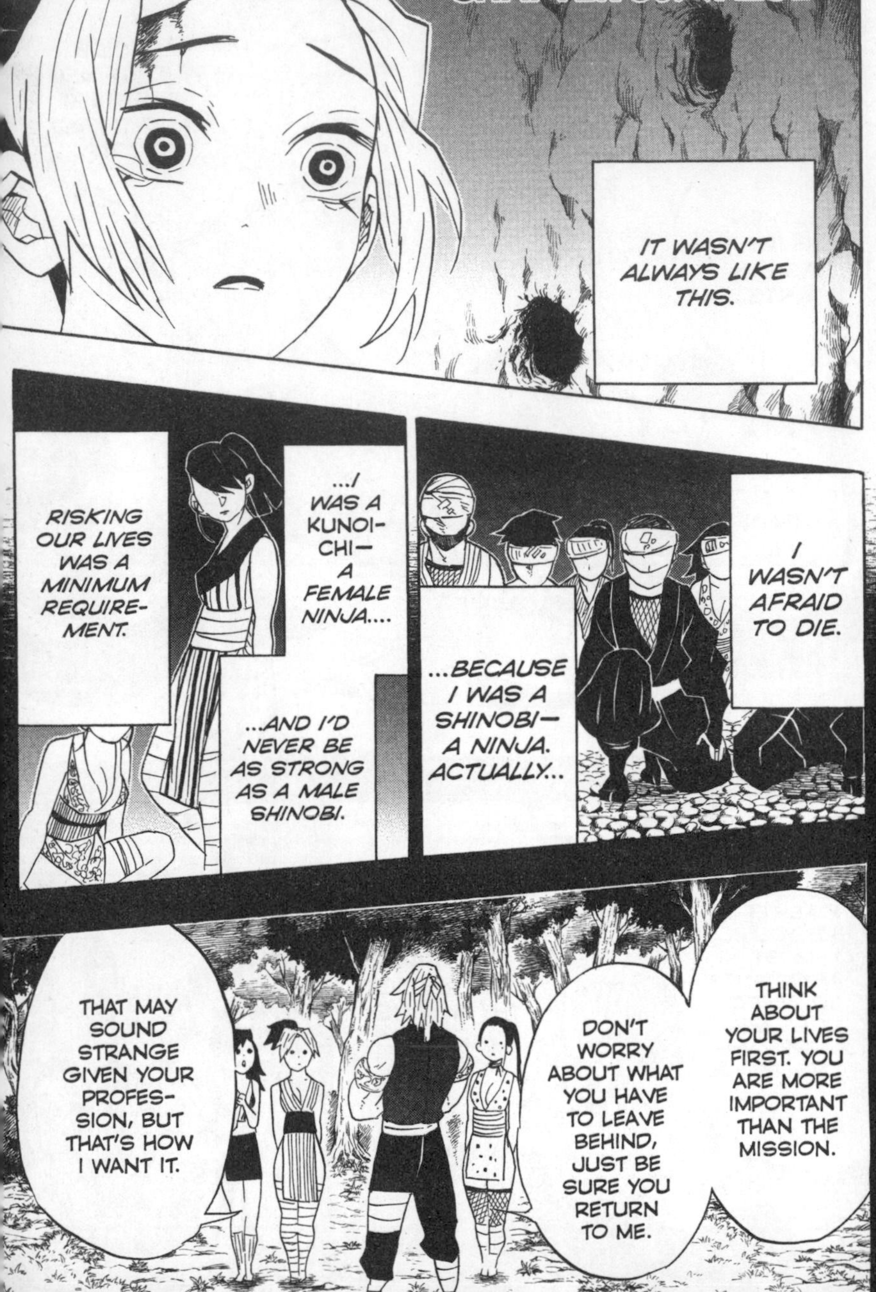

IT WASN'T ALWAYS LIKE THIS.
I WASN'T AFRAID TO DIE.
...BECAUSE I WAS A SHINOBI— A NINJA. ACTUALLY...
...I WAS A KUNOI-CHI— A FEMALE NINJA....
RISKING OUR LIVES WAS A MINIMUM REQUIRE-MENT.
...AND I'D NEVER BE AS STRONG AS A MALE SHINOBI.
THINK ABOUT YOUR LIVES FIRST. YOU ARE MORE IMPORTANT THAN THE MISSION.
DON'T WORRY ABOUT WHAT YOU HAVE TO LEAVE BEHIND, JUST BE SURE YOU RETURN TO ME.
THAT MAY SOUND STRANGE GIVEN YOUR PROFES-SION, BUT THAT'S HOW I WANT IT.

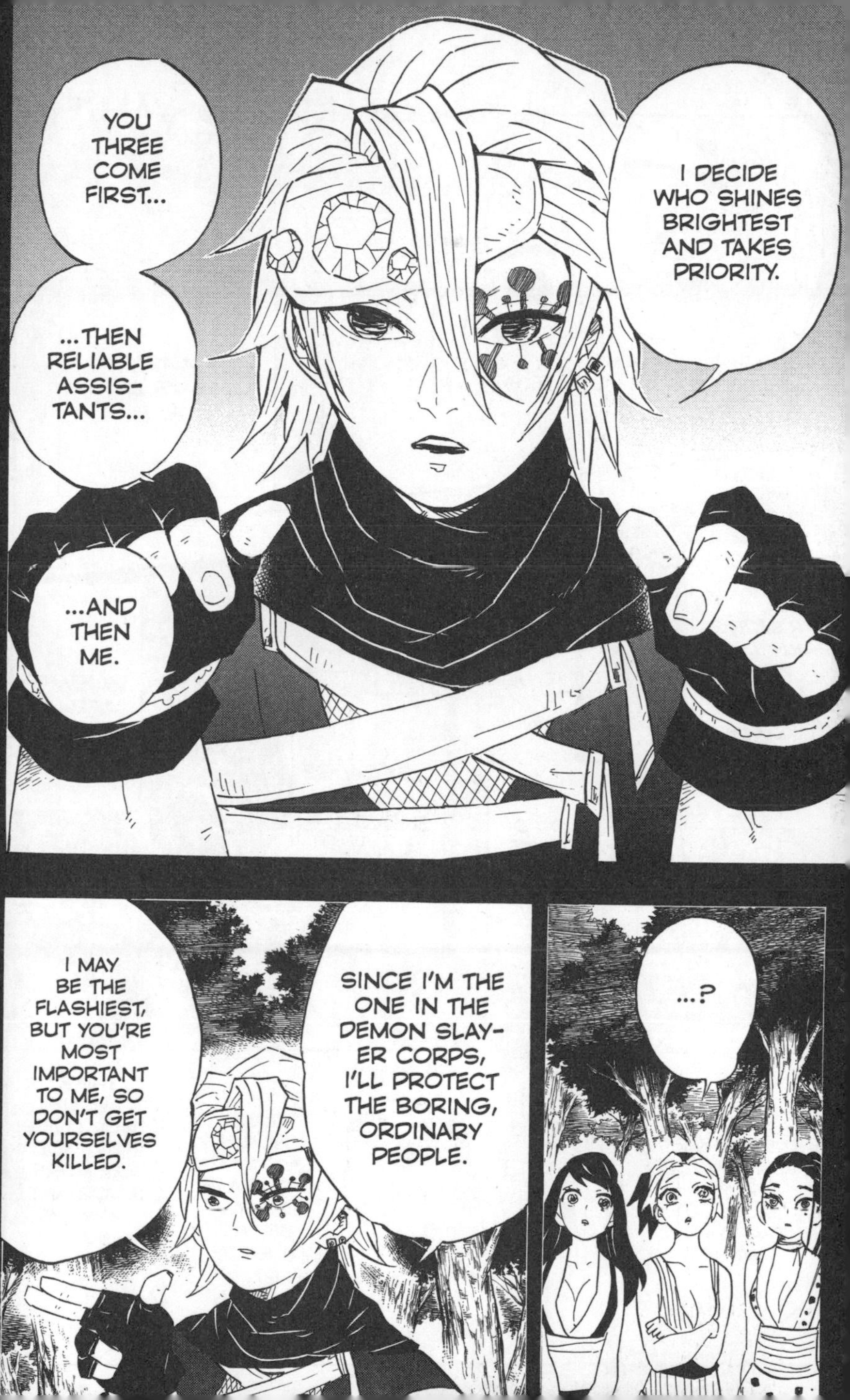
I DECIDE WHO SHINES BRIGHTEST AND TAKES PRIORITY.
YOU THREE COME FIRST...
...THEN RELIABLE ASSIS-TANTS...
...AND THEN ME.
...?
SINCE I'M THE ONE IN THE DEMON SLAY-ER CORPS, I'LL PROTECT THE BORING, ORDINARY PEOPLE.
I MAY BE THE FLASHIEST, BUT YOU'RE MOST IMPORTANT TO ME, SO DON'T GET YOURSELVES KILLED.

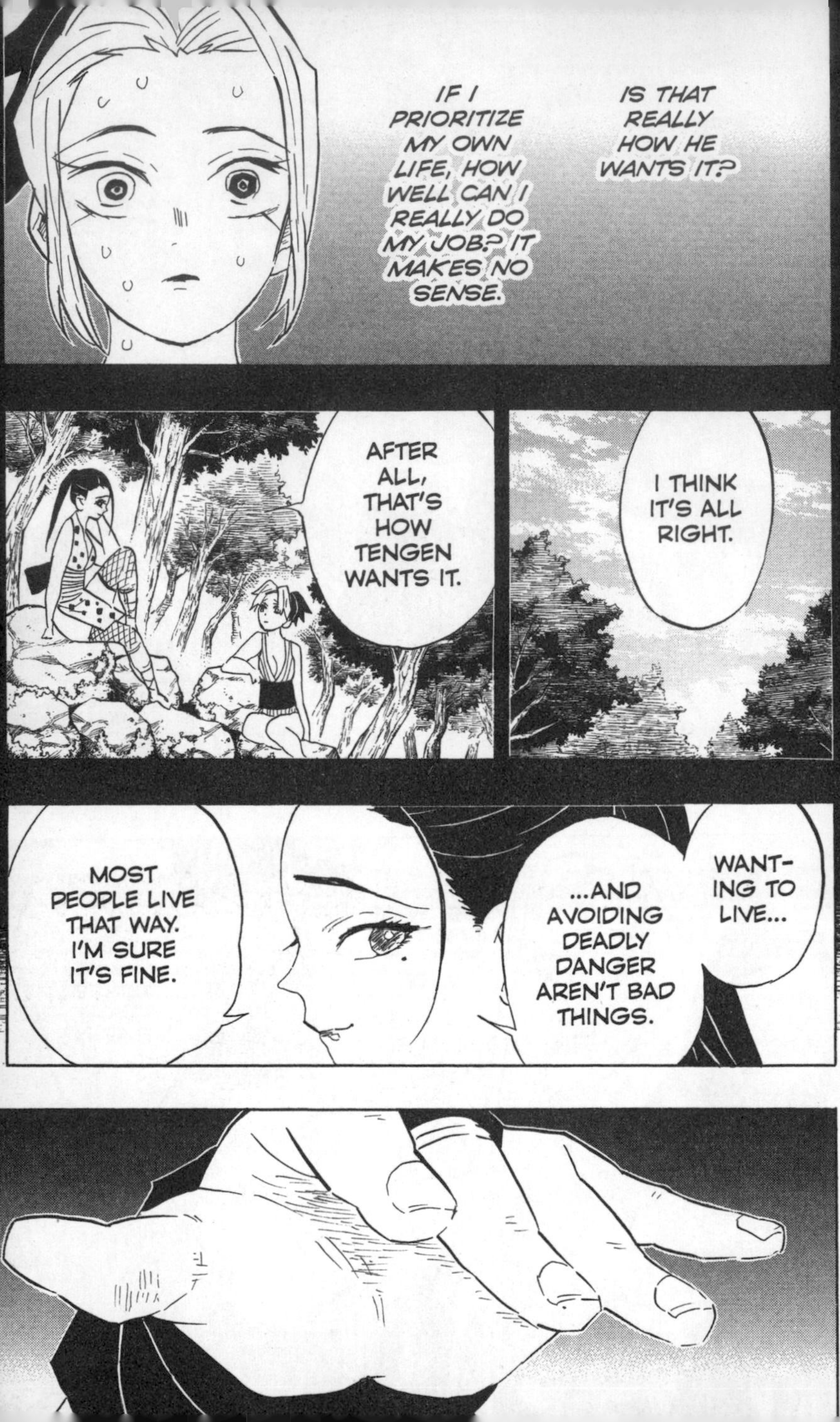
IS THAT REALLY HOW HE WANTS IT?
IF I PRIORITIZE MY OWN LIFE, HOW WELL CAN I REALLY DO MY JOB? IT MAKES NO SENSE.
I THINK IT'S ALL RIGHT.
AFTER ALL, THAT'S HOW TENGEN WANTS IT.
WANT-ING TO LIVE...
...AND AVOIDING DEADLY DANGER AREN'T BAD THINGS.
MOST PEOPLE LIVE THAT WAY. I'M SURE IT'S FINE.

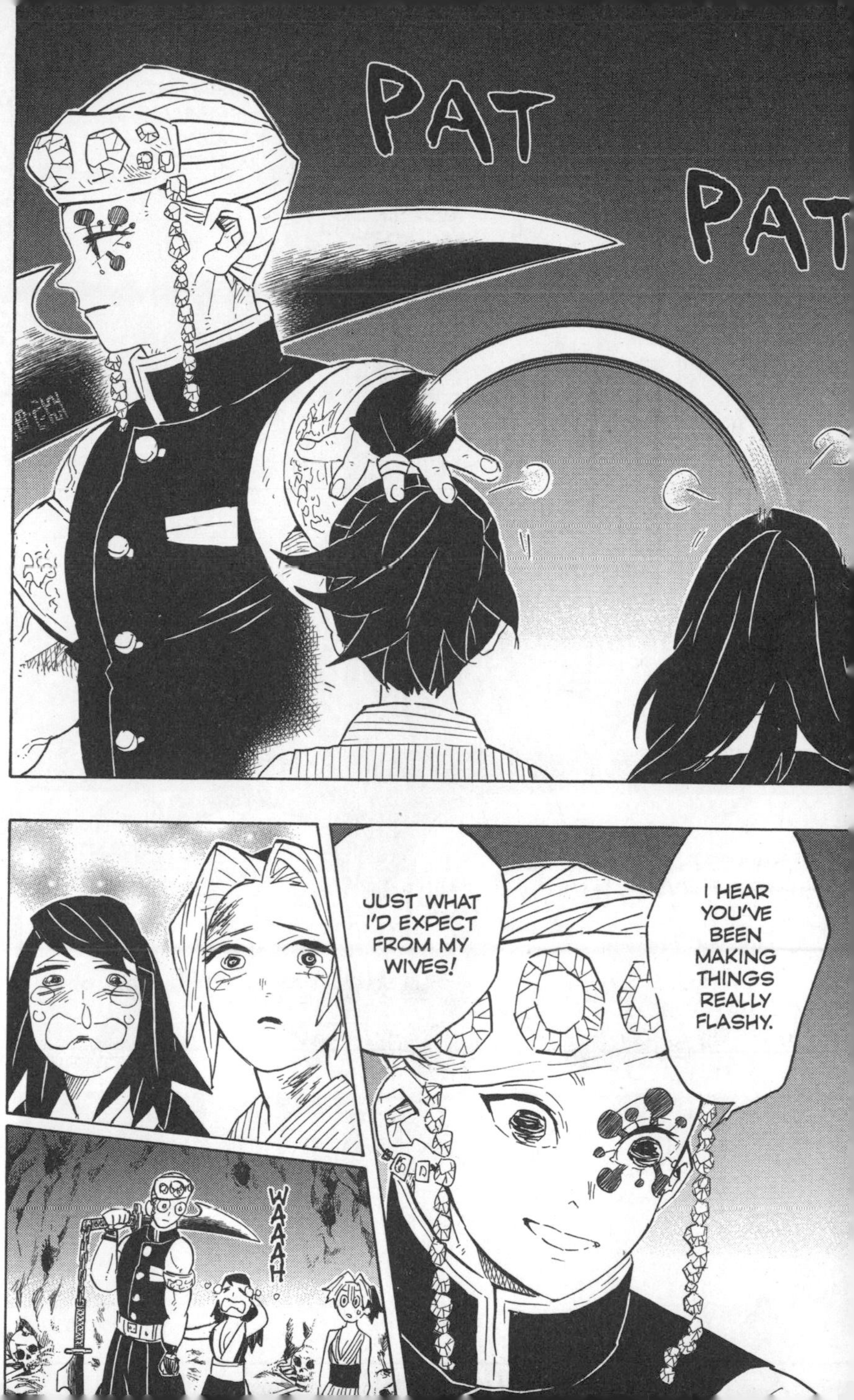
PAT
PAT
I HEAR YOU'VE BEEN MAKING THINGS REALLY FLASHY.
JUST WHAT I'D EXPECT FROM MY WIVES!
WAAAH

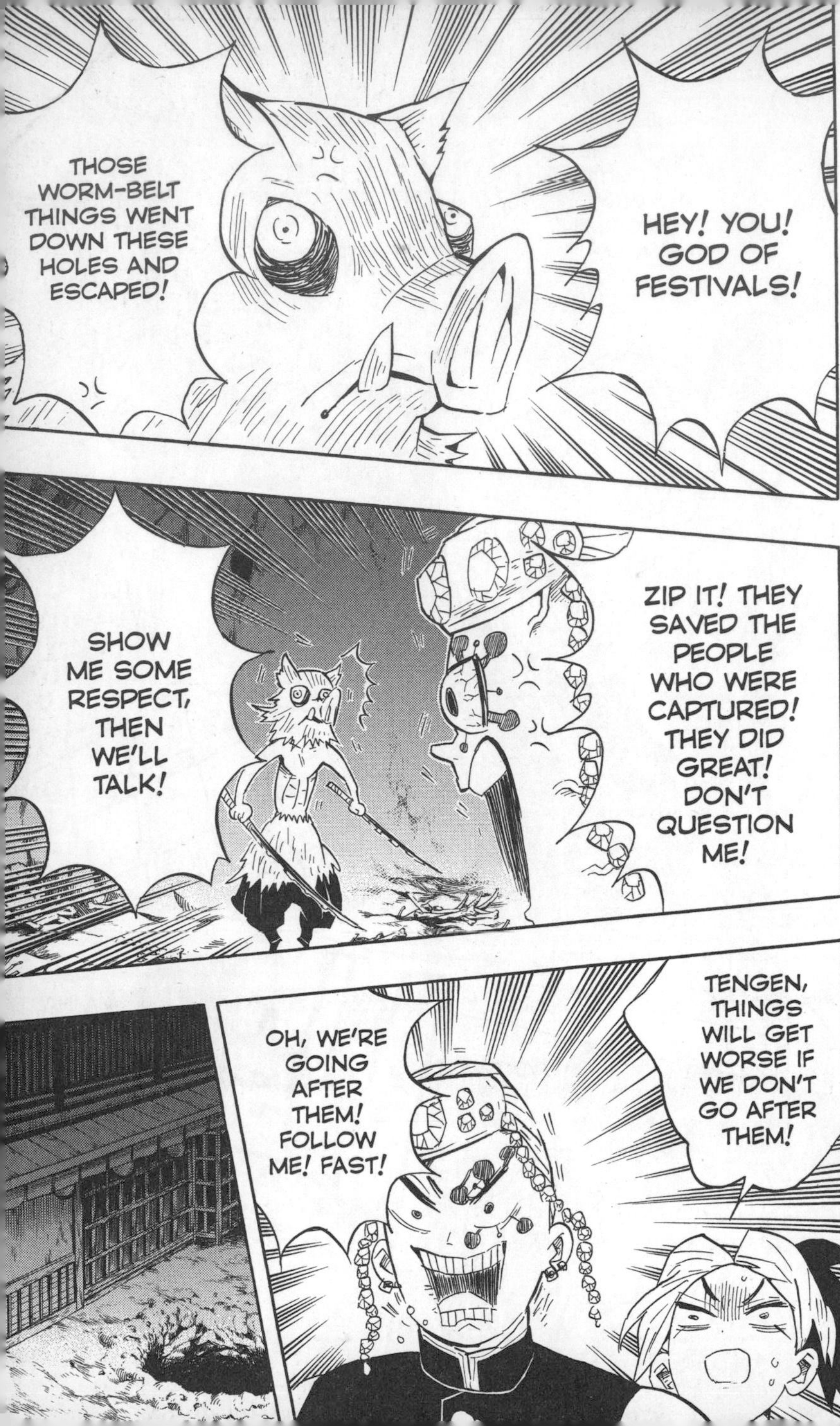
HEY! YOU! GOD OF FESTIVALS!
THOSE WORM-BELT THINGS WENT DOWN THESE HOLES AND ESCAPED!
ZIP IT! THEY SAVED THE PEOPLE WHO WERE CAPTURED! THEY DID GREAT! DON'T QUESTION ME!
SHOW ME SOME RESPECT, THEN WE'LL TALK!
TENGEN, THINGS WILL GET WORSE IF WE DON'T GO AFTER THEM!
OH, WE'RE GOING AFTER THEM! FOLLOW ME! FAST!

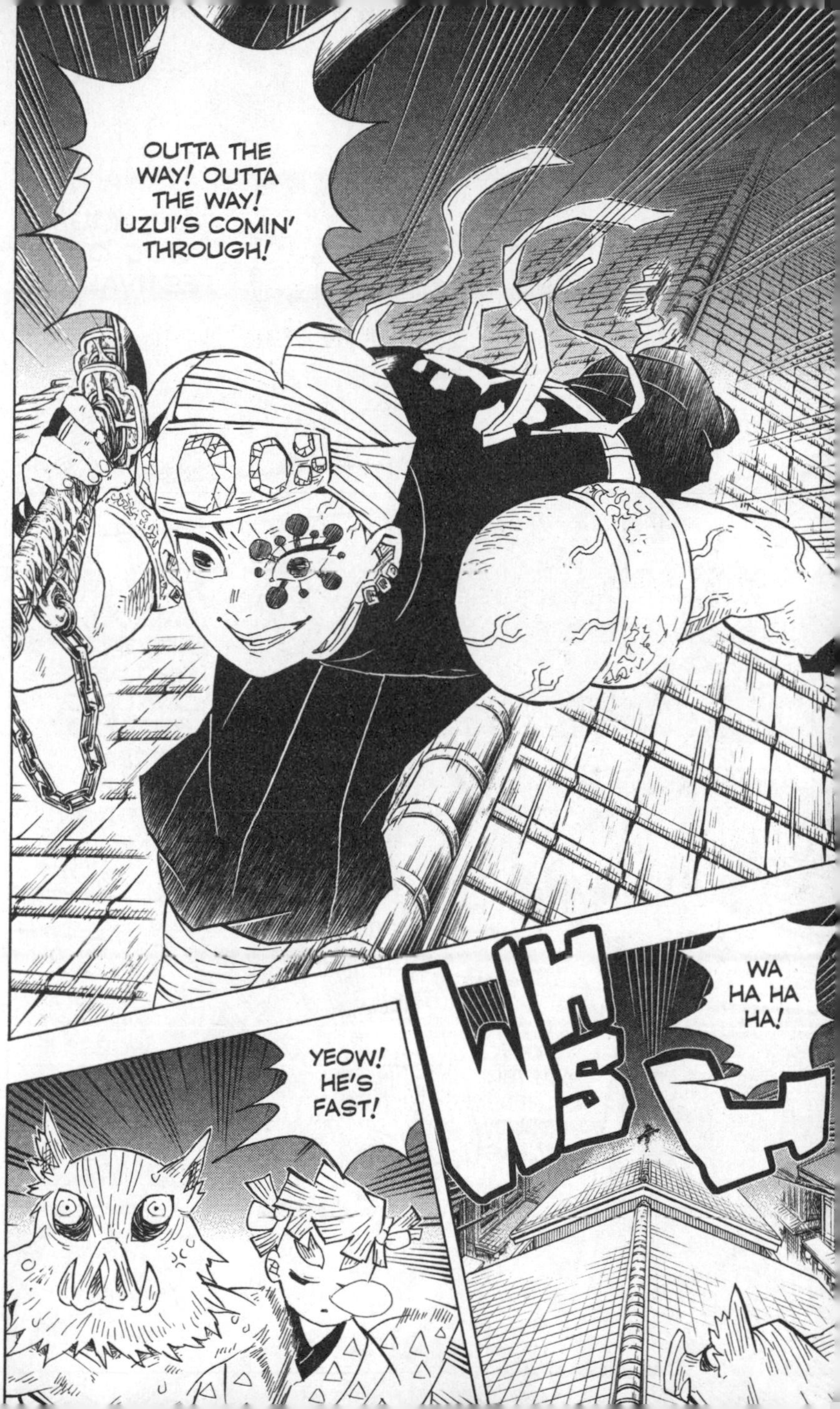
OUTTA THE WAY! OUTTA THE WAY! UZUI'S COMIN' THROUGH!
WA HA HA HA!
YEOW! HE'S FAST!

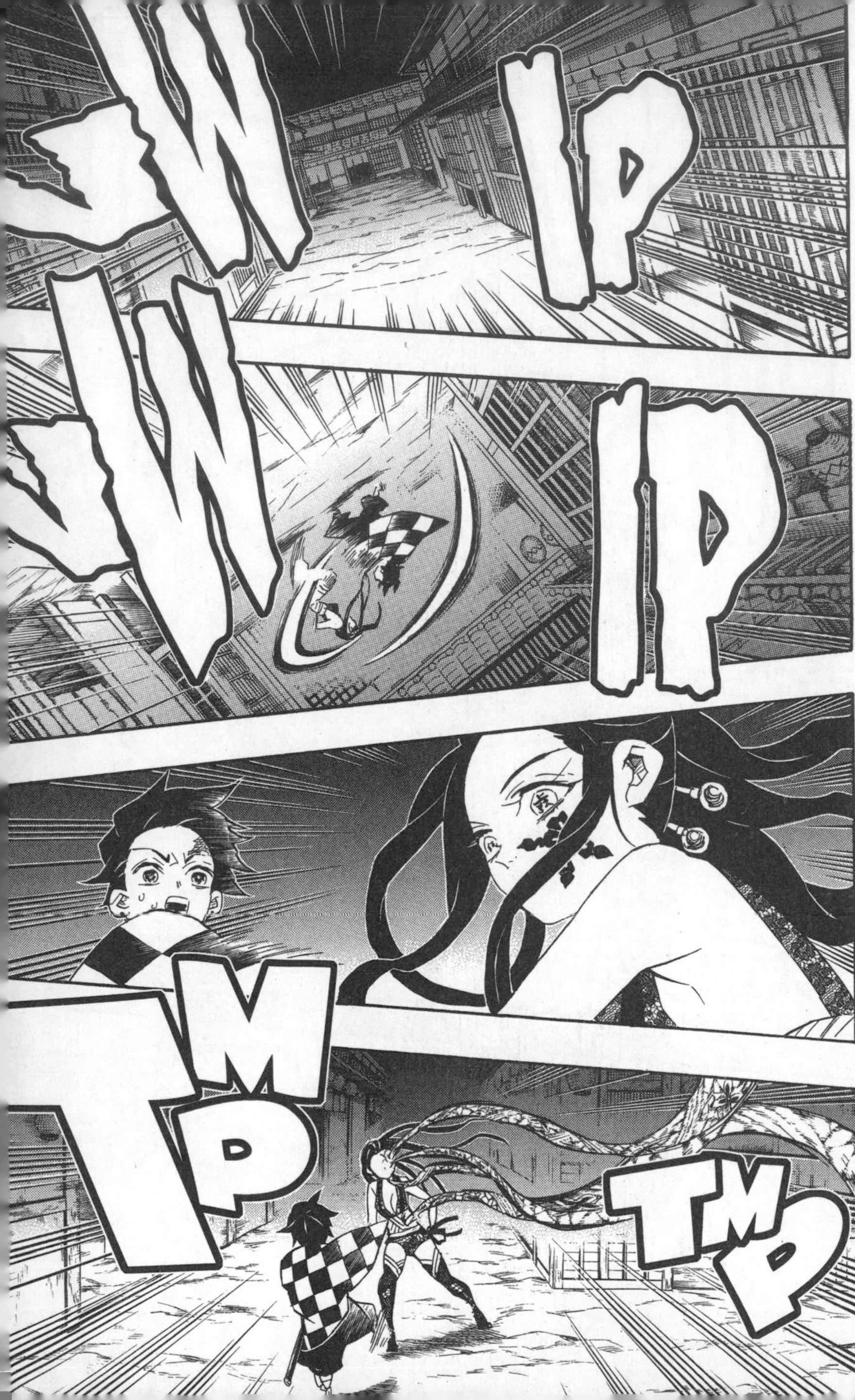
SWIP
SWIP
TMP
TMP

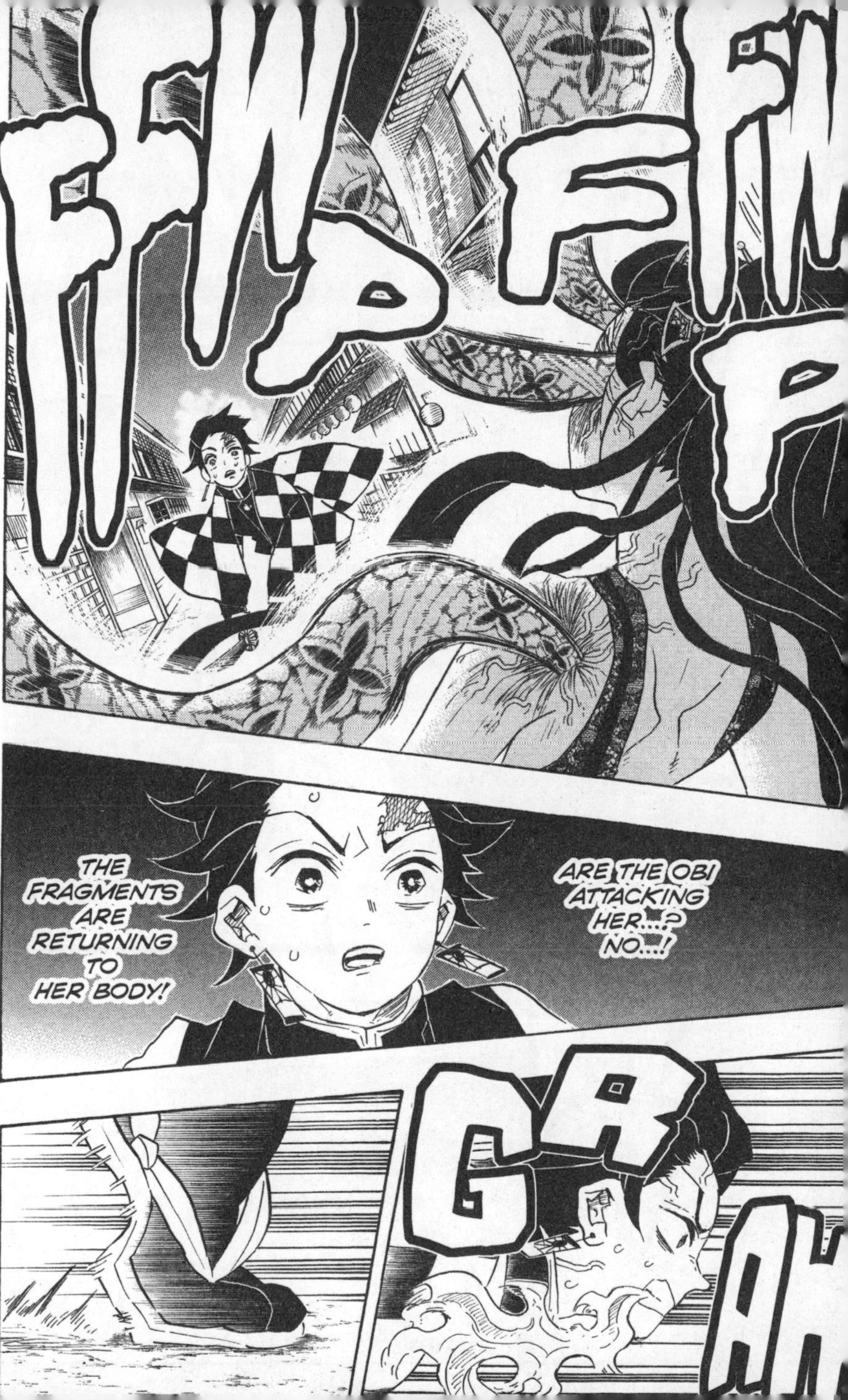
FWP
FWP
ARE THE OBI ATTACKING HER...? NO...!
THE FRAGMENTS ARE RETURNING TO HER BODY!
GR
AH

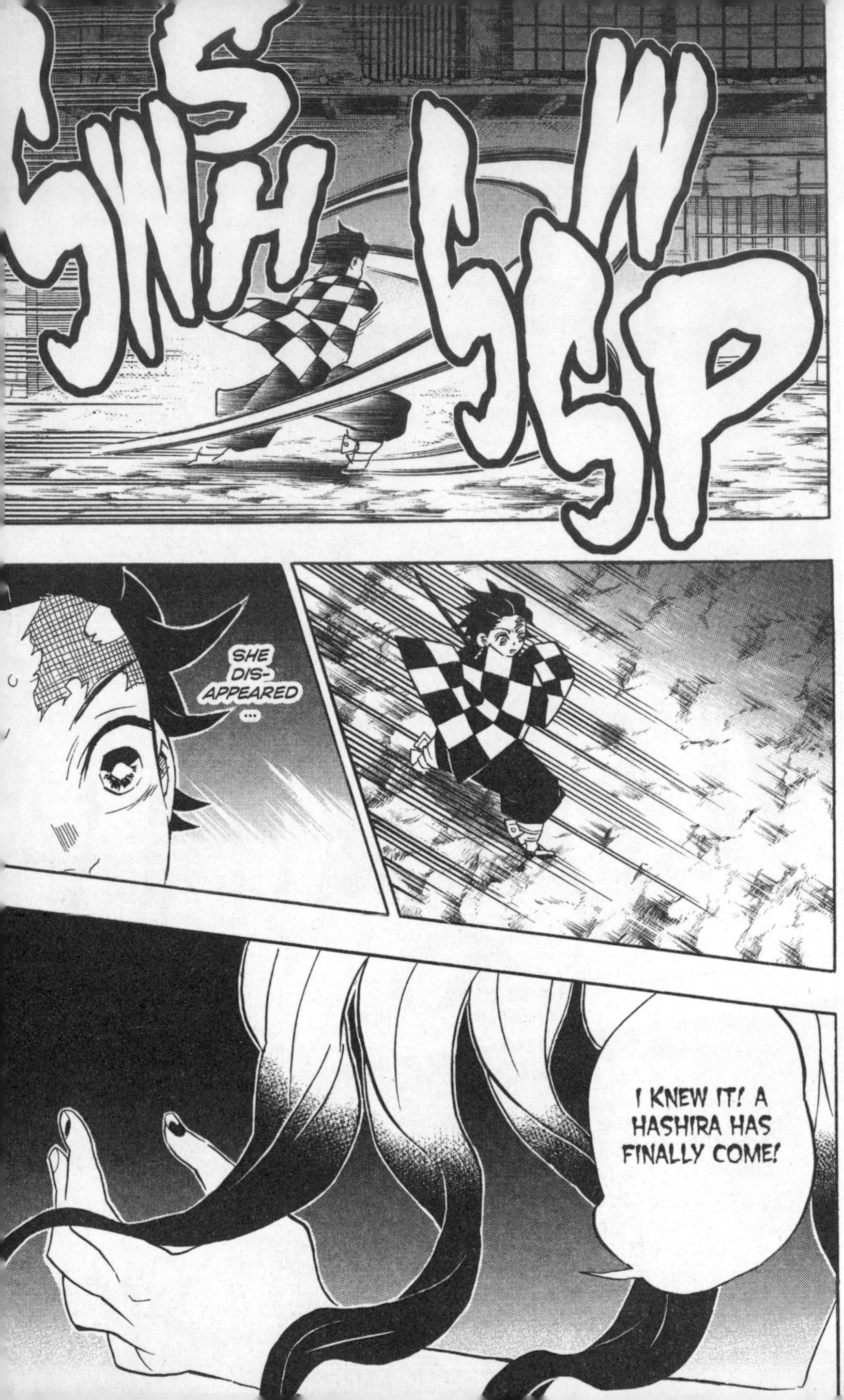
SHE DIS-APPEARED ...
I KNEW IT! A HASHIRA HAS FINALLY COME!

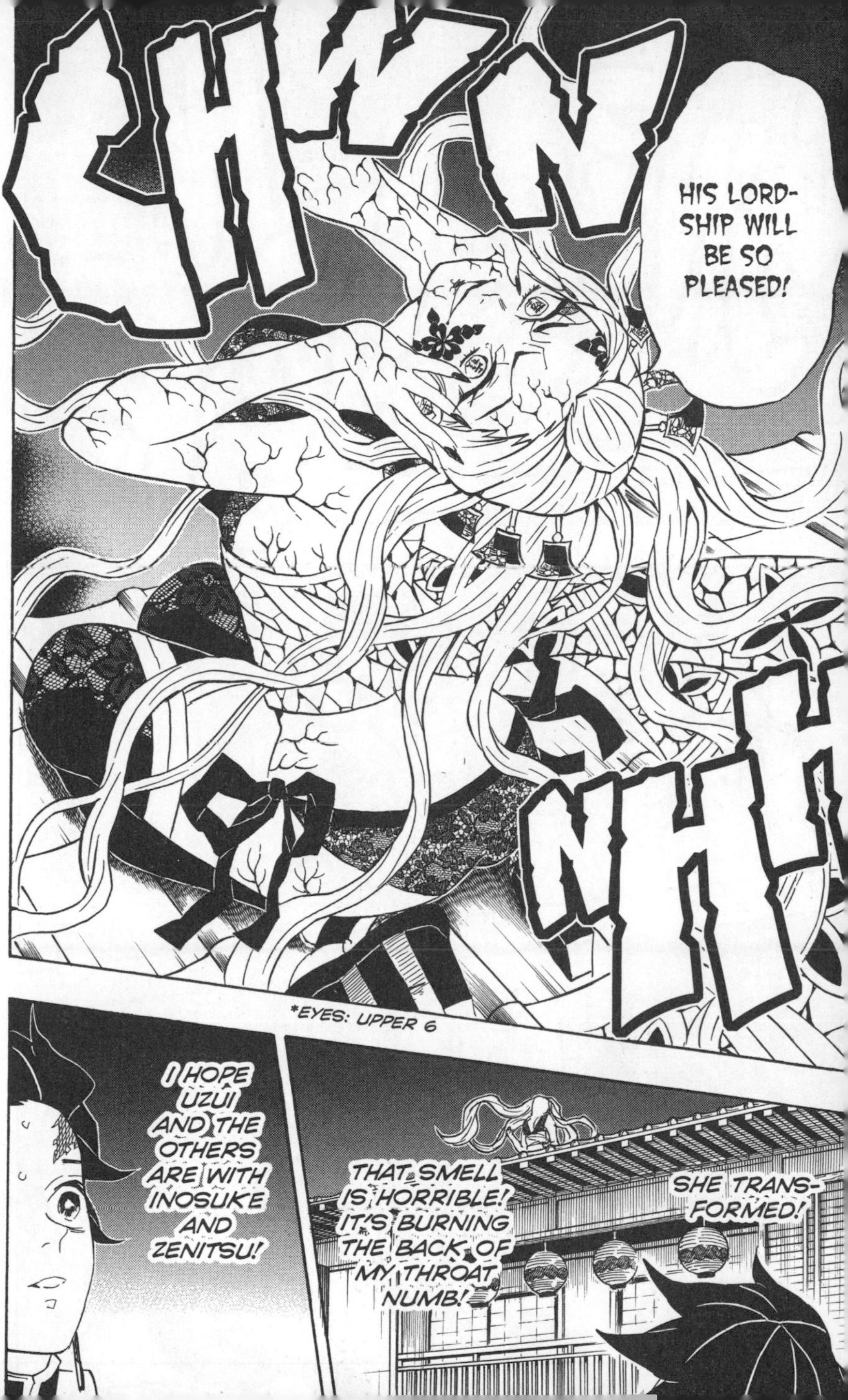
HIS LORD-SHIP WILL BE SO PLEASED!
*EYES: UPPER 6
SHE TRANS-FORMED!
THAT SMELL IS HORRIBLE! IT'S BURNING THE BACK OF MY THROAT NUMB!
I HOPE UZUI AND THE OTHERS ARE WITH INOSUKE AND ZENITSU!

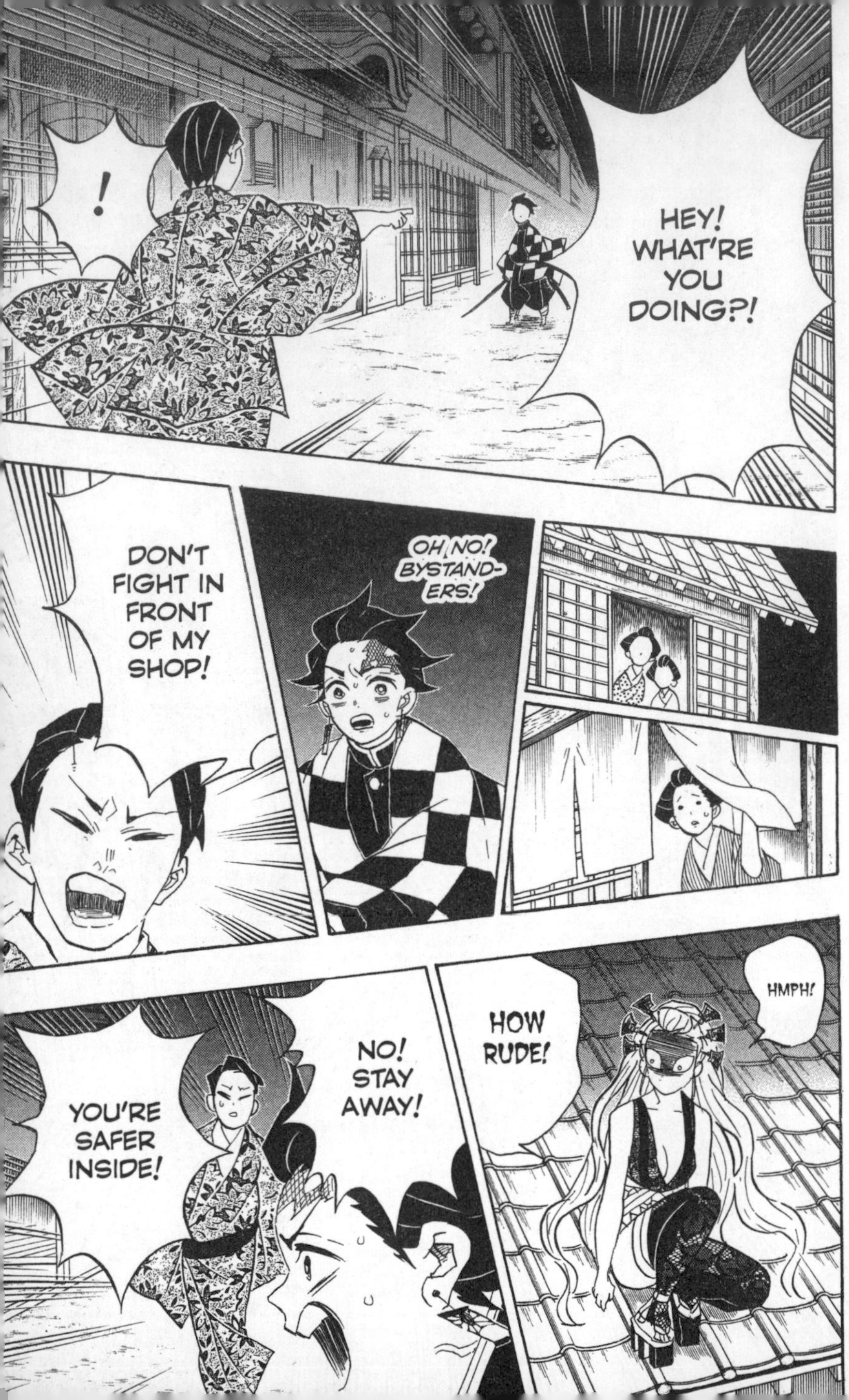
HEY! WHAT'RE YOU DOING?!
!
OH NO! BYSTANDERS!
DON'T FIGHT IN FRONT OF MY SHOP!
HMPH!
HOW RUDE!
NO! STAY AWAY!
YOU'RE SAFER INSIDE!

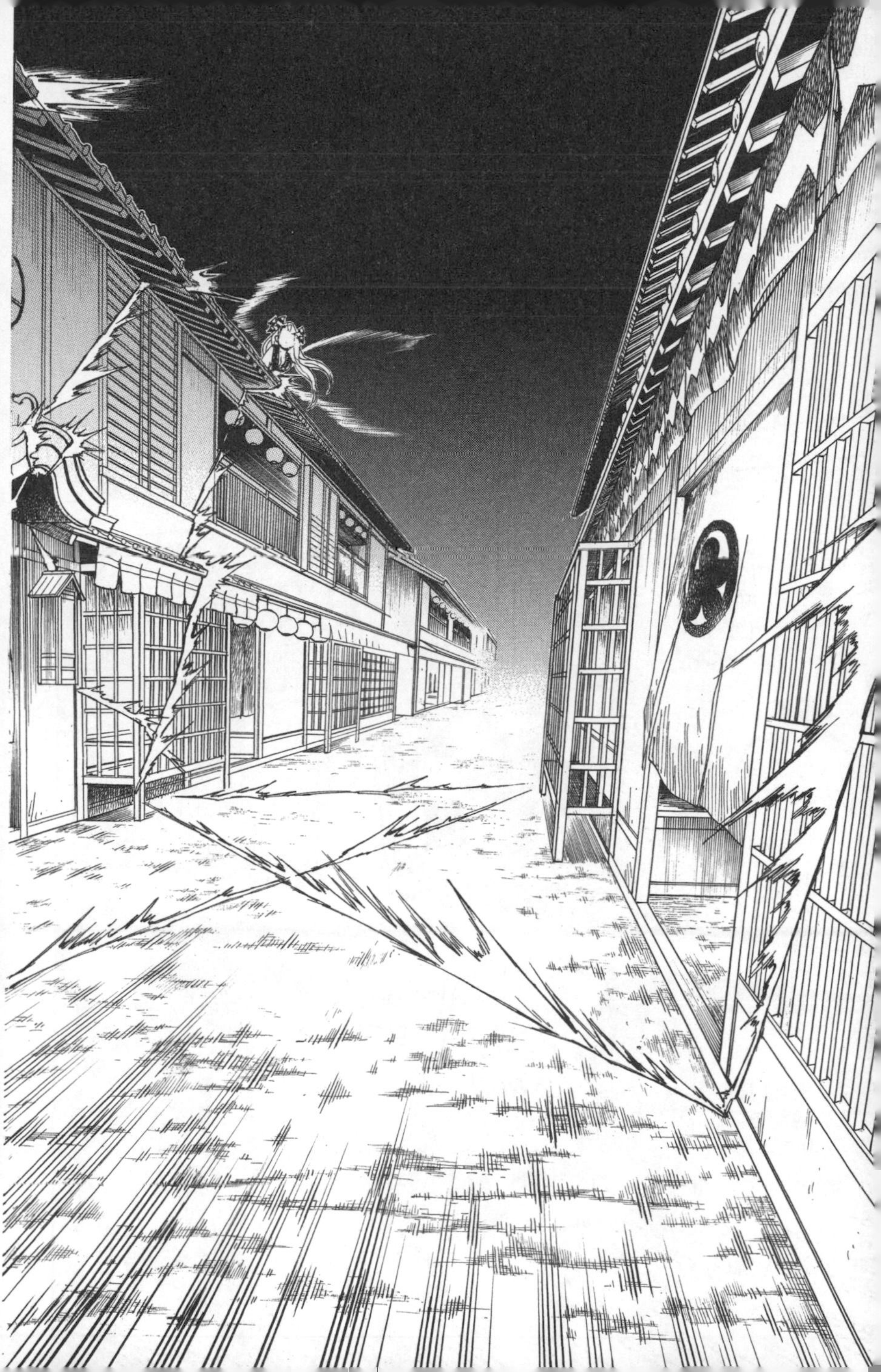

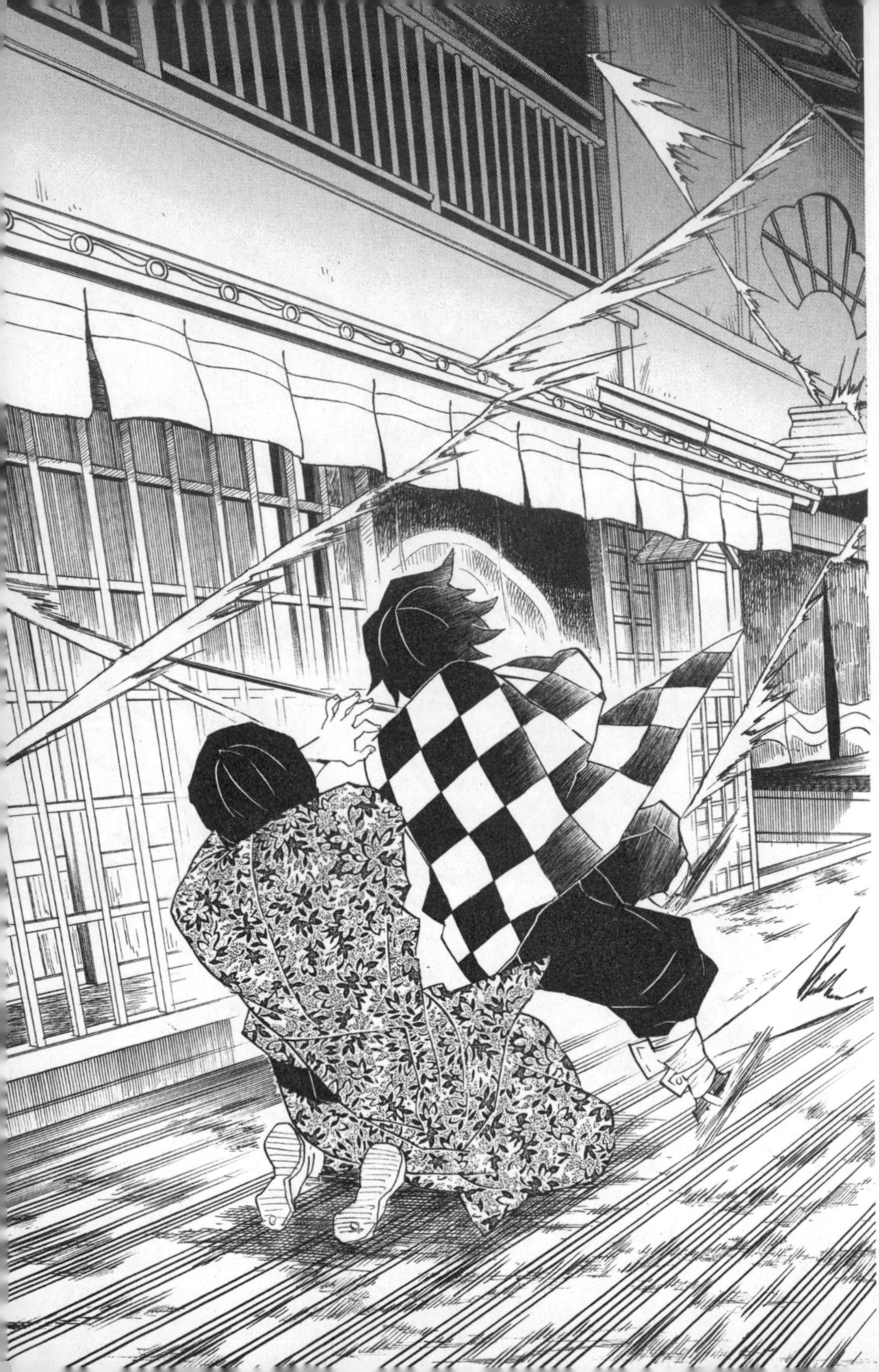

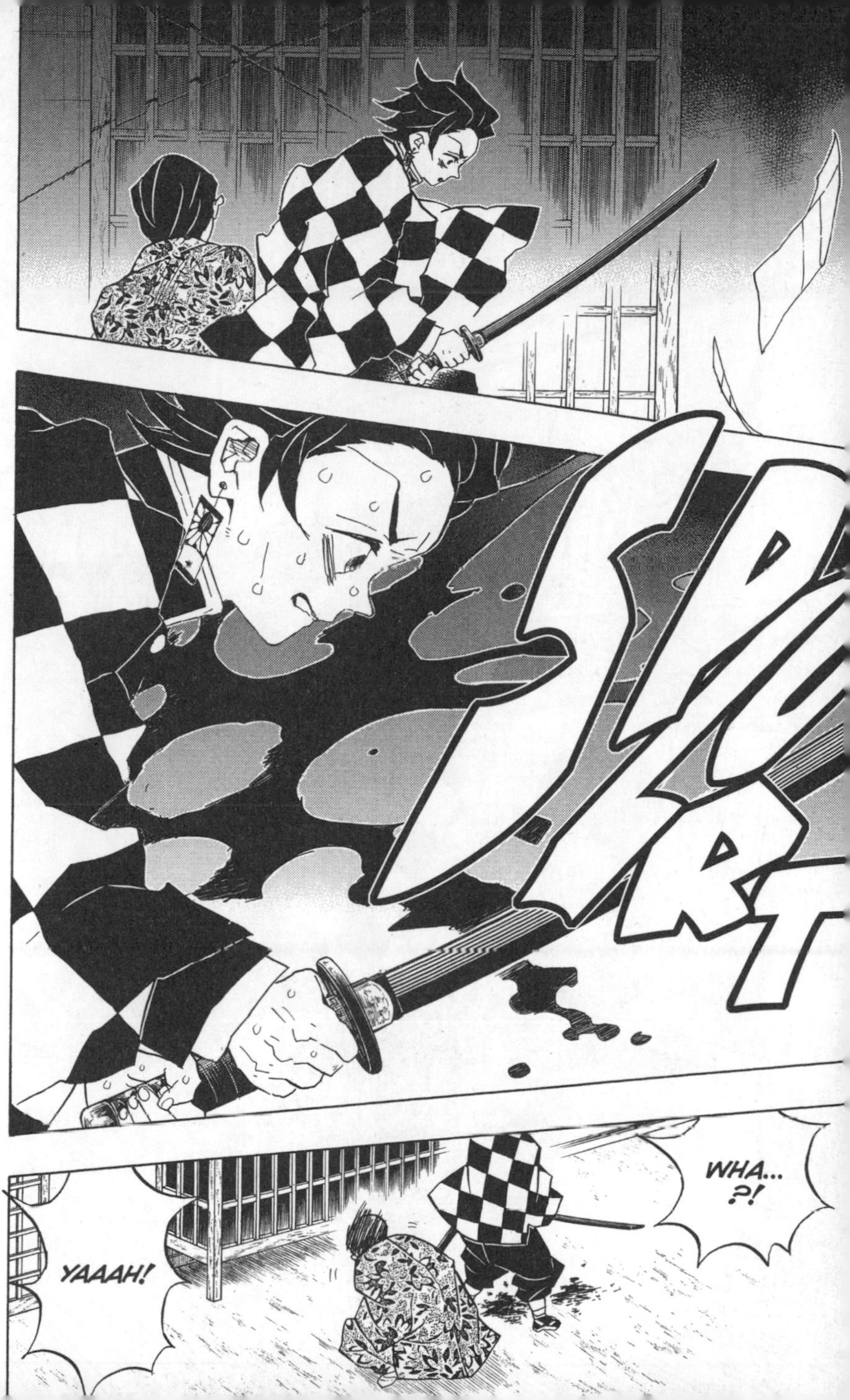
WHA... ?!
YAAAH!

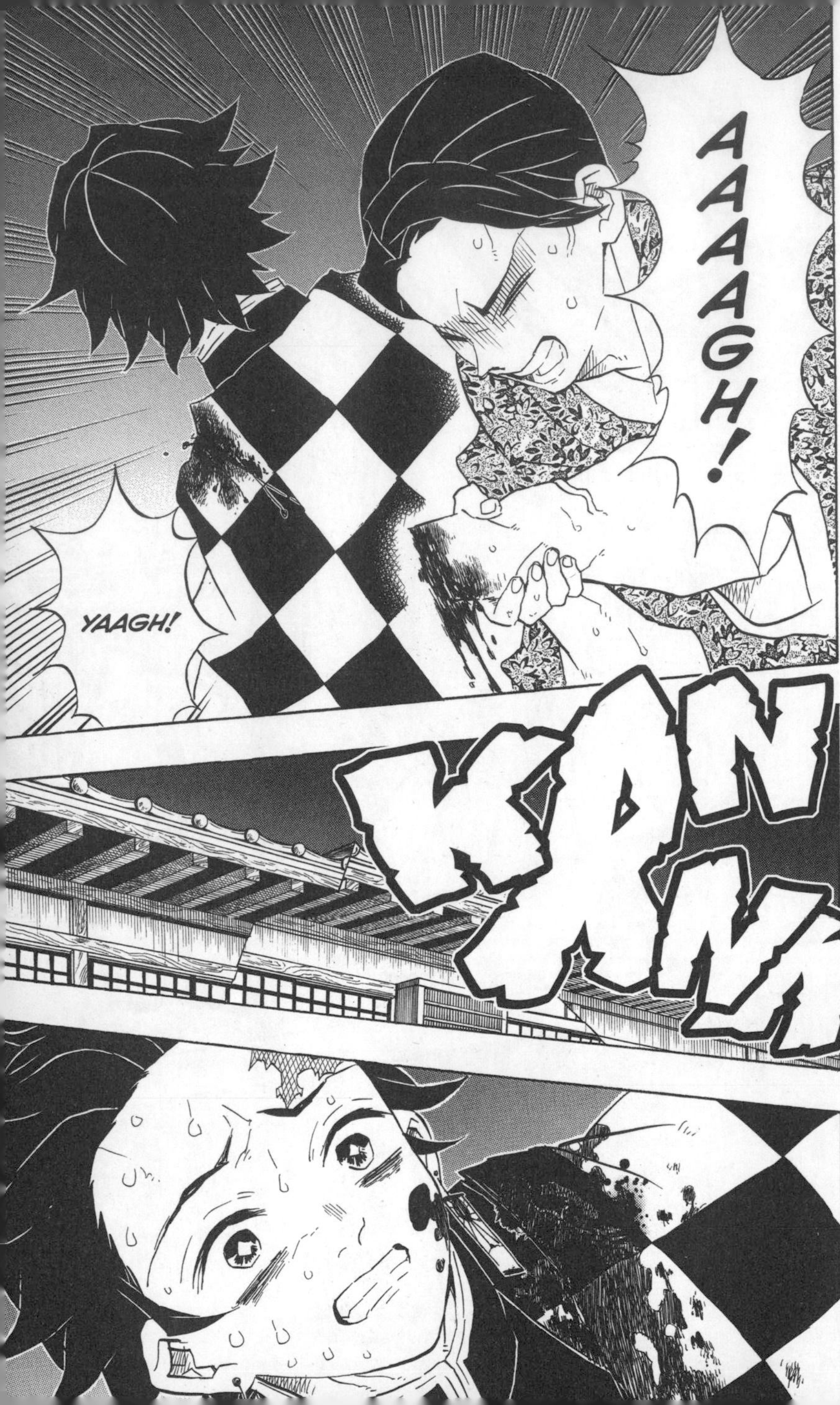
AAAAGH!
YAAGH!
KAN
KAN

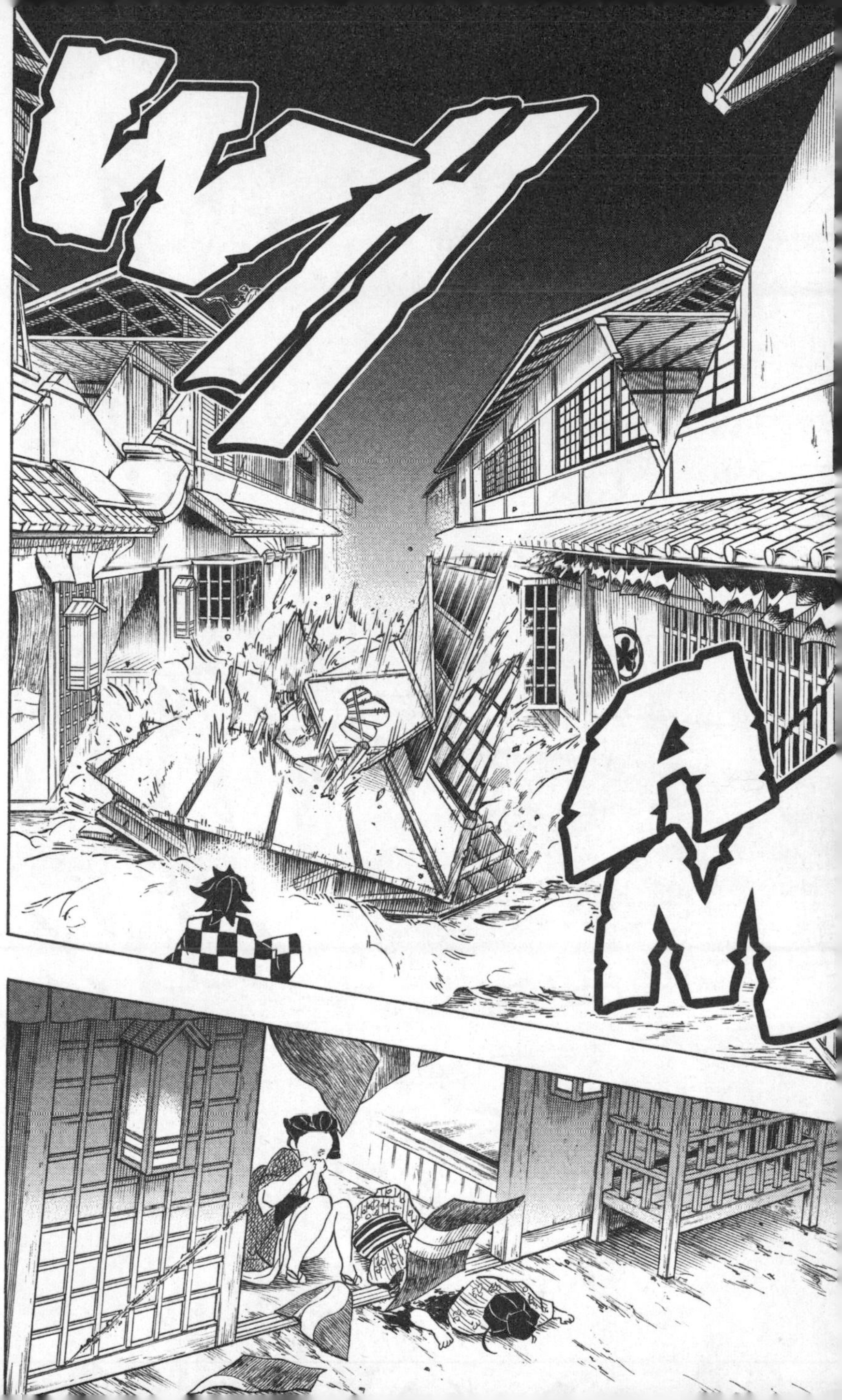
WHAM

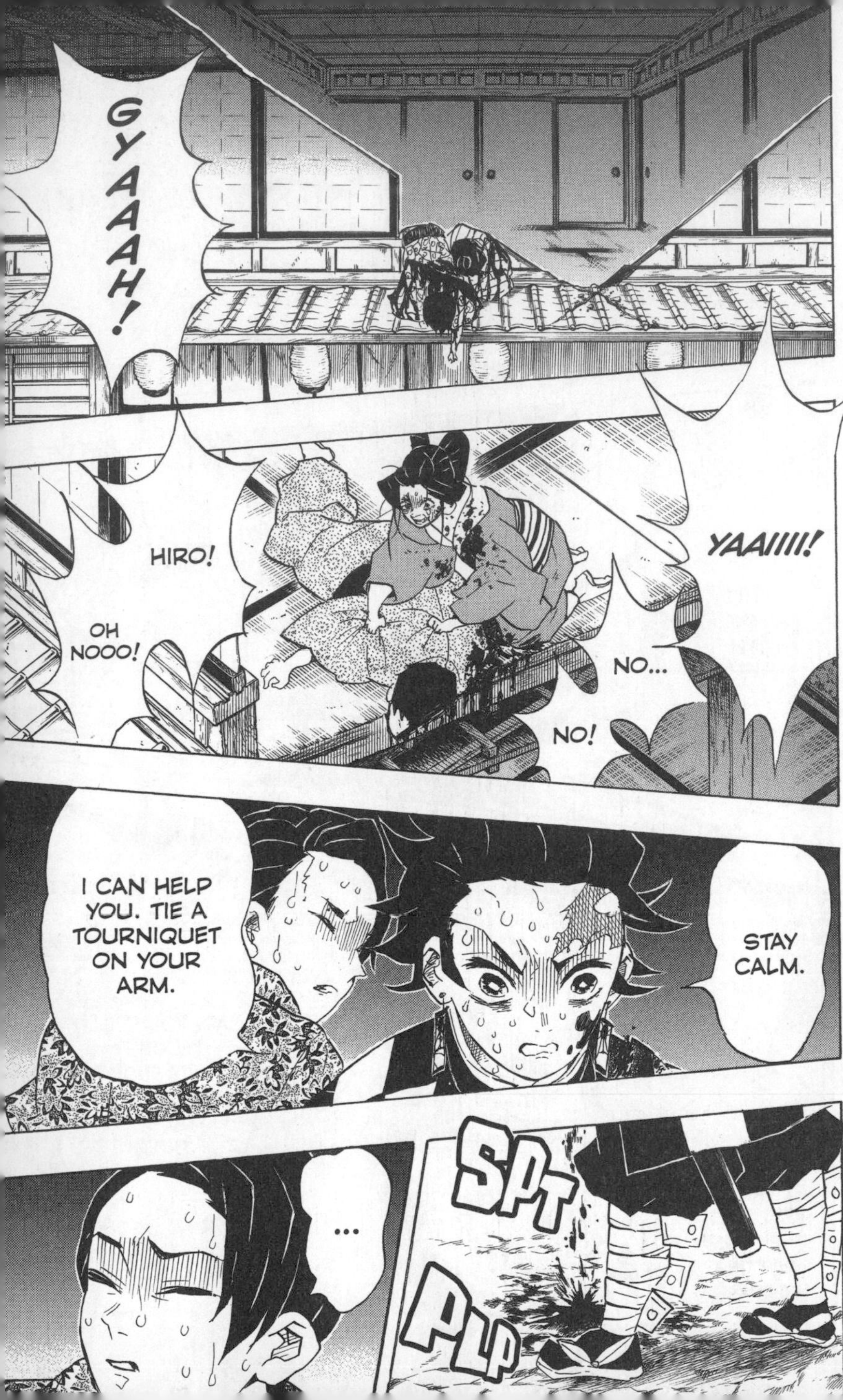
GYAAAH!
YAAIIII!
NO...
NO!
HIRO!
OH NOOO!
STAY CALM.
I CAN HELP YOU. TIE A TOURNIQUET ON YOUR ARM.
SPT
PLP
...

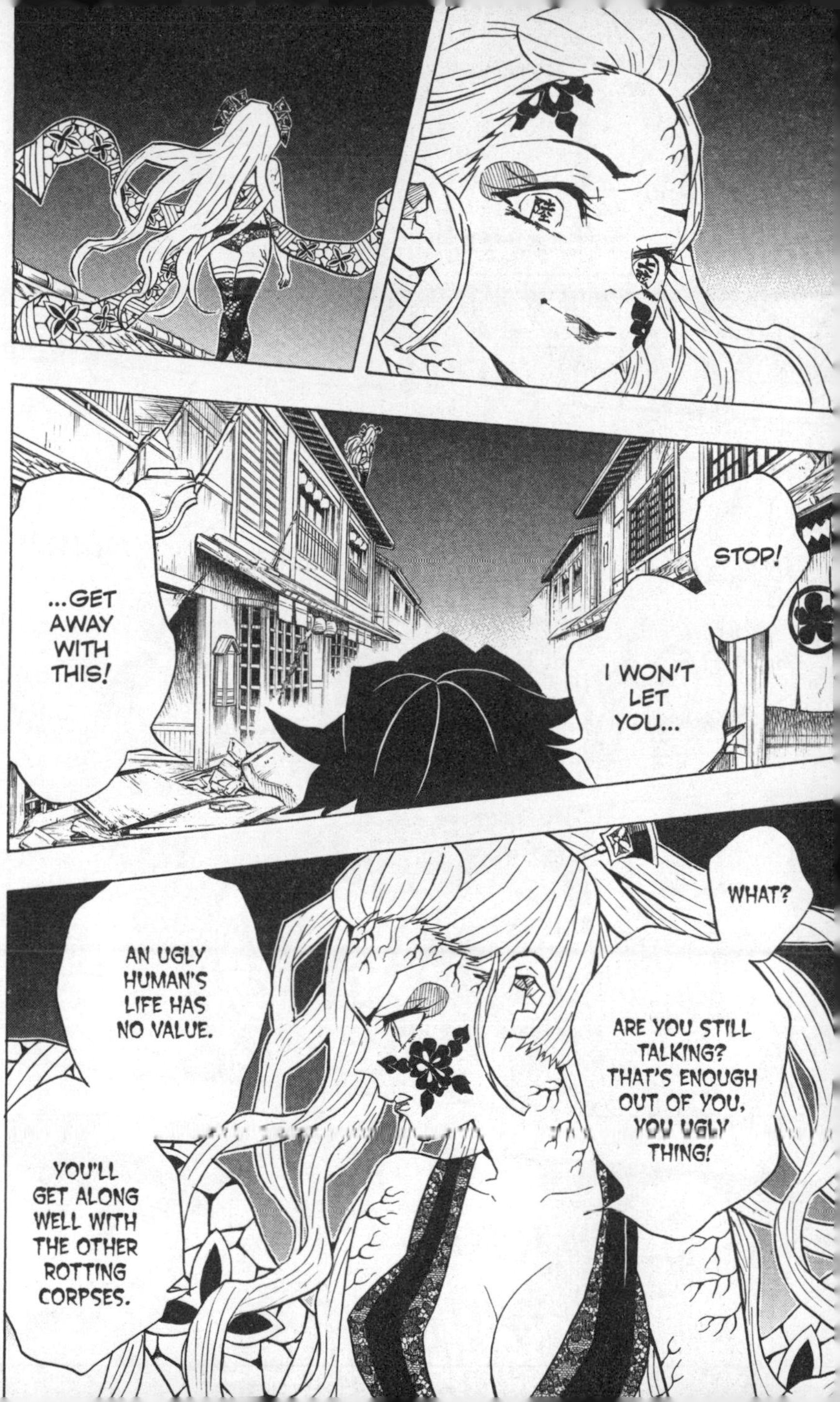
STOP!
I WON'T LET YOU...
...GET AWAY WITH THIS!
WHAT?
ARE YOU STILL TALKING? THAT'S ENOUGH OUT OF YOU, YOU UGLY THING!
AN UGLY HUMAN'S LIFE HAS NO VALUE.
YOU'LL GET ALONG WELL WITH THE OTHER ROTTING CORPSES.

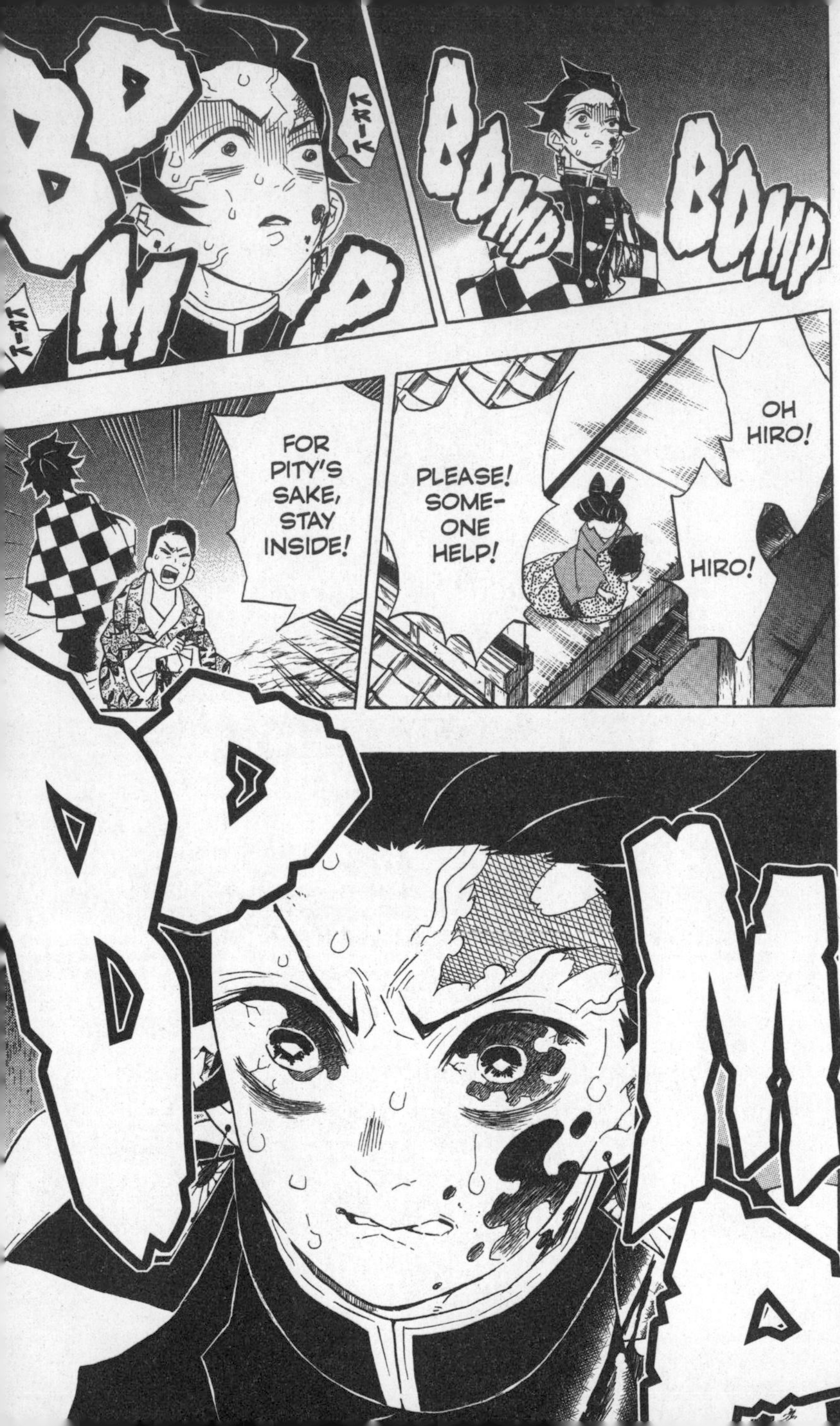
BOMP
BOMP
BOMP
KRIK
KRIK
OH HIRO!
HIRO!
PLEASE! SOME-ONE HELP!
FOR PITY'S SAKE, STAY INSIDE!
BOMP

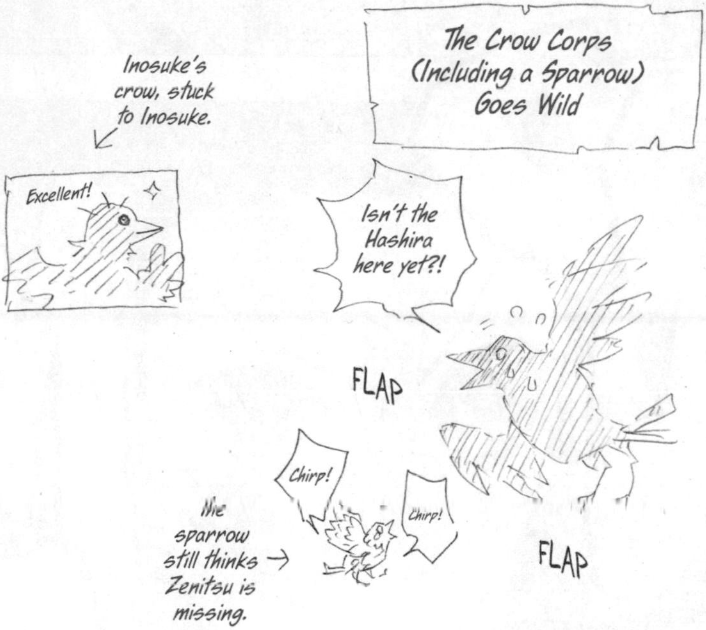
The Crow Corps (Including a Sparrow) Goes Wild
Inosuke's crow, stuck to Inosuke.
Excellent!
Isn't the Hashira here yet?!
FLAP
FLAP
Chirp!
Chirp!
The sparrow still thinks Zenitsu is missing.

CHAPTER 81: LAYERED MEMORIES

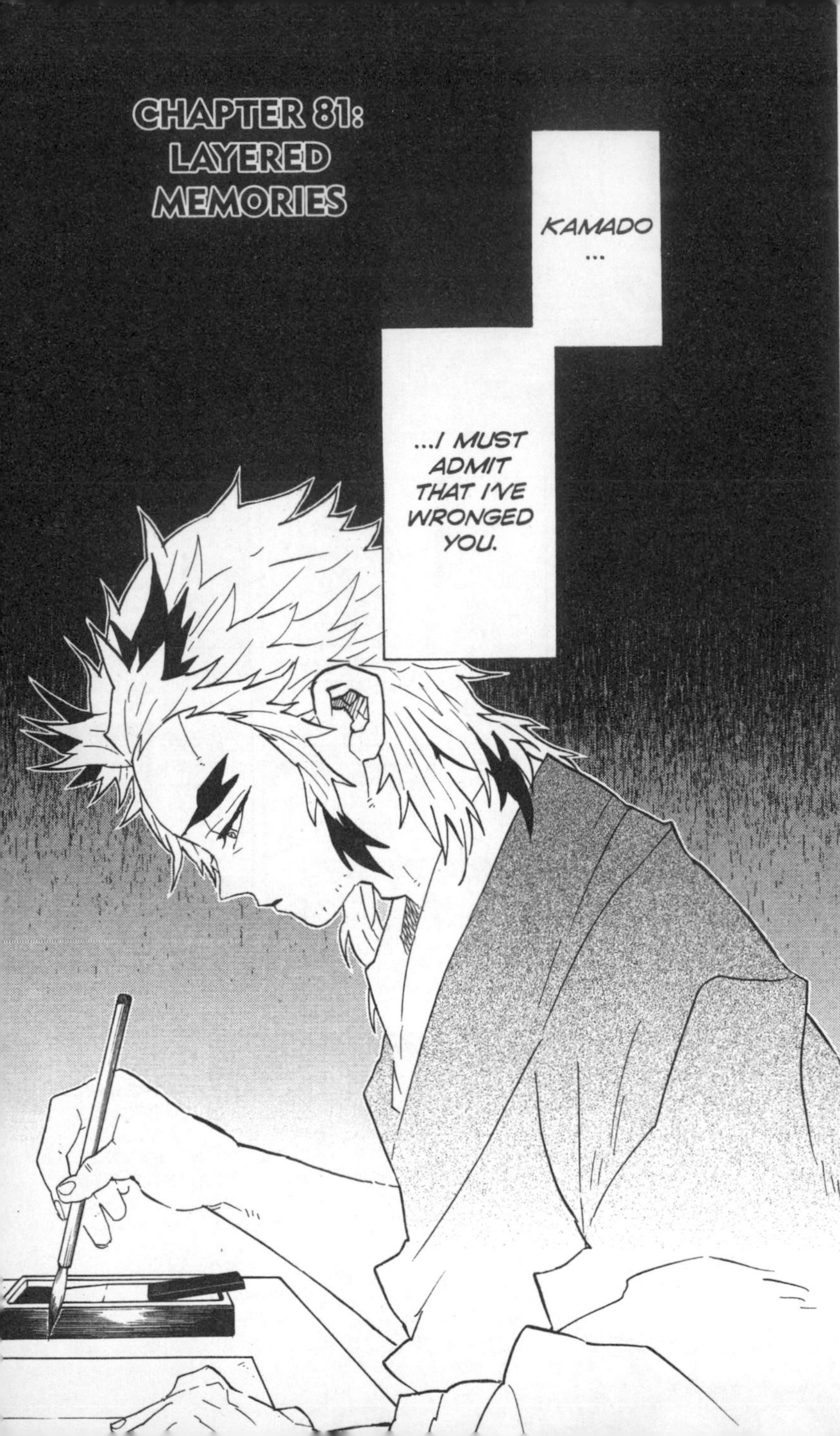
KAMADO ...
...I MUST ADMIT THAT I'VE WRONGED YOU.

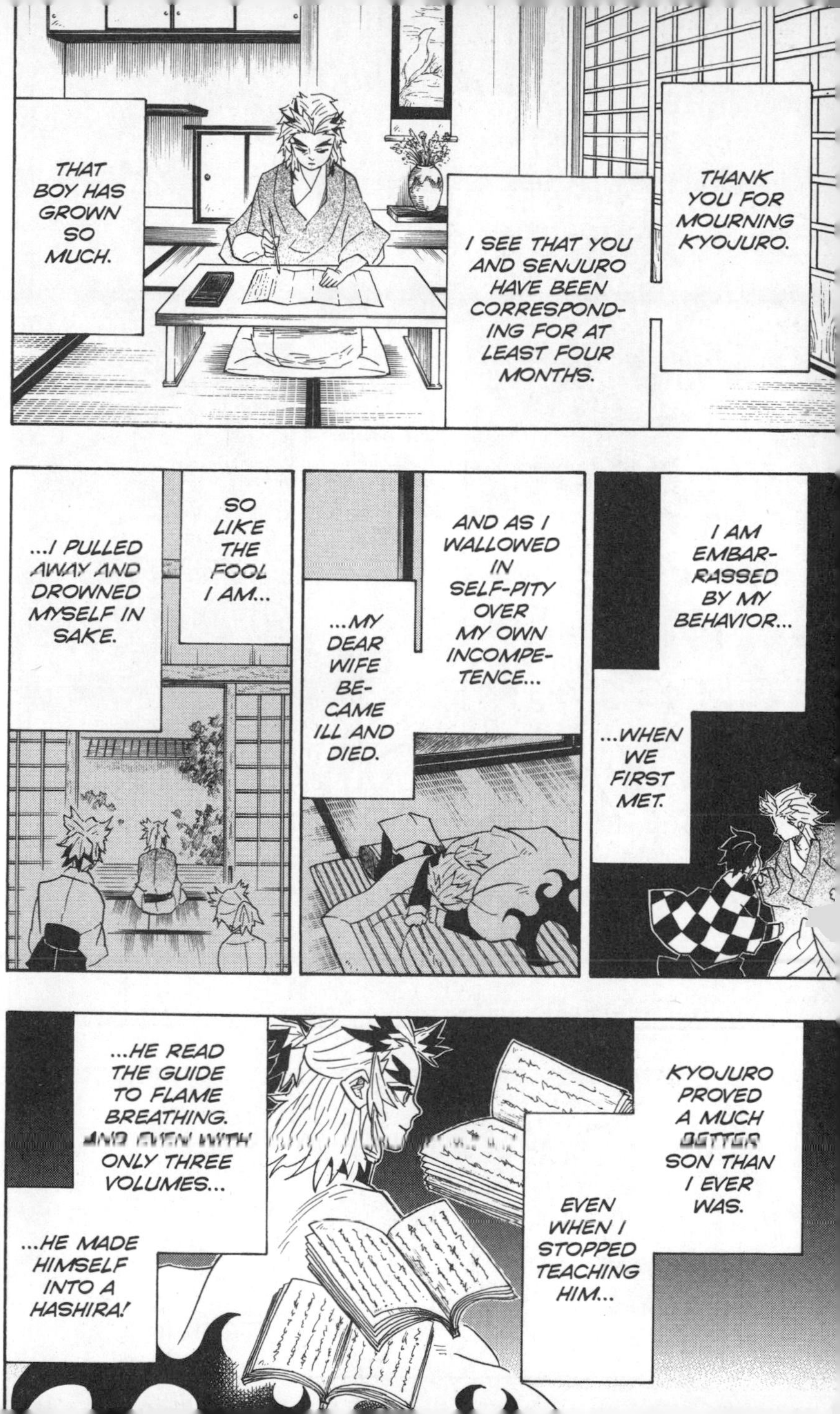
THANK YOU FOR MOURNING KYOJURO.
I SEE THAT YOU AND SENJURO HAVE BEEN CORRESPONDING FOR AT LEAST FOUR MONTHS.
THAT BOY HAS GROWN SO MUCH.
I AM EMBARRASSED BY MY BEHAVIOR...
...WHEN WE FIRST MET.
AND AS I WALLOWED IN SELF-PITY OVER MY OWN INCOMPETENCE...
...MY DEAR WIFE BECAME ILL AND DIED.
SO LIKE THE FOOL I AM...
...I PULLED AWAY AND DROWNED MYSELF IN SAKE.
KYOJURO PROVED A MUCH BETTER SON THAN I EVER WAS.
EVEN WHEN I STOPPED TEACHING HIM...
...HE READ THE GUIDE TO FLAME BREATHING. AND EVEN WITH ONLY THREE VOLUMES...
...HE MADE HIMSELF INTO A HASHIRA!

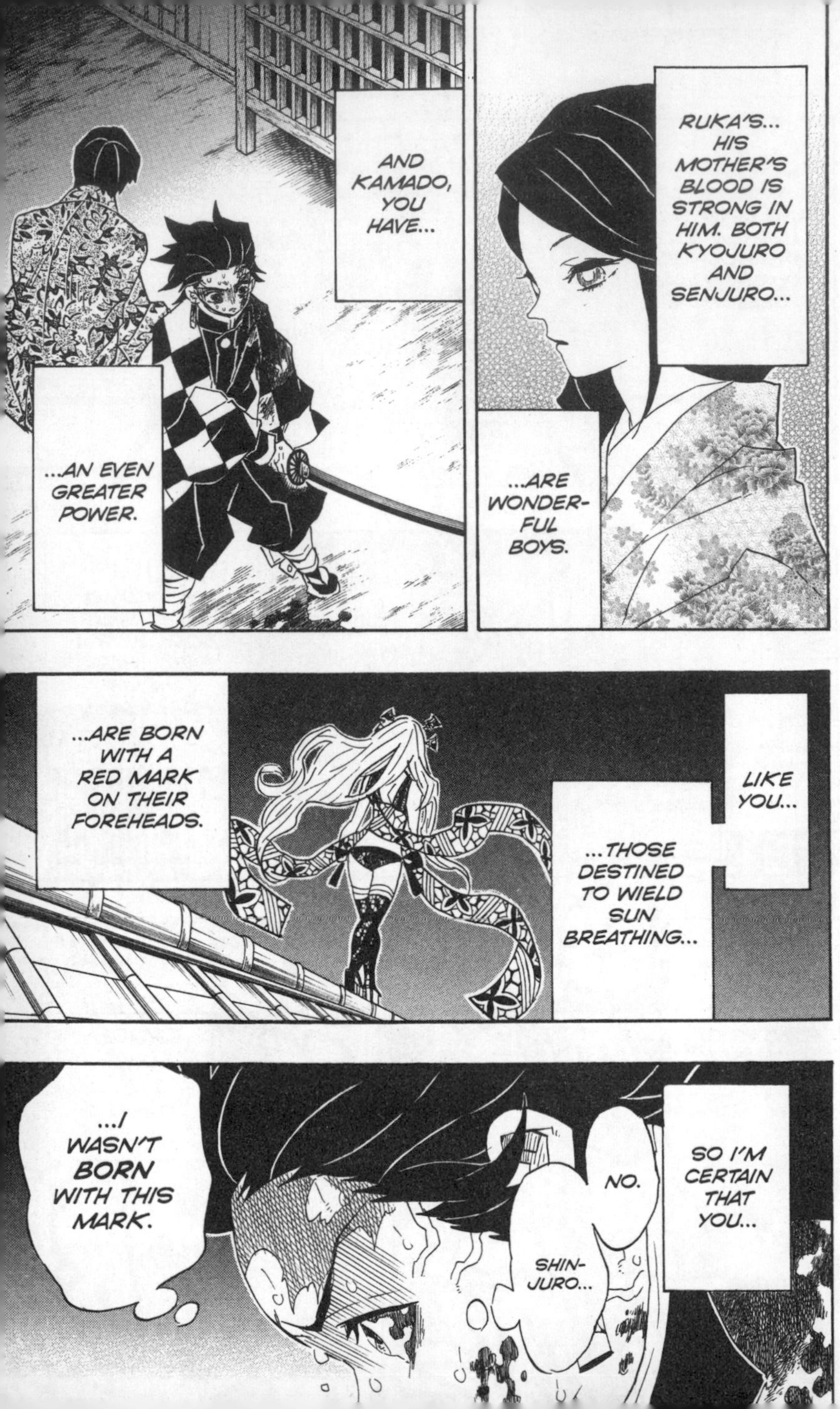
RUKA'S... HIS MOTHER'S BLOOD IS STRONG IN HIM. BOTH KYOJURO AND SENJURO...
...ARE WONDER-FUL BOYS.
AND KAMADO, YOU HAVE...
...AN EVEN GREATER POWER.
LIKE YOU...
...THOSE DESTINED TO WIELD SUN BREATHING...
...ARE BORN WITH A RED MARK ON THEIR FOREHEADS.
SO I'M CERTAIN THAT YOU...
NO.
SHIN-JURO...
...I WASN'T BORN WITH THIS MARK.

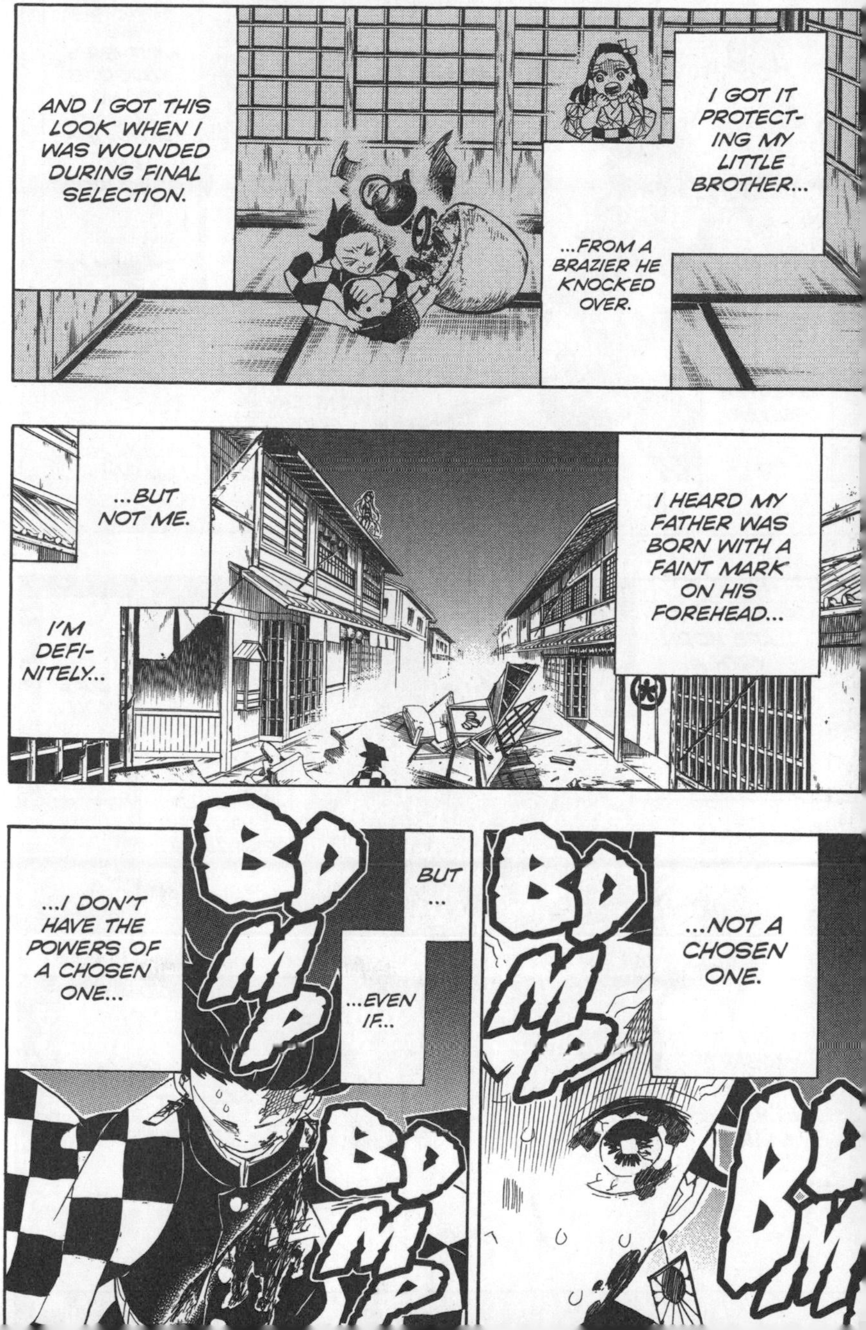
I GOT IT PROTECTING MY LITTLE BROTHER...
...FROM A BRAZIER HE KNOCKED OVER.
AND I GOT THIS LOOK WHEN I WAS WOUNDED DURING FINAL SELECTION.
I HEARD MY FATHER WAS BORN WITH A FAINT MARK ON HIS FOREHEAD...
...BUT NOT ME.
I'M DEFINITELY...
...NOT A CHOSEN ONE.
BDMP
BUT...
...EVEN IF...
...I DON'T HAVE THE POWERS OF A CHOSEN ONE...
BDMP
BDMP

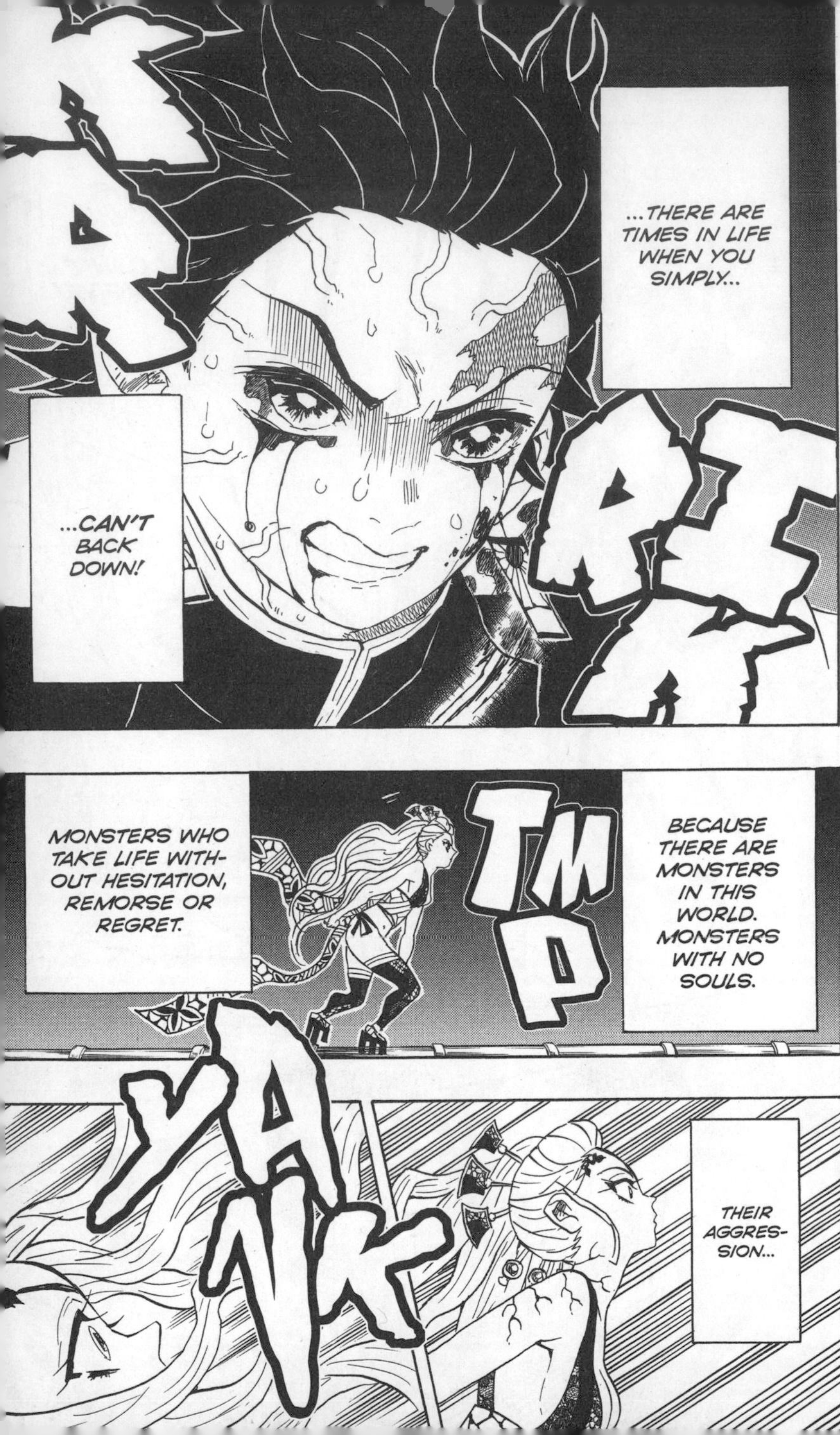
...THERE ARE TIMES IN LIFE WHEN YOU SIMPLY...
...CAN'T BACK DOWN!
BECAUSE THERE ARE MONSTERS IN THIS WORLD. MONSTERS WITH NO SOULS.
TMP
MONSTERS WHO TAKE LIFE WITH-OUT HESITATION, REMORSE OR REGRET.
THEIR AGGRES-SION...
YANK

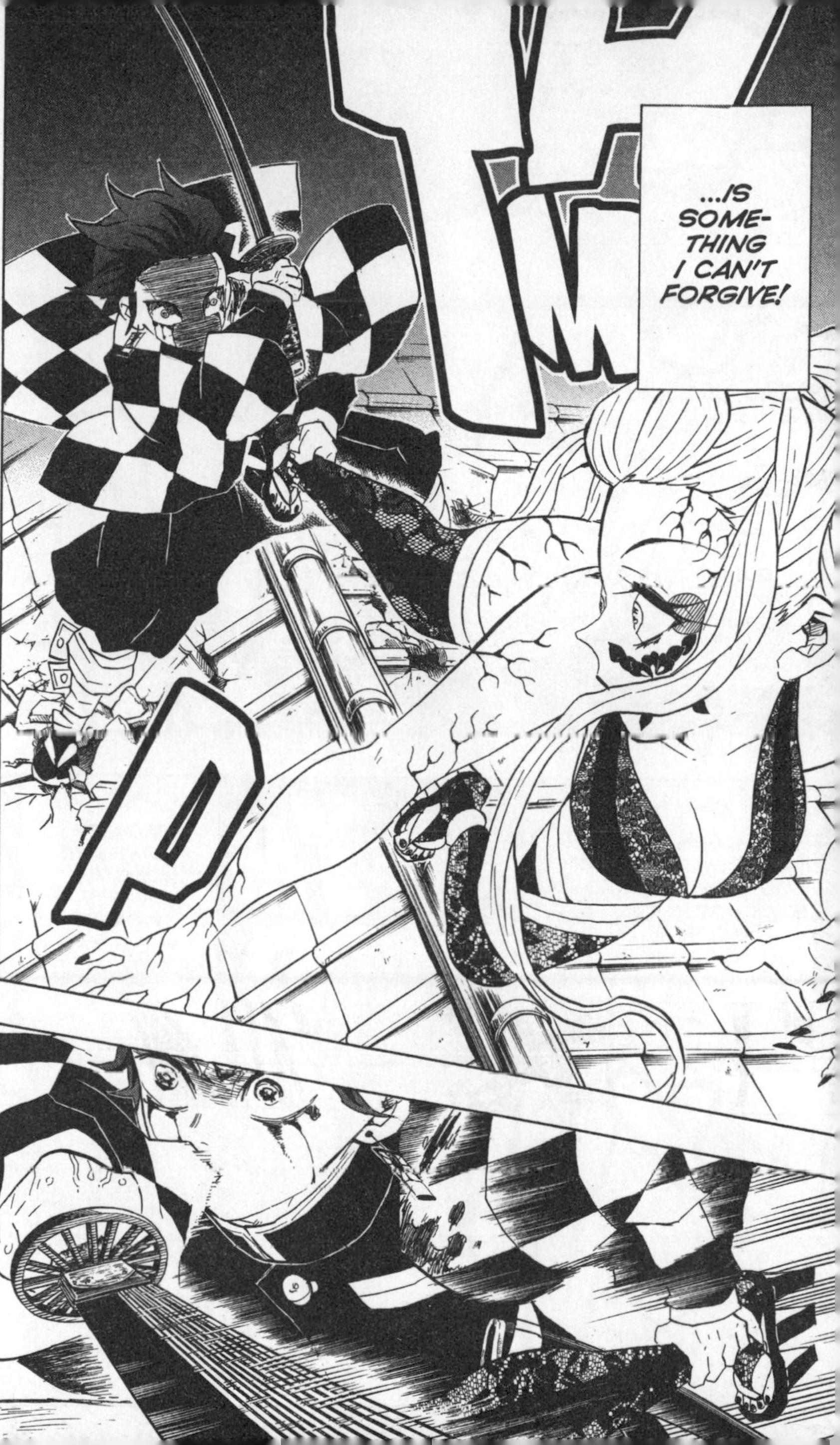
...IS SOMETHING I CAN'T FORGIVE!

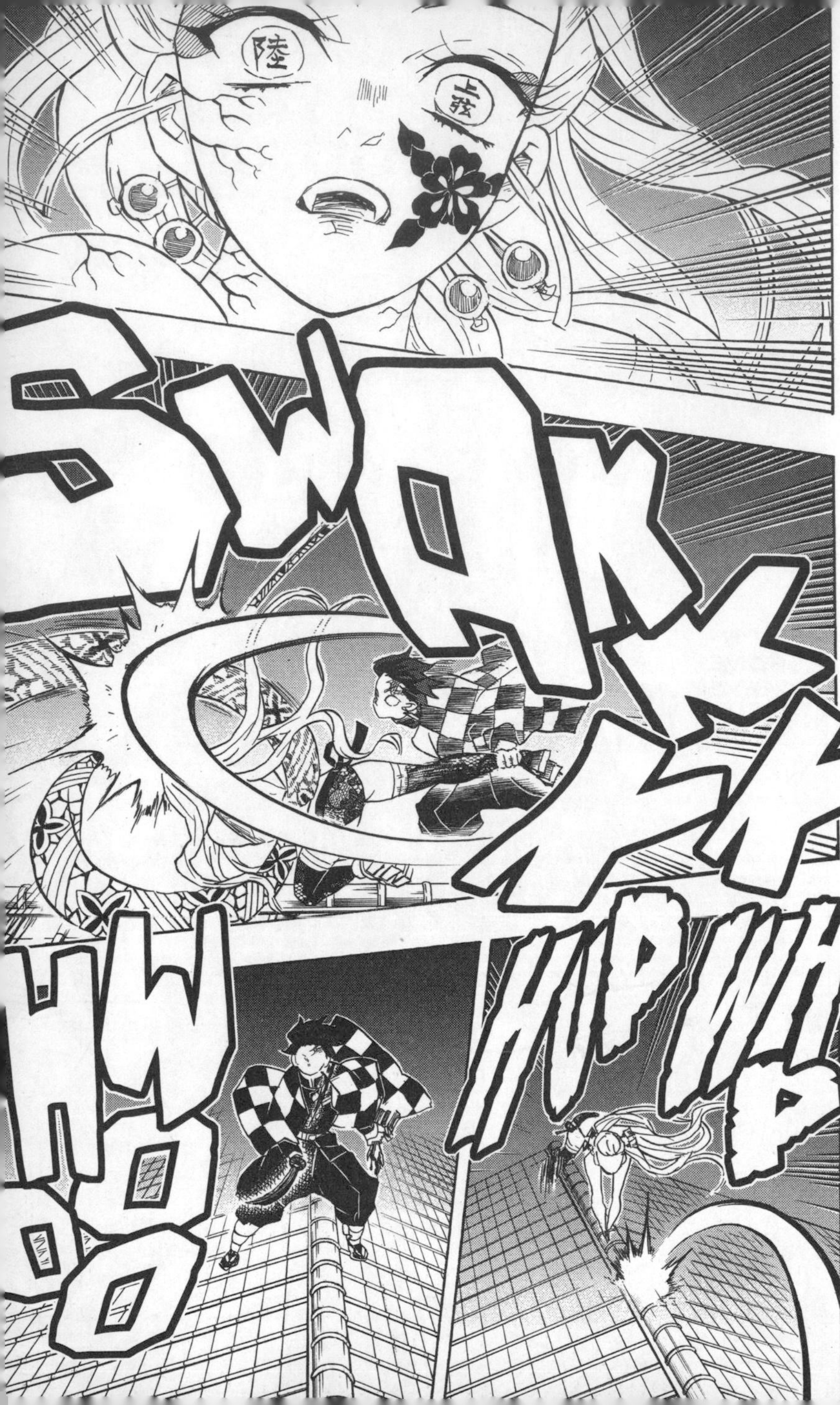
上弦
陸

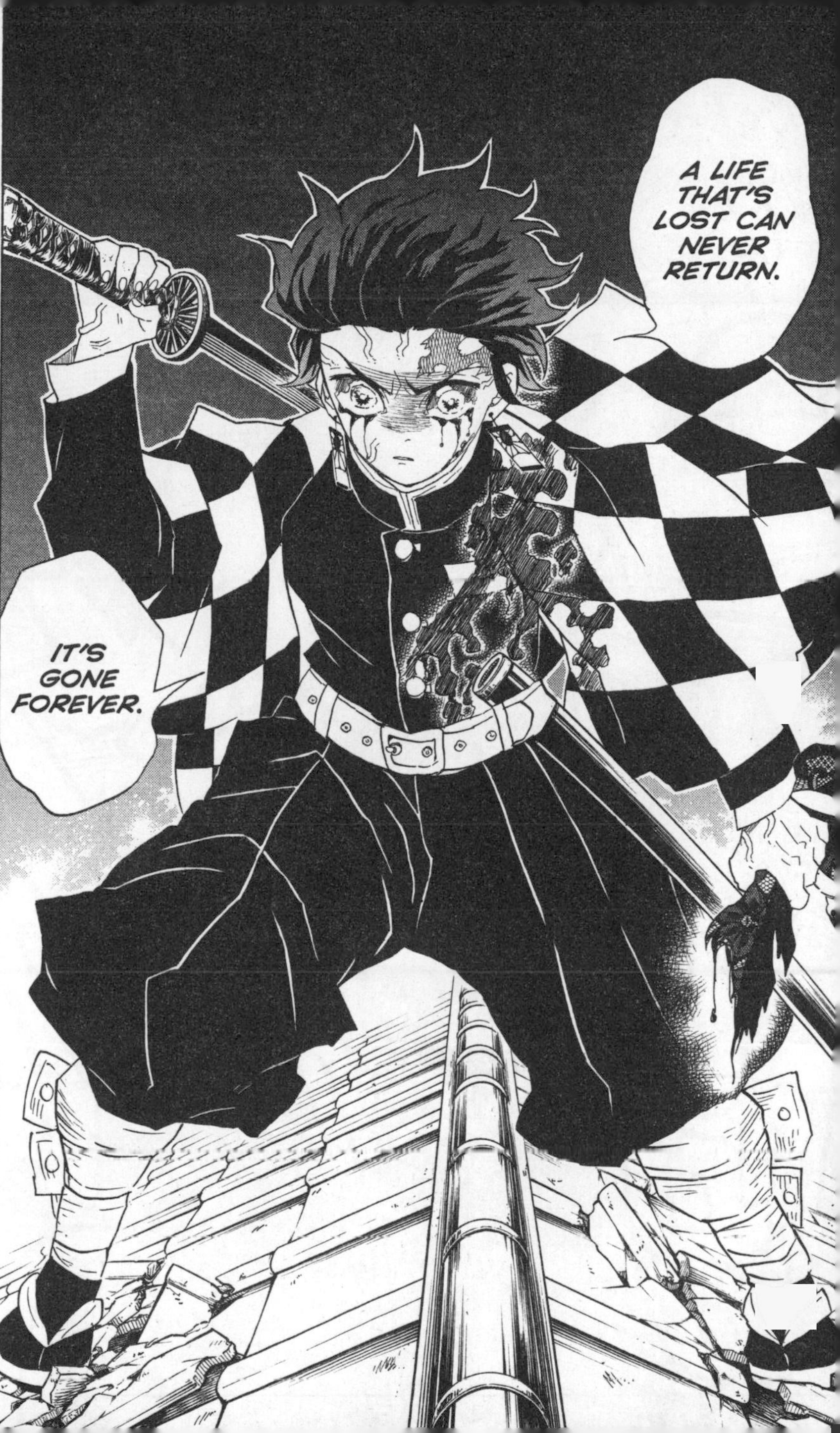
A LIFE THAT'S LOST CAN NEVER RETURN.
IT'S GONE FOREVER.

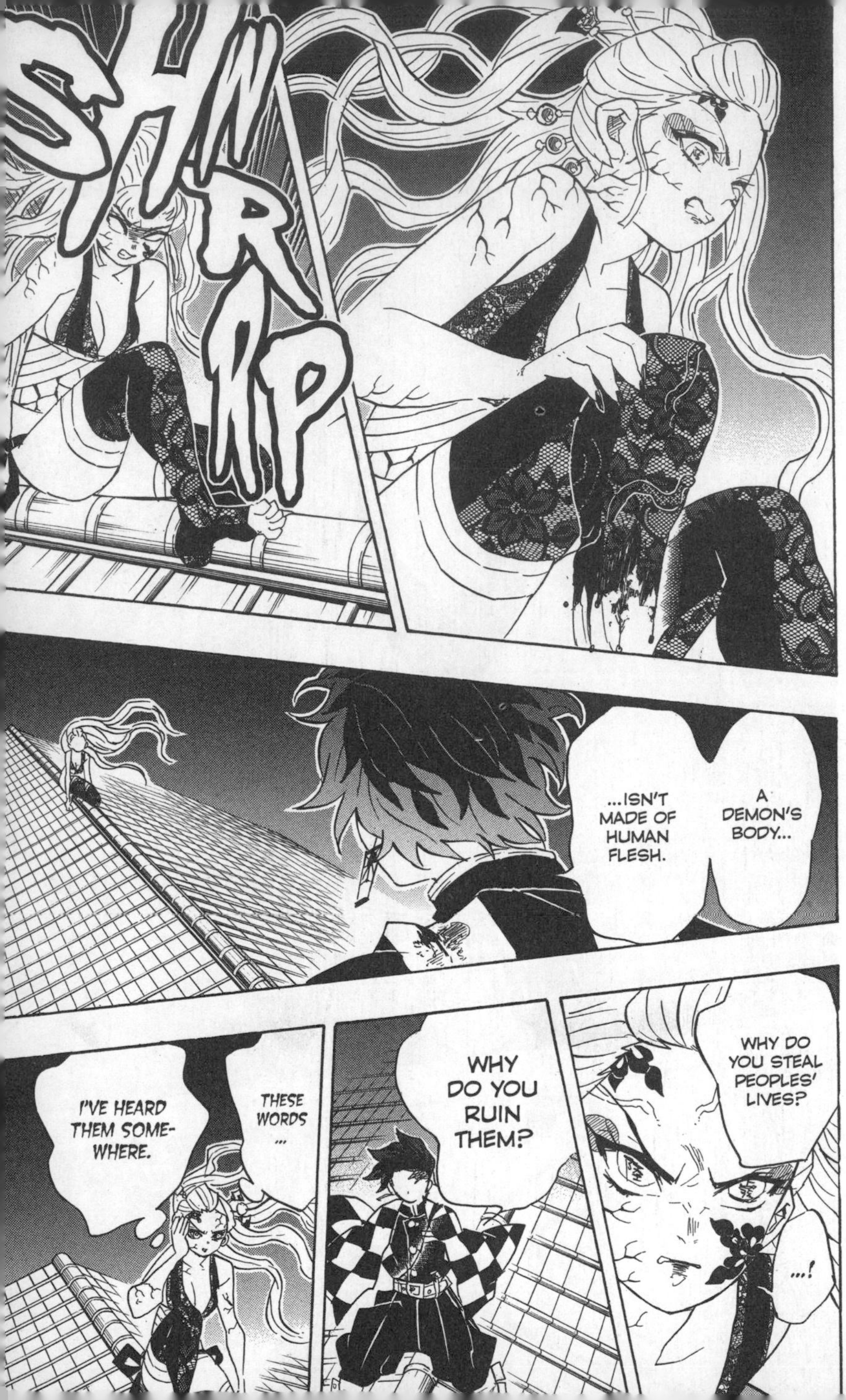
A DEMON'S BODY...
...ISN'T MADE OF HUMAN FLESH.
WHY DO YOU STEAL PEOPLES' LIVES?
...!
WHY DO YOU RUIN THEM?
THESE WORDS...
I'VE HEARD THEM SOME-WHERE.

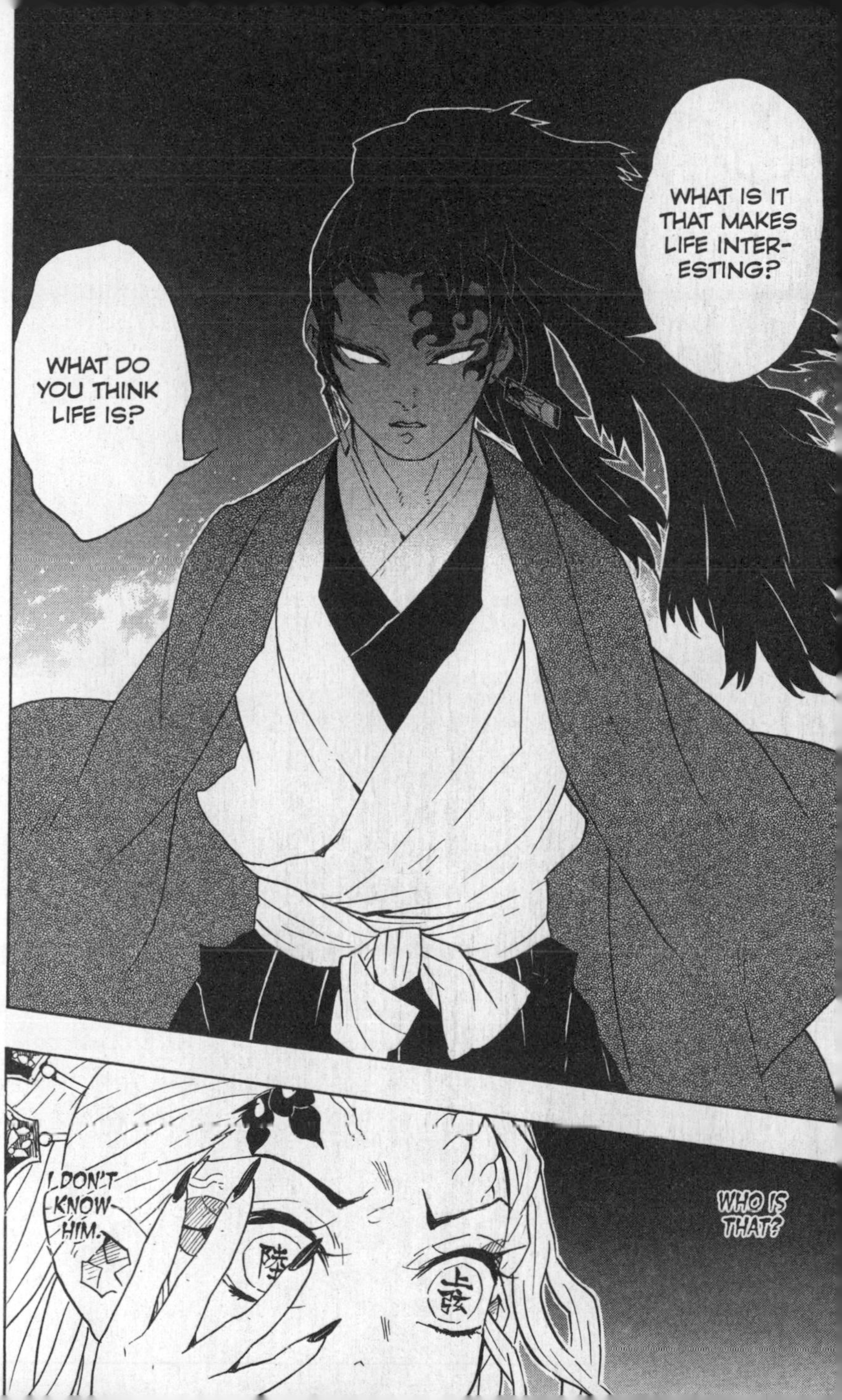
WHAT IS IT THAT MAKES LIFE INTER-ESTING?
WHAT DO YOU THINK LIFE IS?
WHO IS THAT?
上弦
陸
I DON'T KNOW HIM.

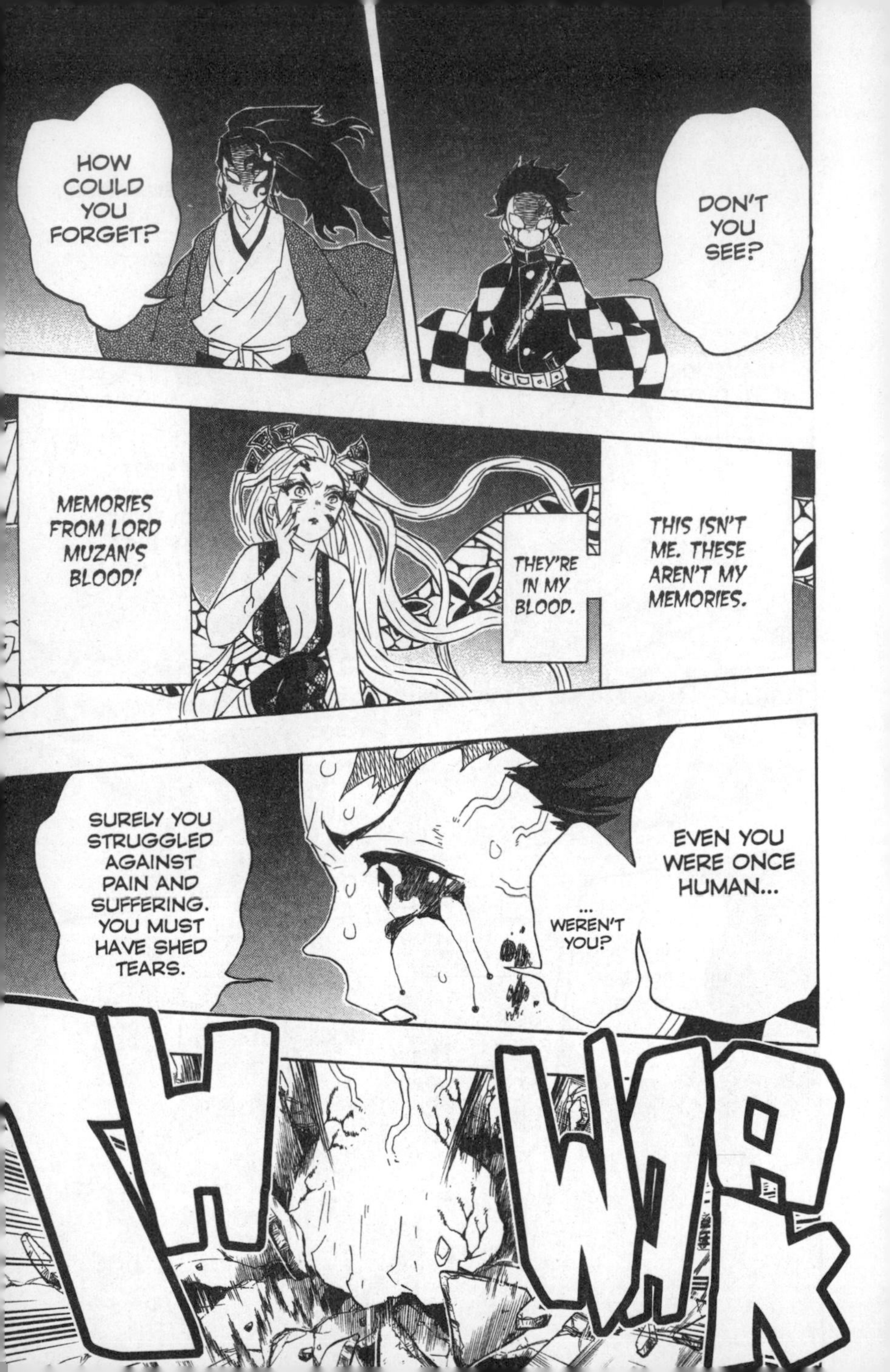
DON'T YOU SEE?
HOW COULD YOU FORGET?
THIS ISN'T ME. THESE AREN'T MY MEMORIES.
THEY'RE IN MY BLOOD.
MEMORIES FROM LORD MUZAN'S BLOOD!
EVEN YOU WERE ONCE HUMAN...
...WEREN'T YOU?
SURELY YOU STRUGGLED AGAINST PAIN AND SUFFERING. YOU MUST HAVE SHED TEARS.

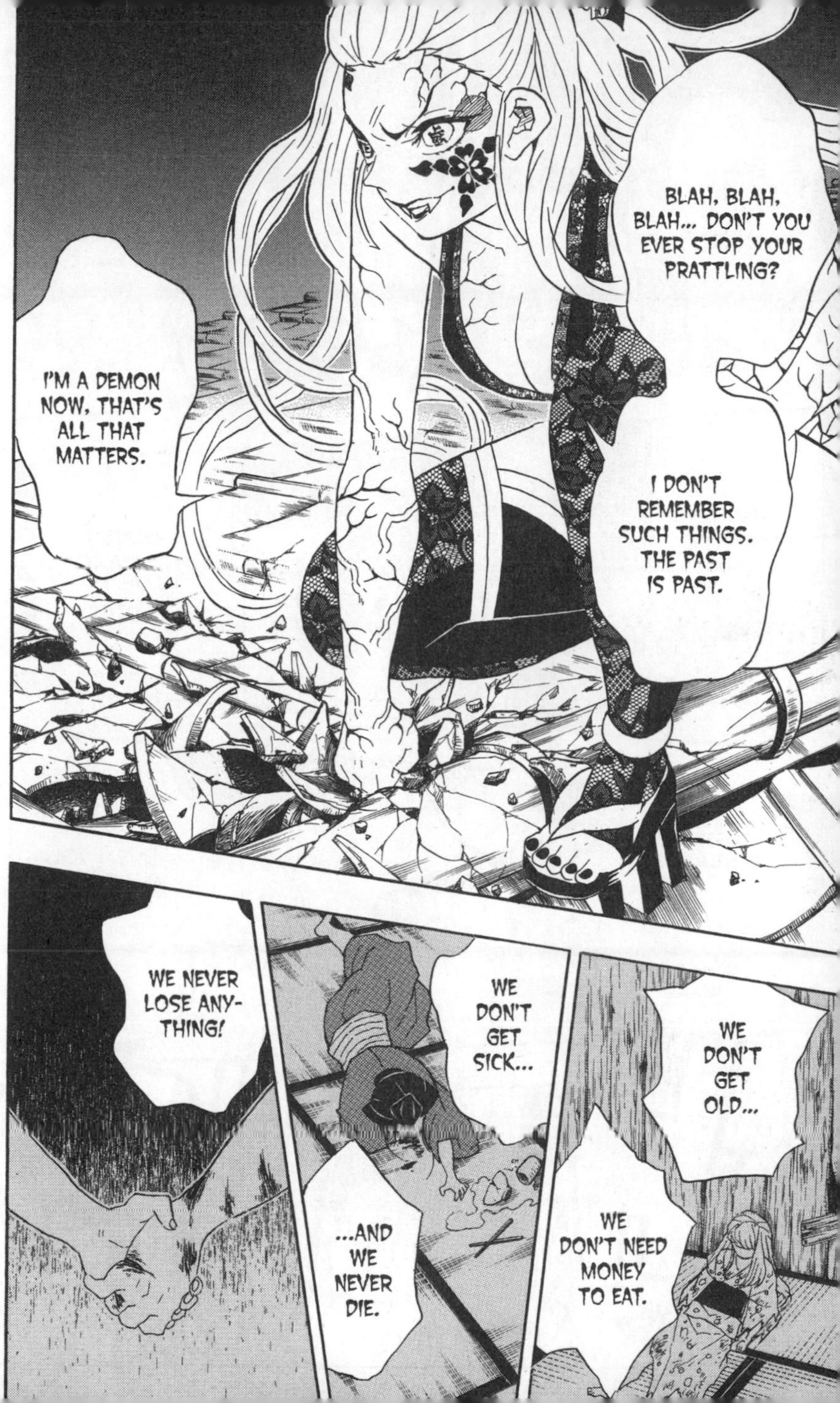
BLAH, BLAH, BLAH... DON'T YOU EVER STOP YOUR PRATTLING?
I DON'T REMEMBER SUCH THINGS. THE PAST IS PAST.
I'M A DEMON NOW, THAT'S ALL THAT MATTERS.
WE DON'T GET OLD...
WE DON'T NEED MONEY TO EAT.
WE DON'T GET SICK...
...AND WE NEVER DIE.
WE NEVER LOSE ANY-THING!

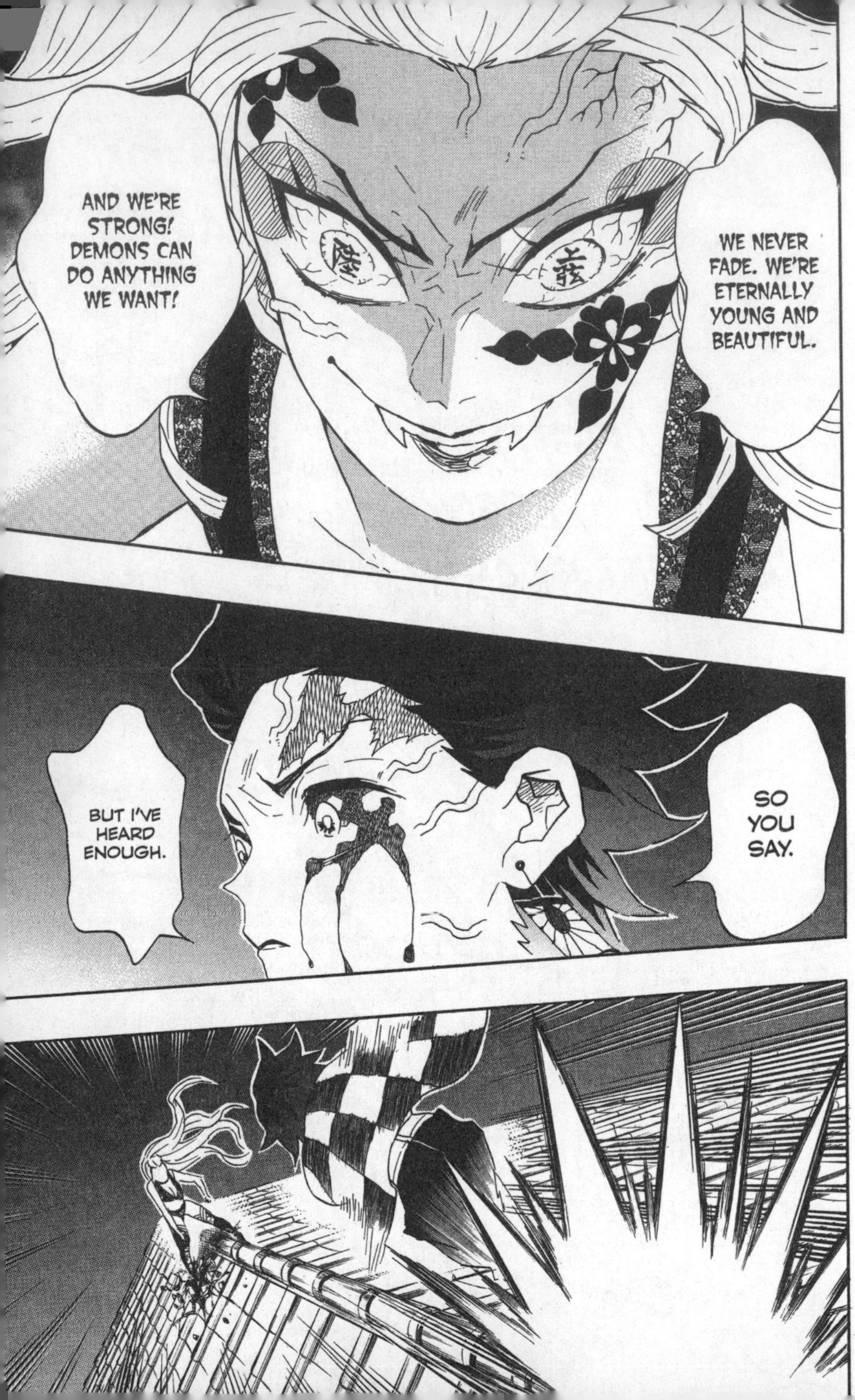
WE NEVER FADE. WE'RE ETERNALLY YOUNG AND BEAUTIFUL.
AND WE'RE STRONG! DEMONS CAN DO ANYTHING WE WANT!
SO YOU SAY.
BUT I'VE HEARD ENOUGH.

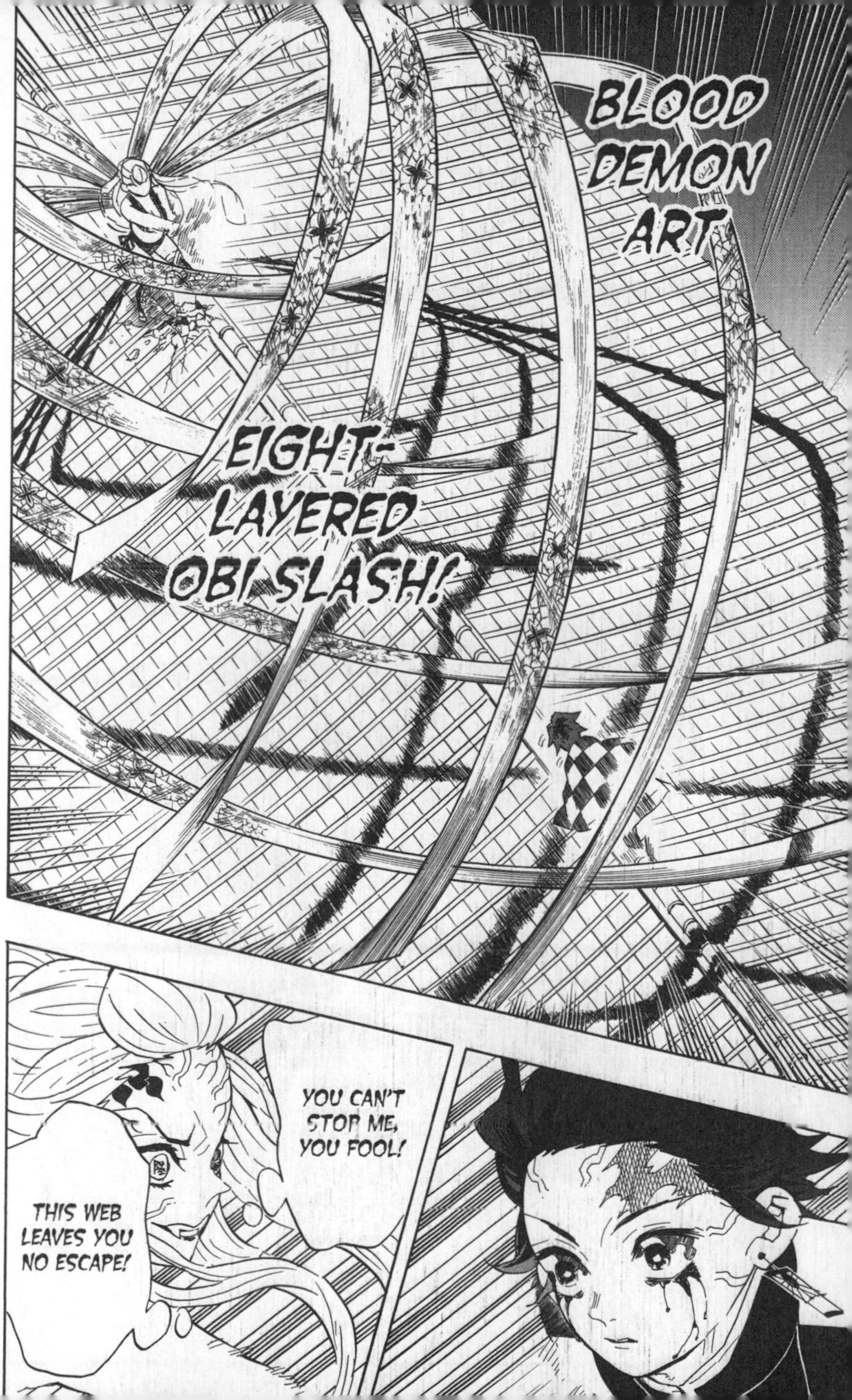
BLOOD DEMON ART
EIGHT-LAYERED OBI SLASH!
YOU CAN'T STOP ME, YOU FOOL!
THIS WEB LEAVES YOU NO ESCAPE!

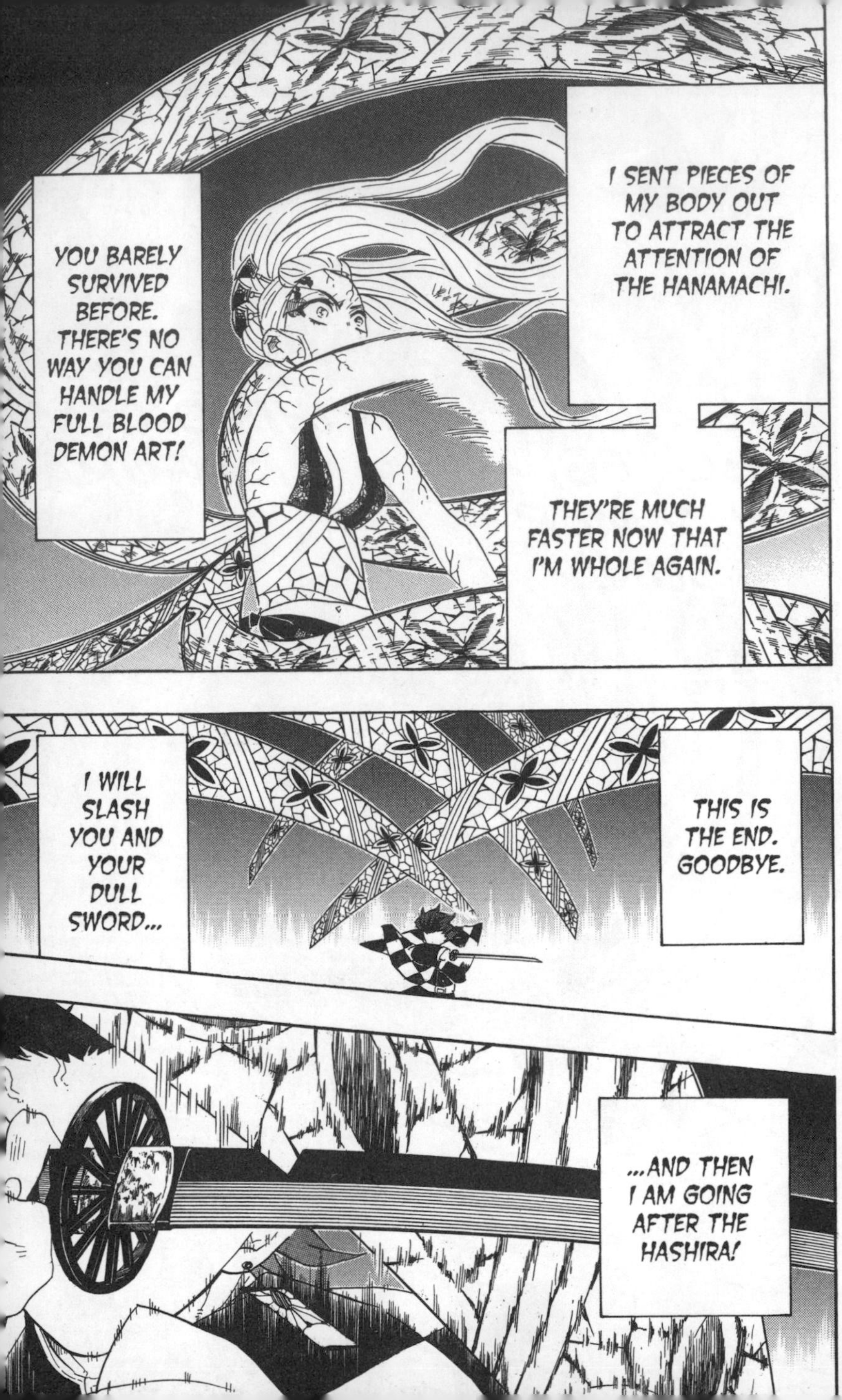
I SENT PIECES OF MY BODY OUT TO ATTRACT THE ATTENTION OF THE HANAMACHI.
THEY'RE MUCH FASTER NOW THAT I'M WHOLE AGAIN.
YOU BARELY SURVIVED BEFORE. THERE'S NO WAY YOU CAN HANDLE MY FULL BLOOD DEMON ART!
THIS IS THE END. GOODBYE.
I WILL SLASH YOU AND YOUR DULL SWORD...
...AND THEN I AM GOING AFTER THE HASHIRA!

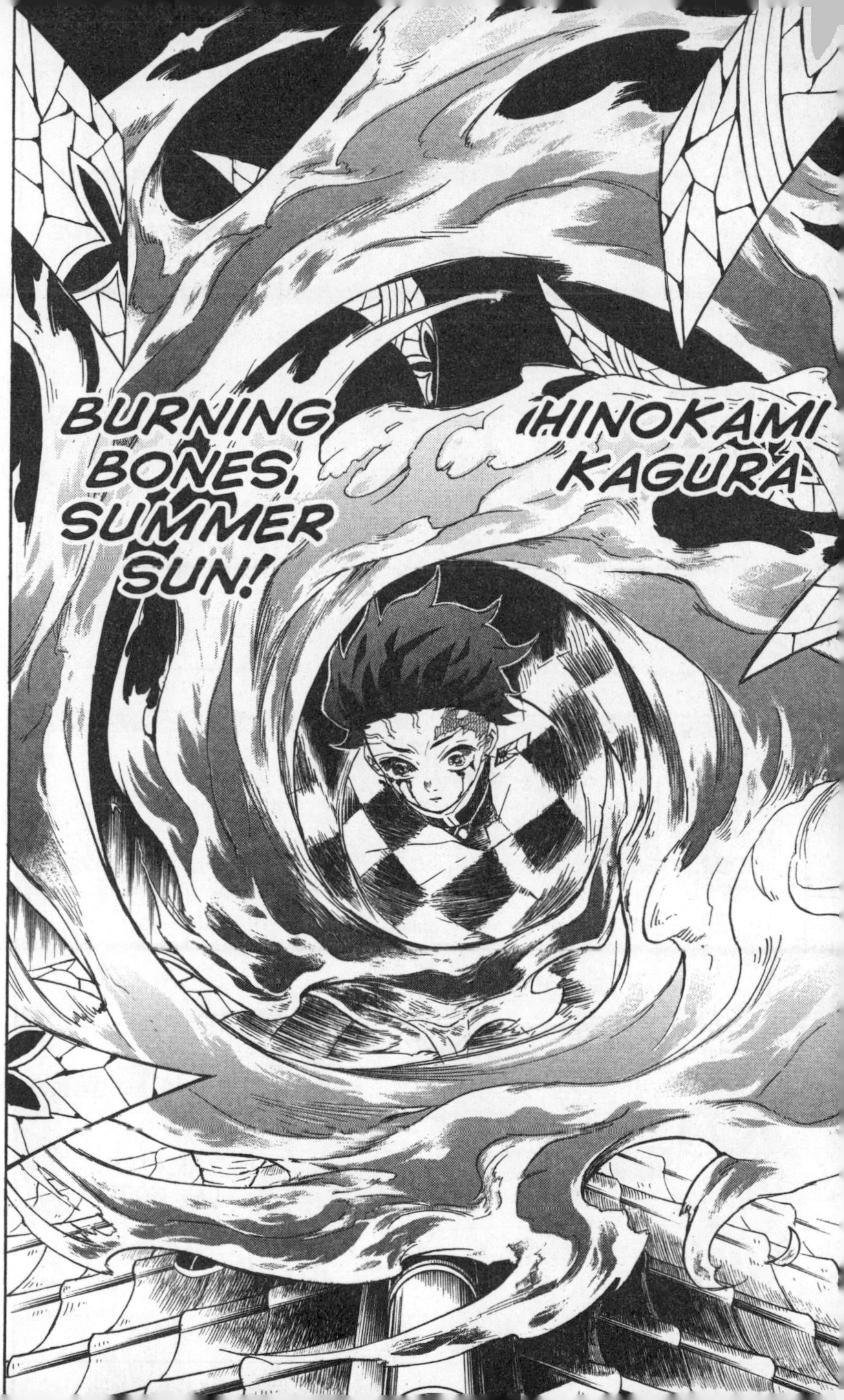
HINOKAMI KAGURA
BURNING BONES, SUMMER SUN!

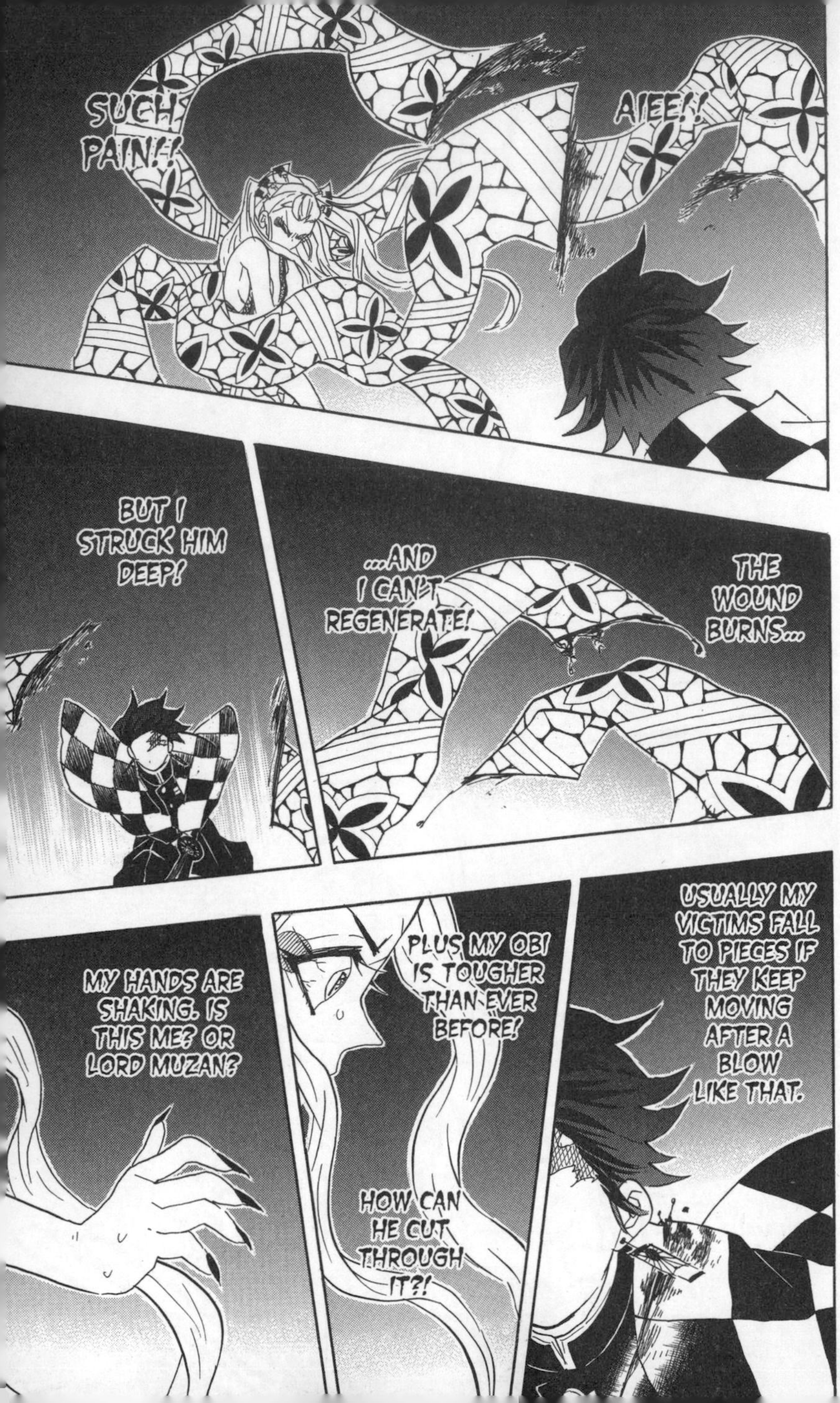
AIEE!!
SUCH PAIN!!
THE WOUND BURNS...
...AND I CAN'T REGENERATE!
BUT I STRUCK HIM DEEP!
USUALLY MY VICTIMS FALL TO PIECES IF THEY KEEP MOVING AFTER A BLOW LIKE THAT.
PLUS MY OBI IS TOUGHER THAN EVER BEFORE!
HOW CAN HE CUT THROUGH IT?!
MY HANDS ARE SHAKING. IS THIS ME? OR LORD MUZAN?

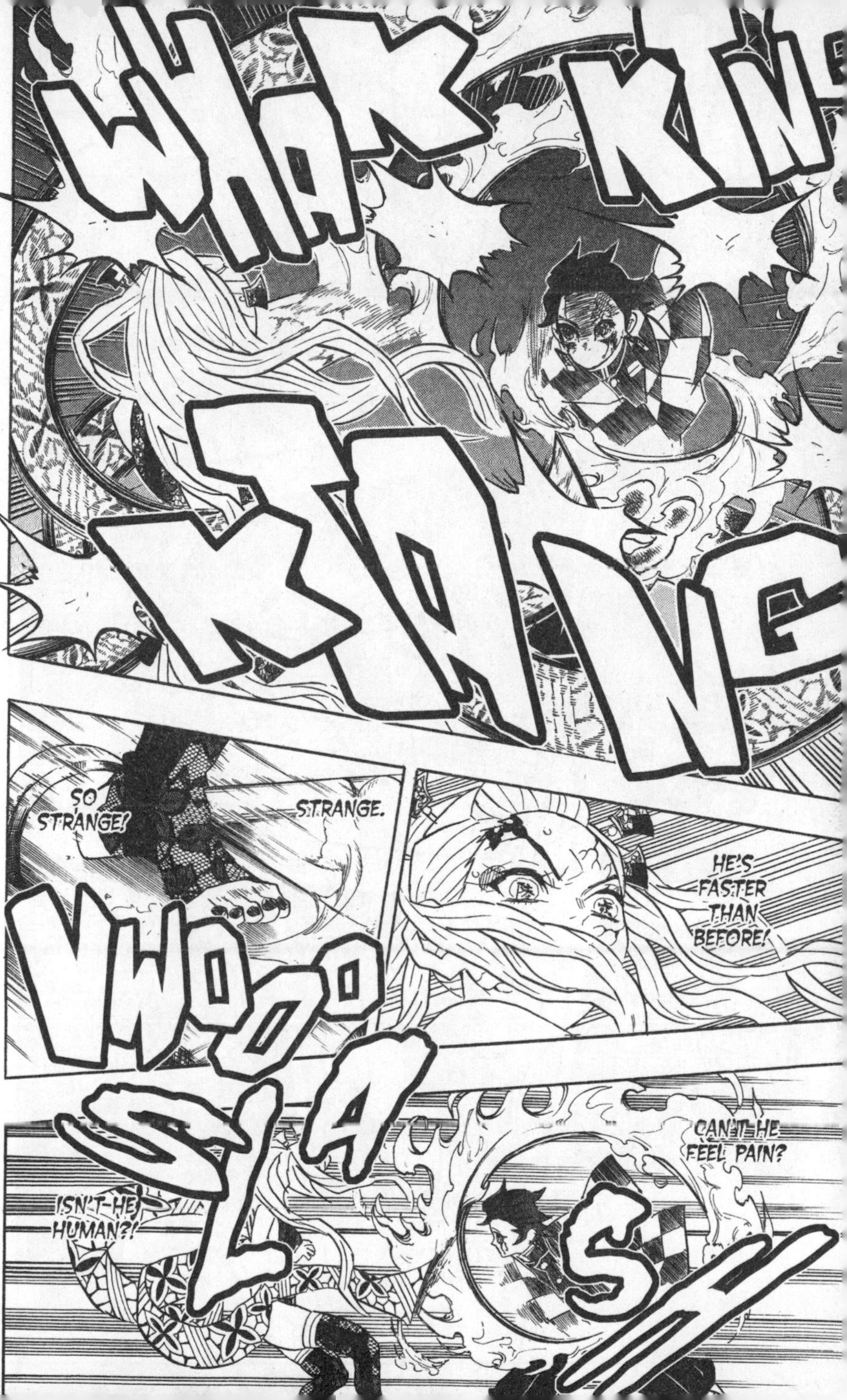
HE'S FASTER THAN BEFORE!
STRANGE.
SO STRANGE!
CAN'T HE FEEL PAIN?
ISN'T HE HUMAN?!

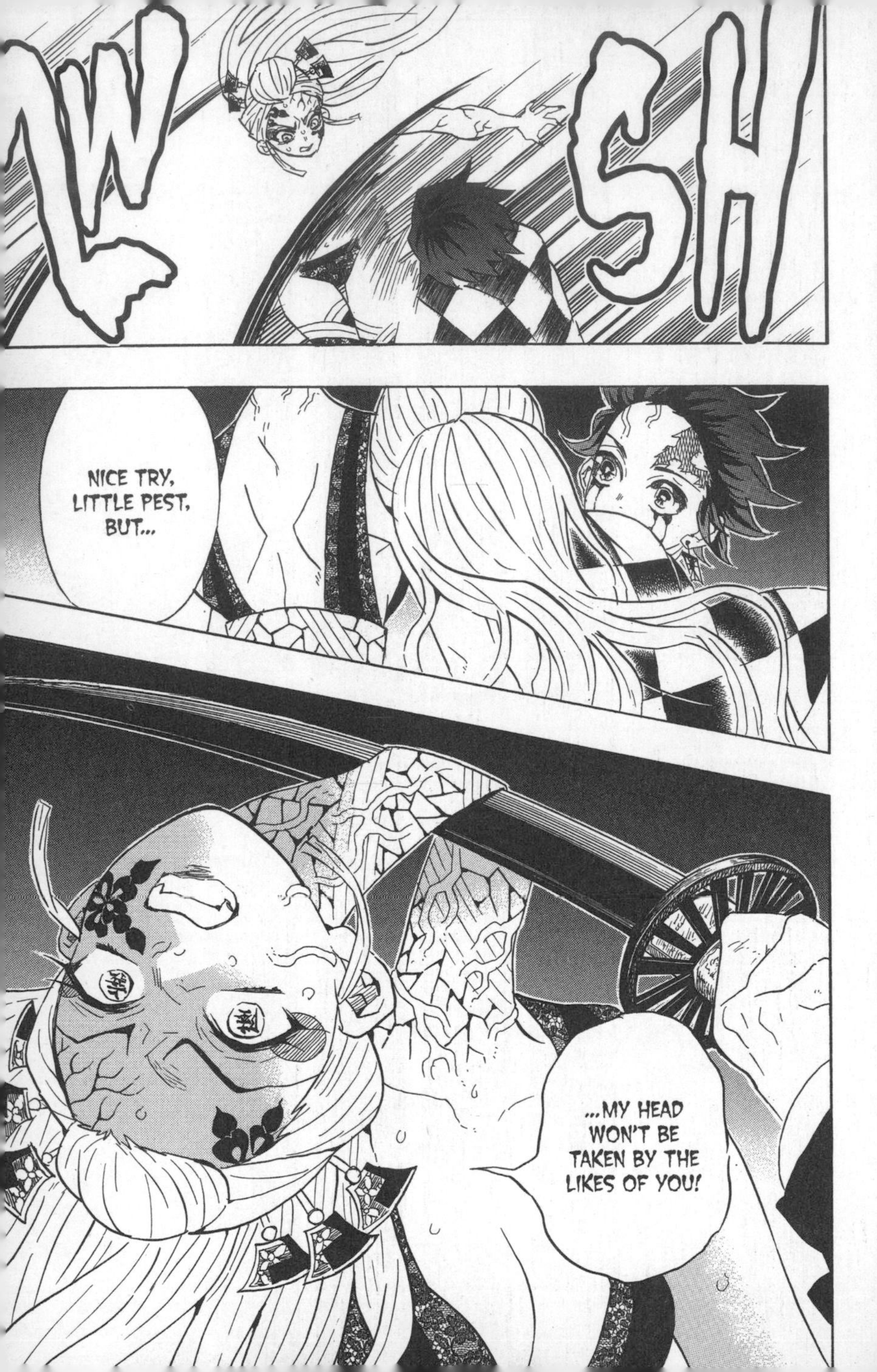

WSH
NICE TRY, LITTLE PEST, BUT...
...MY HEAD WON'T BE TAKEN BY THE LIKES OF YOU!

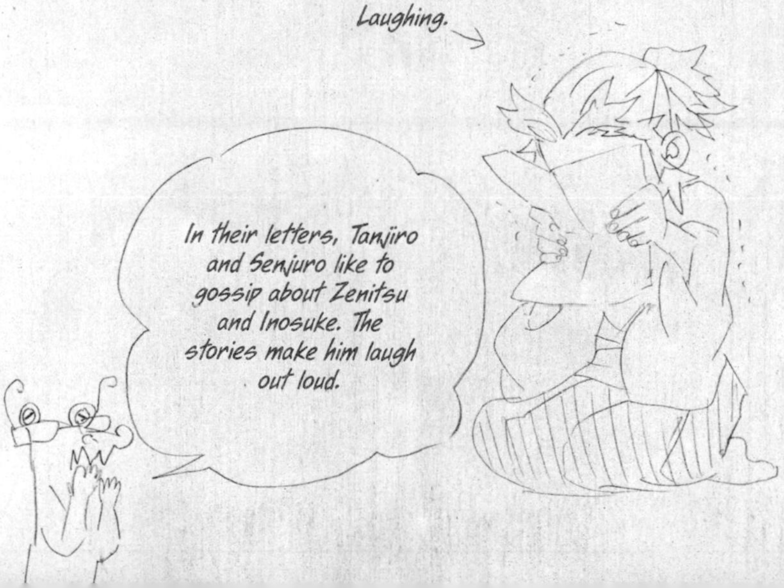
Laughing.
In their letters, Tanjiro and Senjuro like to gossip about Zenitsu and Inosuke. The stories make him laugh out loud.

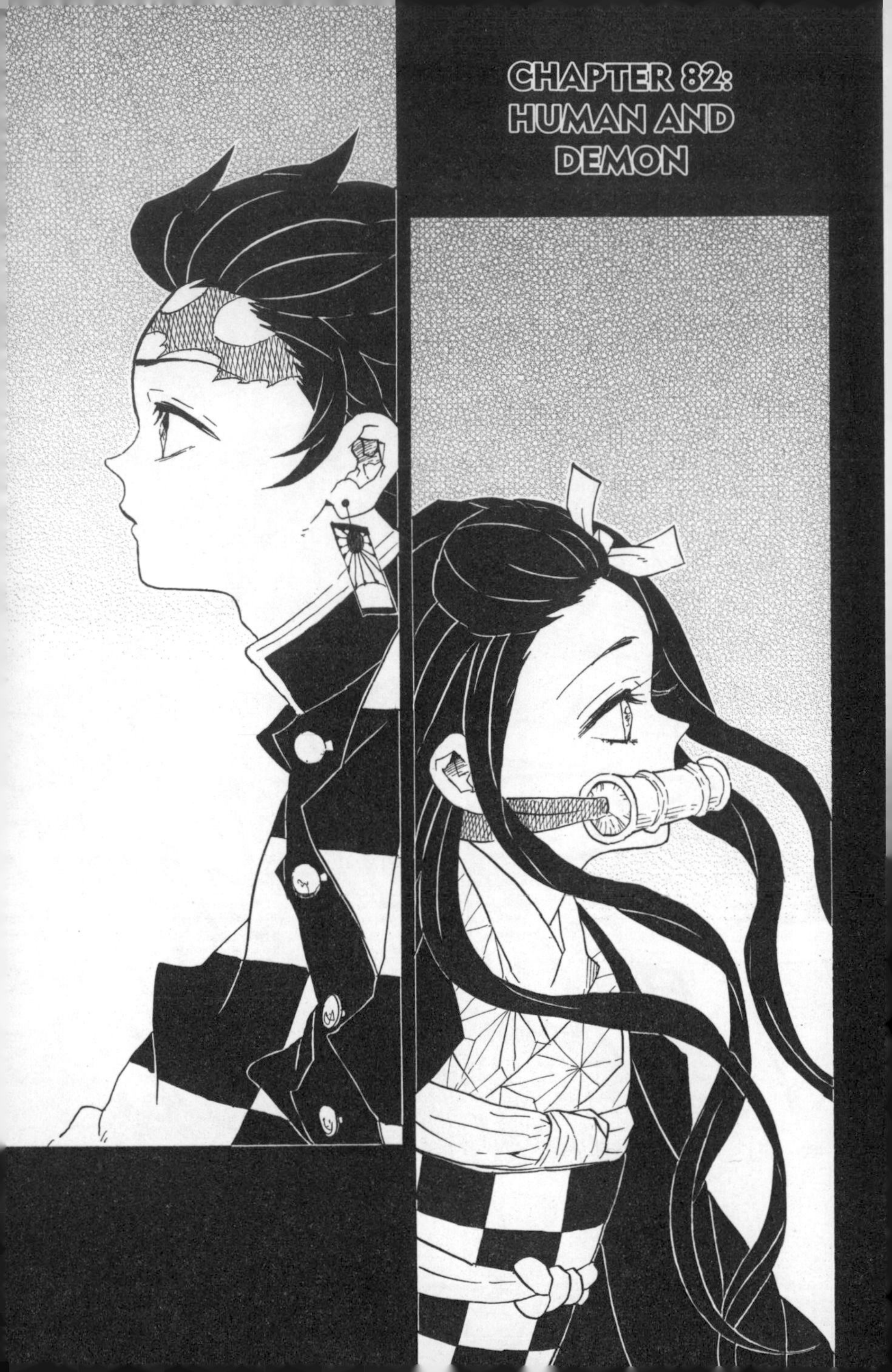
CHAPTER 82:
HUMAN AND
DEMON

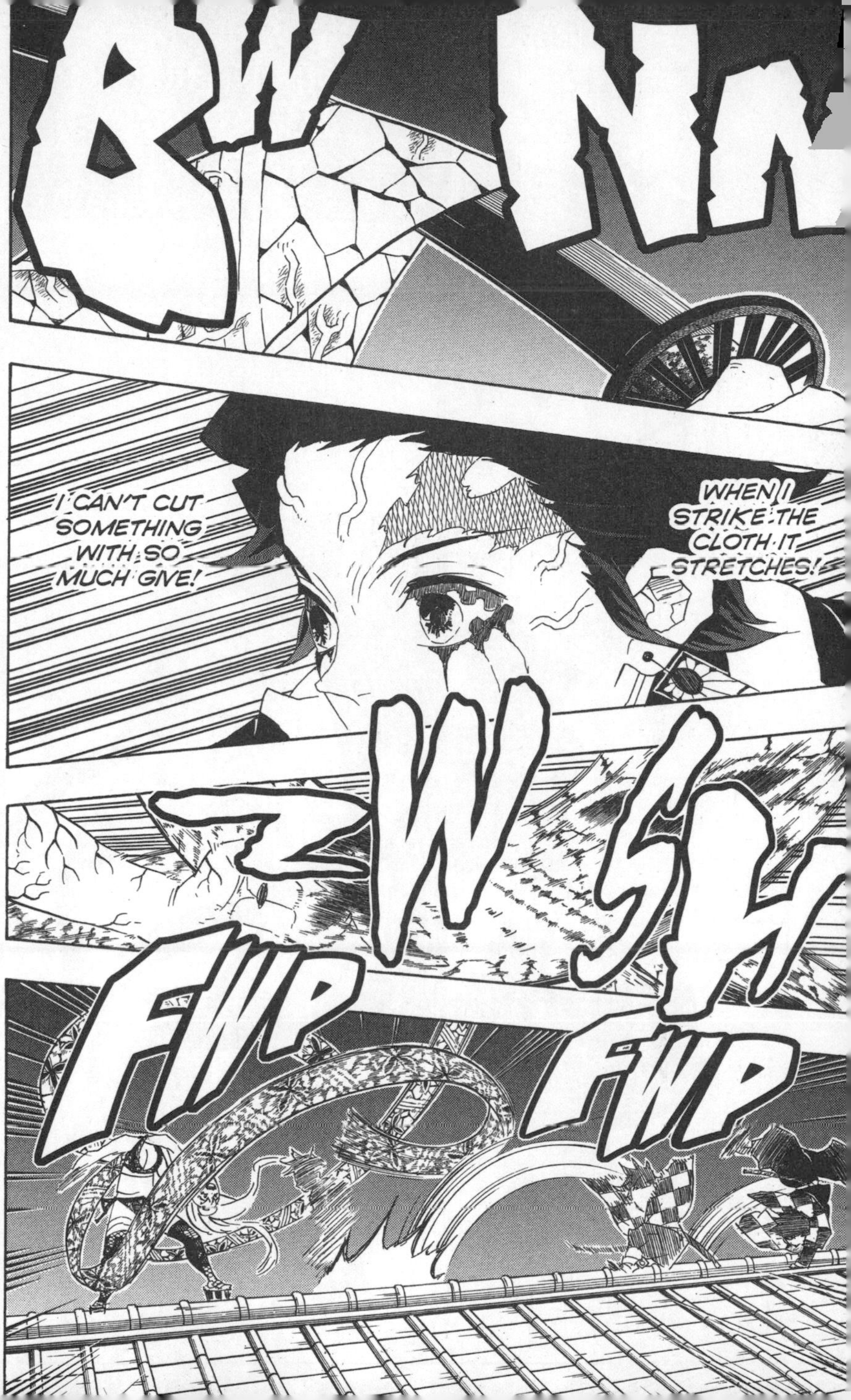
BWN
WHEN I STRIKE THE CLOTH IT STRETCHES!
I CAN'T CUT SOMETHING WITH SO MUCH GIVE!
ZWSH
FWP
FWP

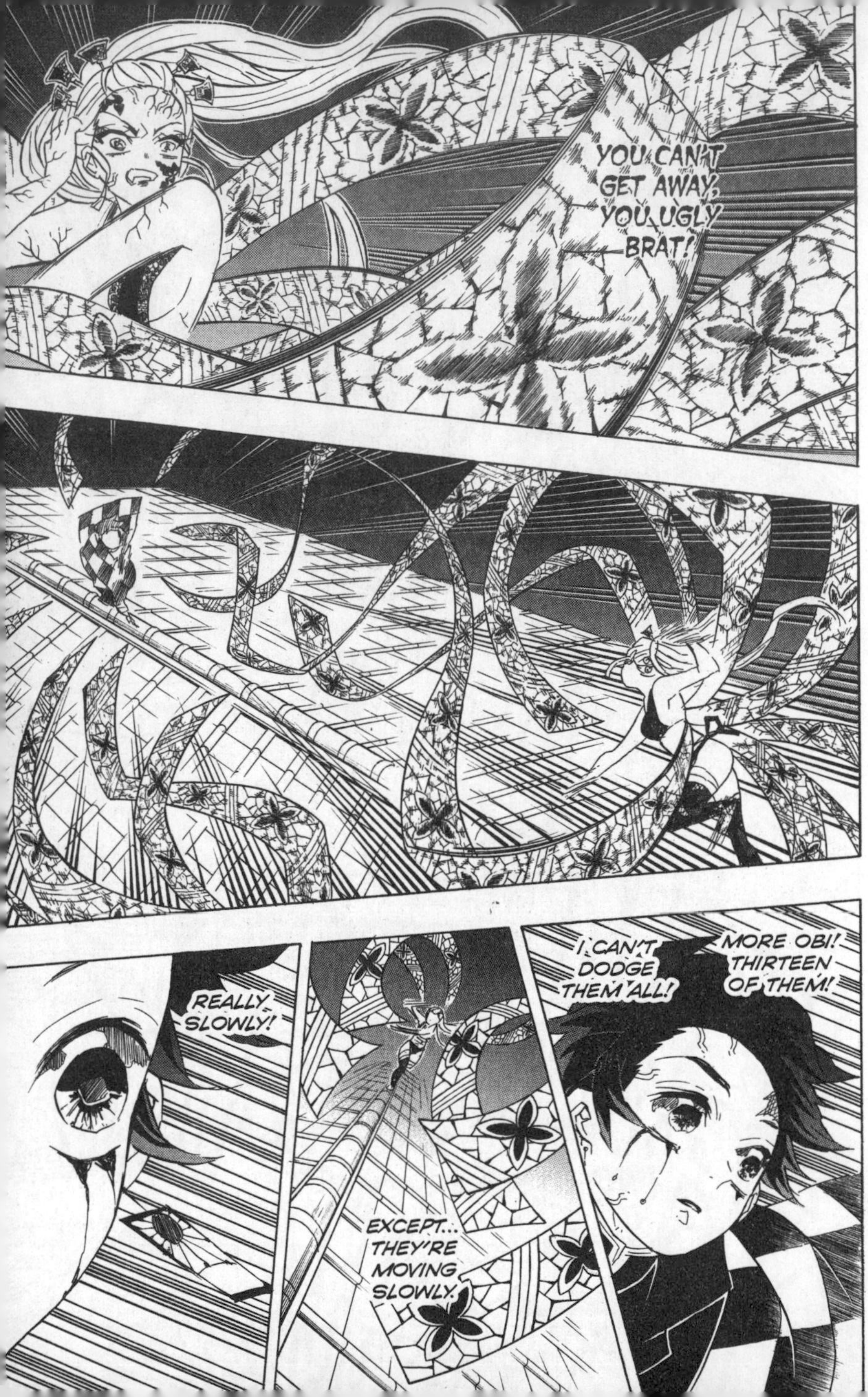
YOU CAN'T GET AWAY, YOU UGLY BRAT!
MORE OBI! THIRTEEN OF THEM!
I CAN'T DODGE THEM ALL!
EXCEPT... THEY'RE MOVING SLOWLY.
REALLY SLOWLY!

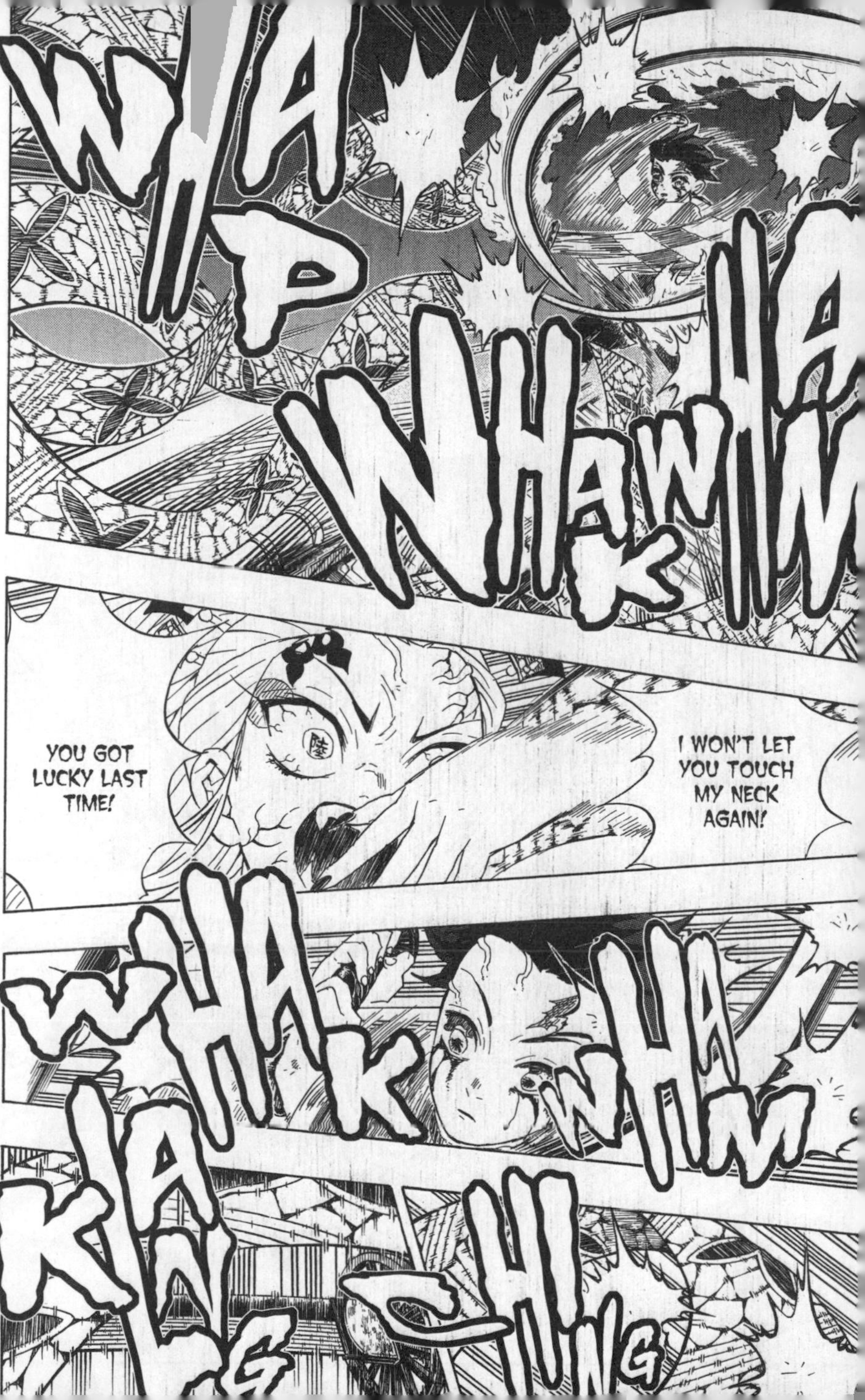
WAP
I WON'T LET YOU TOUCH MY NECK AGAIN!
YOU GOT LUCKY LAST TIME!

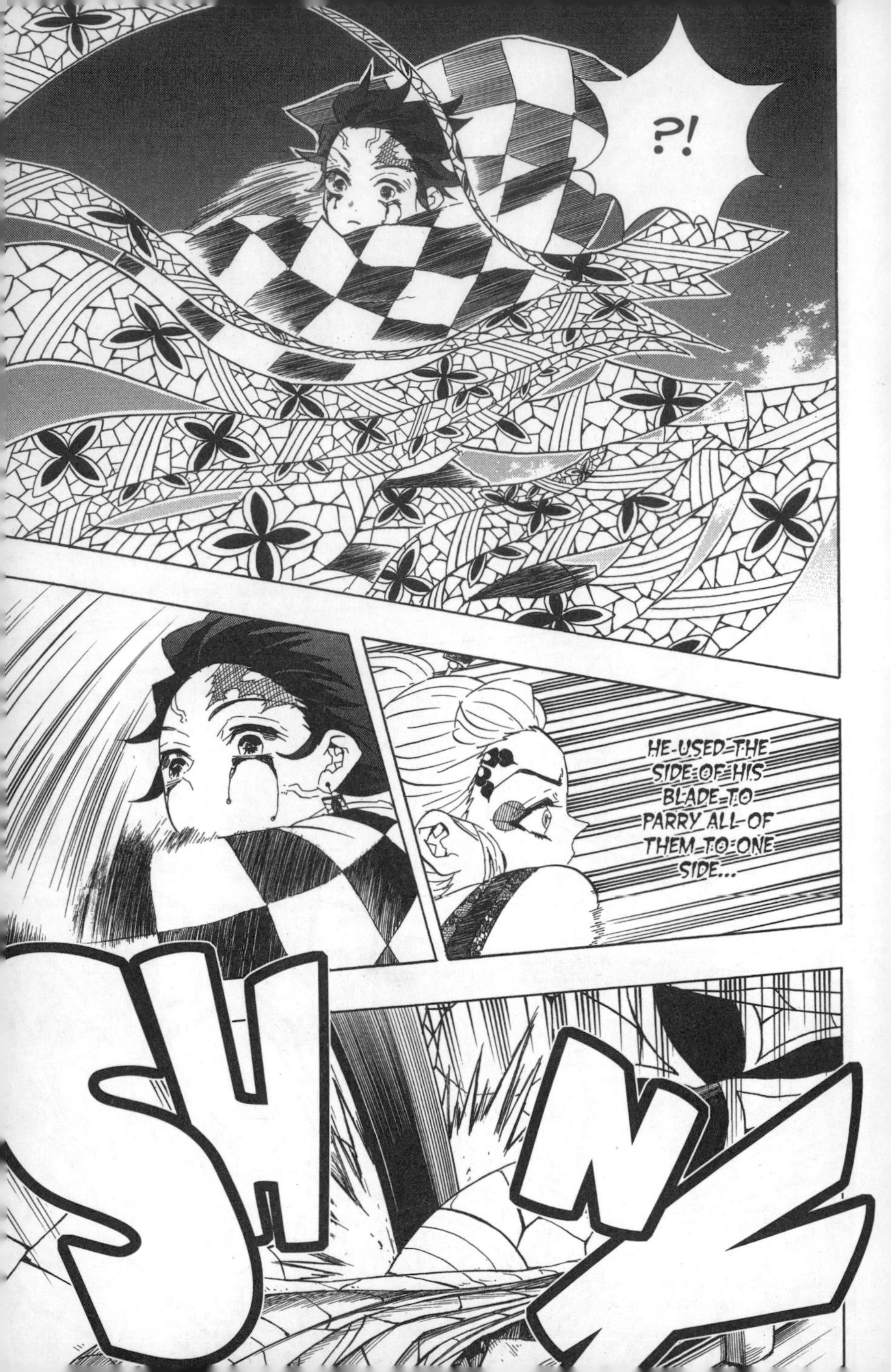
?!
HE USED THE SIDE OF HIS BLADE TO PARRY ALL OF THEM TO ONE SIDE...
SHNK

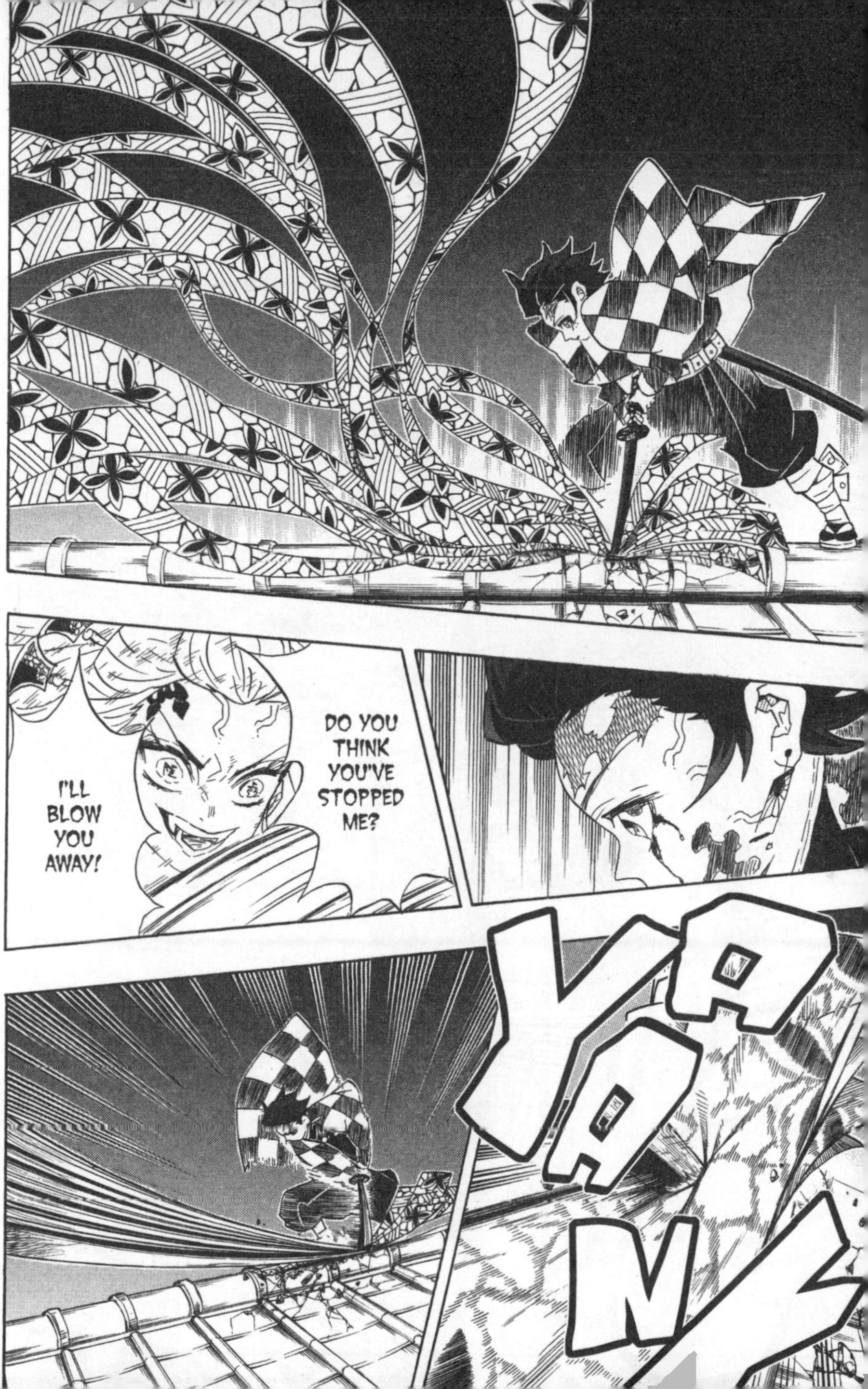
DO YOU THINK YOU'VE STOPPED ME?
I'LL BLOW YOU AWAY!

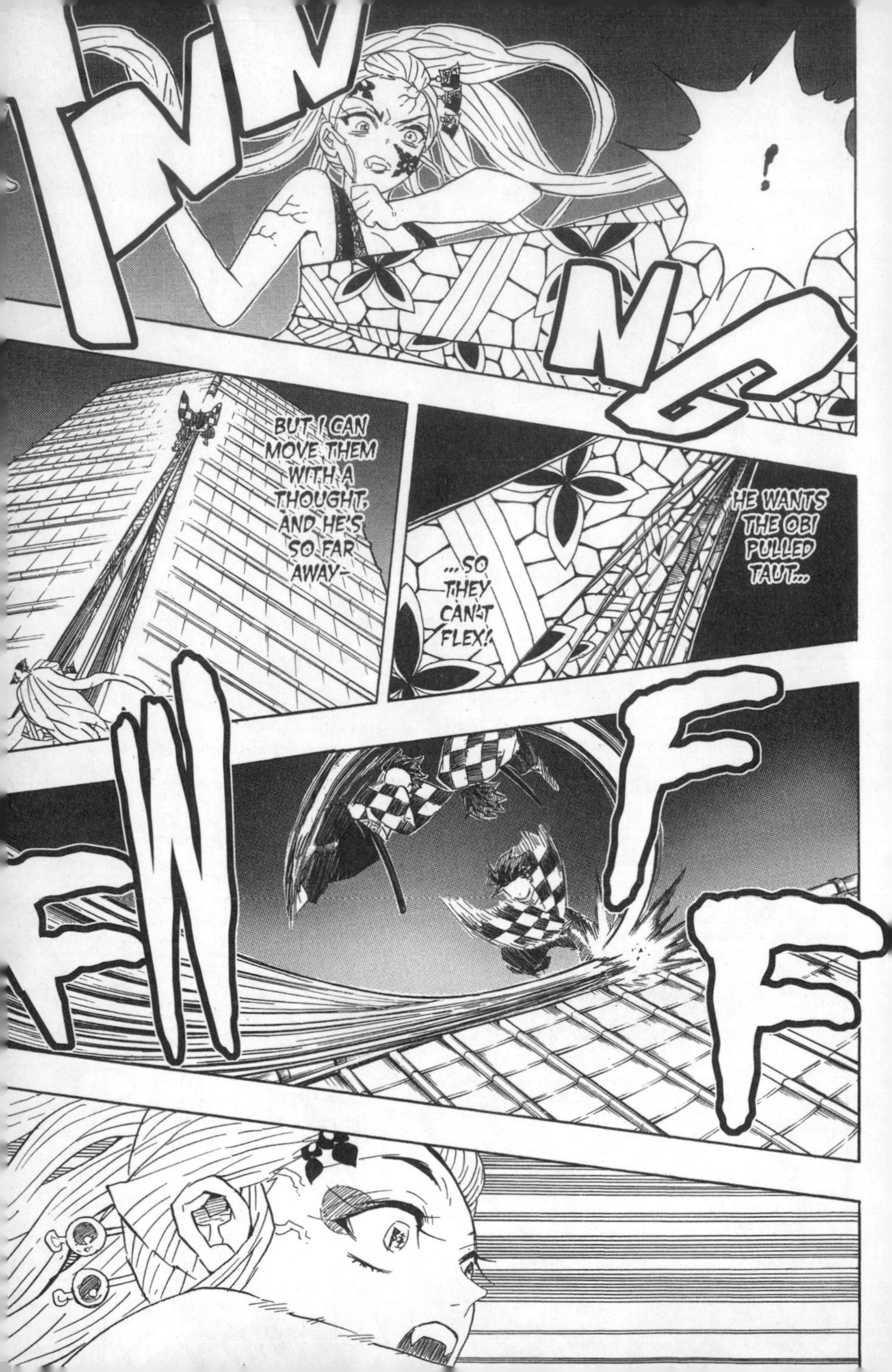
!
HE WANTS THE OBI PULLED TAUT...
...SO THEY CAN'T FLEX!!
BUT I CAN MOVE THEM WITH A THOUGHT, AND HE'S SO FAR AWAY–

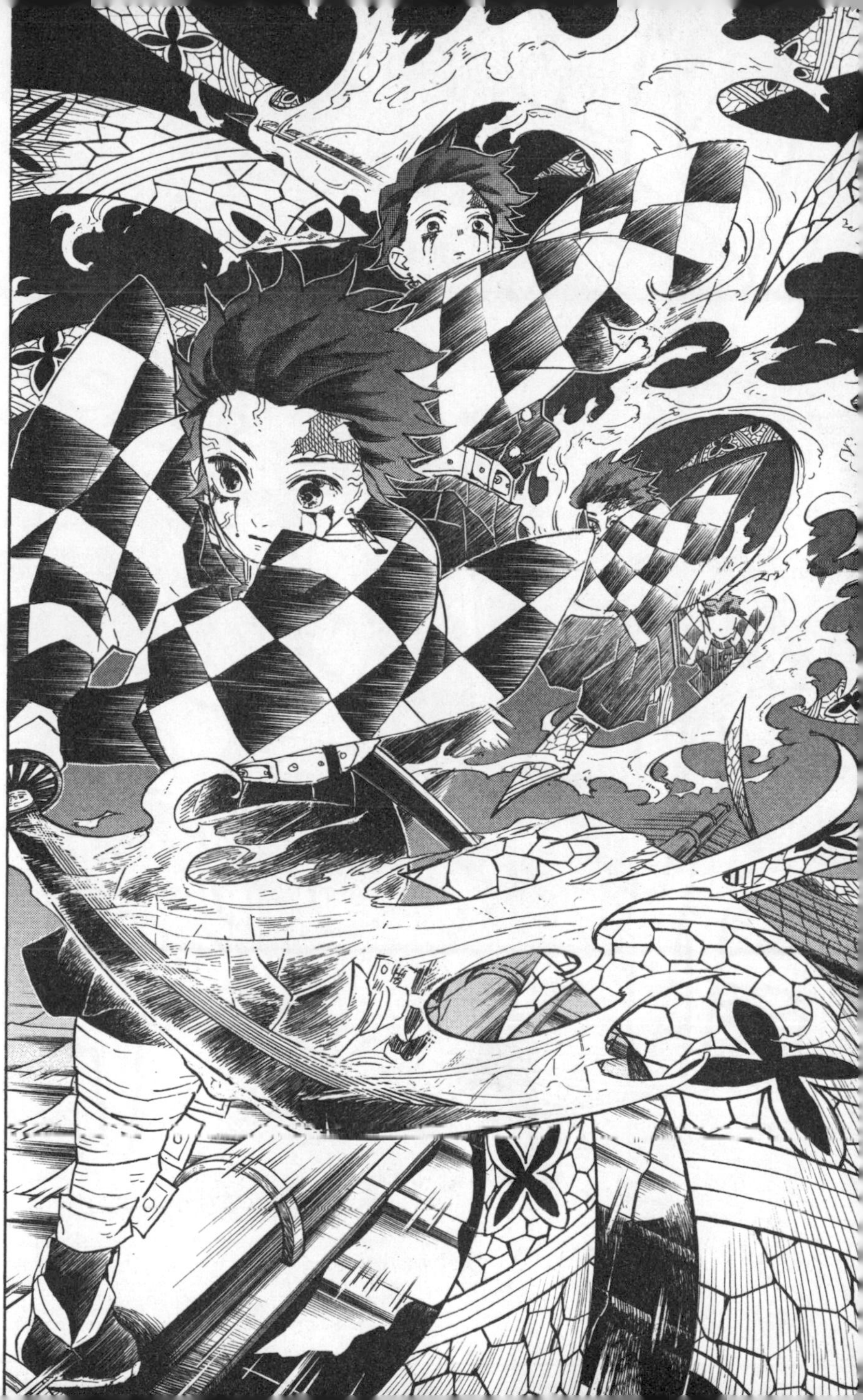

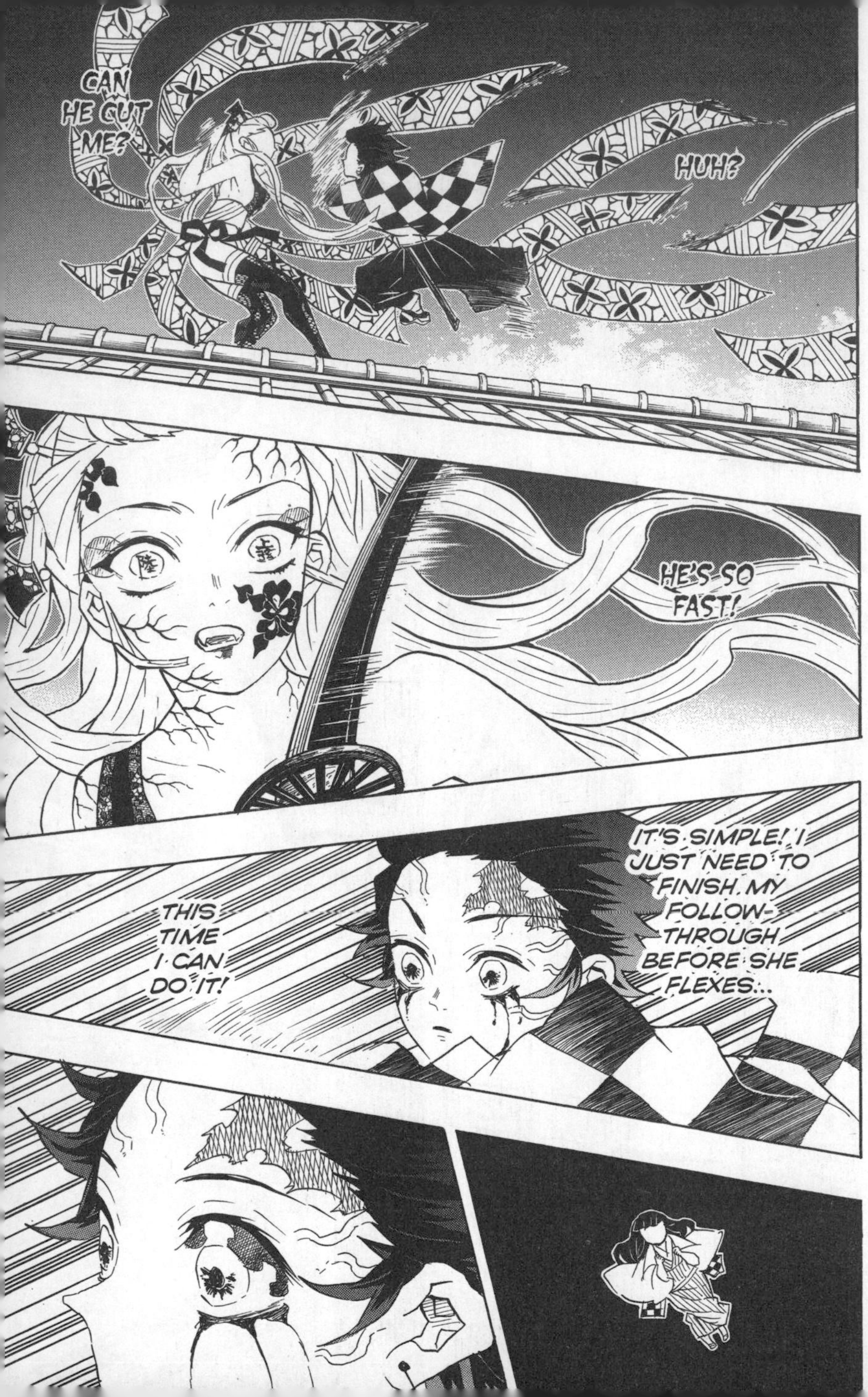
HUH?
CAN HE CUT ME?
HE'S SO FAST!
IT'S SIMPLE! I JUST NEED TO FINISH MY FOLLOW-THROUGH BEFORE SHE FLEXES...
THIS TIME I CAN DO IT!

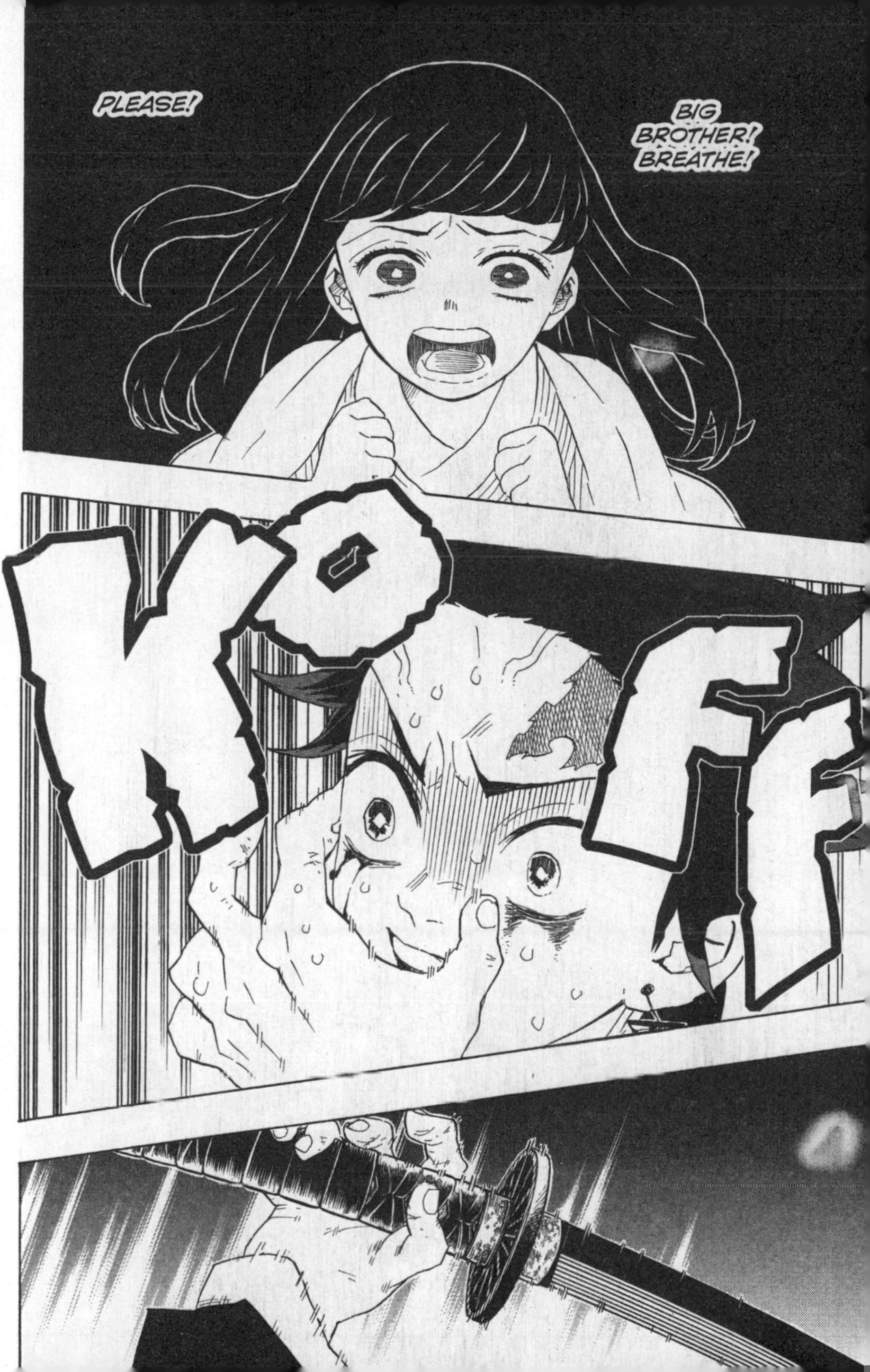
BIG BROTHER! BREATHE!
PLEASE!
KOFF

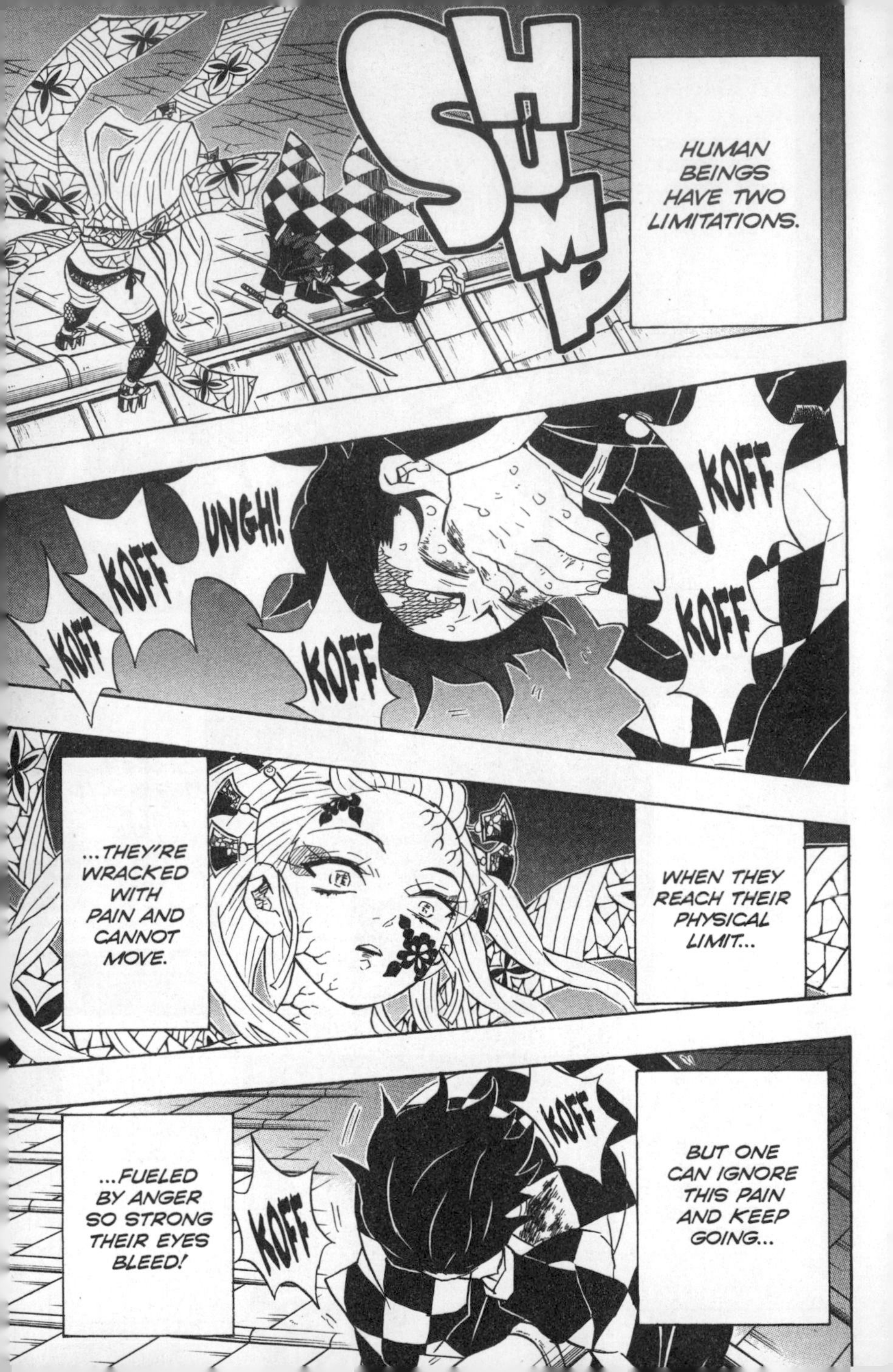
HUMAN BEINGS HAVE TWO LIMITATIONS.
SHUMP
KOFF
KOFF
UNGH!
KOFF
KOFF
KOFF
WHEN THEY REACH THEIR PHYSICAL LIMIT...
...THEY'RE WRACKED WITH PAIN AND CANNOT MOVE.
BUT ONE CAN IGNORE THIS PAIN AND KEEP GOING...
KOFF
KOFF
...FUELED BY ANGER SO STRONG THEIR EYES BLEED!

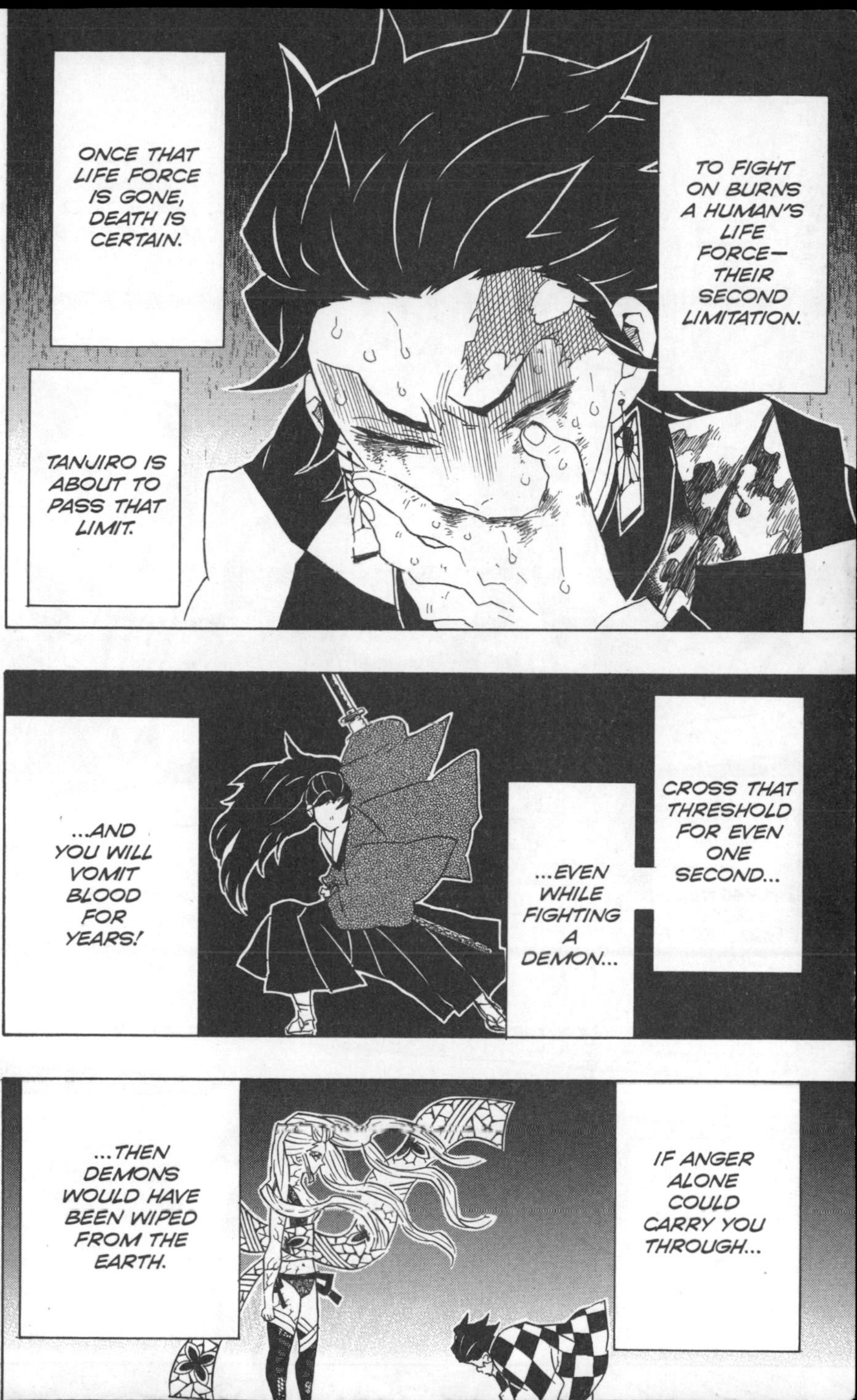
TO FIGHT ON BURNS A HUMAN'S LIFE FORCE—THEIR SECOND LIMITATION.
ONCE THAT LIFE FORCE IS GONE, DEATH IS CERTAIN.
TANJIRO IS ABOUT TO PASS THAT LIMIT.
CROSS THAT THRESHOLD FOR EVEN ONE SECOND...
...EVEN WHILE FIGHTING A DEMON...
...AND YOU WILL VOMIT BLOOD FOR YEARS!
IF ANGER ALONE COULD CARRY YOU THROUGH...
...THEN DEMONS WOULD HAVE BEEN WIPED FROM THE EARTH.

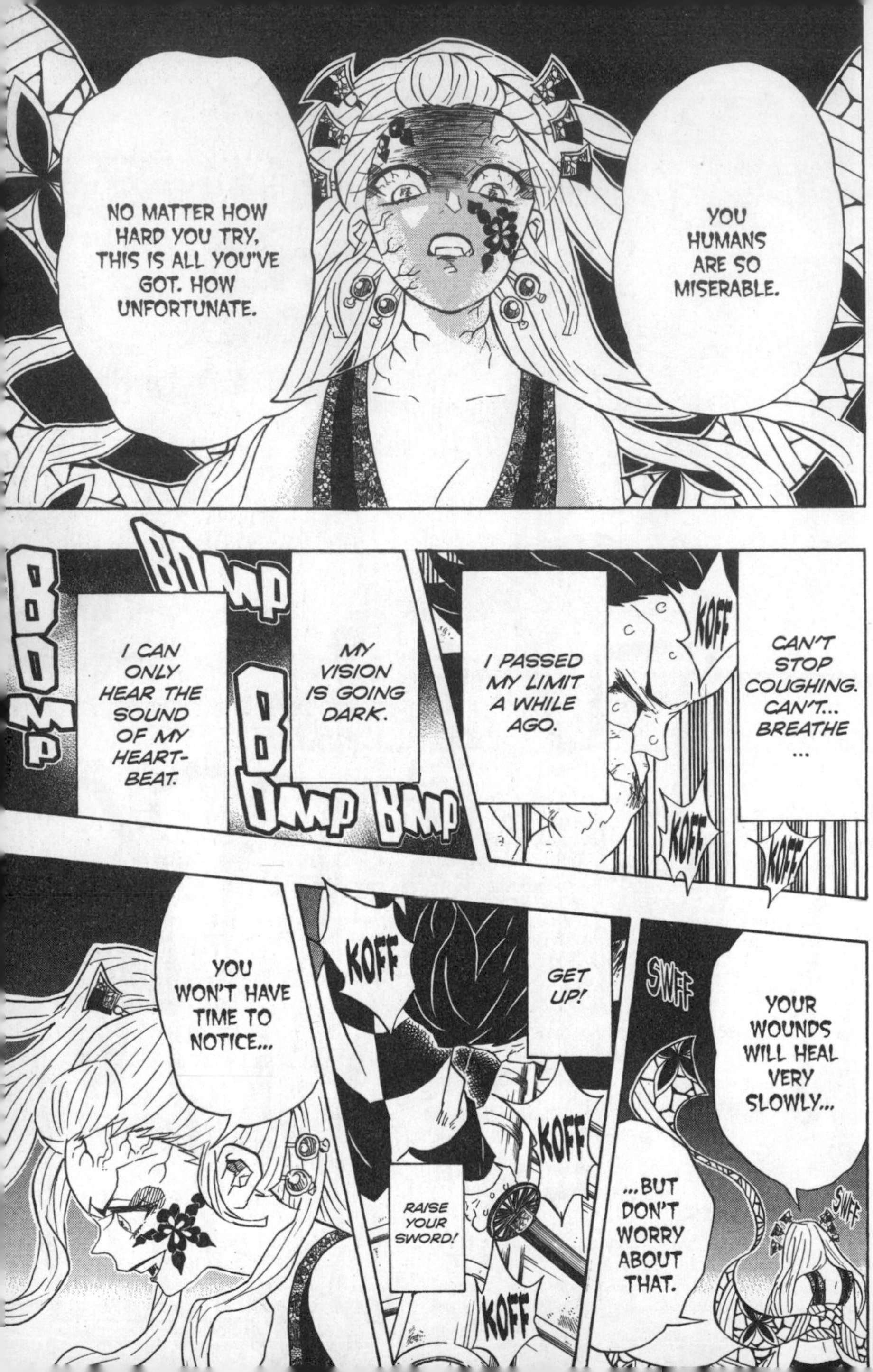
YOU HUMANS ARE SO MISERABLE.
NO MATTER HOW HARD YOU TRY, THIS IS ALL YOU'VE GOT. HOW UNFORTUNATE.
CAN'T STOP COUGHING. CAN'T... BREATHE ...
KOFF
KOFF
KOFF
I PASSED MY LIMIT A WHILE AGO.
BDMP BMP
MY VISION IS GOING DARK.
BDMP
I CAN ONLY HEAR THE SOUND OF MY HEART-BEAT.
BDMP
SWFF
YOUR WOUNDS WILL HEAL VERY SLOWLY...
...BUT DON'T WORRY ABOUT THAT.
SWFF
GET UP!
KOFF
KOFF
RAISE YOUR SWORD!
KOFF
YOU WON'T HAVE TIME TO NOTICE...

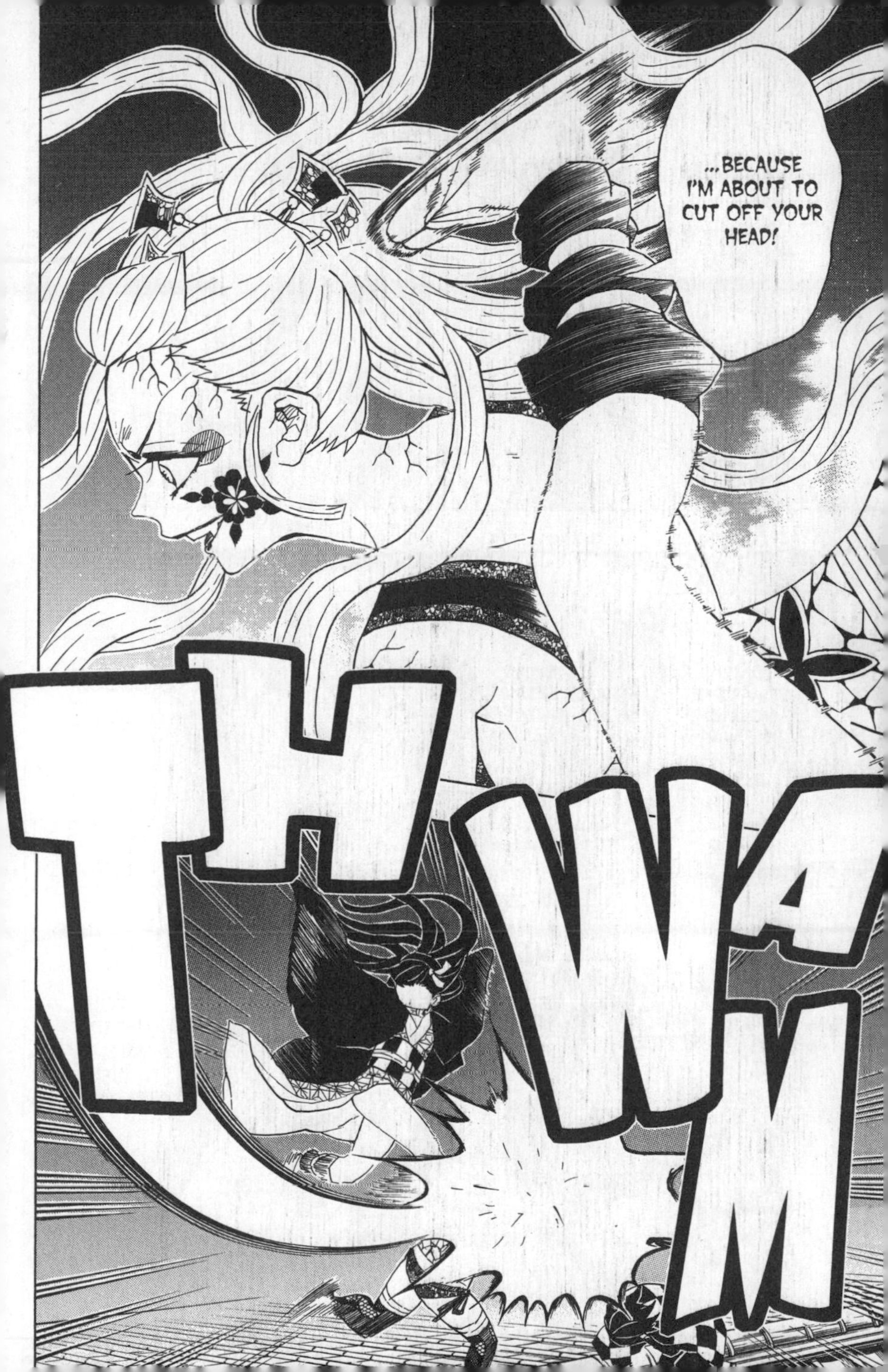
...BECAUSE I'M ABOUT TO CUT OFF YOUR HEAD!
THWAM

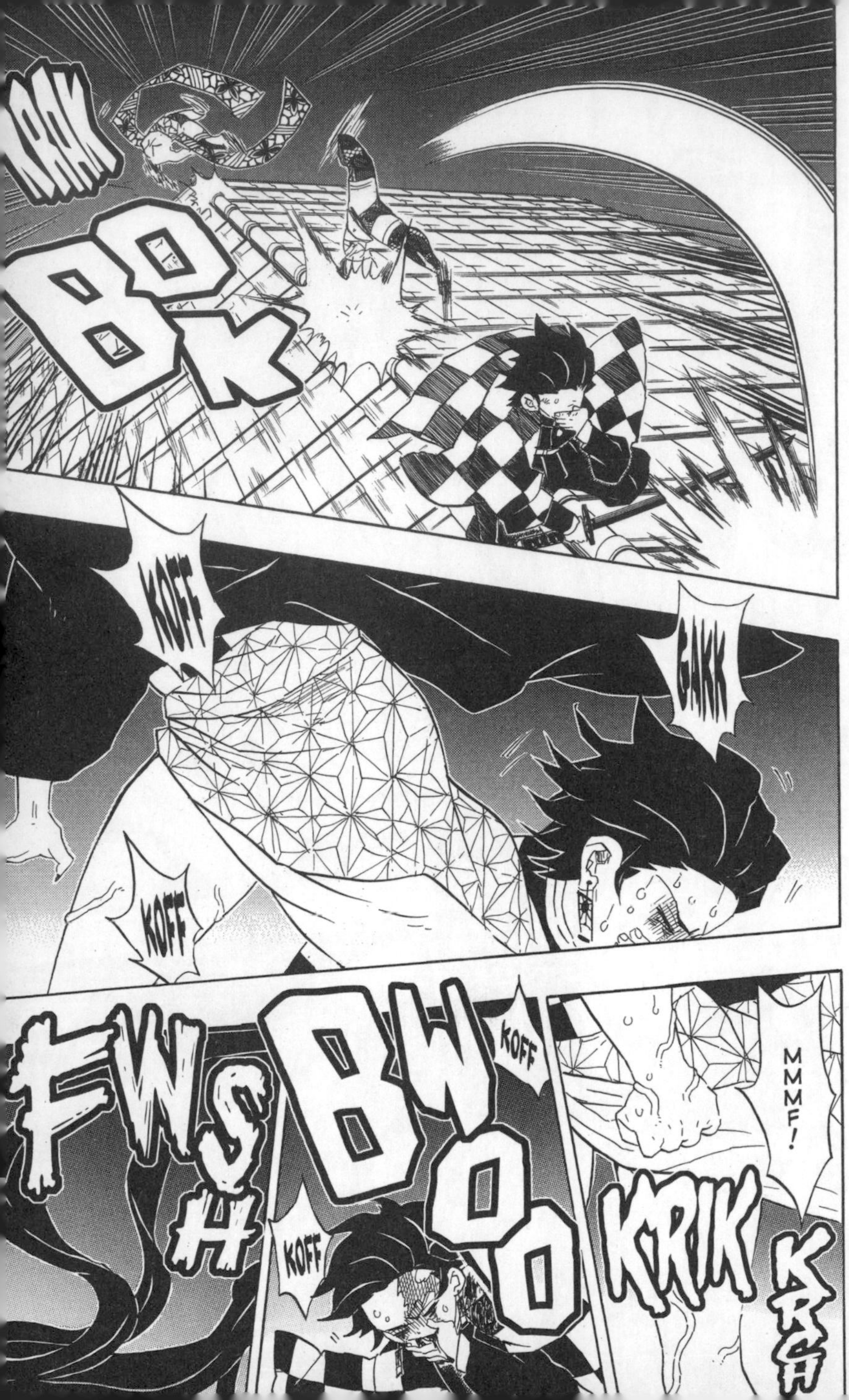

RAK
BOK
GAKK
KOFF
KOFF
MMMF!
KRIK
KRCH
KOFF
BWOO
FWSH
KOFF

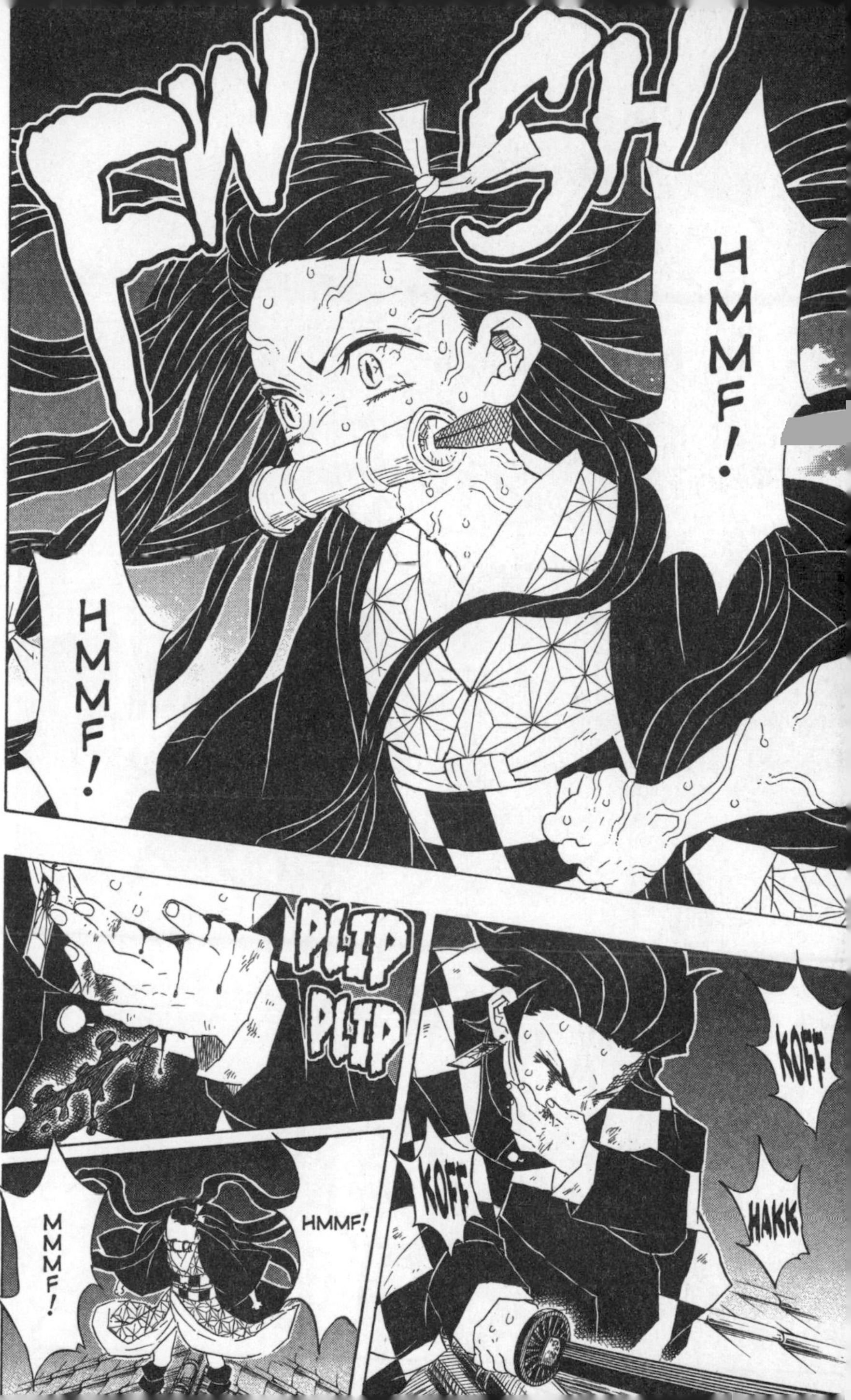
FWISH
HMMF!
HMMF!
KOFF
KOFF
HAKK
PLIP
PLIP
HMMF!
MMMF!

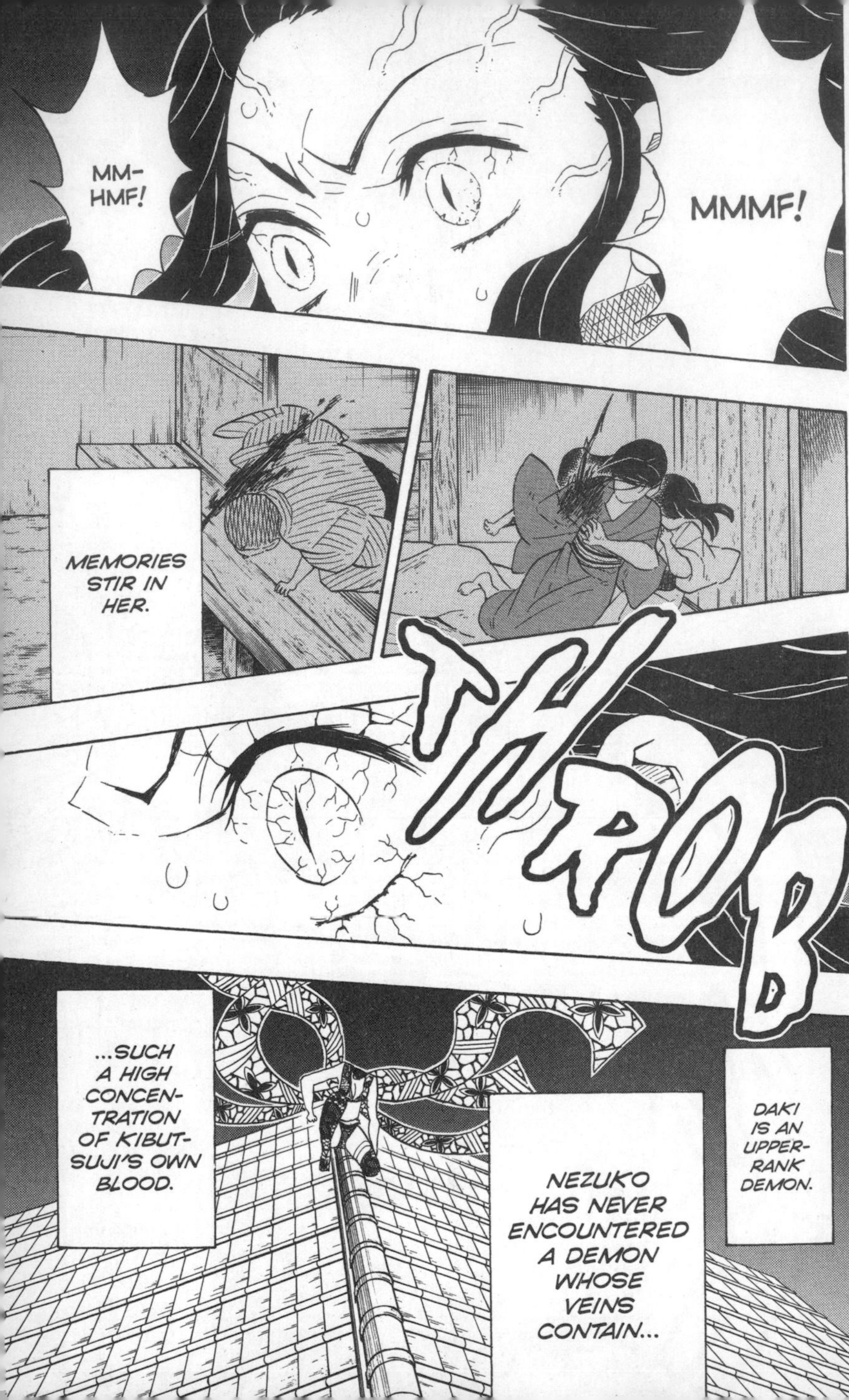
MMMF!
MM-HMF!
MEMORIES STIR IN HER.
THROB
DAKI IS AN UPPER-RANK DEMON.
NEZUKO HAS NEVER ENCOUNTERED A DEMON WHOSE VEINS CONTAIN...
...SUCH A HIGH CONCENTRATION OF KIBUTSUJI'S OWN BLOOD.

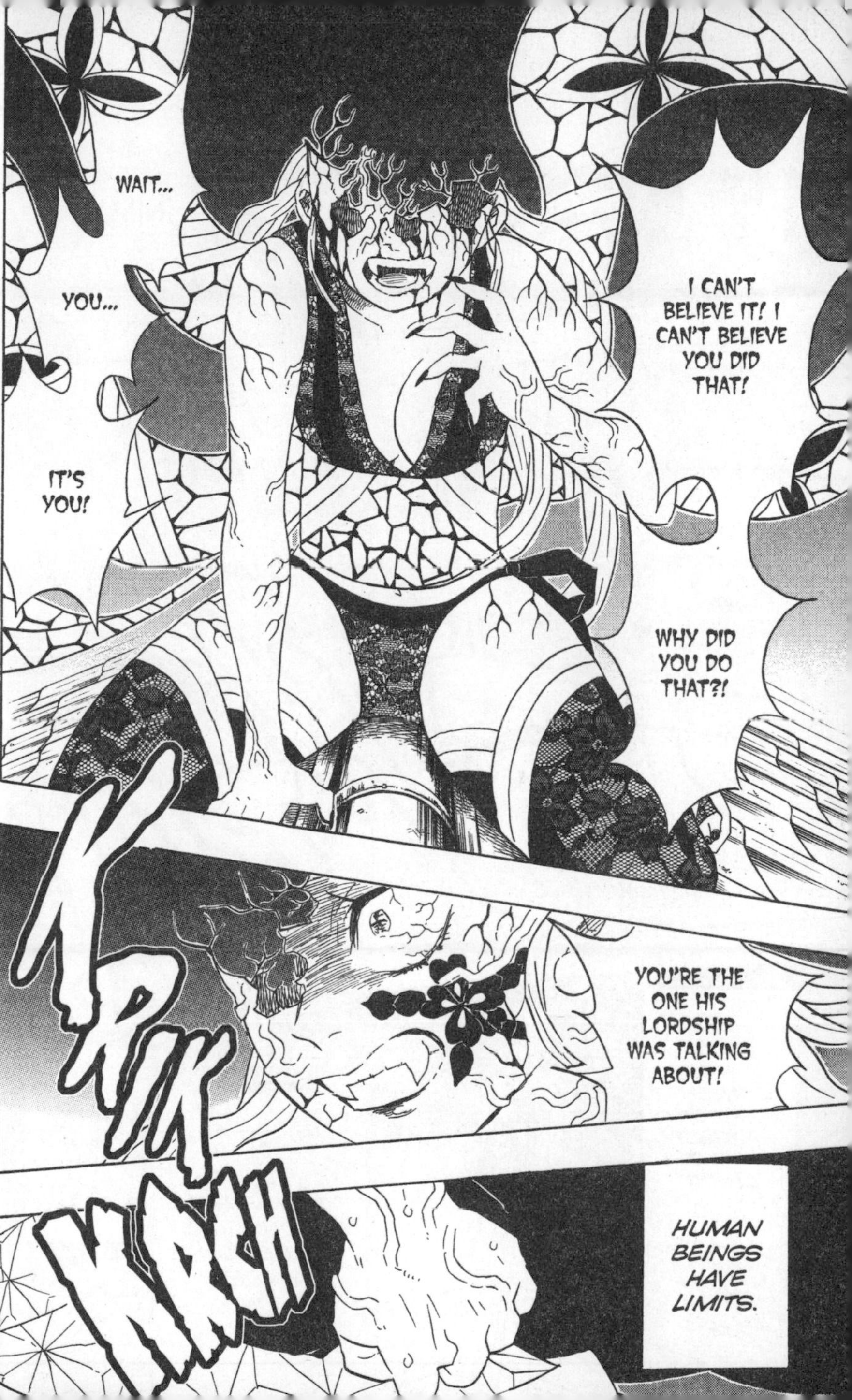
I CAN'T BELIEVE IT! I CAN'T BELIEVE YOU DID THAT!
WHY DID YOU DO THAT?!
WAIT...
YOU...
IT'S YOU!
YOU'RE THE ONE HIS LORDSHIP WAS TALKING ABOUT!
KRAK
HUMAN BEINGS HAVE LIMITS.
KRACH

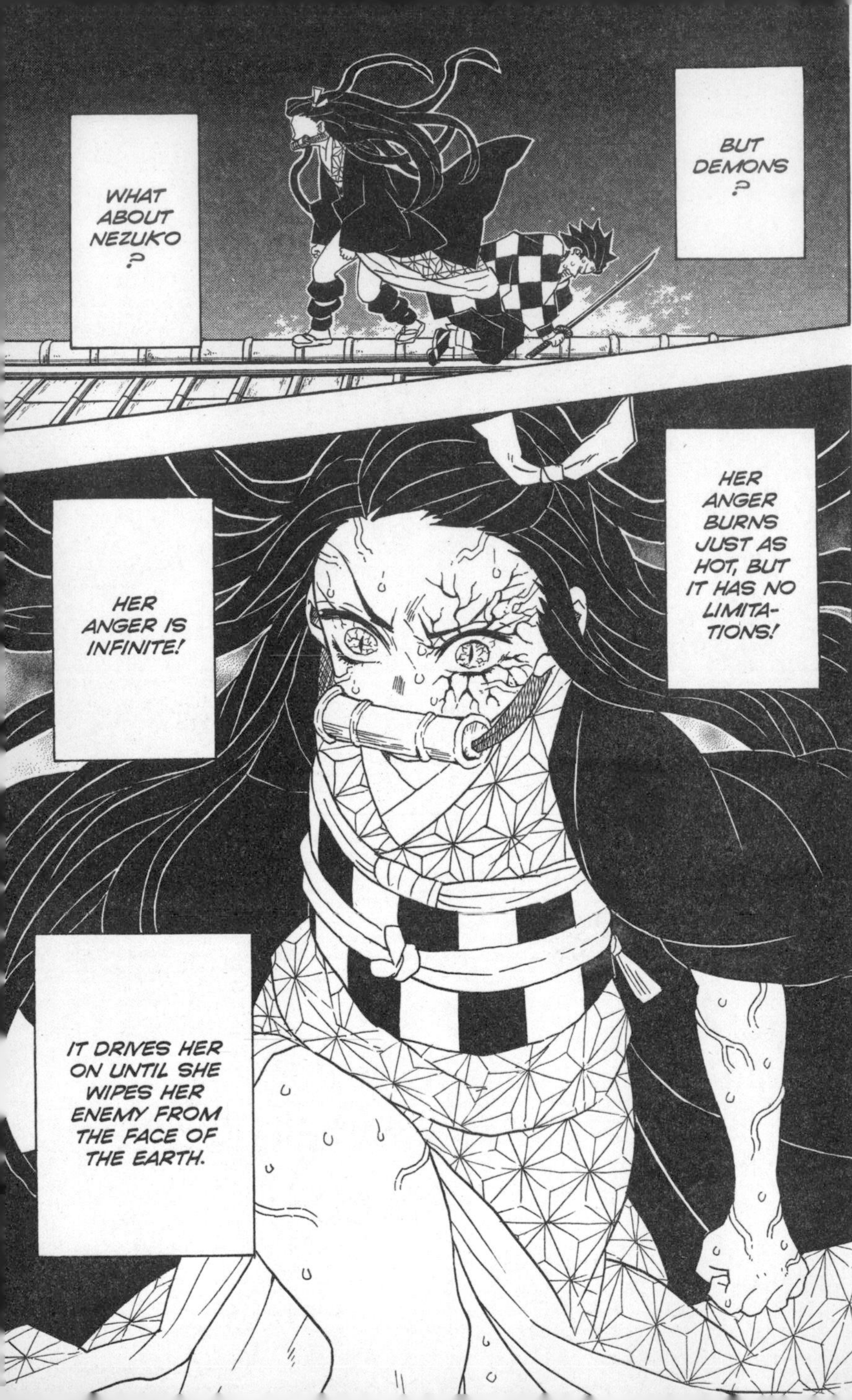
BUT DEMONS?
WHAT ABOUT NEZUKO?
HER ANGER BURNS JUST AS HOT, BUT IT HAS NO LIMITATIONS!
HER ANGER IS INFINITE!
IT DRIVES HER ON UNTIL SHE WIPES HER ENEMY FROM THE FACE OF THE EARTH.

CHAPTER 83: TRANSFORMATION

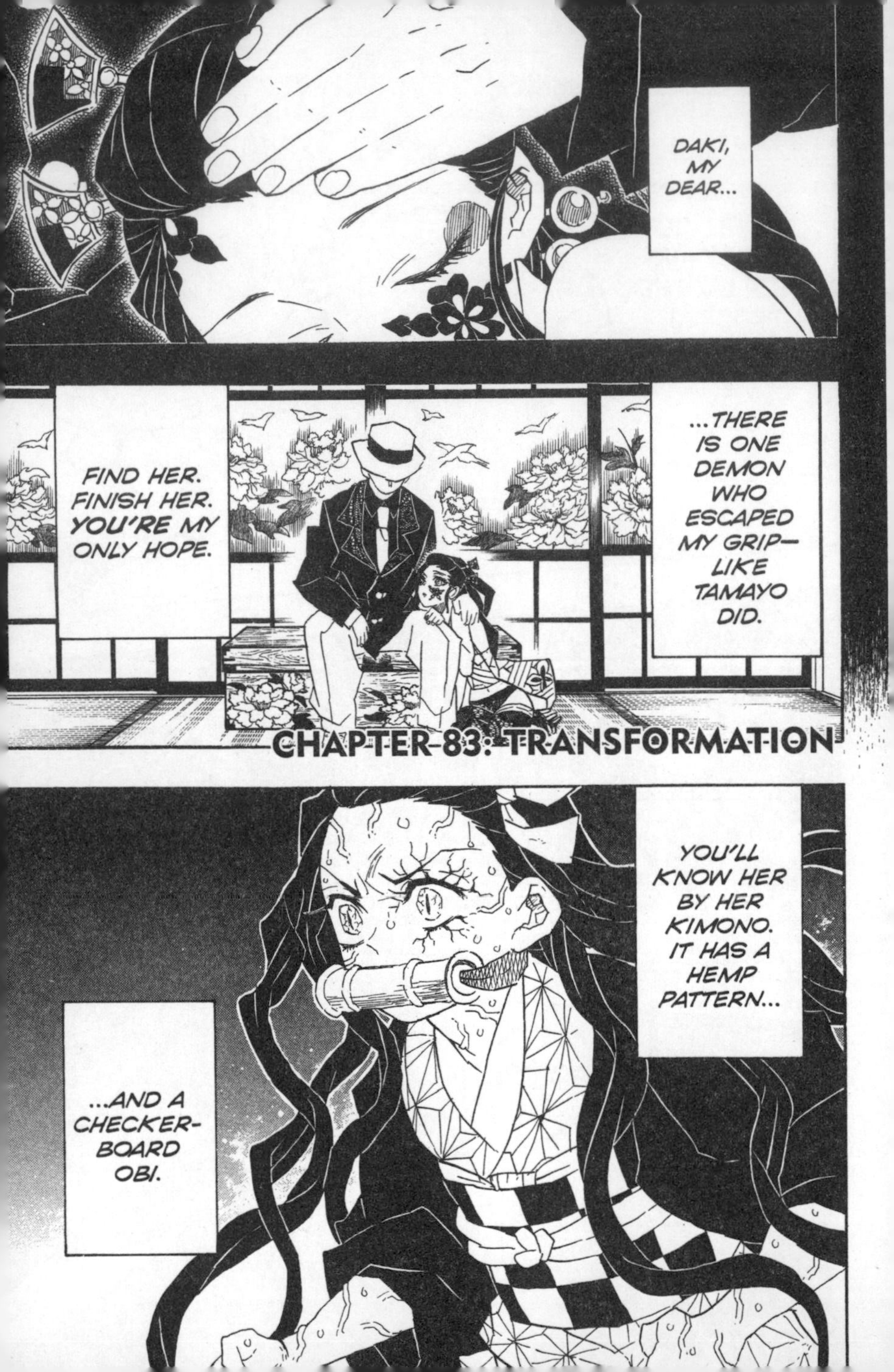
DAKI, MY DEAR...
...THERE IS ONE DEMON WHO ESCAPED MY GRIP—LIKE TAMAYO DID.
FIND HER. FINISH HER. YOU'RE MY ONLY HOPE.
YOU'LL KNOW HER BY HER KIMONO. IT HAS A HEMP PATTERN...
...AND A CHECKER-BOARD OBI.

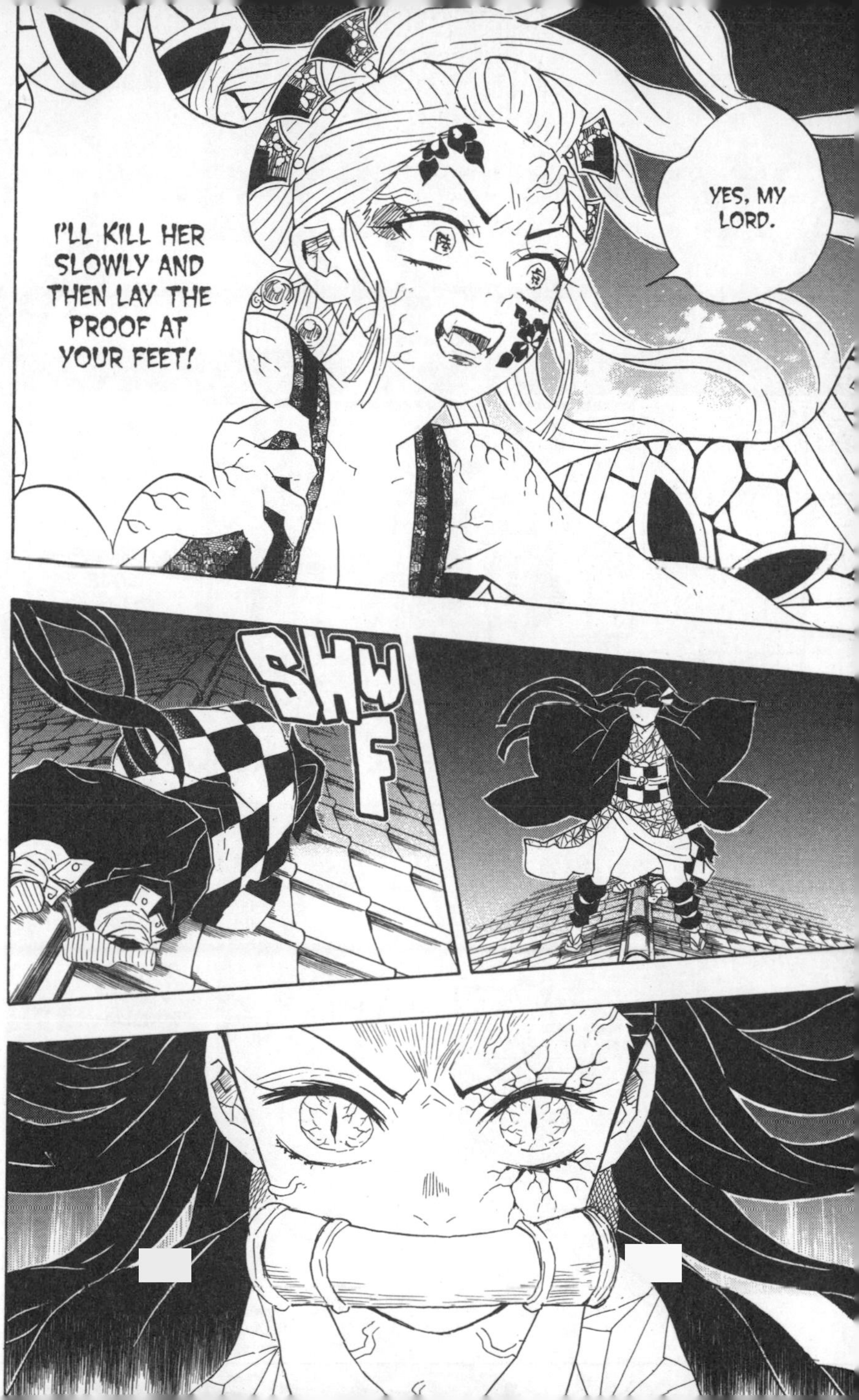
YES, MY LORD.
I'LL KILL HER SLOWLY AND THEN LAY THE PROOF AT YOUR FEET!
SHWF

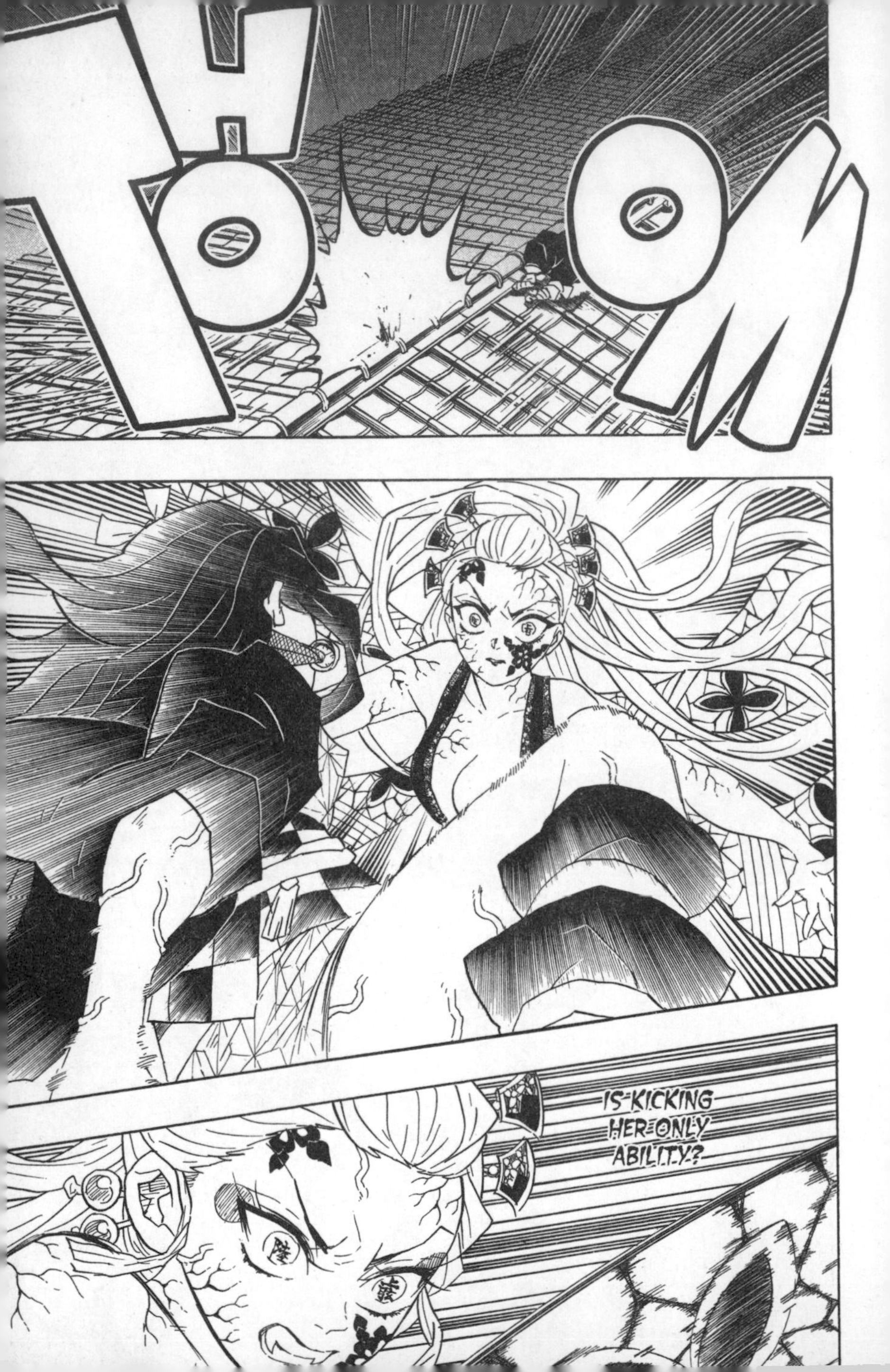
IS KICKING HER ONLY ABILITY?

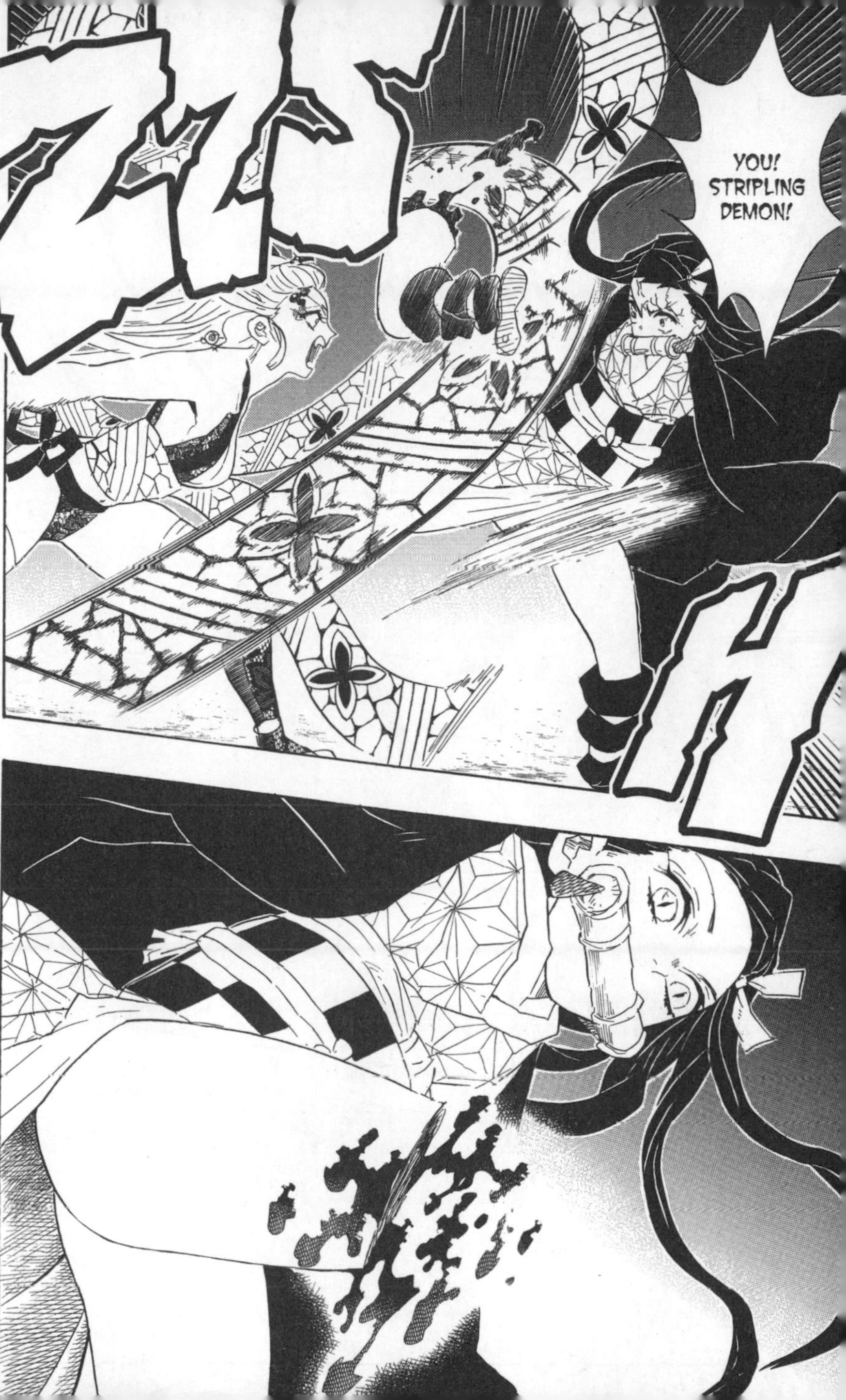
YOU! STRIPLING DEMON!

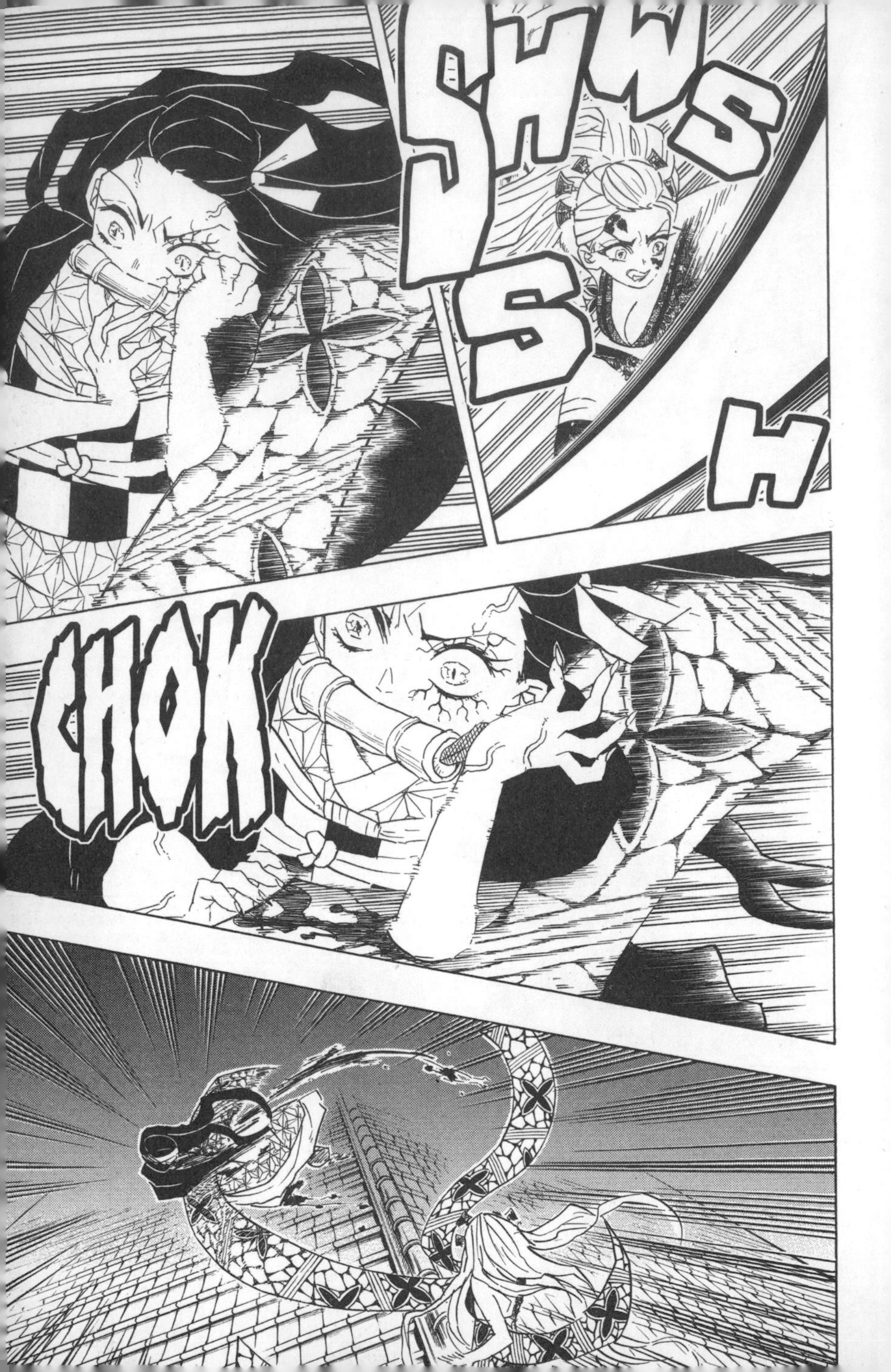
SHWSSH
CHOK

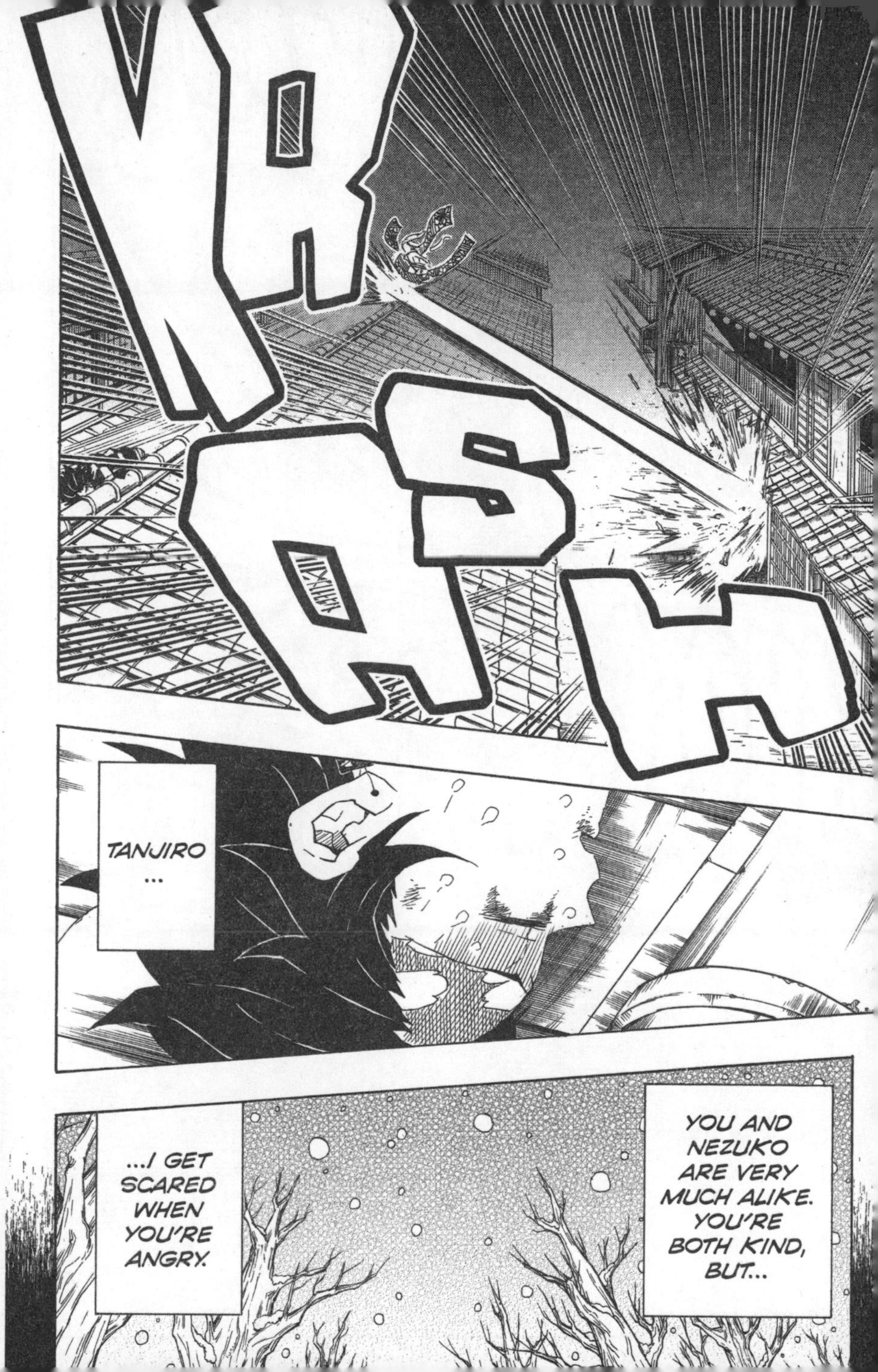
TANJIRO ...
YOU AND NEZUKO ARE VERY MUCH ALIKE. YOU'RE BOTH KIND, BUT...
...I GET SCARED WHEN YOU'RE ANGRY.

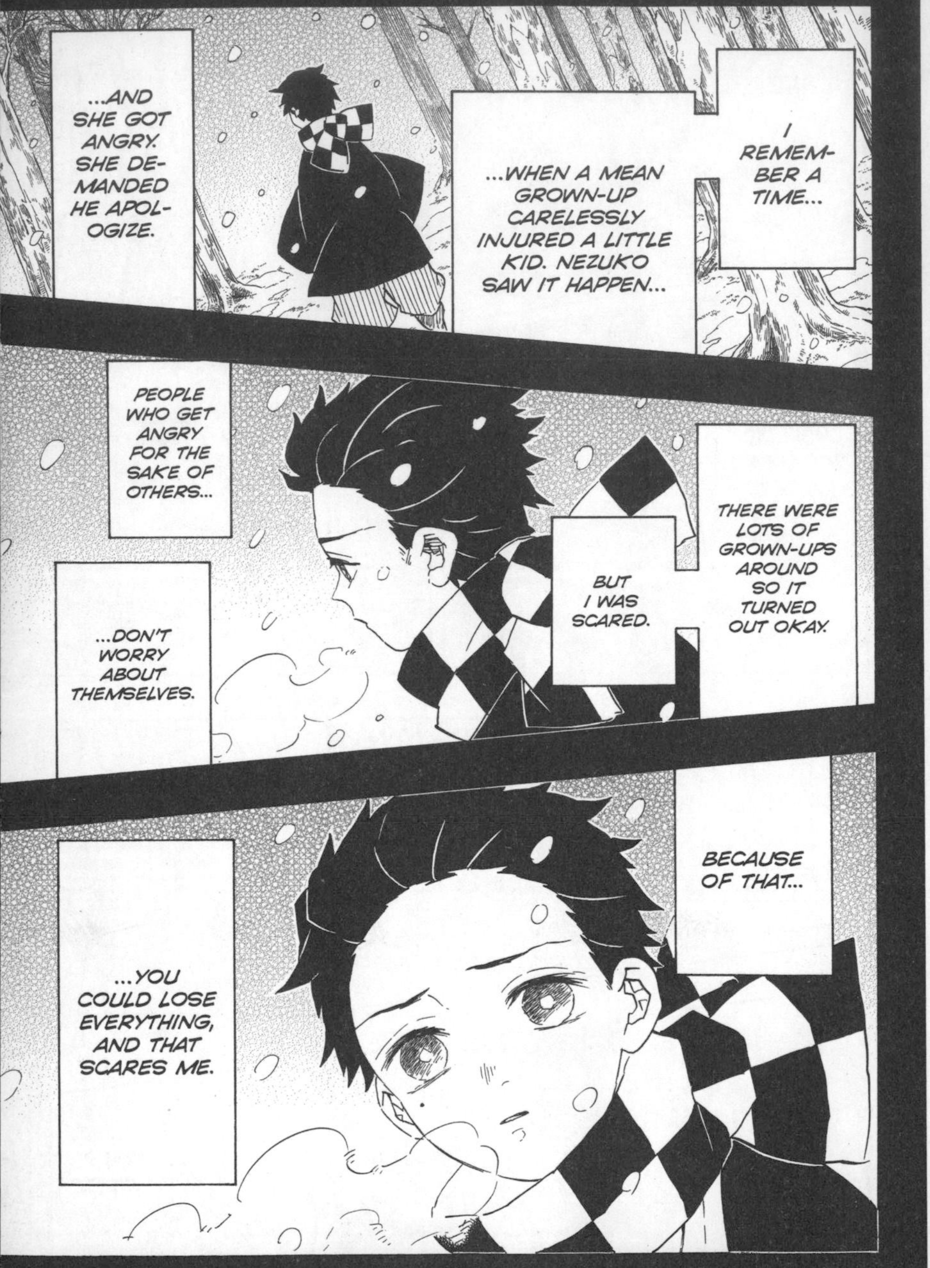
I REMEMBER A TIME...
...WHEN A MEAN GROWN-UP CARELESSLY INJURED A LITTLE KID. NEZUKO SAW IT HAPPEN...
...AND SHE GOT ANGRY. SHE DEMANDED HE APOLOGIZE.
THERE WERE LOTS OF GROWN-UPS AROUND SO IT TURNED OUT OKAY.
BUT I WAS SCARED.
PEOPLE WHO GET ANGRY FOR THE SAKE OF OTHERS...
...DON'T WORRY ABOUT THEMSELVES.
BECAUSE OF THAT...
...YOU COULD LOSE EVERYTHING, AND THAT SCARES ME.

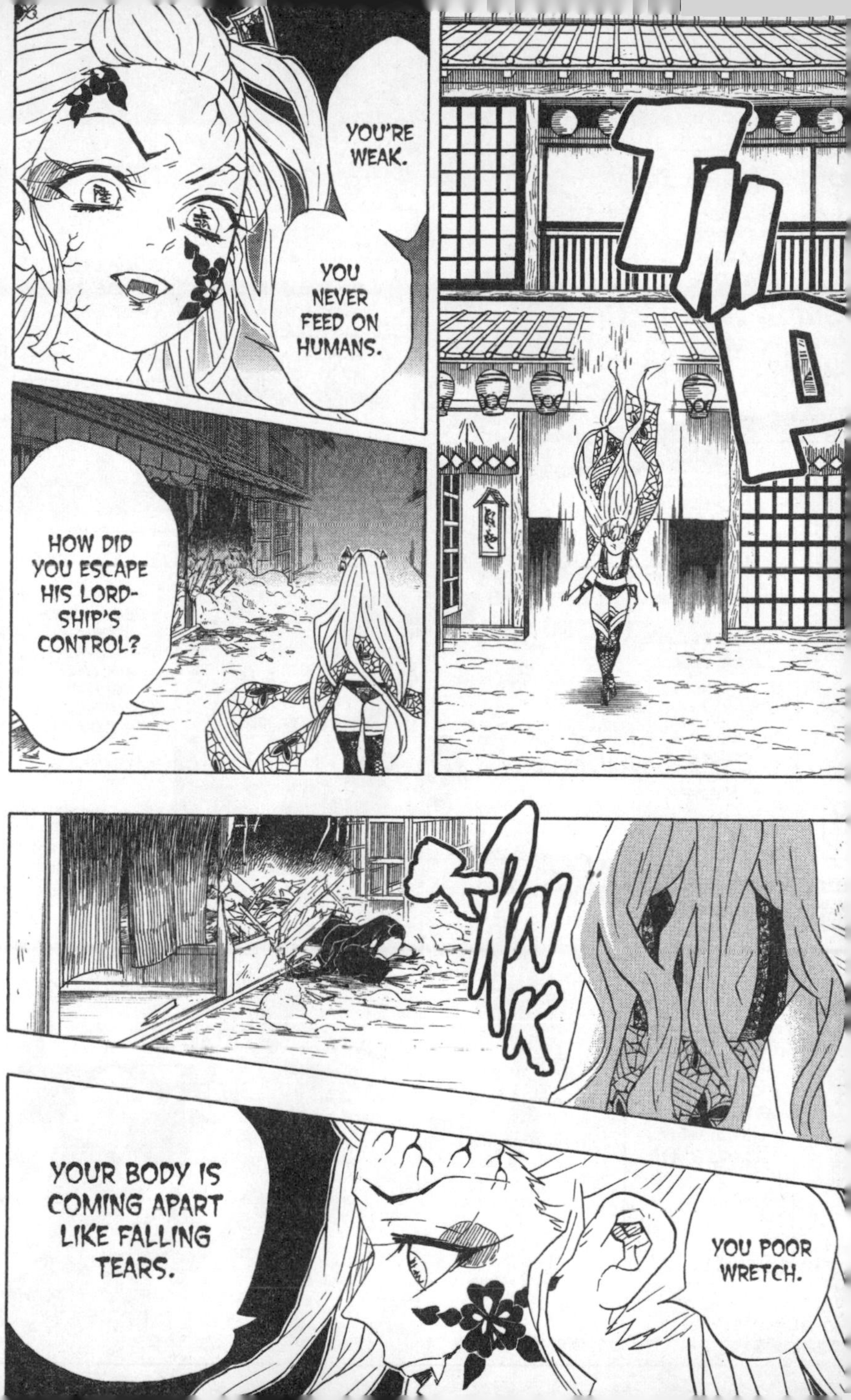
TMP
YOU'RE WEAK.
YOU NEVER FEED ON HUMANS.
HOW DID YOU ESCAPE HIS LORD-SHIP'S CONTROL?
YOU POOR WRETCH.
YOUR BODY IS COMING APART LIKE FALLING TEARS.

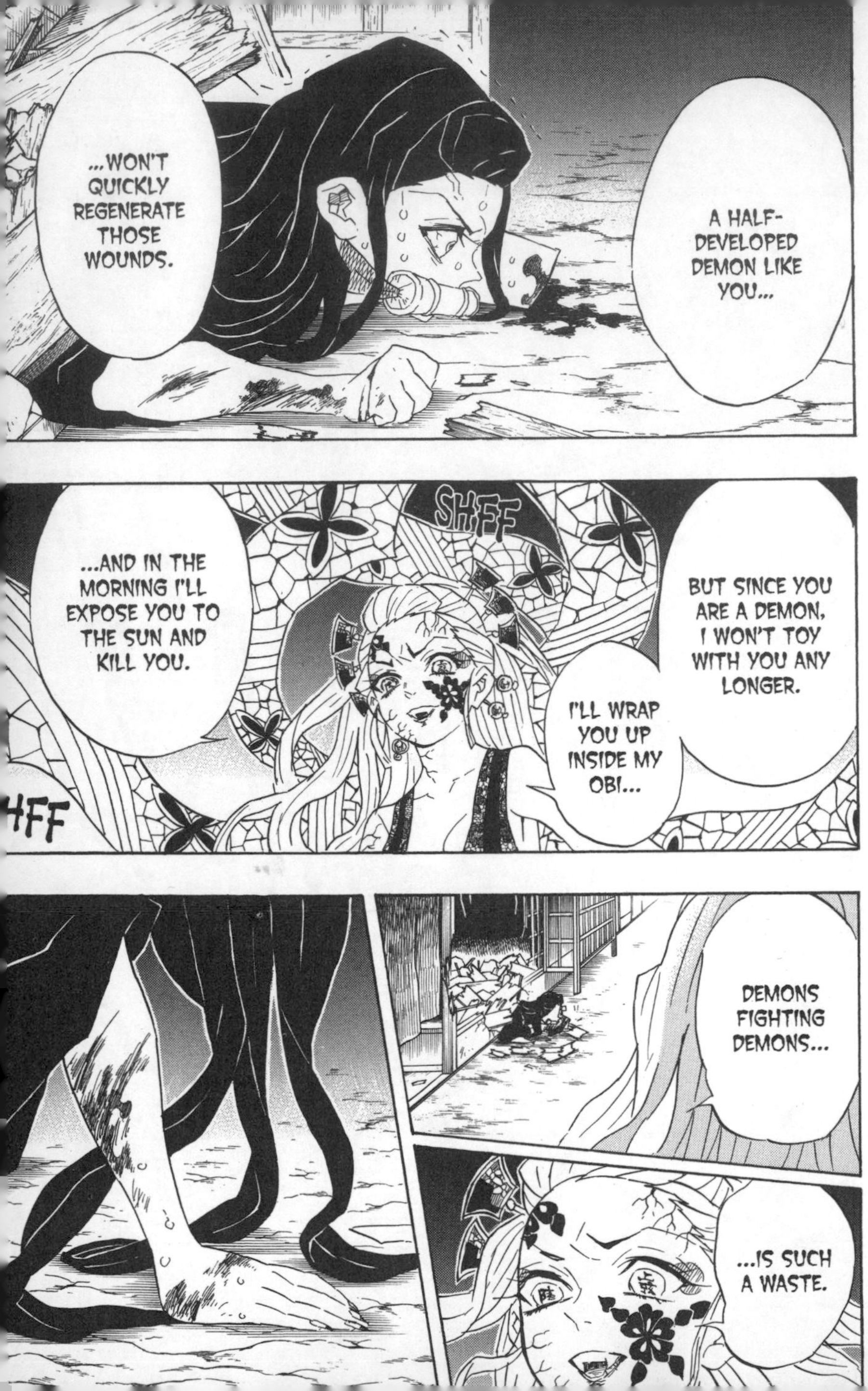
A HALF-DEVELOPED DEMON LIKE YOU...
...WON'T QUICKLY REGENERATE THOSE WOUNDS.
BUT SINCE YOU ARE A DEMON, I WON'T TOY WITH YOU ANY LONGER.
I'LL WRAP YOU UP INSIDE MY OBI...
SHFF
...AND IN THE MORNING I'LL EXPOSE YOU TO THE SUN AND KILL YOU.
DEMONS FIGHTING DEMONS...
...IS SUCH A WASTE.

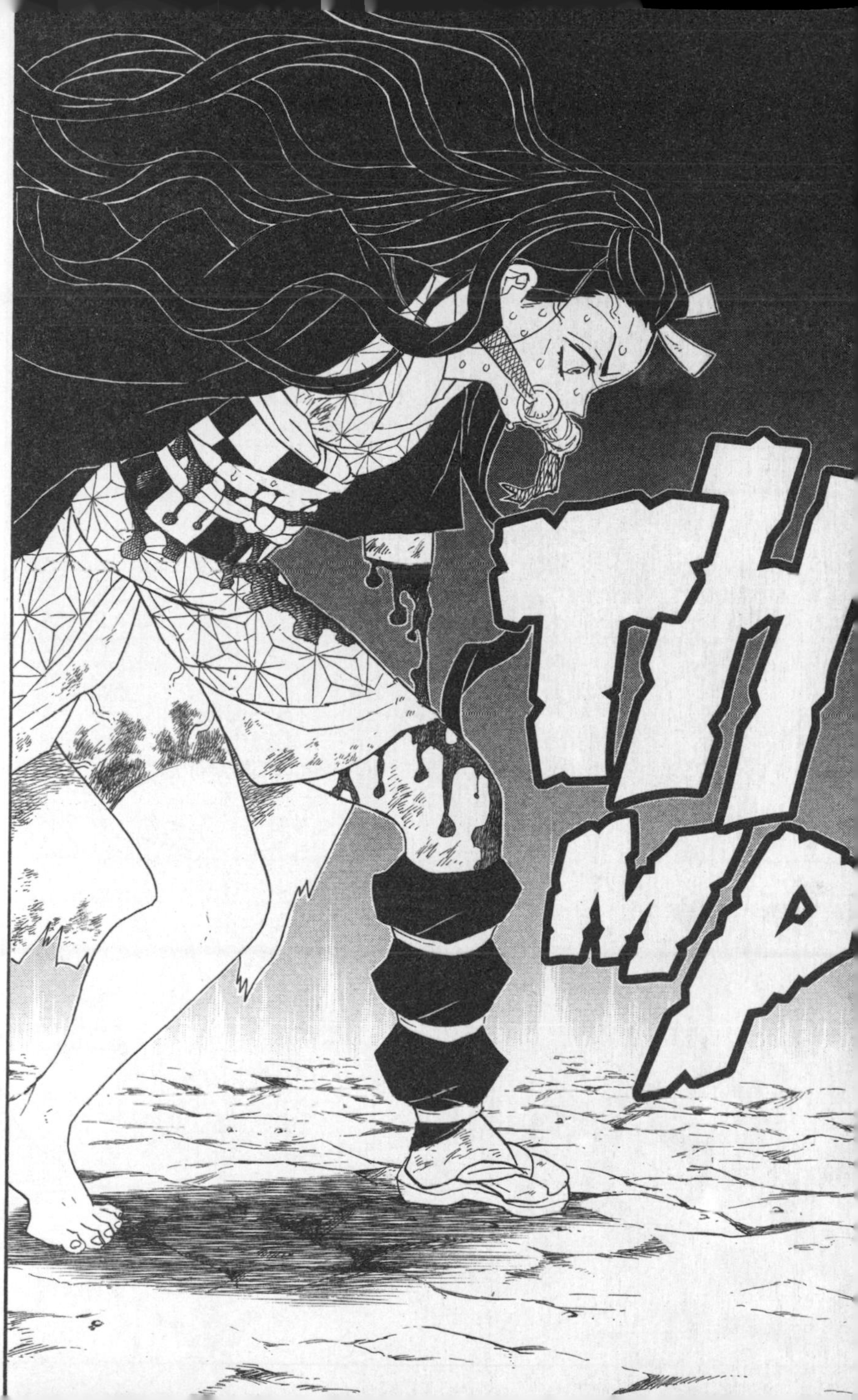
TH
MP

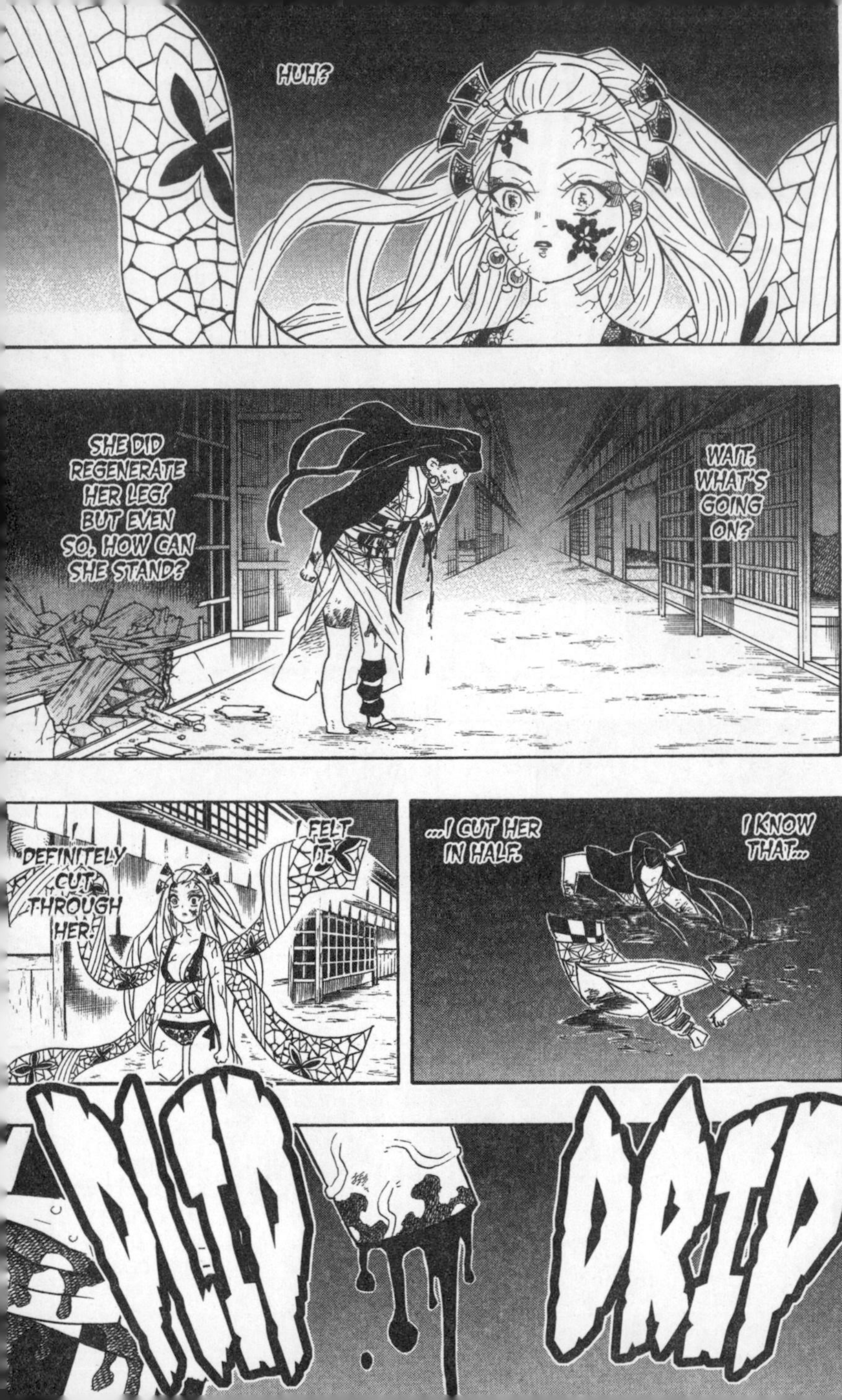
HUH?
WAIT. WHAT'S GOING ON?
SHE DID REGENERATE HER LEG! BUT EVEN SO, HOW CAN SHE STAND?
I KNOW THAT...
...I CUT HER IN HALF.
I FELT IT.
DEFINITELY CUT THROUGH HER.
DRIP
DRIP

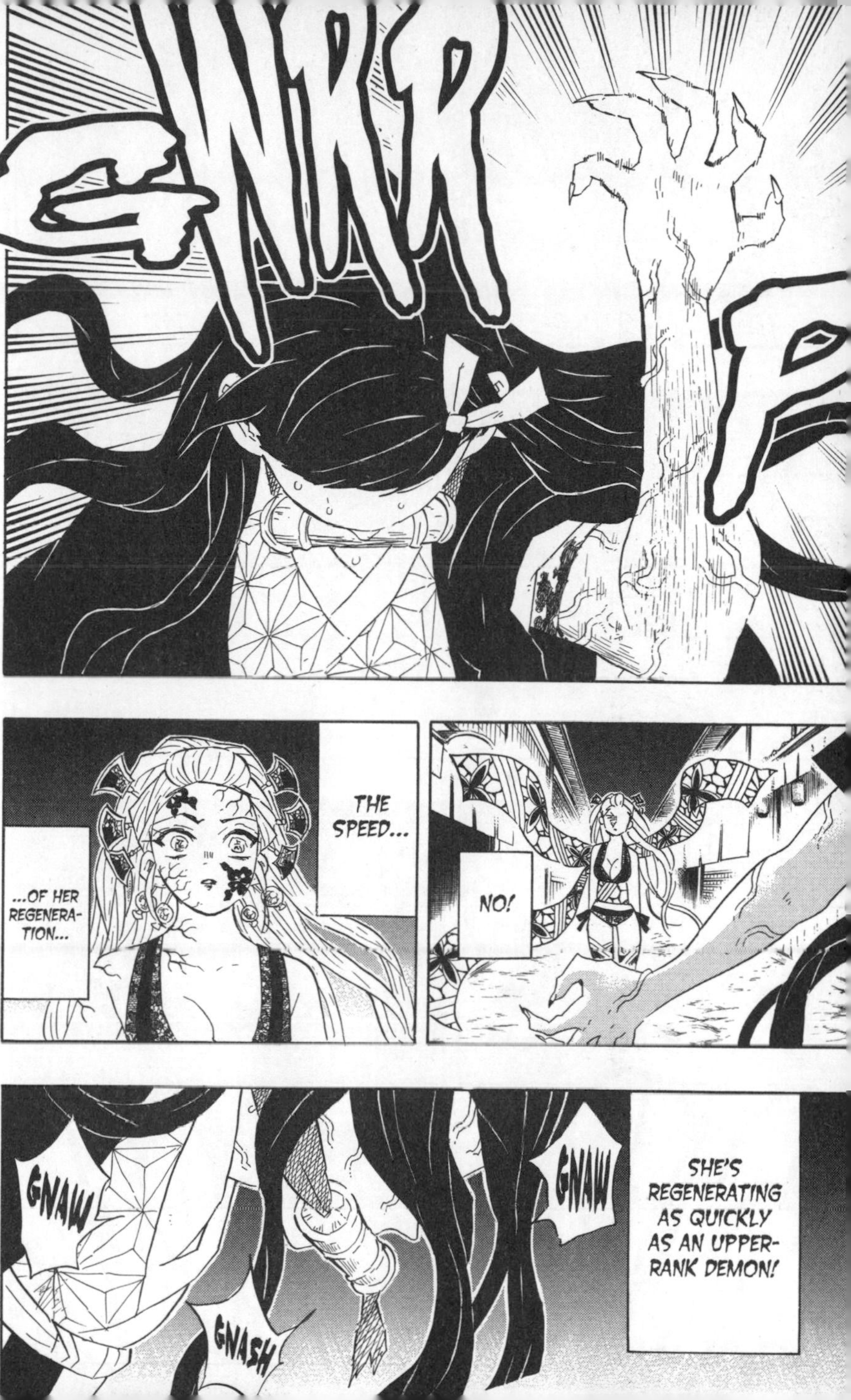
NO!
THE SPEED...
...OF HER REGENERATION...
SHE'S REGENERATING AS QUICKLY AS AN UPPER-RANK DEMON!
GNAW
GNAW
GNASH

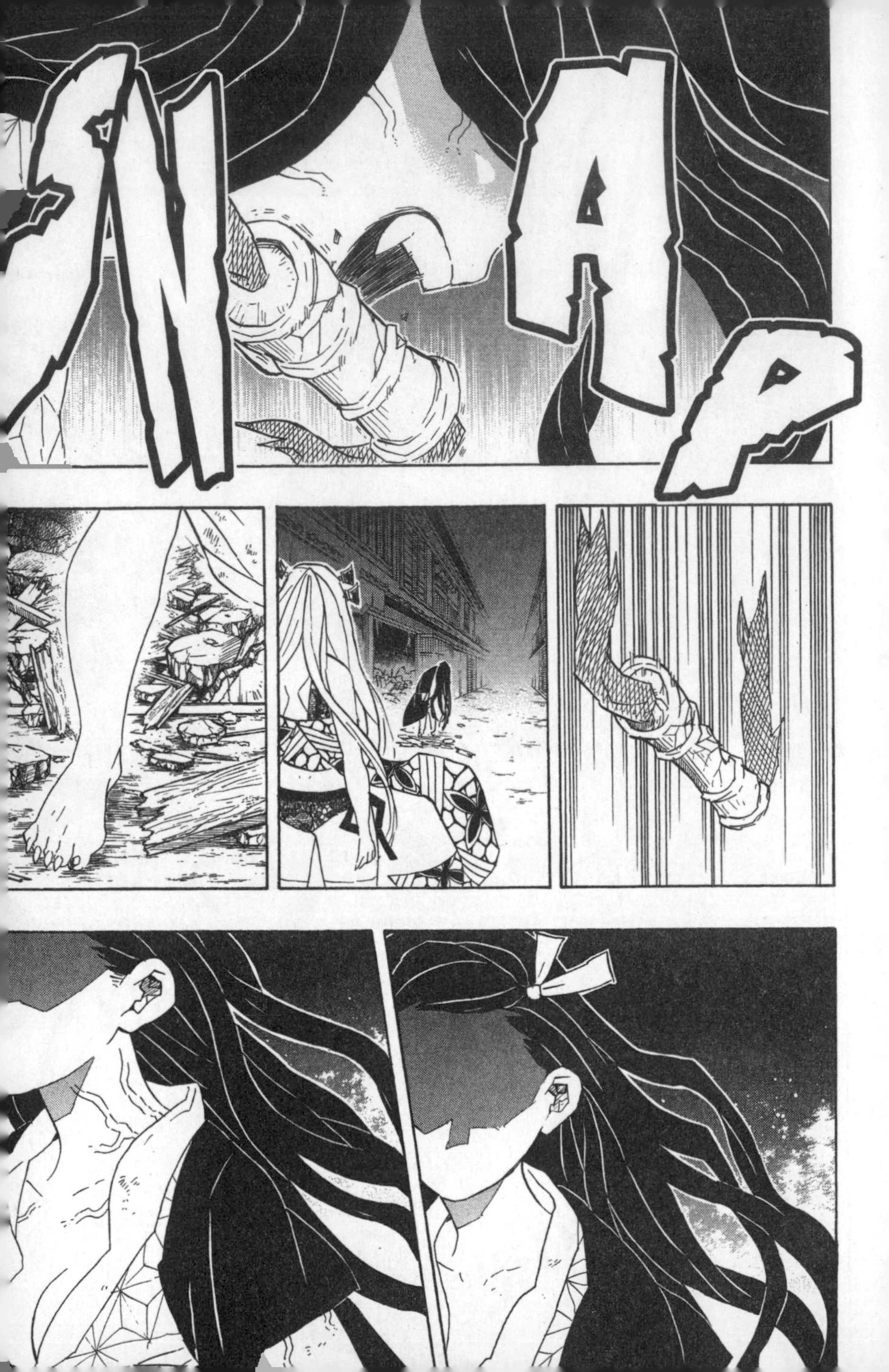
SNAP

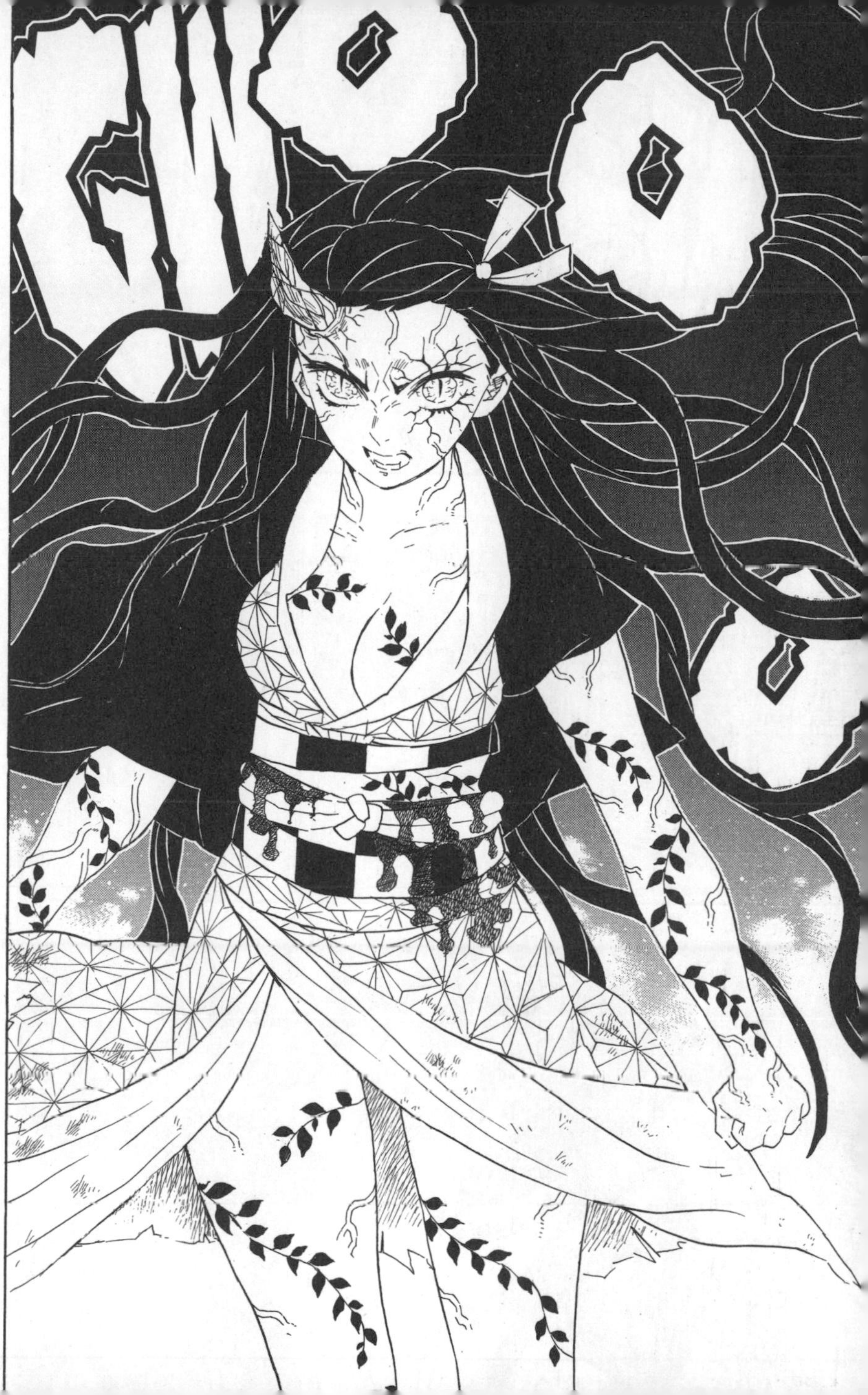

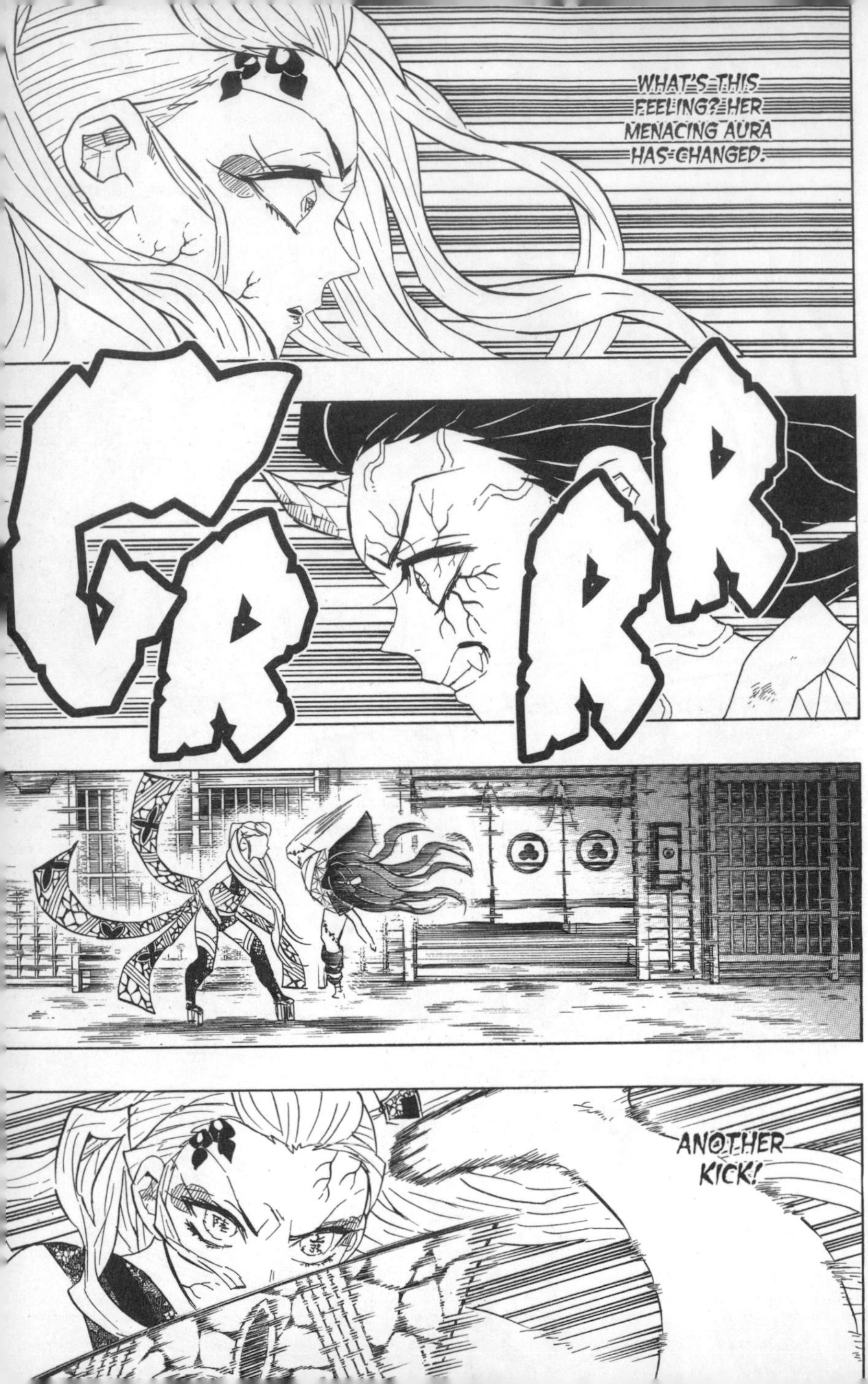
WHAT'S THIS FEELING? HER MENACING AURA HAS CHANGED.
GRRR
ANOTHER KICK!

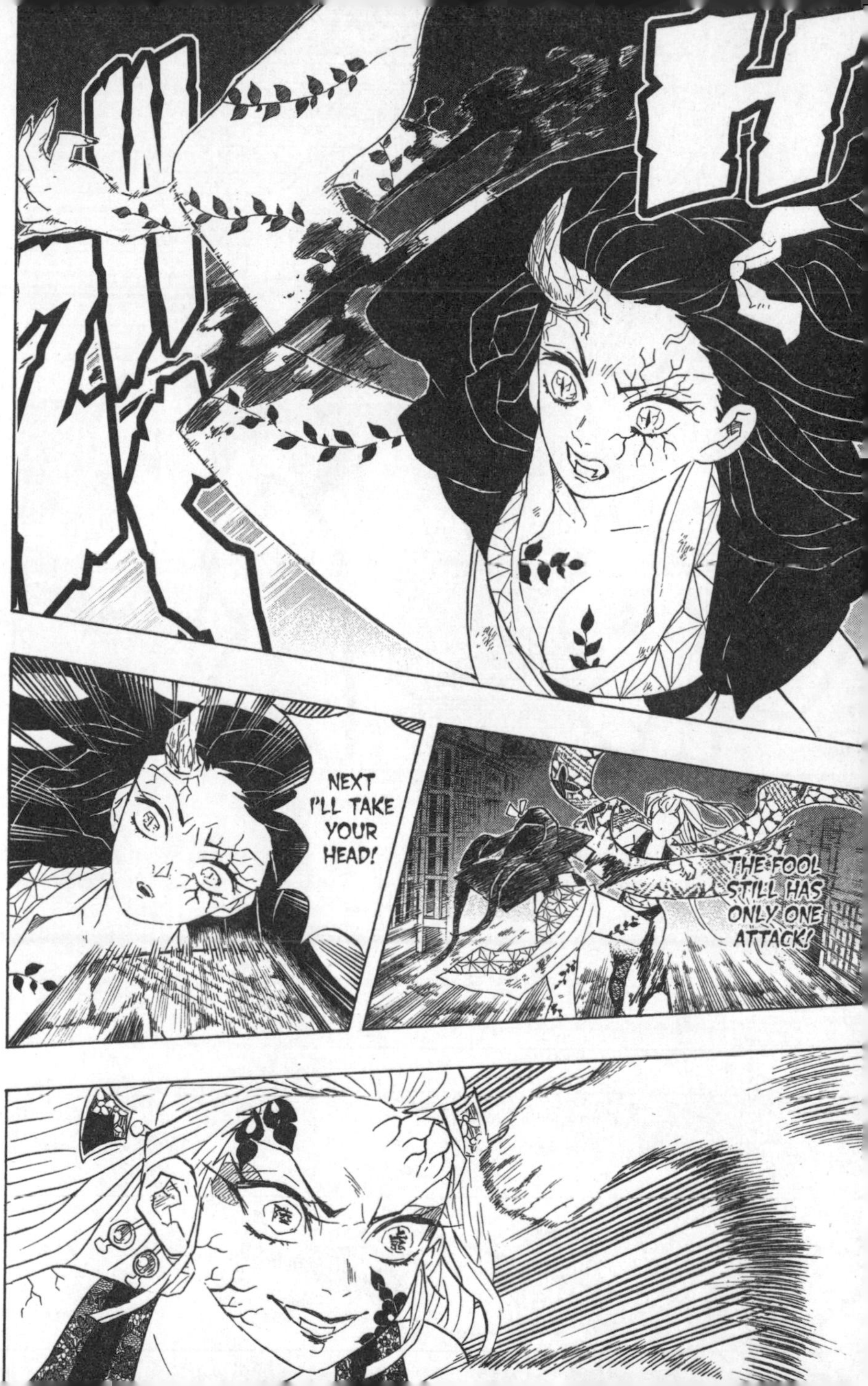
THE FOOL STILL HAS ONLY ONE ATTACK!
NEXT I'LL TAKE YOUR HEAD!

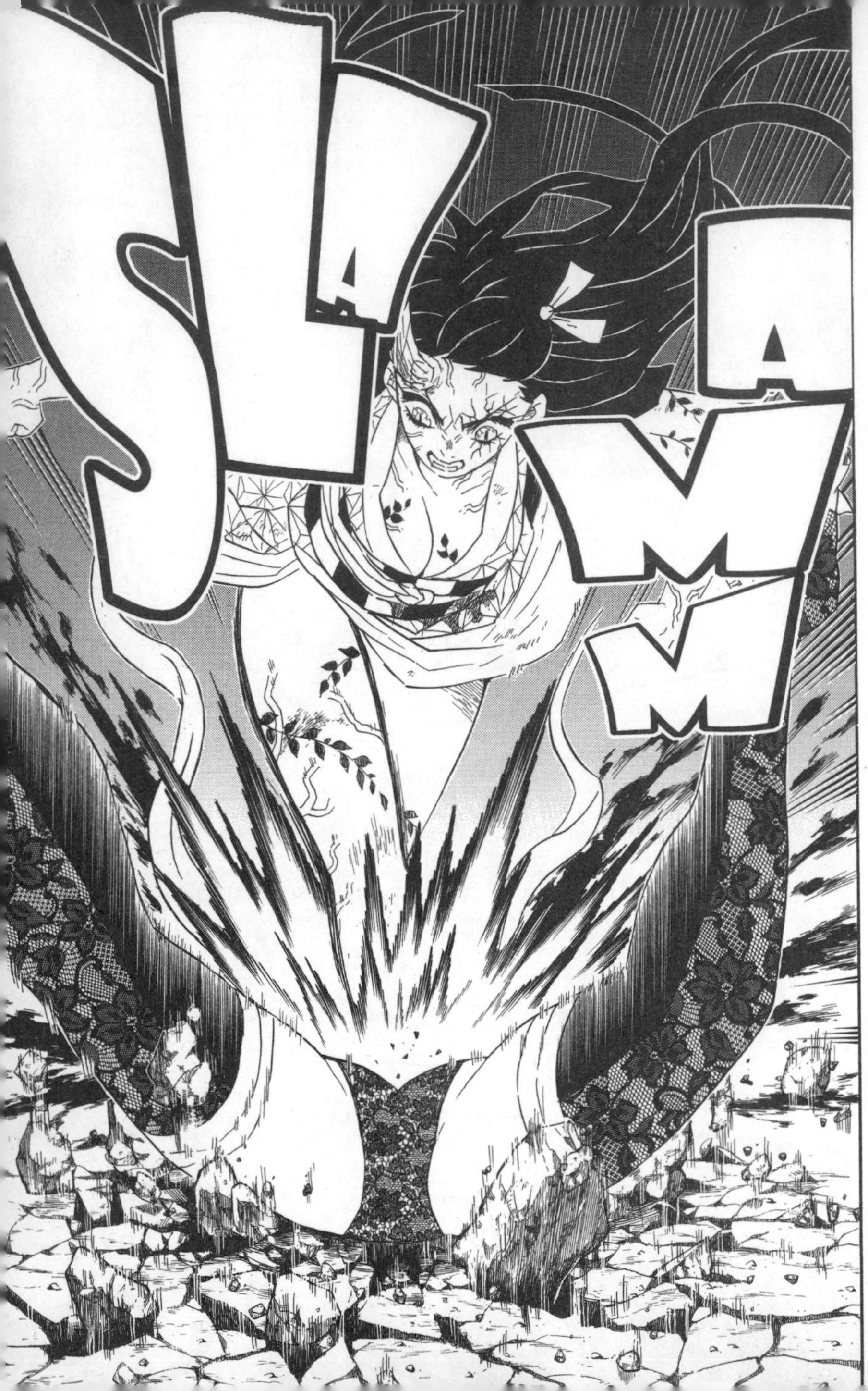
SLAM

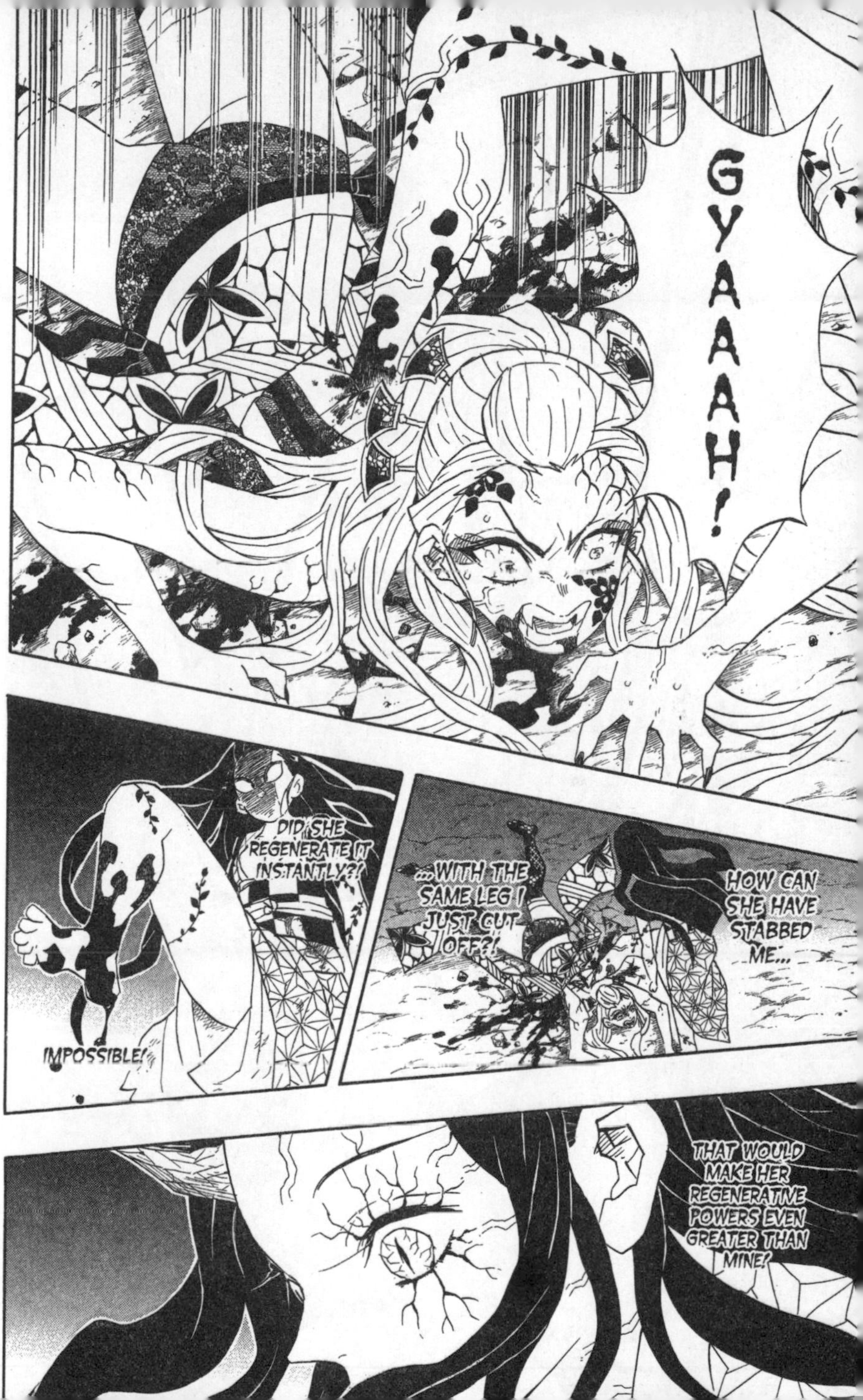
GYAAAH!
HOW CAN SHE HAVE STABBED ME...
...WITH THE SAME LEG I JUST CUT OFF?!
DID SHE REGENERATE IT INSTANTLY?!
IMPOSSIBLE!
THAT WOULD MAKE HER REGENERATIVE POWERS EVEN GREATER THAN MINE!

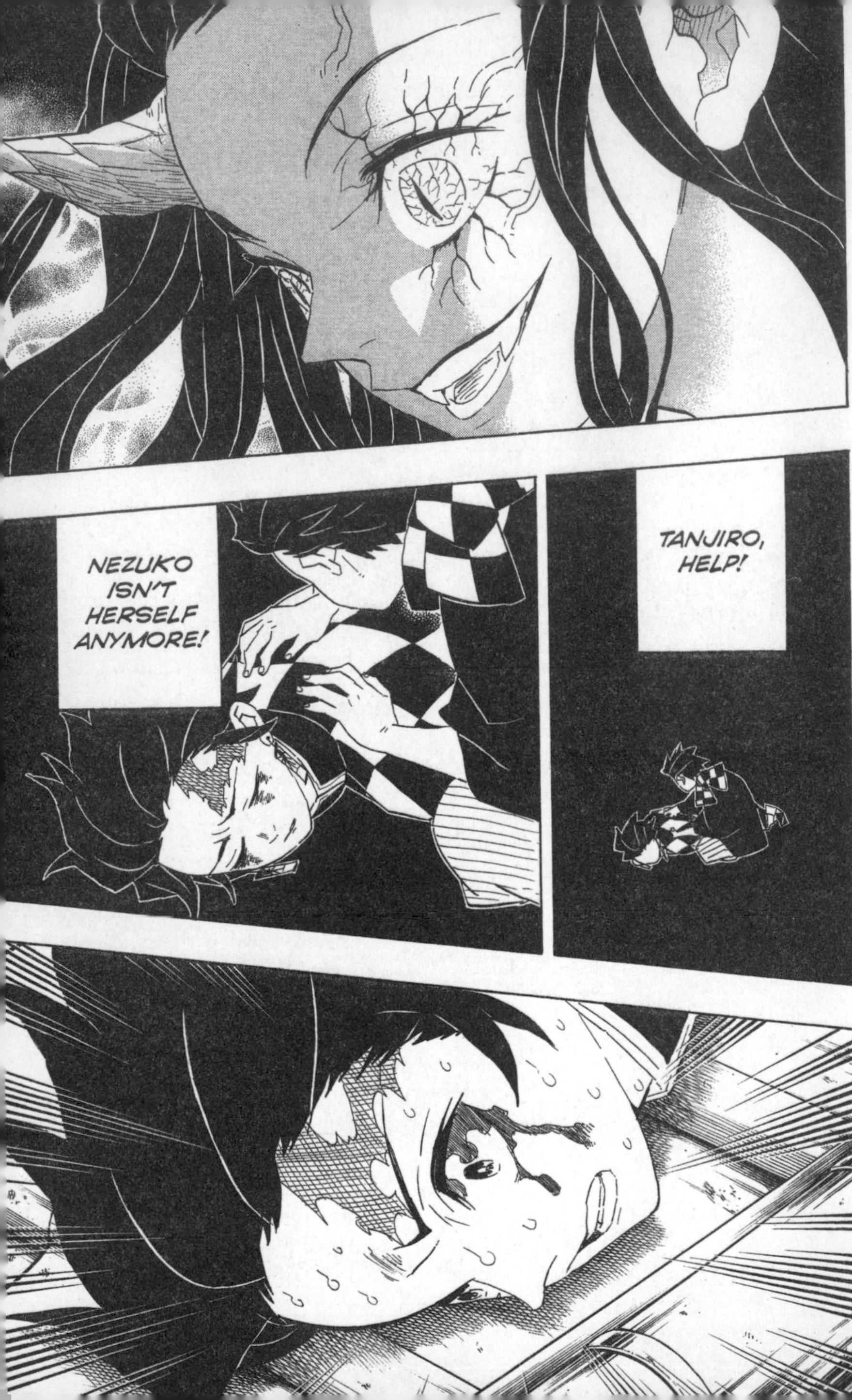
TANJIRO, HELP!
NEZUKO ISN'T HERSELF ANYMORE!

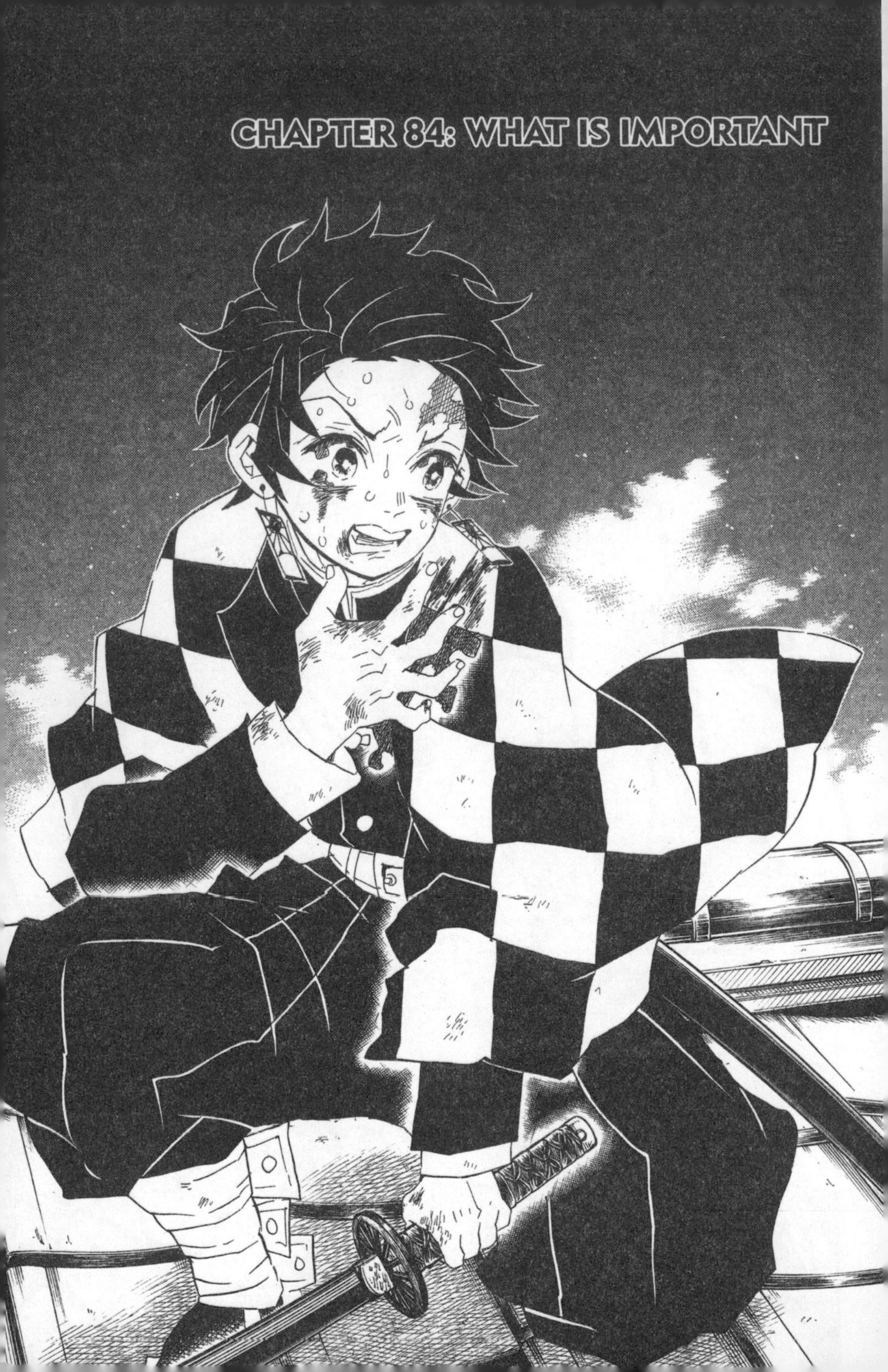
CHAPTER 84: WHAT IS IMPORTANT

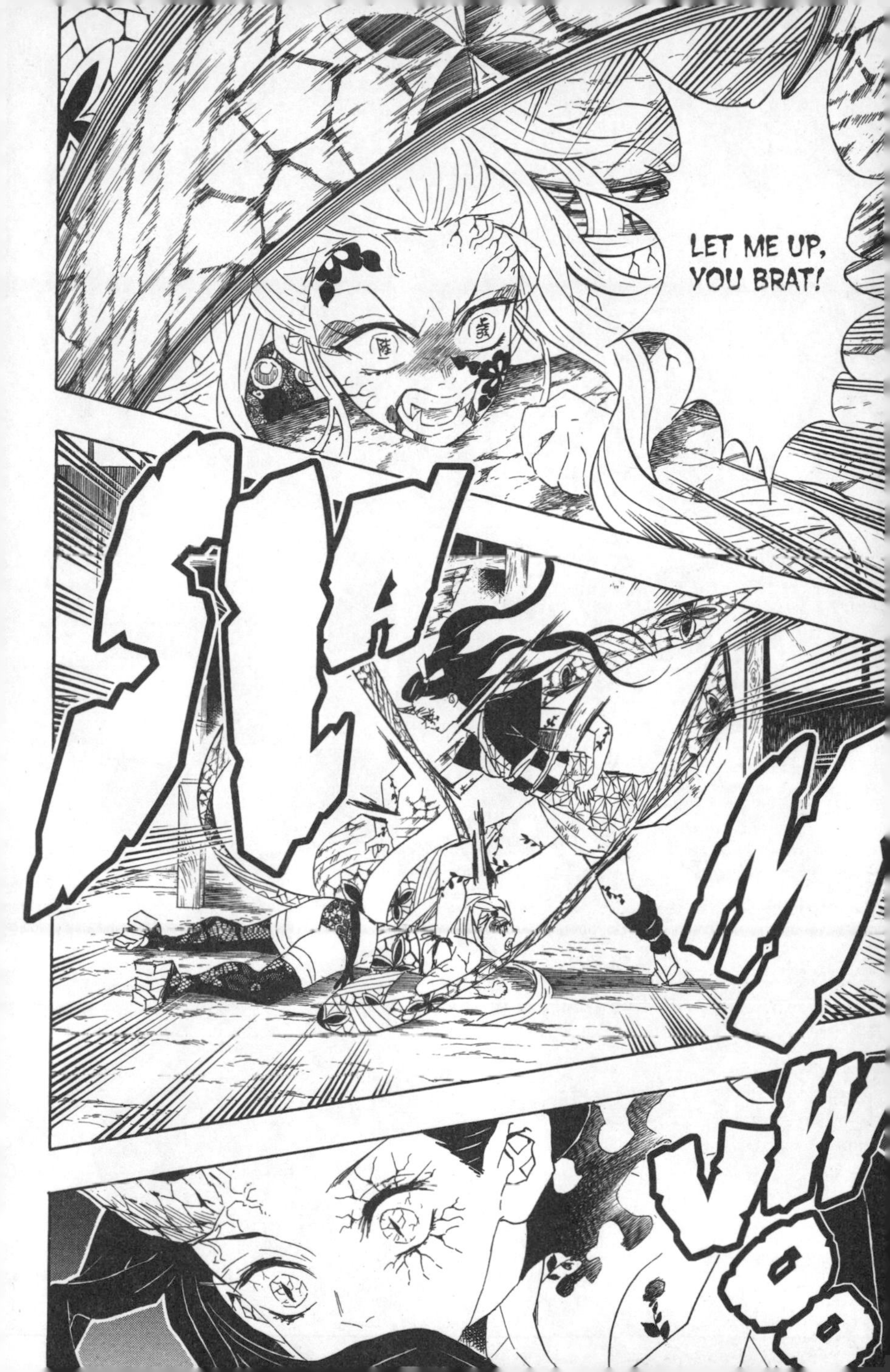
LET ME UP, YOU BRAT!
SLAM

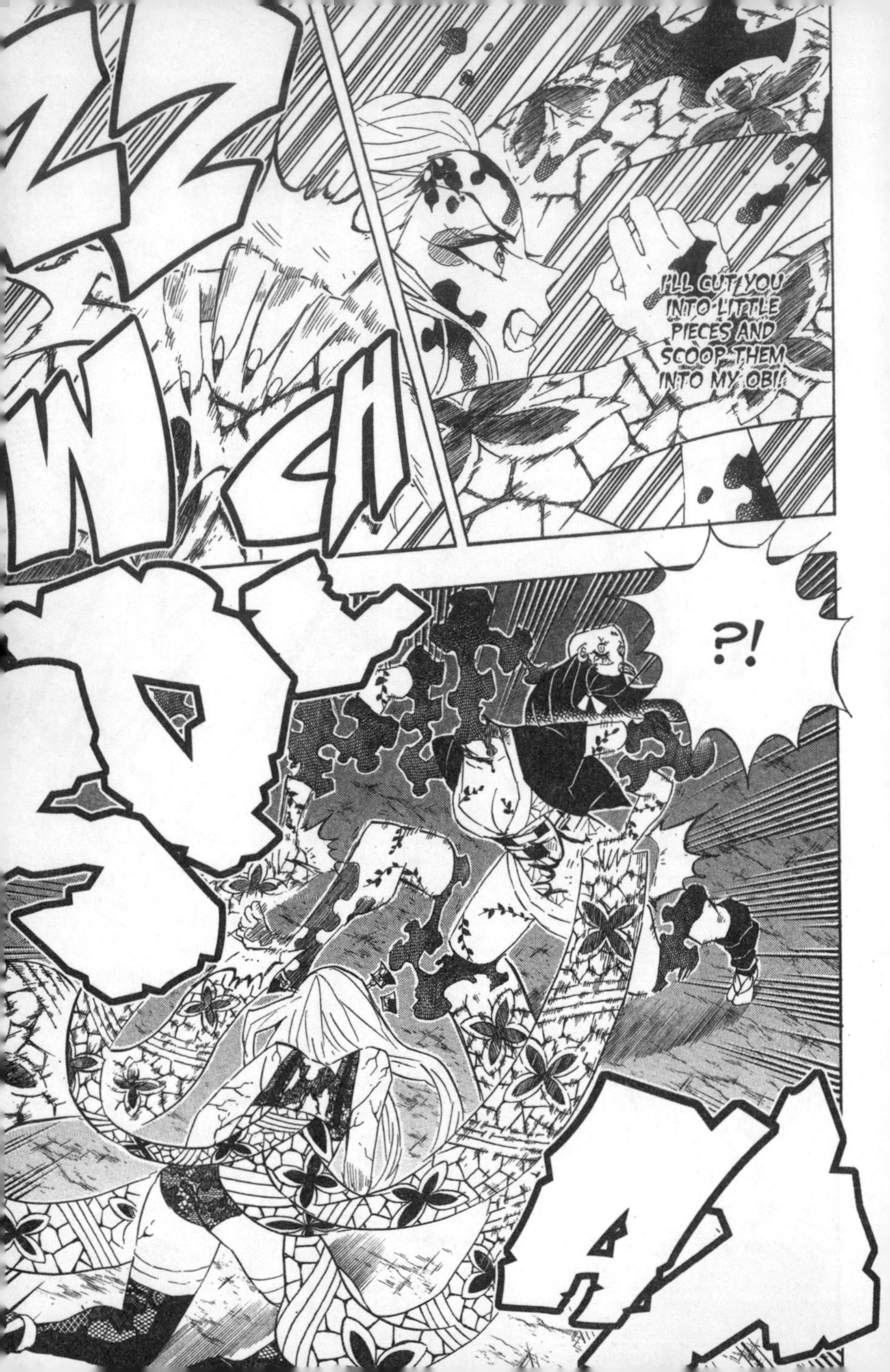
I'LL CUT YOU INTO LITTLE PIECES AND SCOOP THEM INTO MY OBI!
?!

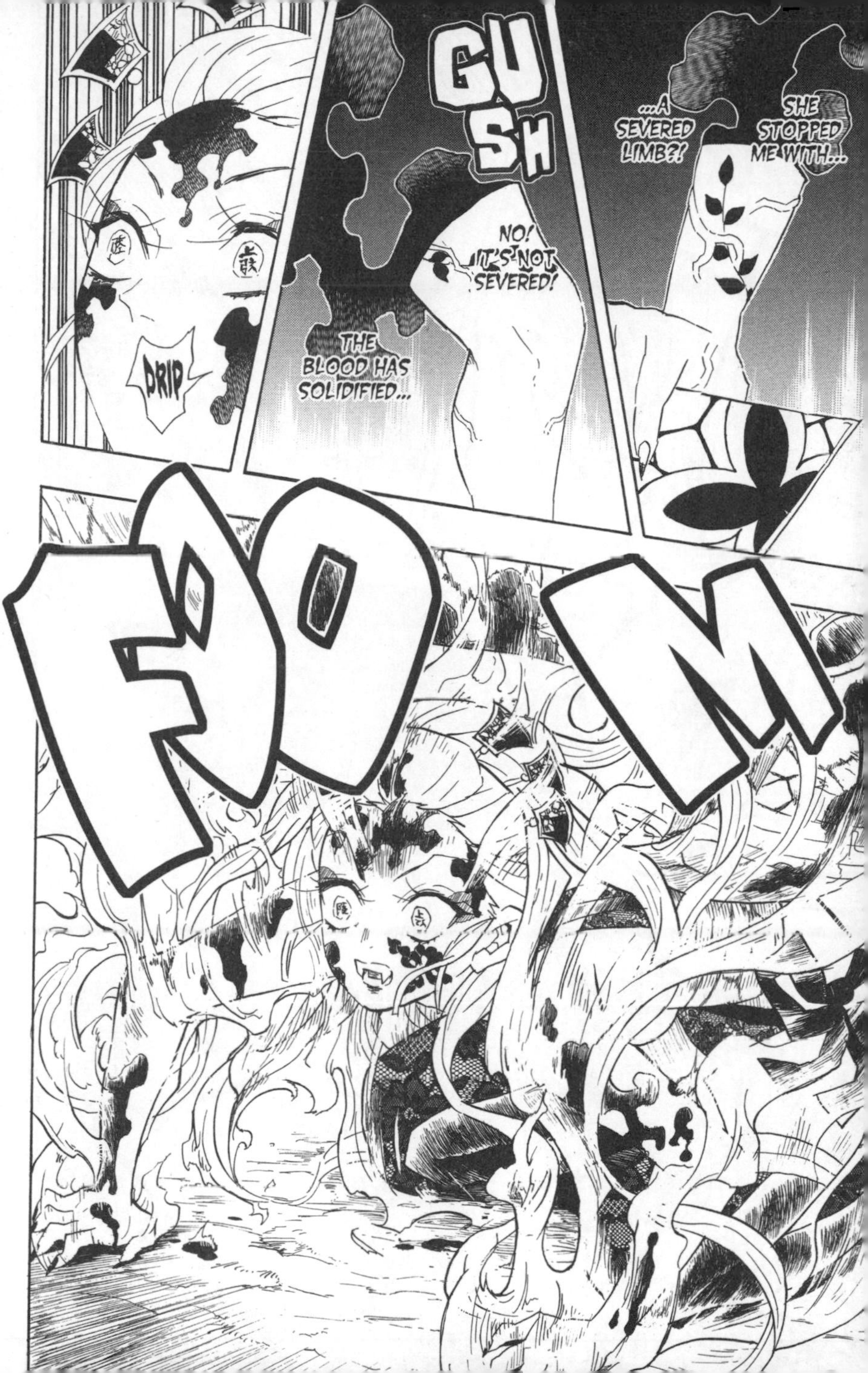
SHE STOPPED ME WITH...
...A SEVERED LIMB?!
GUSH
NO! IT'S NOT SEVERED!
THE BLOOD HAS SOLIDIFIED...
DRIP
FOOM

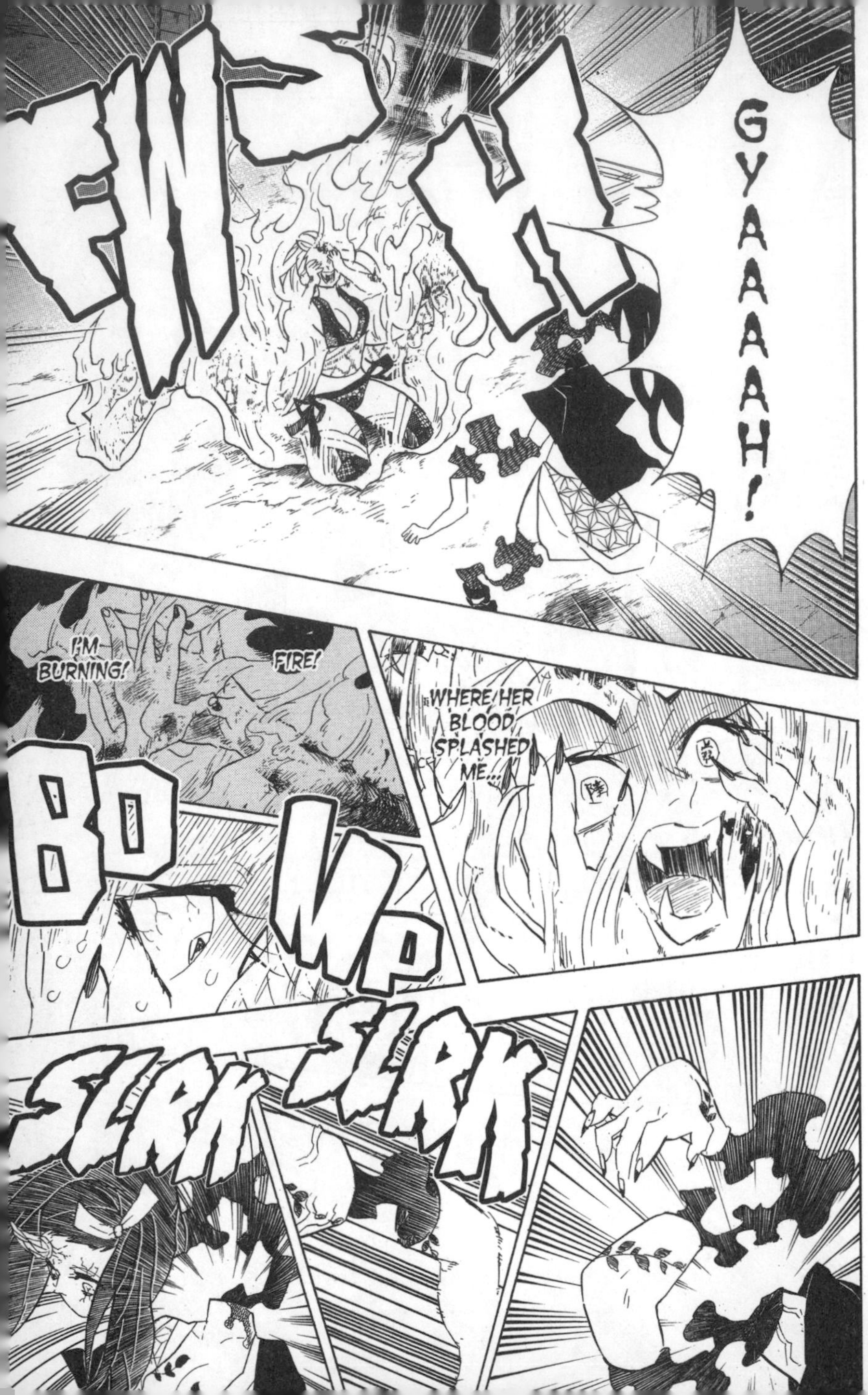
GYAAAAH!
WHERE HER BLOOD SPLASHED ME...
FIRE!
I'M BURNING!
BOMP
SLRK
SLRK

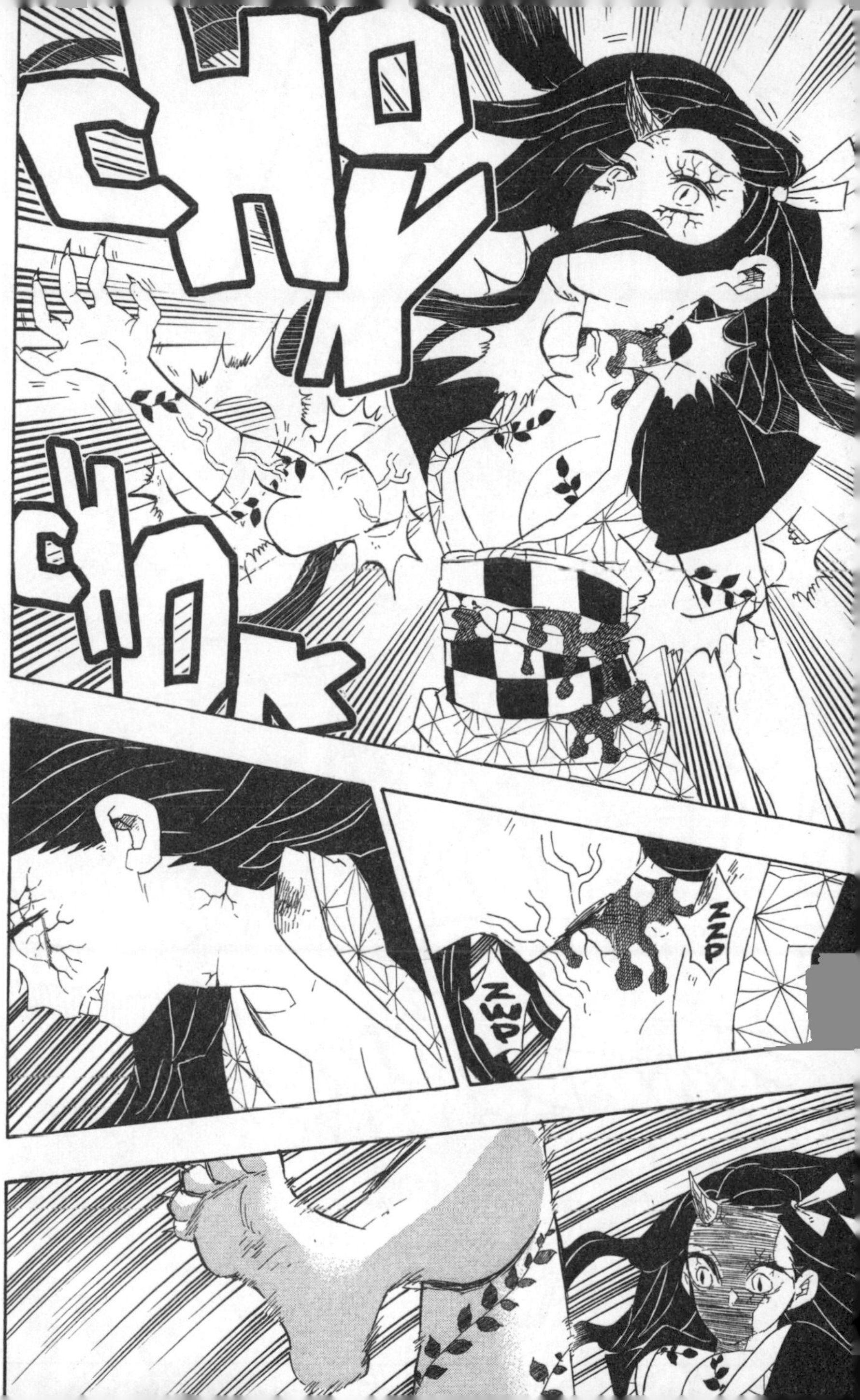
CHOK
CHOK

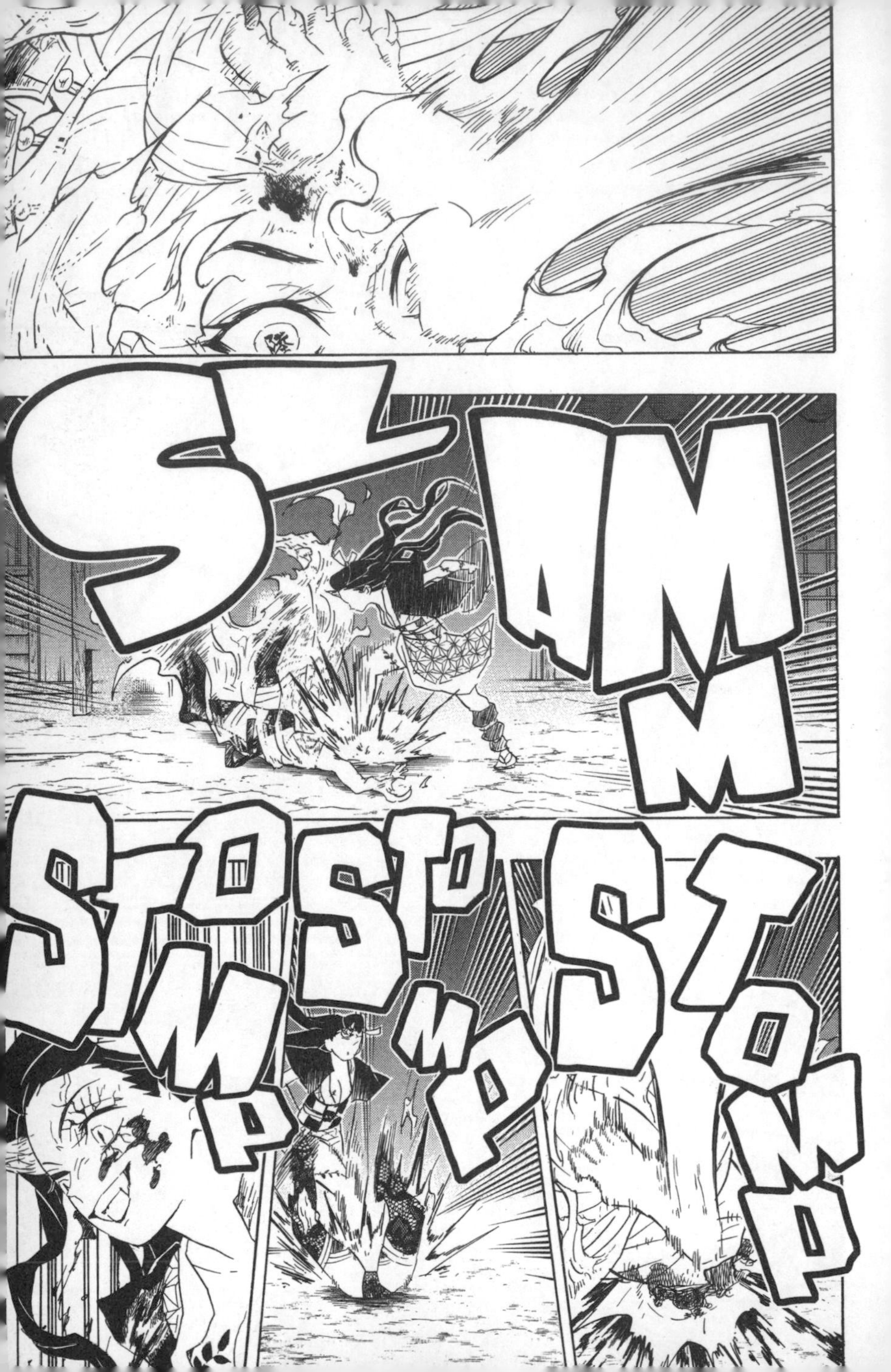
SLAMM
STOMP
STOMP
STOMP

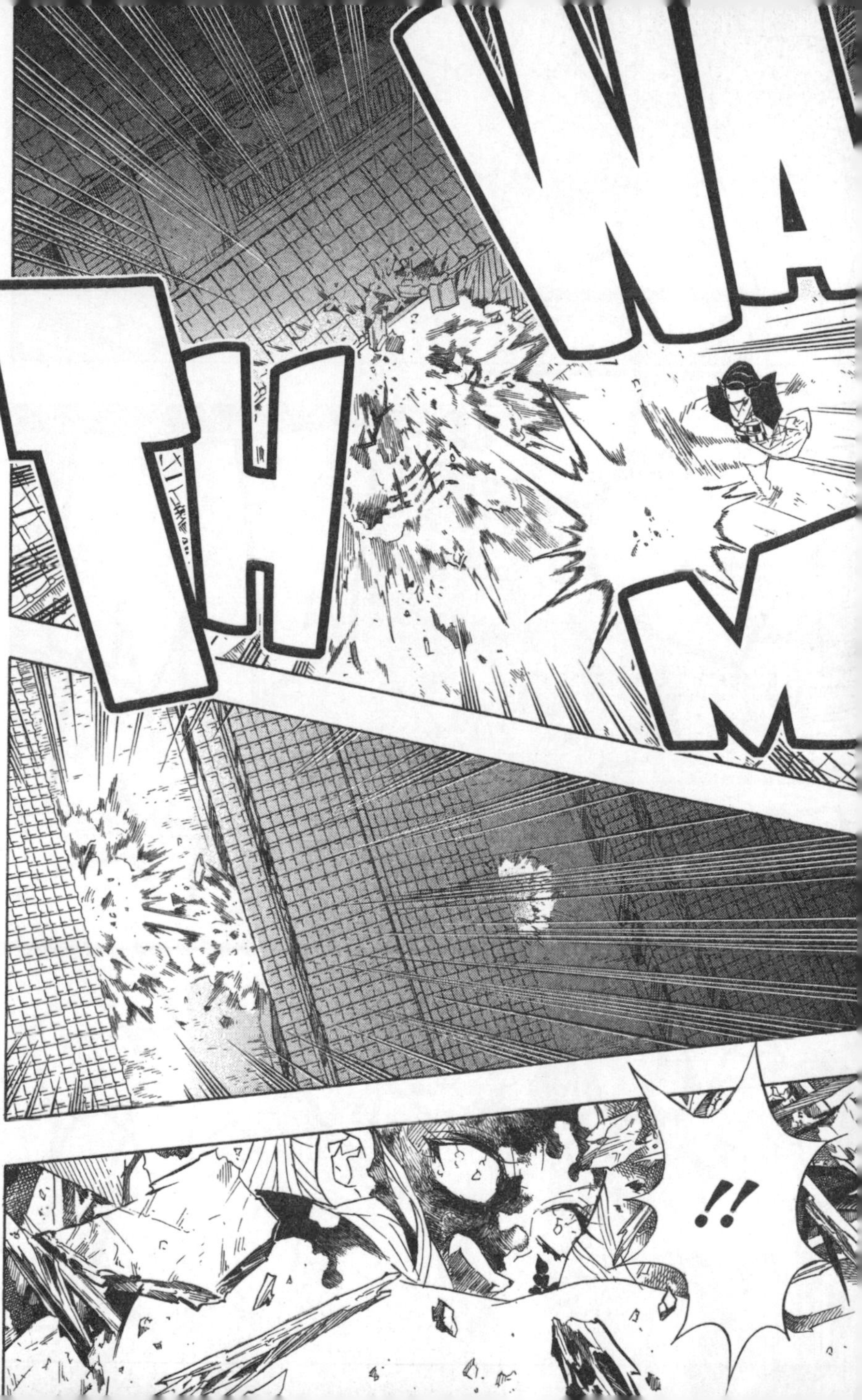
THWAM
!!

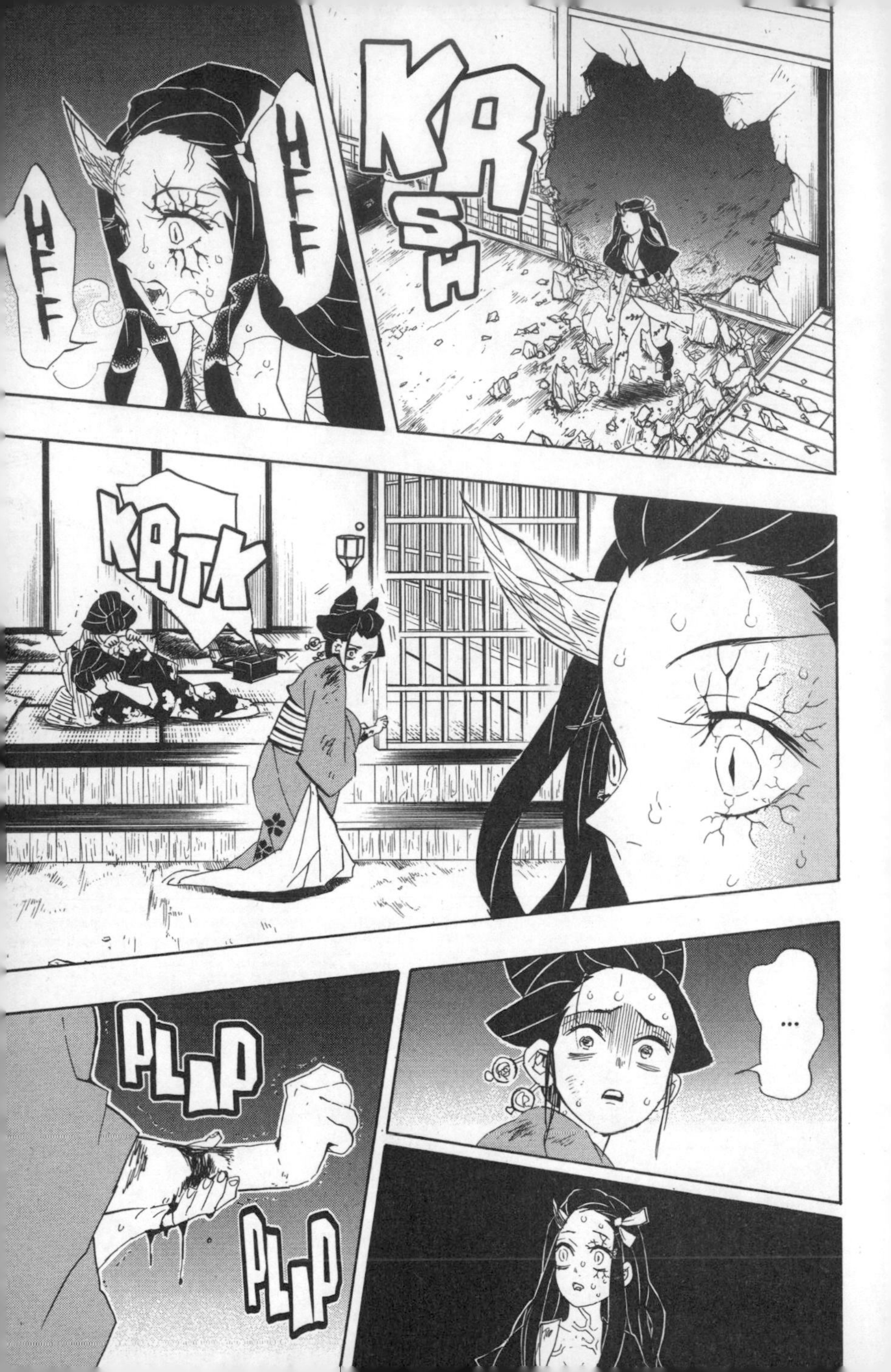
KRSH
HFFF
HFFF
KRTK
...
PLIP
PLIP

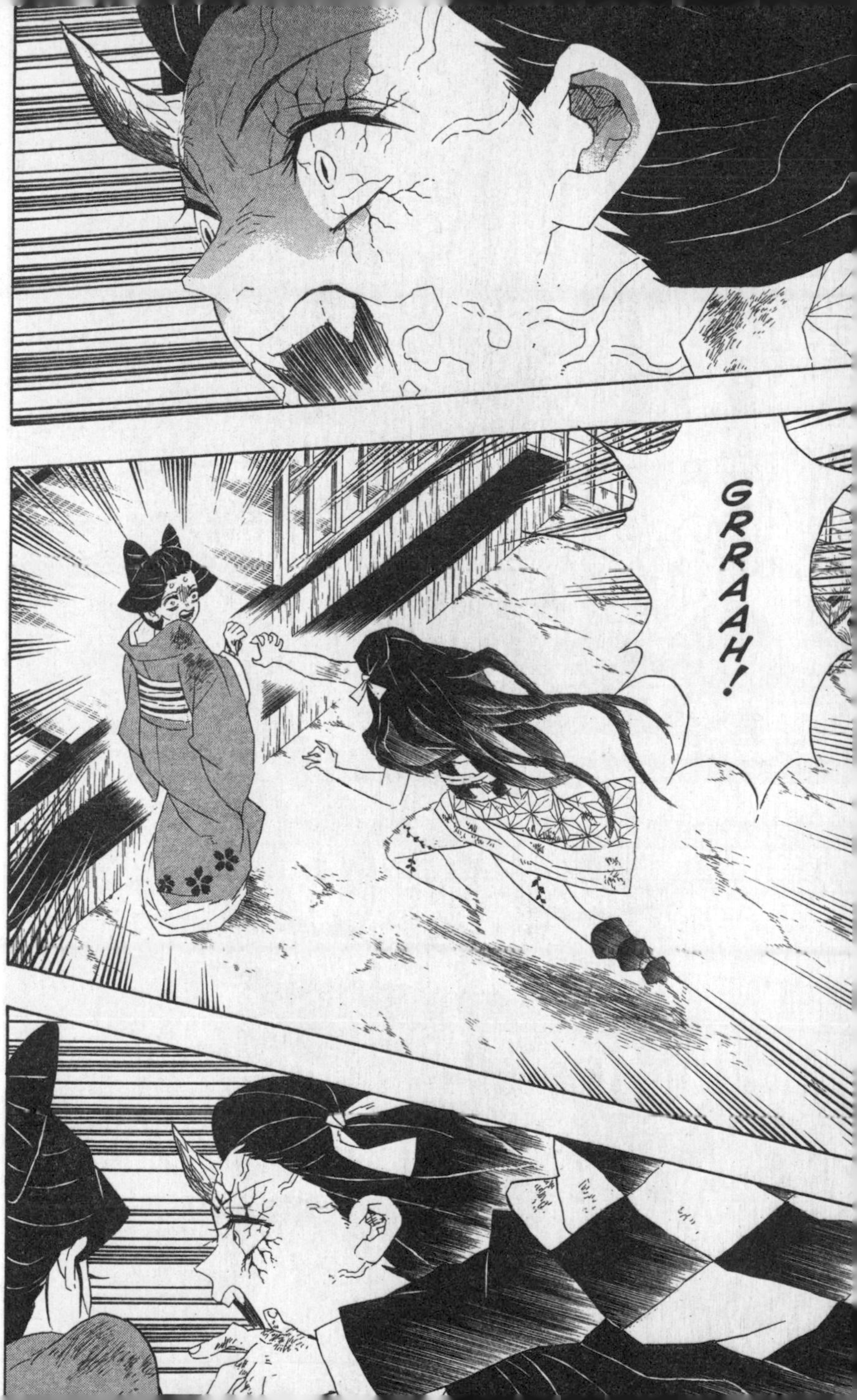
GRRAAAH!

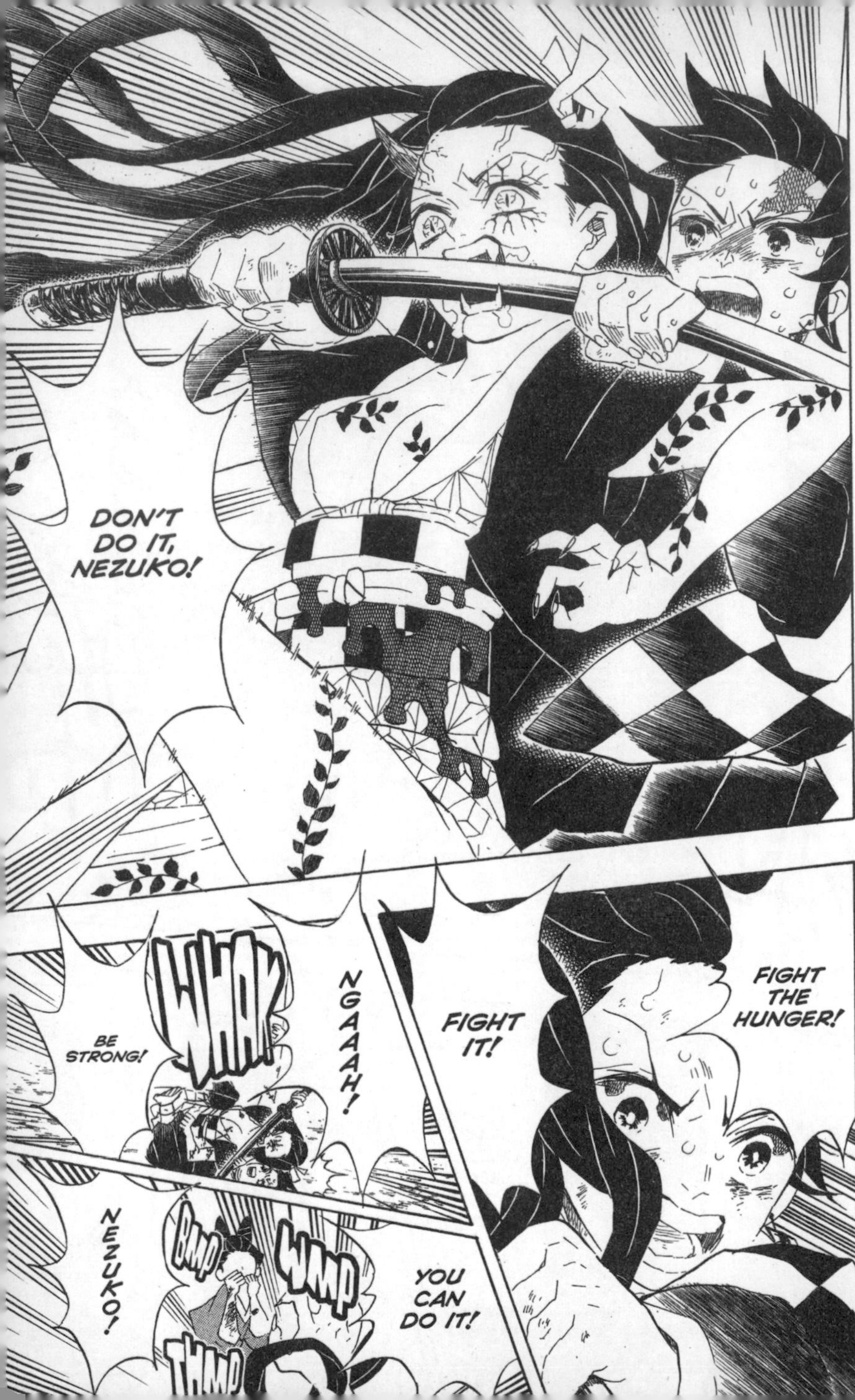
DON'T DO IT, NEZUKO!
FIGHT THE HUNGER!
FIGHT IT!
YOU CAN DO IT!
NGAAAAH!
WHAK
BE STRONG!
NEZUKO!
WMP
BAMP
THMP

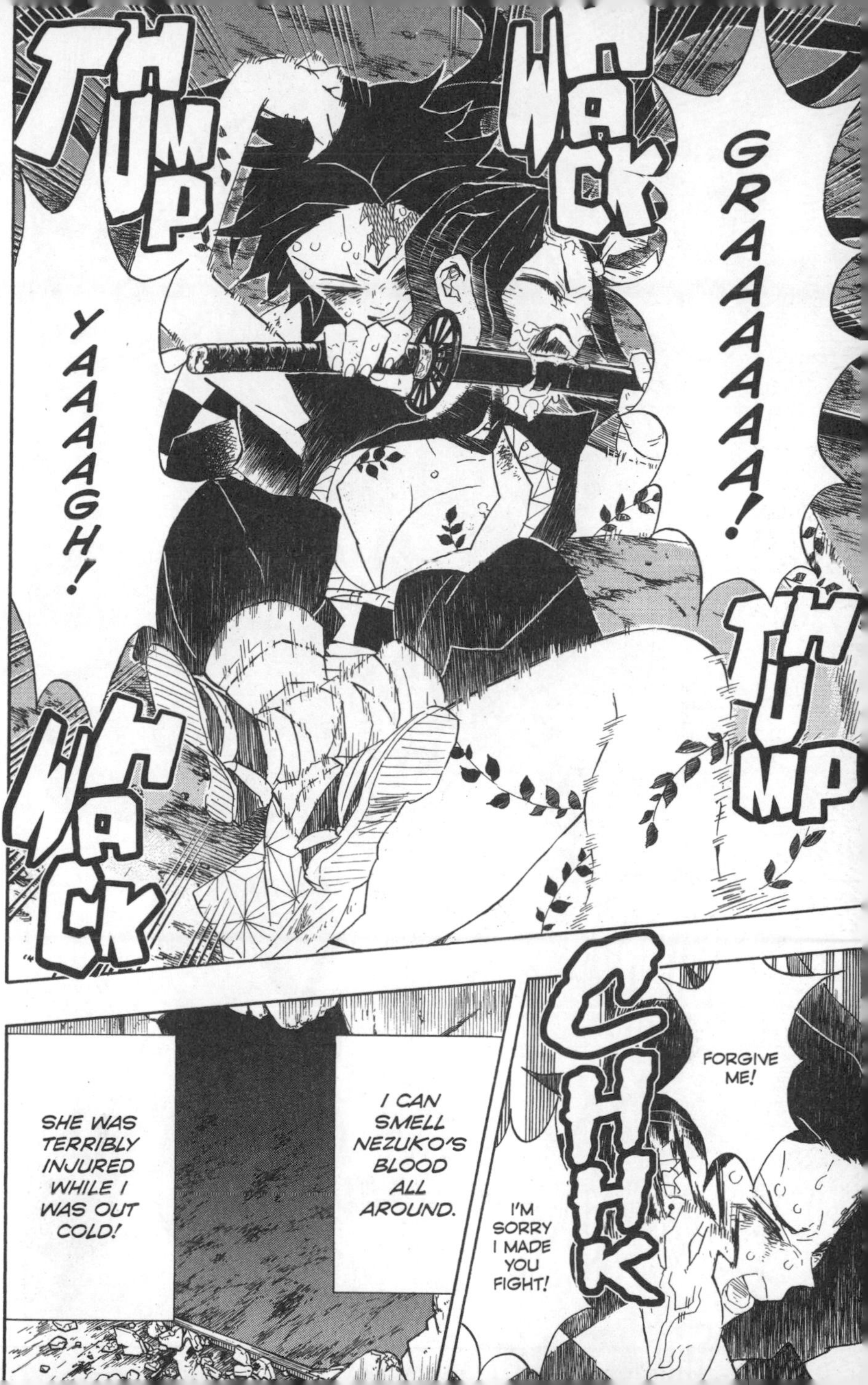
WHACK
GRAAAAAAAA!
THUMP
YAAAAAGH!
THUMP
WHACK
CHK
FORGIVE ME!
I'M SORRY I MADE YOU FIGHT!
I CAN SMELL NEZUKO'S BLOOD ALL AROUND.
SHE WAS TERRIBLY INJURED WHILE I WAS OUT COLD!

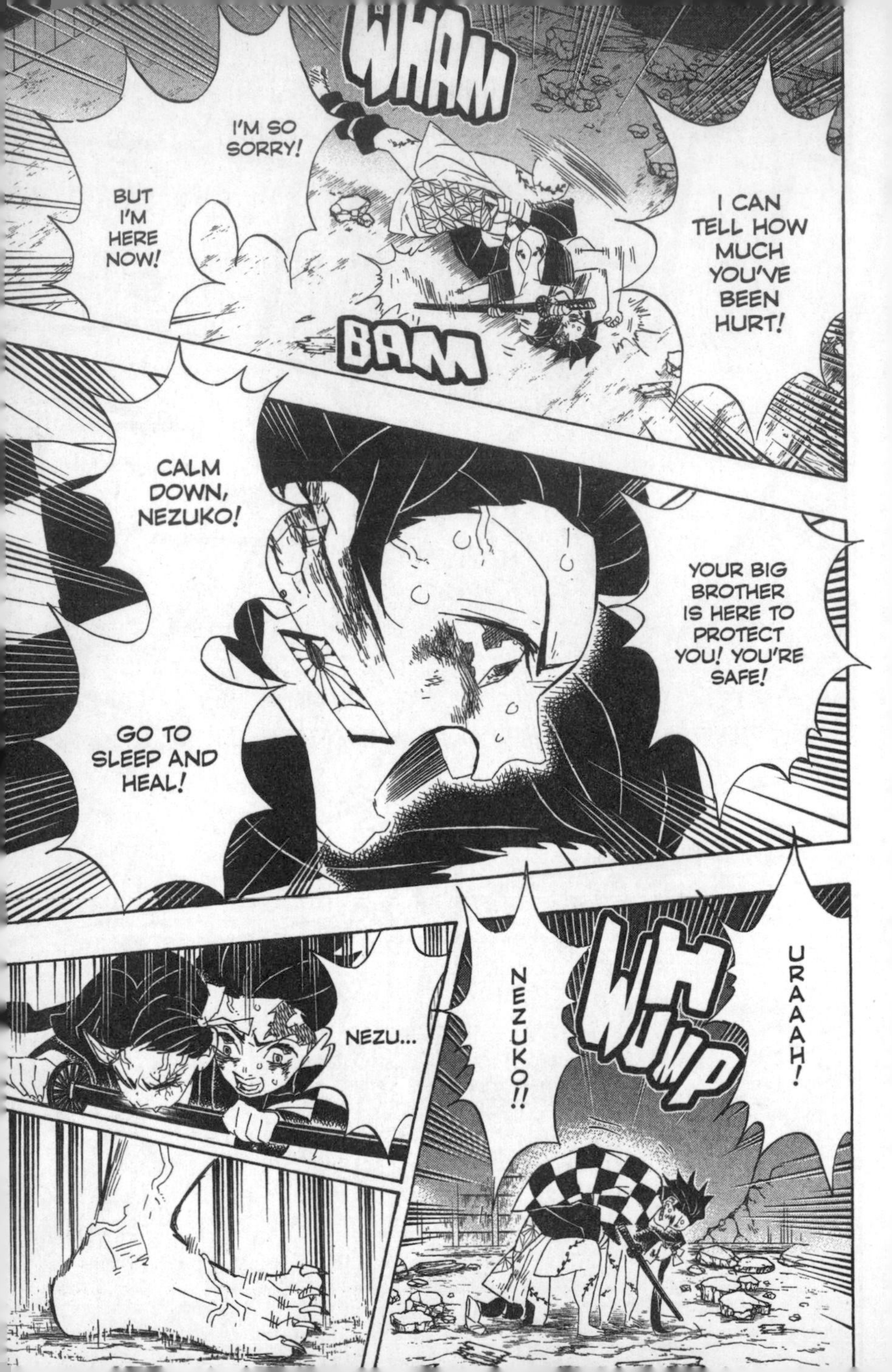
I CAN TELL HOW MUCH YOU'VE BEEN HURT!
WHAM
I'M SO SORRY!
BUT I'M HERE NOW!
BAM
YOUR BIG BROTHER IS HERE TO PROTECT YOU! YOU'RE SAFE!
CALM DOWN, NEZUKO!
GO TO SLEEP AND HEAL!
URAAAH!
WHUMP
NEZUKO!!
NEZU...

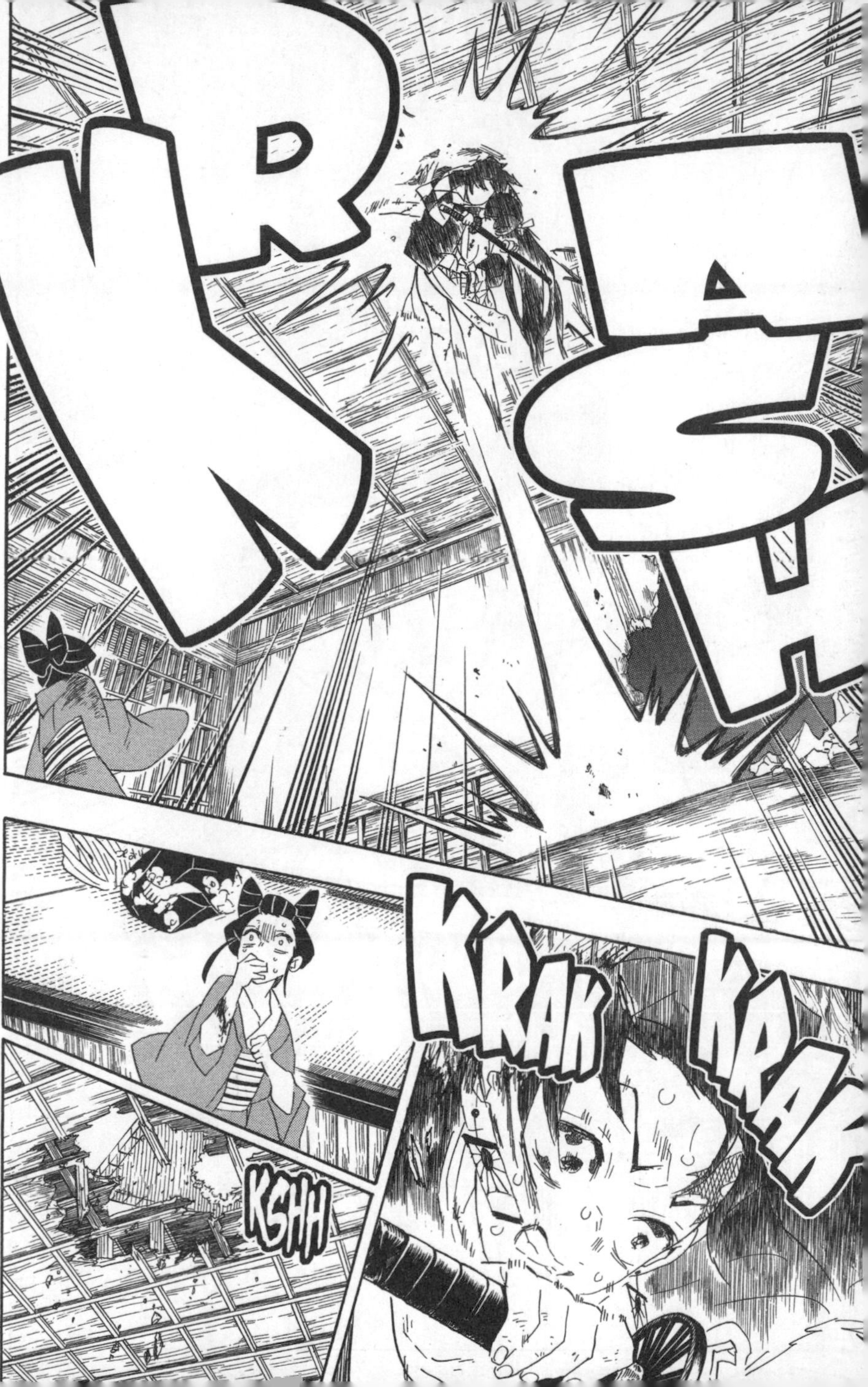
KRASH
KRAK KRAK
KSHH

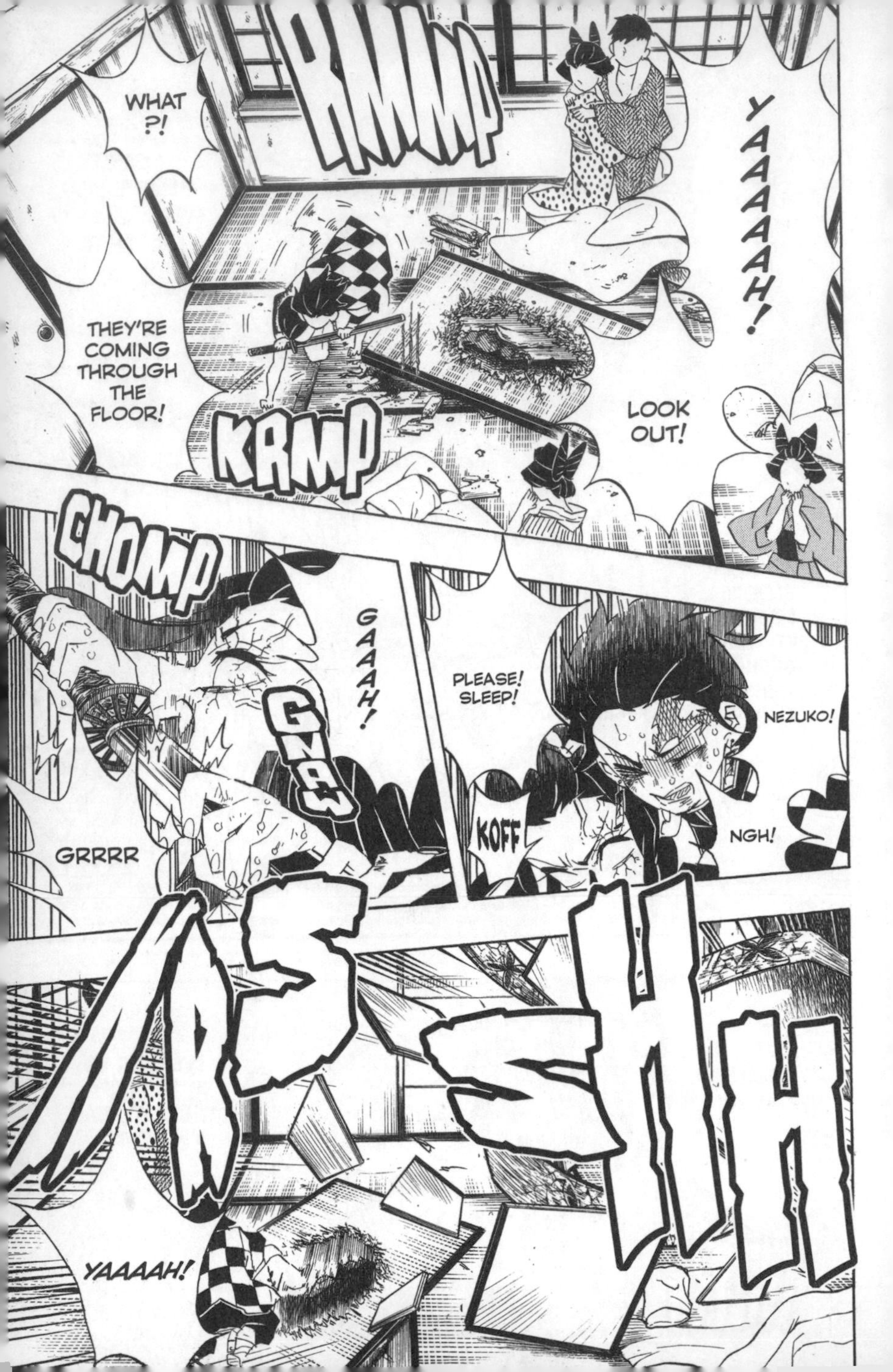
YAAAAAAH!
WHAT?!
LOOK OUT!
THEY'RE COMING THROUGH THE FLOOR!
KRAMP
NEZUKO!
NGH!
PLEASE! SLEEP!
KOFF
GAAAAH!
GNAW
CHOMP
GRRRR
YAAAAH!

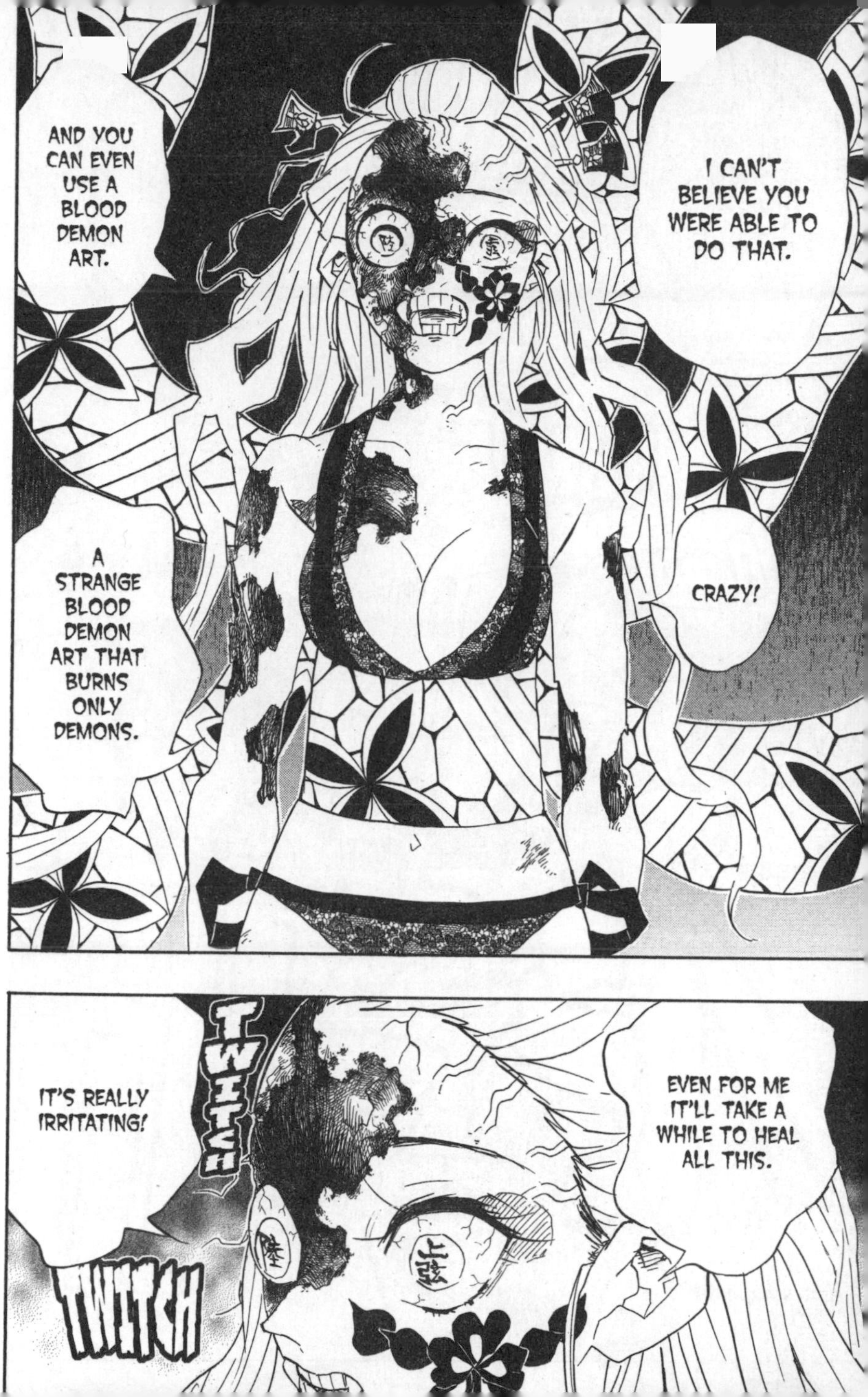
I CAN'T BELIEVE YOU WERE ABLE TO DO THAT.
CRAZY!
AND YOU CAN EVEN USE A BLOOD DEMON ART.
A STRANGE BLOOD DEMON ART THAT BURNS ONLY DEMONS.
EVEN FOR ME IT'LL TAKE A WHILE TO HEAL ALL THIS.
TWITCH!!
IT'S REALLY IRRITATING!
TWITCH

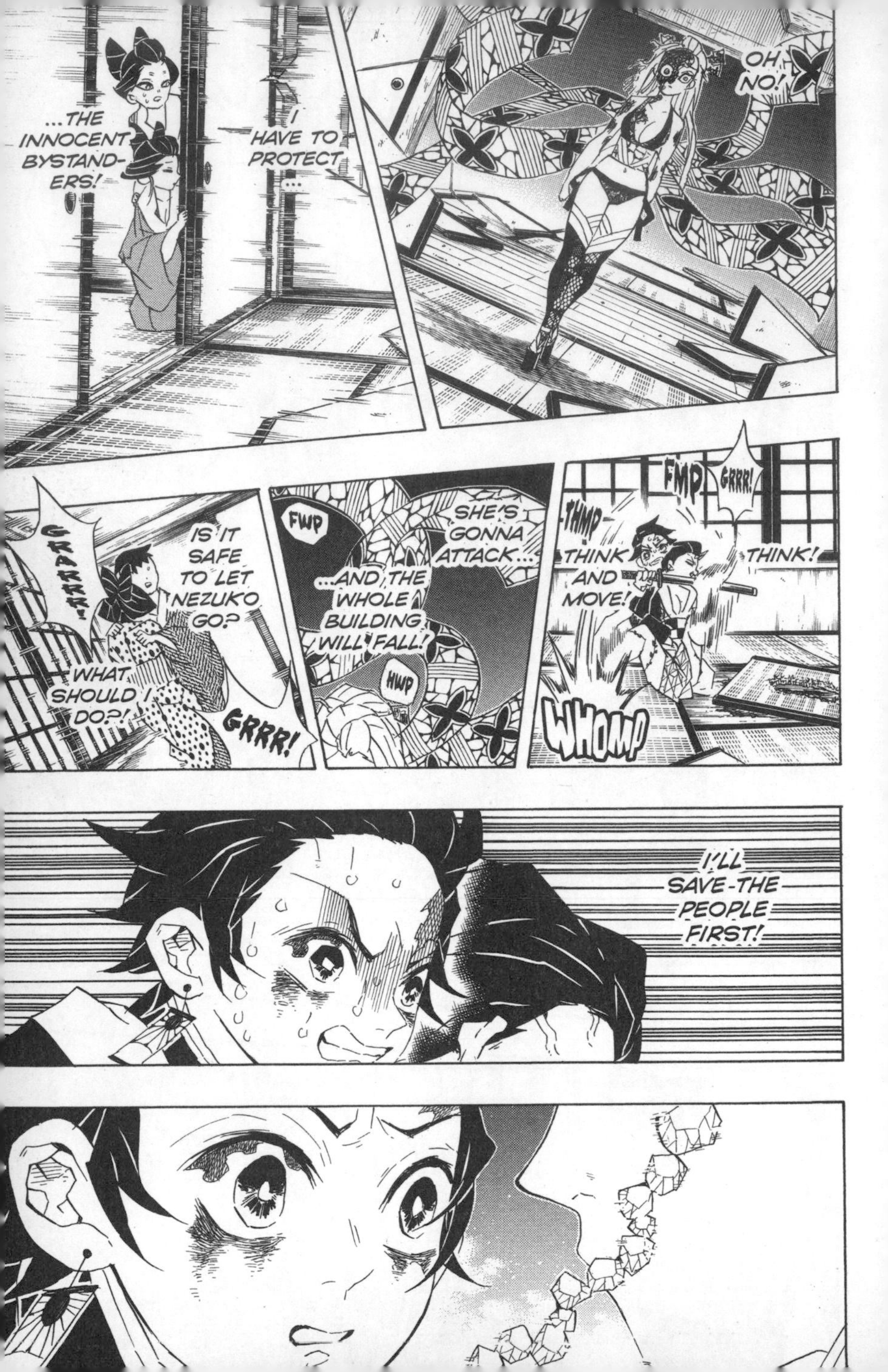
OH NO!
I HAVE TO PROTECT...
...THE INNOCENT BYSTANDERS!
FMP
GRRR!
THMP
THINK!
THINK AND MOVE!
WHOMP
SHE'S GONNA ATTACK...
FWP
...AND THE WHOLE BUILDING WILL FALL!
HWP
GRARRR!
IS IT SAFE TO LET NEZUKO GO?
WHAT SHOULD I DO?!
GRRRR!
I'LL SAVE THE PEOPLE FIRST!

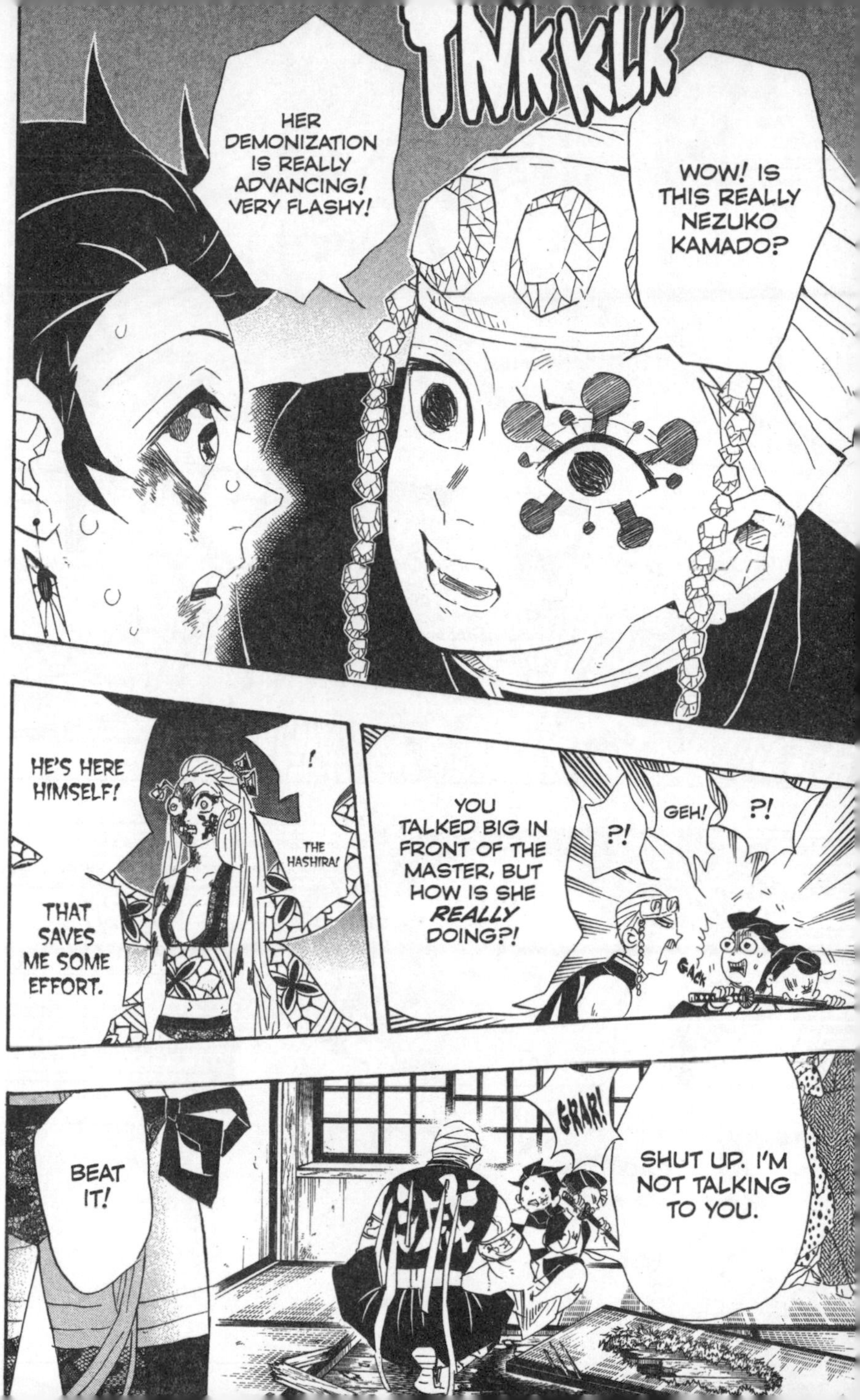
TNK KLK
WOW! IS THIS REALLY NEZUKO KAMADO?
HER DEMONIZATION IS REALLY ADVANCING! VERY FLASHY!
?!
GEH!
?!
YOU TALKED BIG IN FRONT OF THE MASTER, BUT HOW IS SHE *REALLY* DOING?!
GACK
!
HE'S HERE HIMSELF!
THE HASHIRA!
THAT SAVES ME SOME EFFORT.
SHUT UP. I'M NOT TALKING TO YOU.
GRAR!
BEAT IT!

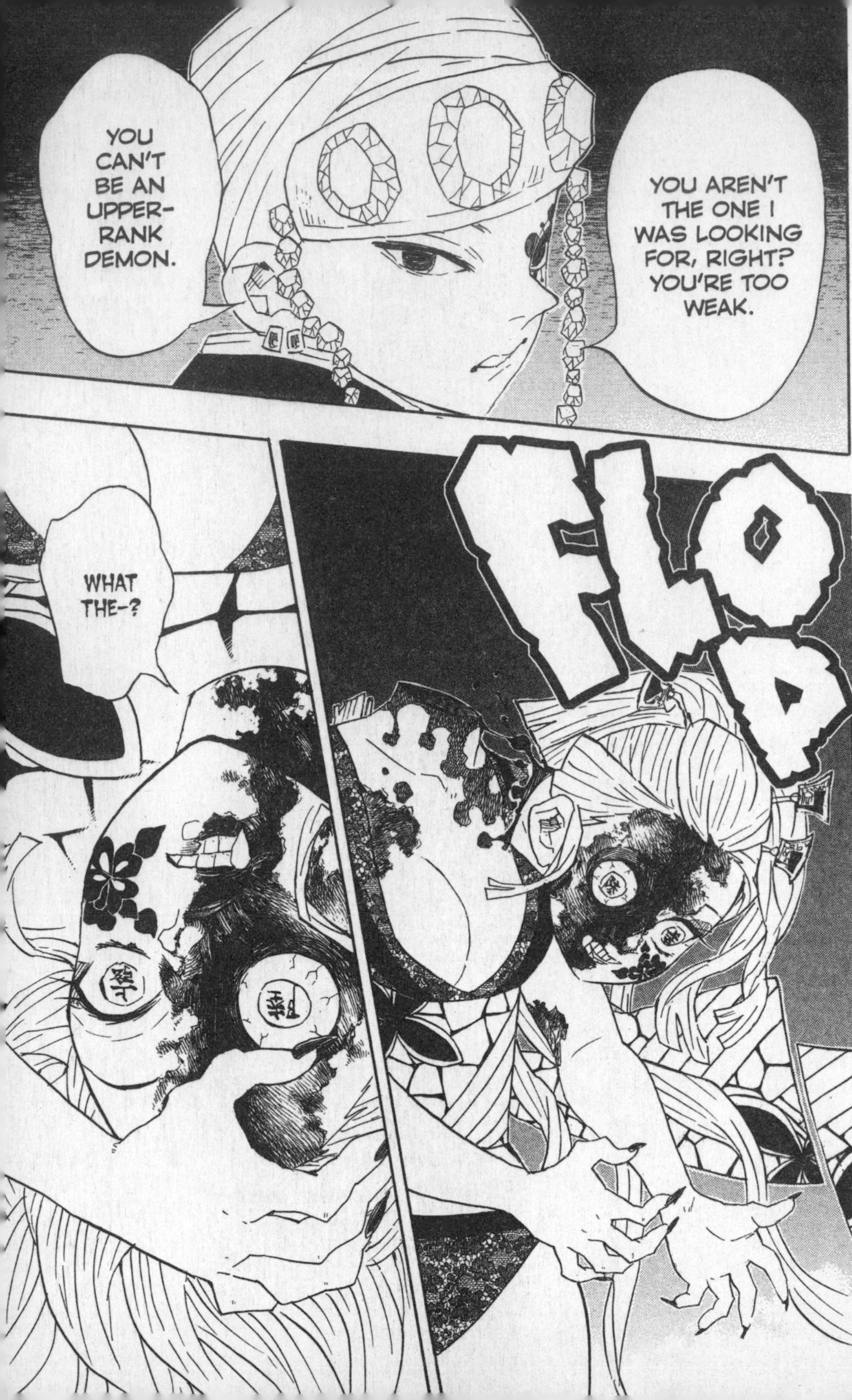
YOU AREN'T THE ONE I WAS LOOKING FOR, RIGHT? YOU'RE TOO WEAK.
YOU CAN'T BE AN UPPER-RANK DEMON.
FLOP
WHAT THE-?

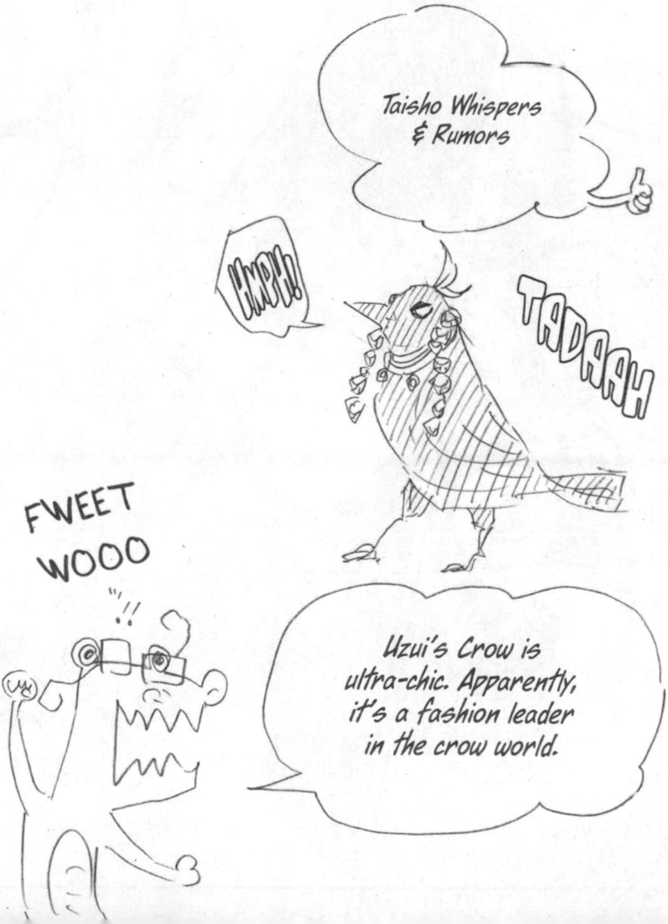
Taisho Whispers
& Rumors
TADAAAH
HMPH!
FWEET
WOOO
!!
Uzui's Crow is ultra-chic. Apparently, it's a fashion leader in the crow world.

CHAPTER 85: WEEPING

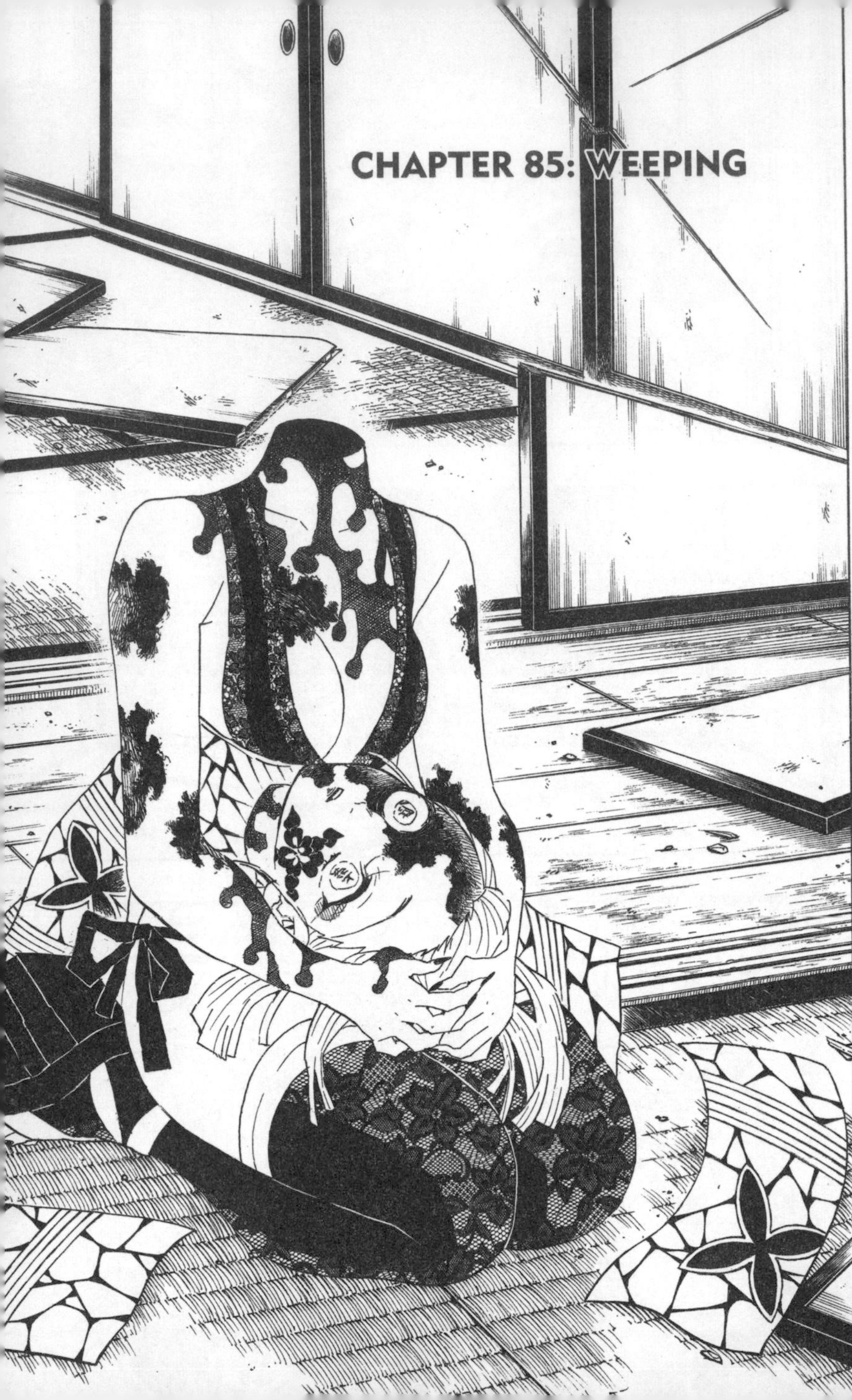

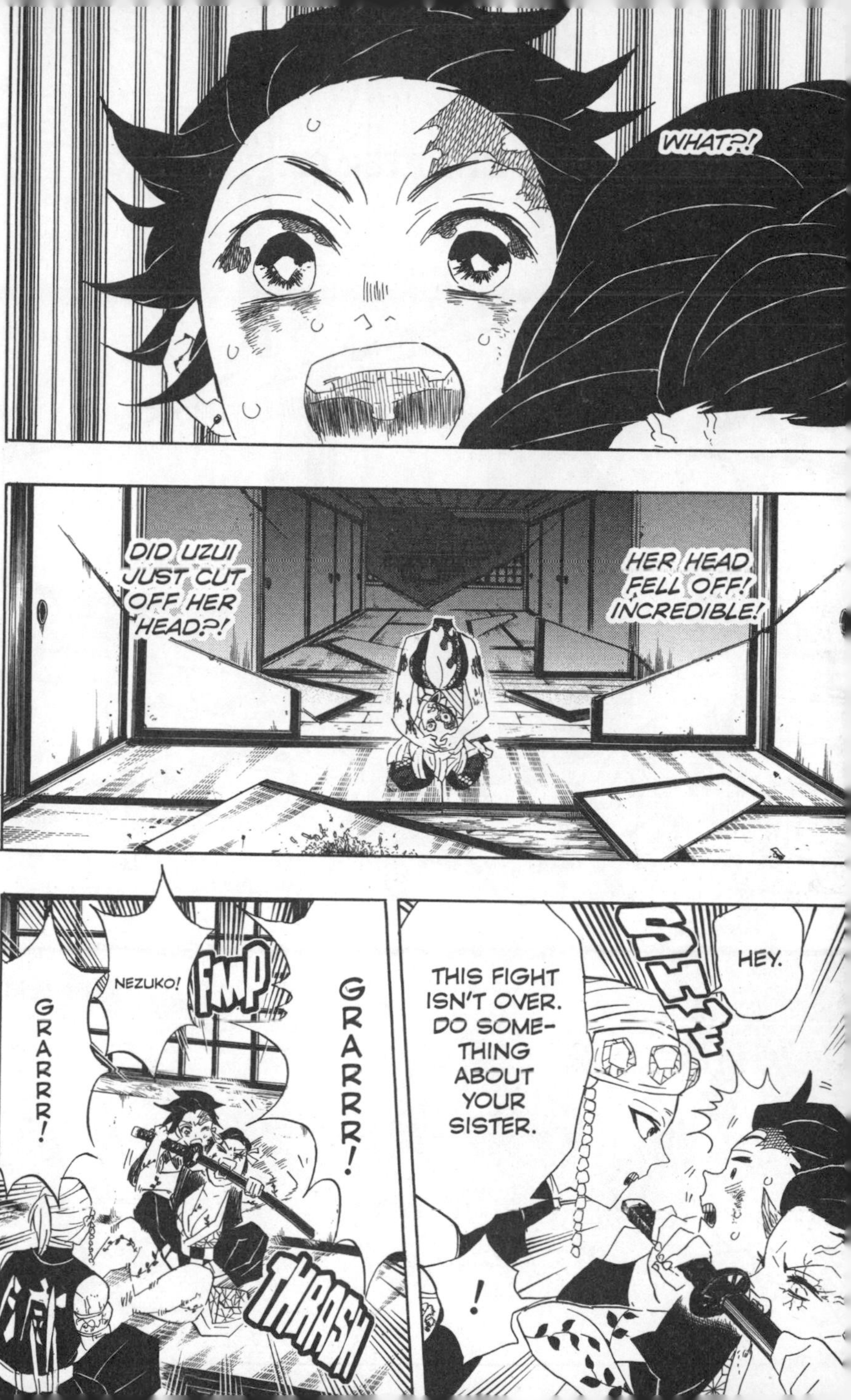
WHAT?!
HER HEAD FELL OFF! INCREDIBLE!
DID UZUI JUST CUT OFF HER HEAD?!
HEY.
SHWF
THIS FIGHT ISN'T OVER. DO SOME-THING ABOUT YOUR SISTER.
!
GRARRR!
FMP
NEZUKO!
GRARRR!
THRASH

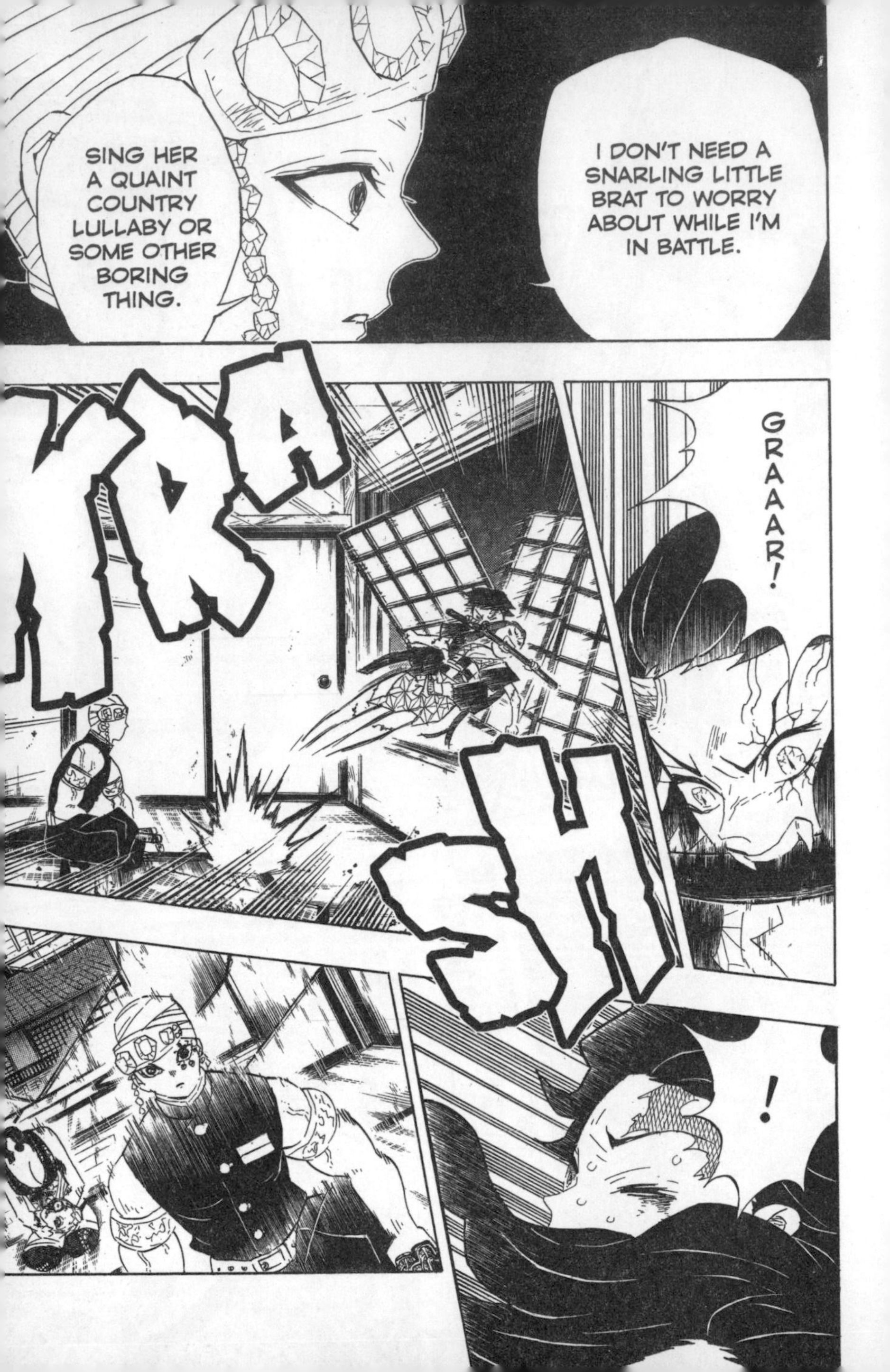
I DON'T NEED A SNARLING LITTLE BRAT TO WORRY ABOUT WHILE I'M IN BATTLE.
SING HER A QUAINT COUNTRY LULLABY OR SOME OTHER BORING THING.
GRAAAR!
KRASH
!

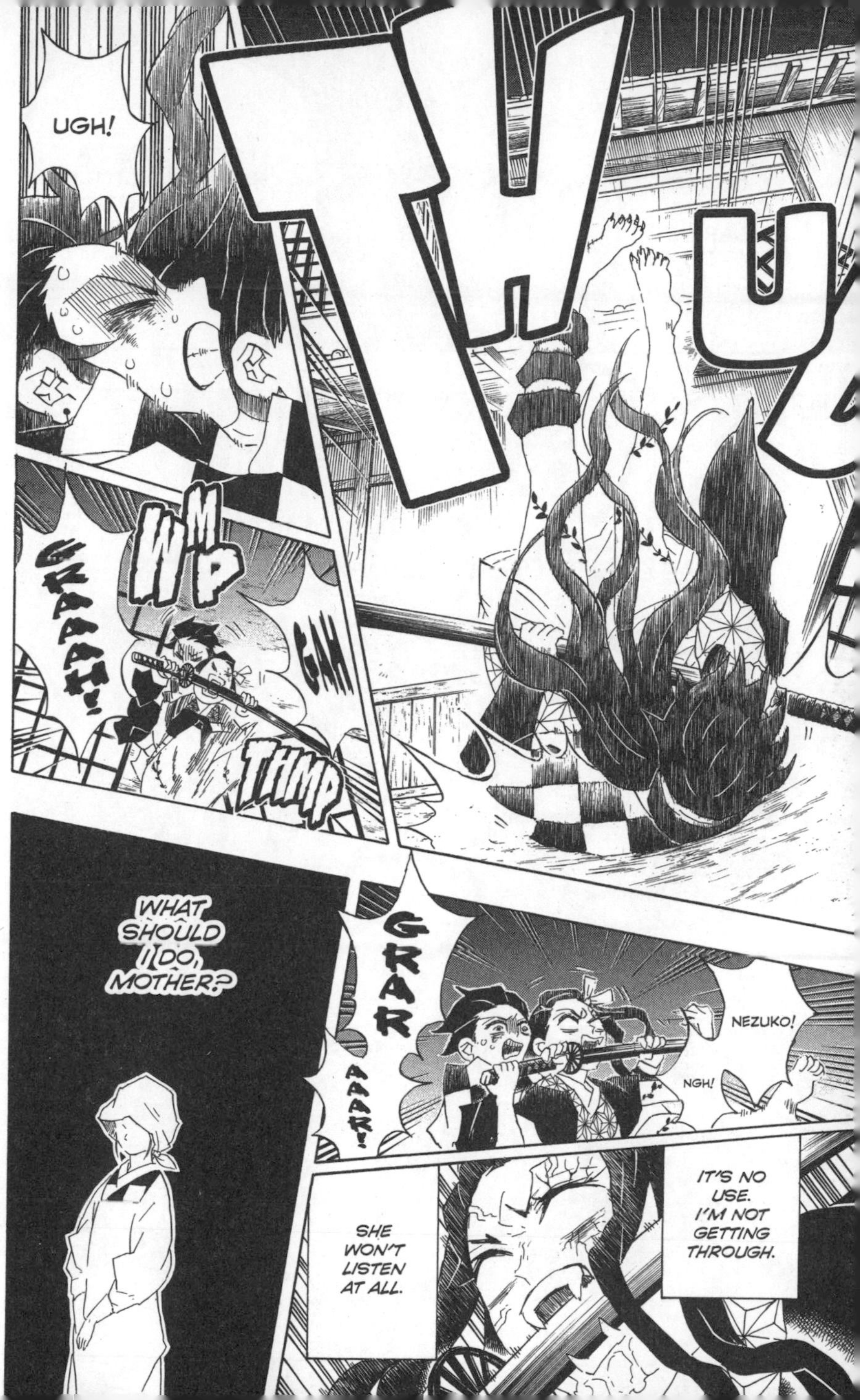
THU
UGH!
WMP
GRAAAAH!
GAH
THMP
NEZUKO!
NGH!
GRAR
AAAAK!
IT'S NO USE. I'M NOT GETTING THROUGH.
SHE WON'T LISTEN AT ALL.
WHAT SHOULD I DO, MOTHER?

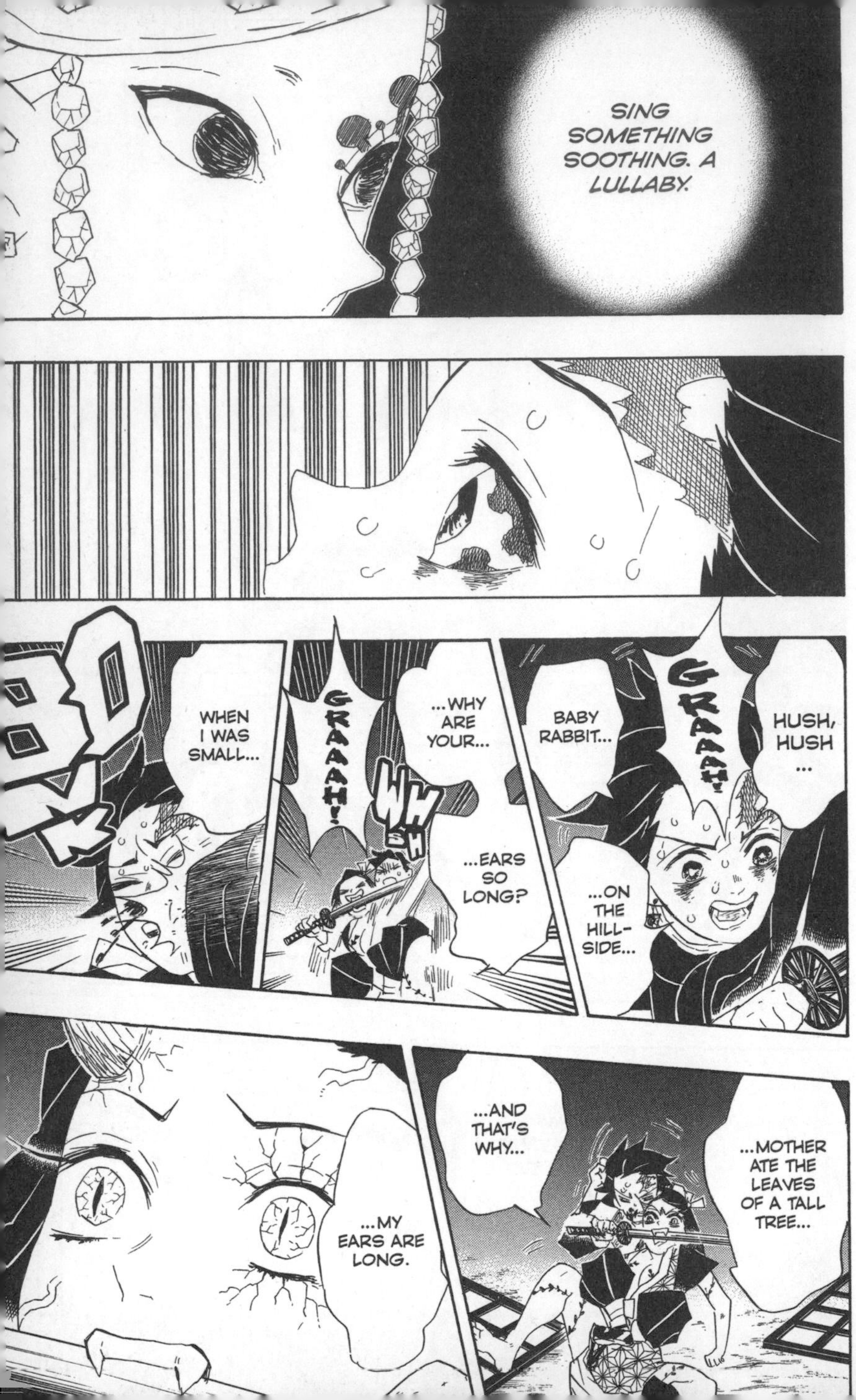
SING SOMETHING SOOTHING. A LULLABY.
HUSH, HUSH ...
GRAAAAH!
BABY RABBIT...
...ON THE HILL-SIDE...
...WHY ARE YOUR...
GRAAAAH!
WHSH
...EARS SO LONG?
WHEN I WAS SMALL...
BOK
...MOTHER ATE THE LEAVES OF A TALL TREE...
...AND THAT'S WHY...
...MY EARS ARE LONG.

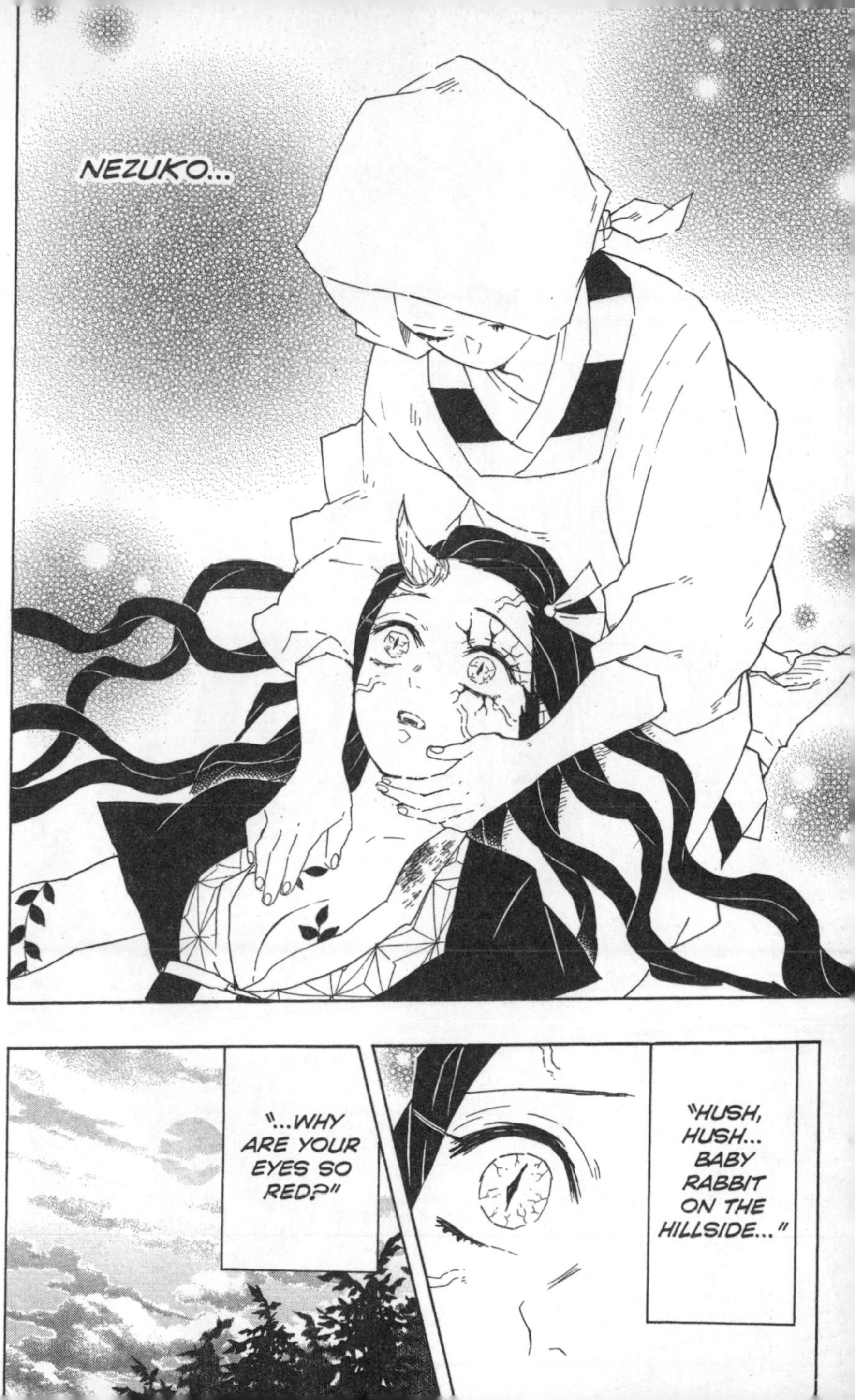
NEZUKO...
"HUSH, HUSH... BABY RABBIT ON THE HILLSIDE..."
"...WHY ARE YOUR EYES SO RED?"

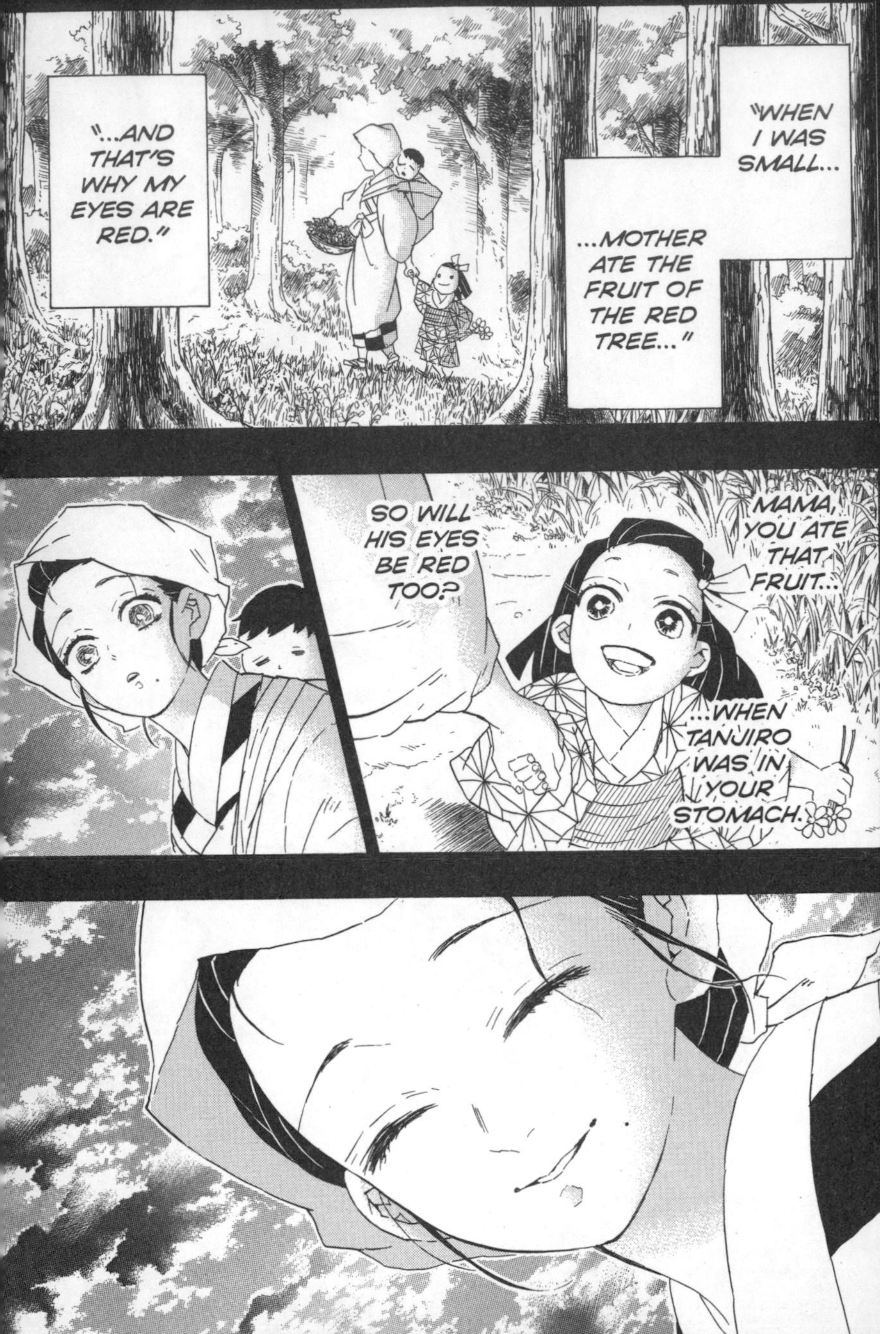
"WHEN I WAS SMALL...
...MOTHER ATE THE FRUIT OF THE RED TREE..."
"...AND THAT'S WHY MY EYES ARE RED."
MAMA, YOU ATE THAT FRUIT...
...WHEN TANJIRO WAS IN YOUR STOMACH.
SO WILL HIS EYES BE RED TOO?

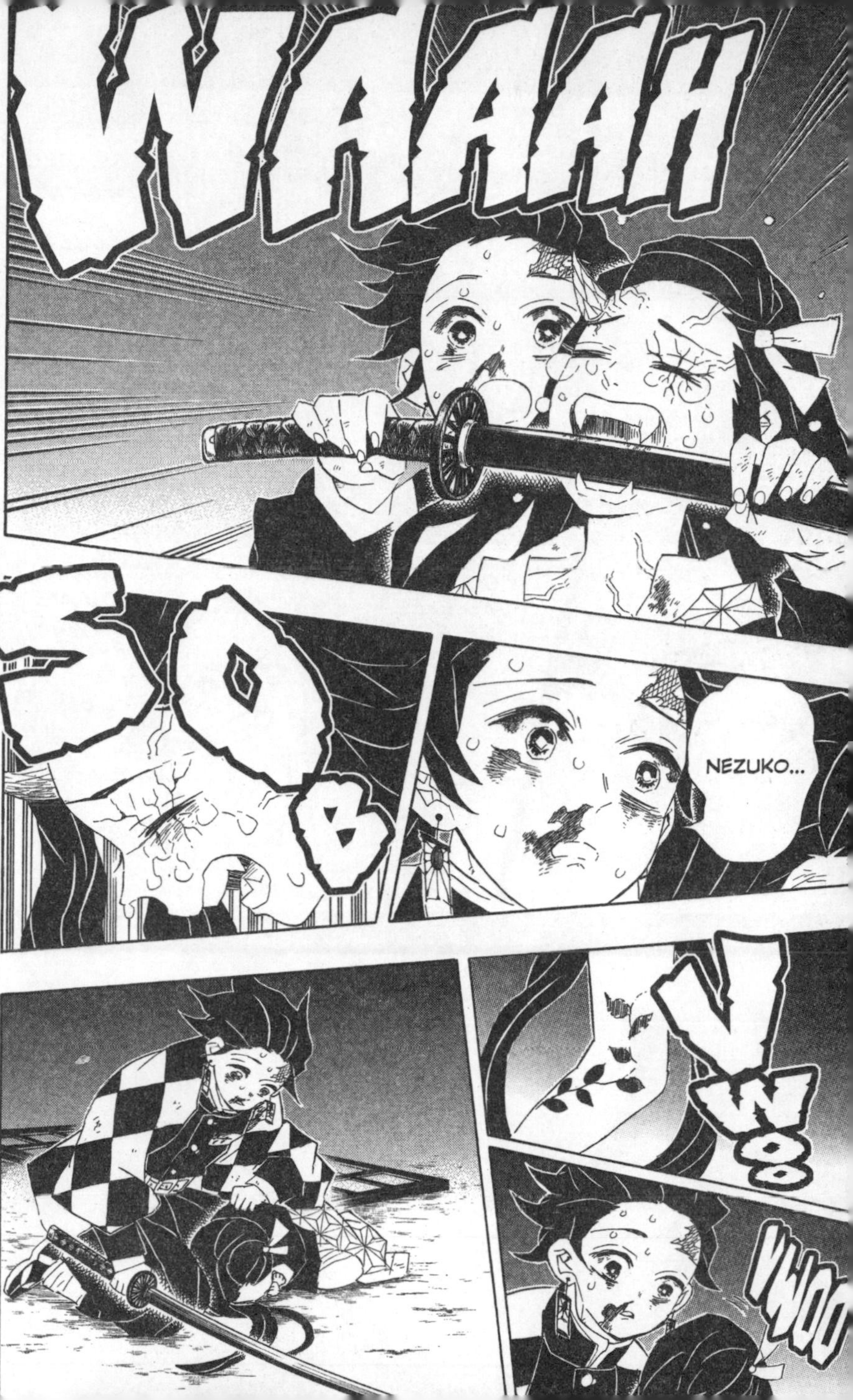
WAAAH
NEZUKO...
SOB
VWOO
VWOO

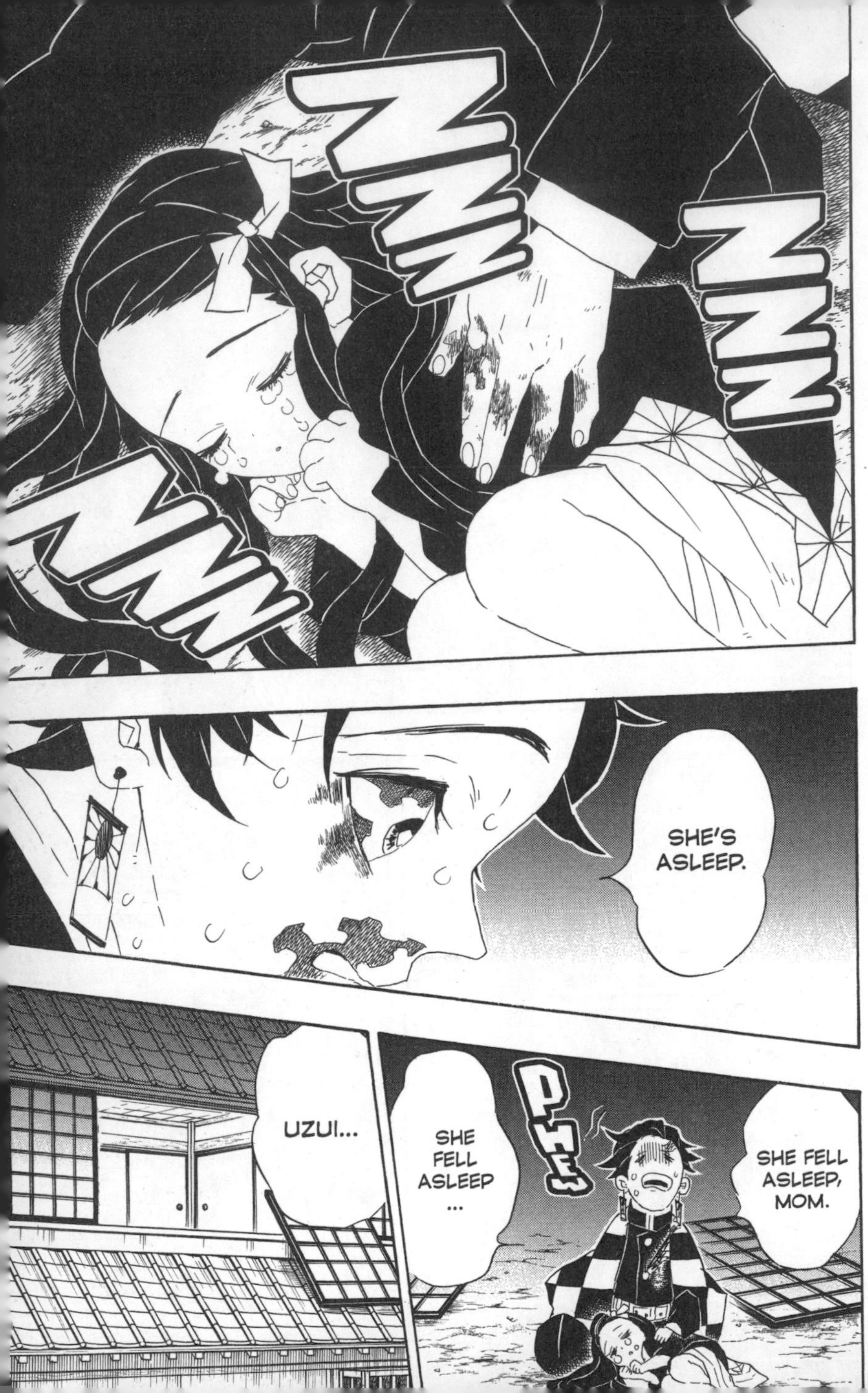

NNN
NNN
NNN
SHE'S ASLEEP.
SHE FELL ASLEEP, MOM.
PHEW
SHE FELL ASLEEP ...
UZUI...

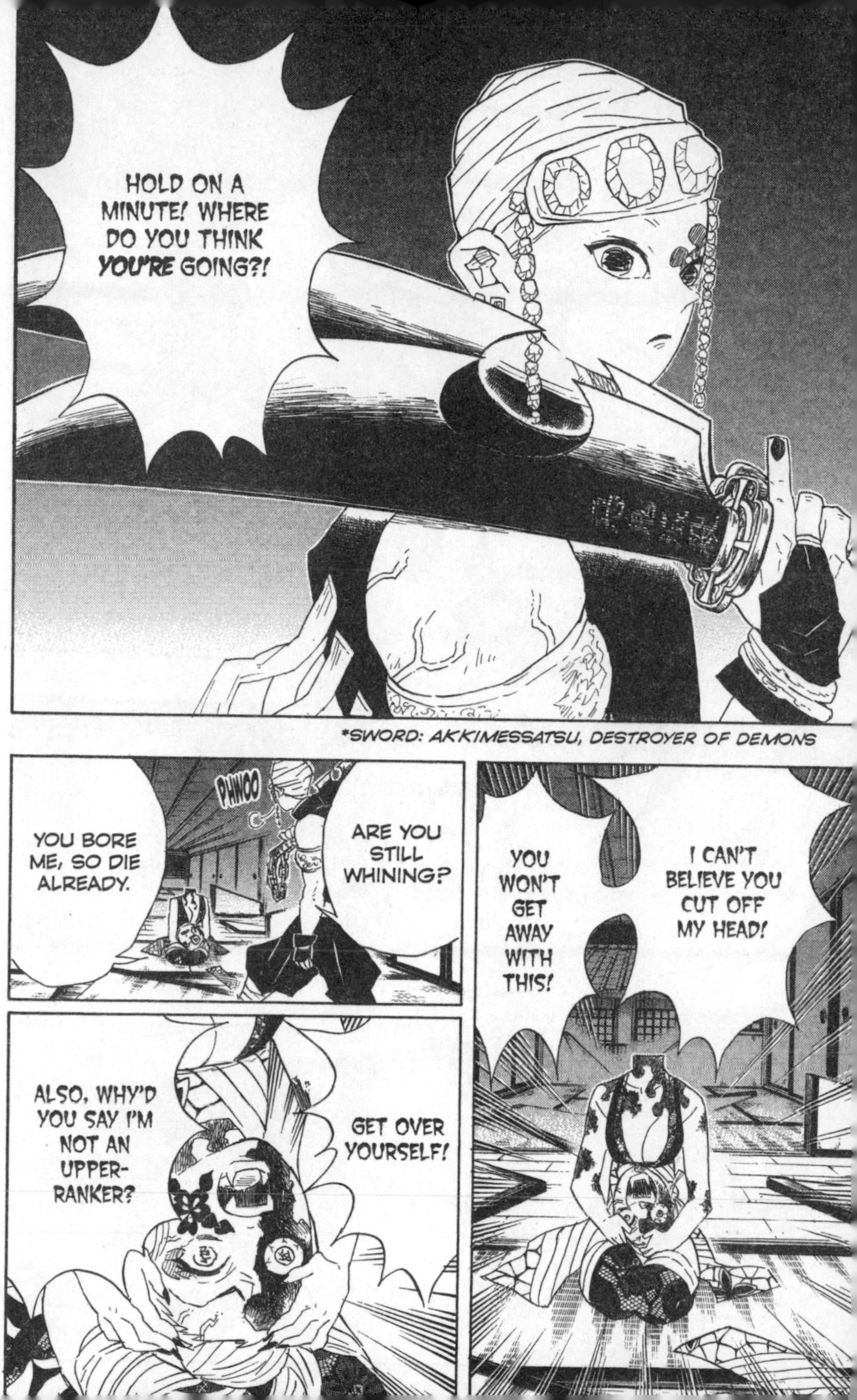
HOLD ON A MINUTE! WHERE DO YOU THINK YOU'RE GOING?!
*SWORD: AKKIMESSATSU, DESTROYER OF DEMONS
I CAN'T BELIEVE YOU CUT OFF MY HEAD!
YOU WON'T GET AWAY WITH THIS!
PHWOO
ARE YOU STILL WHINING?
YOU BORE ME, SO DIE ALREADY.
GET OVER YOURSELF!
ALSO, WHY'D YOU SAY I'M NOT AN UPPER-RANKER?

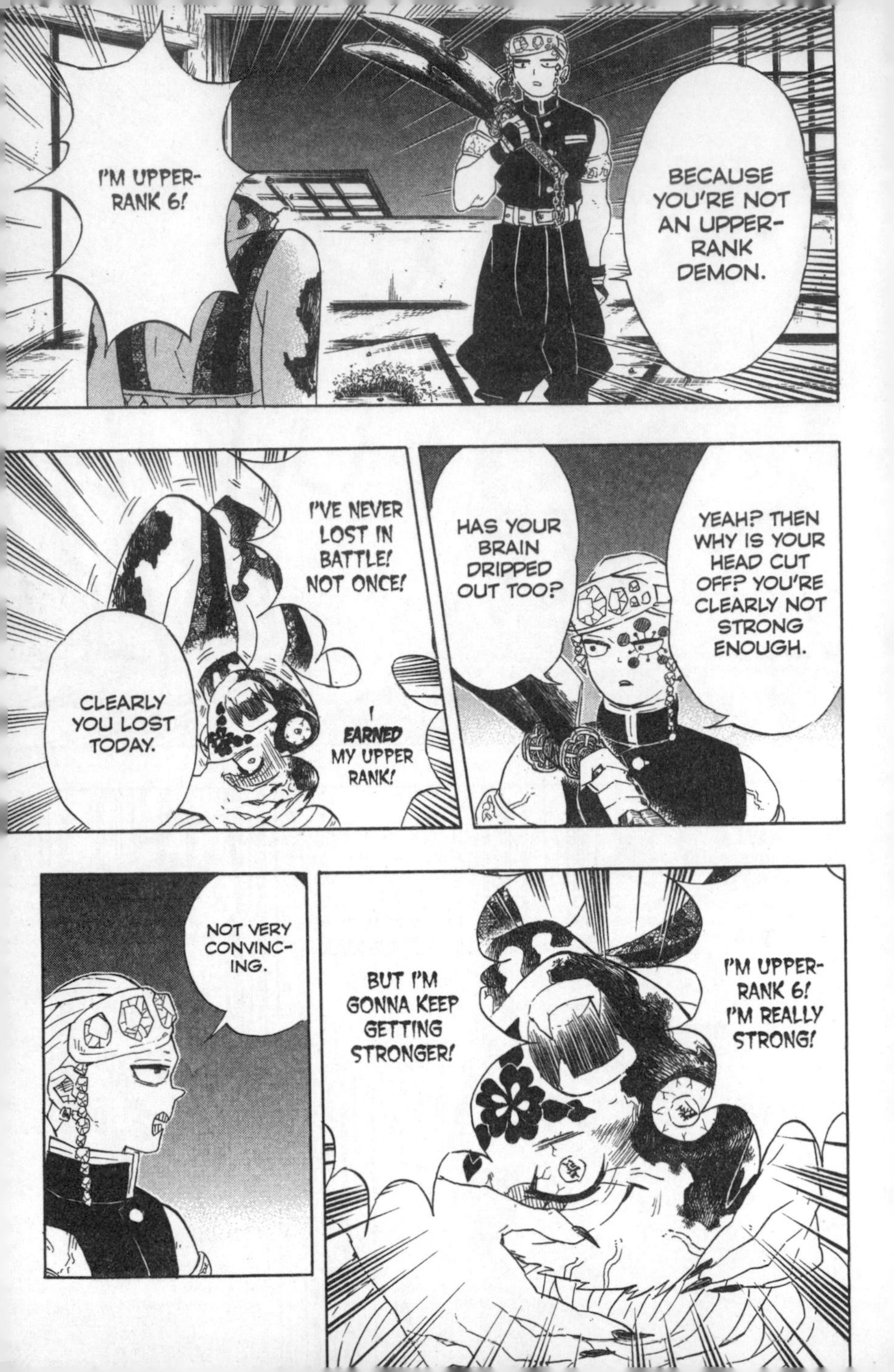
BECAUSE YOU'RE NOT AN UPPER-RANK DEMON.
I'M UPPER-RANK 6!
YEAH? THEN WHY IS YOUR HEAD CUT OFF? YOU'RE CLEARLY NOT STRONG ENOUGH.
HAS YOUR BRAIN DRIPPED OUT TOO?
I'VE NEVER LOST IN BATTLE! NOT ONCE!
I *EARNED* MY UPPER RANK!
CLEARLY YOU LOST TODAY.
I'M UPPER-RANK 6! I'M REALLY STRONG!
BUT I'M GONNA KEEP GETTING STRONGER!
NOT VERY CONVINCING.

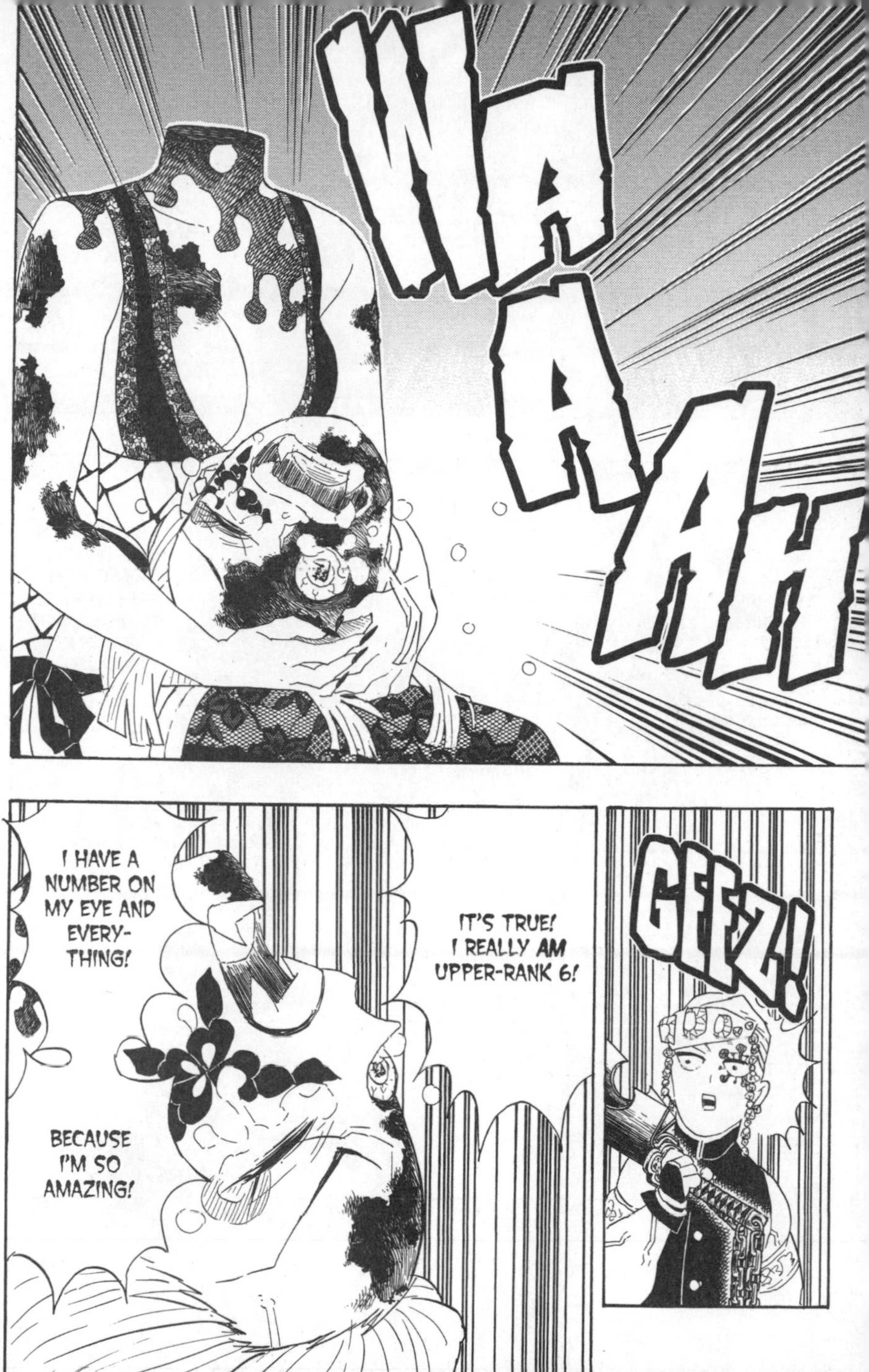
WAAAH
GEEZ!
IT'S TRUE! I REALLY AM UPPER-RANK 6!
I HAVE A NUMBER ON MY EYE AND EVERY-THING!
BECAUSE I'M SO AMAZING!

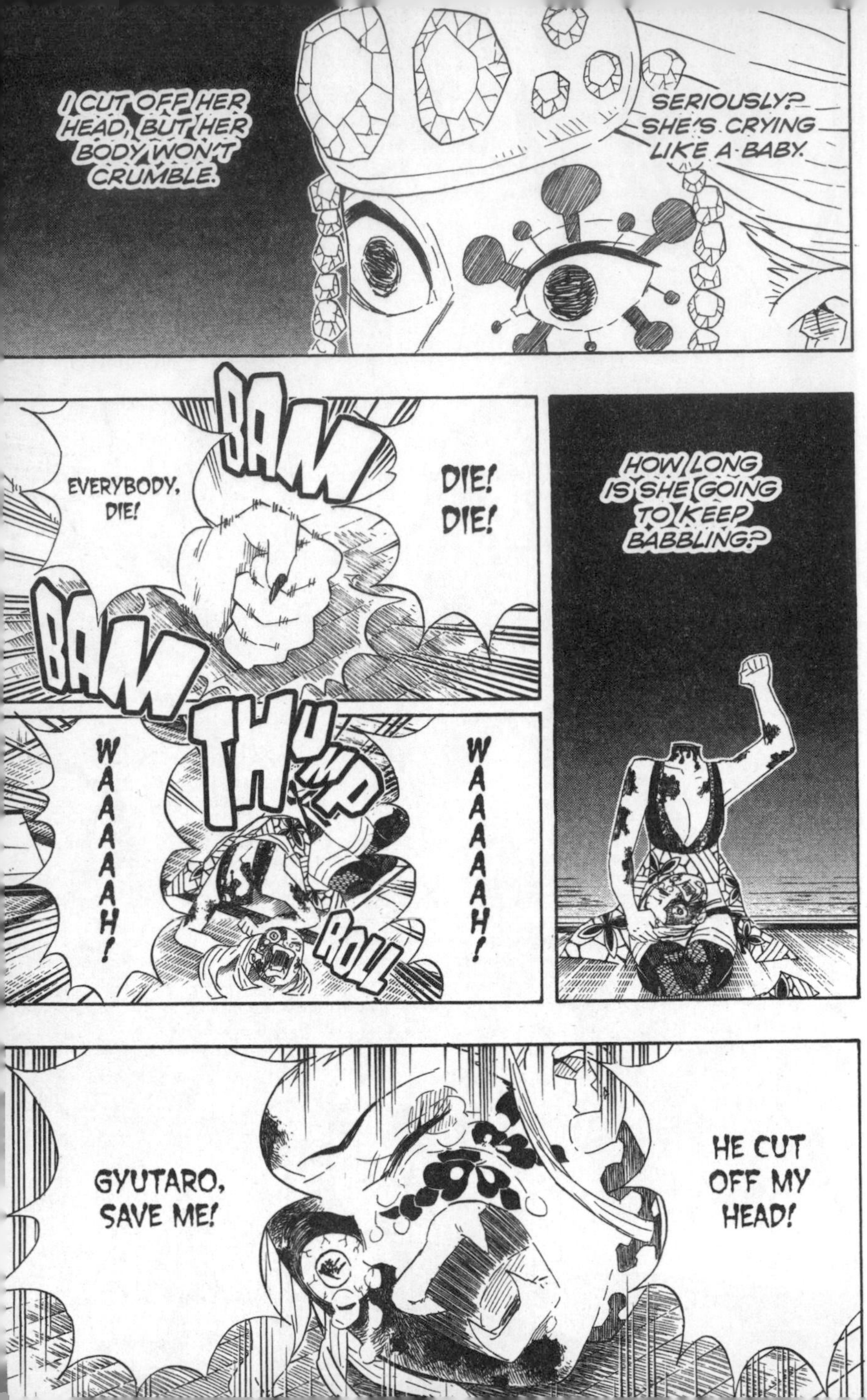
SERIOUSLY? SHE'S CRYING LIKE A BABY.
I CUT OFF HER HEAD, BUT HER BODY WON'T CRUMBLE.
HOW LONG IS SHE GOING TO KEEP BABBLING?
DIE! DIE!
BAM
EVERYBODY, DIE!
BAM
WAAAAAAH!
THUMP
ROLL
WAAAAAAH!
HE CUT OFF MY HEAD!
GYUTARO, SAVE ME!

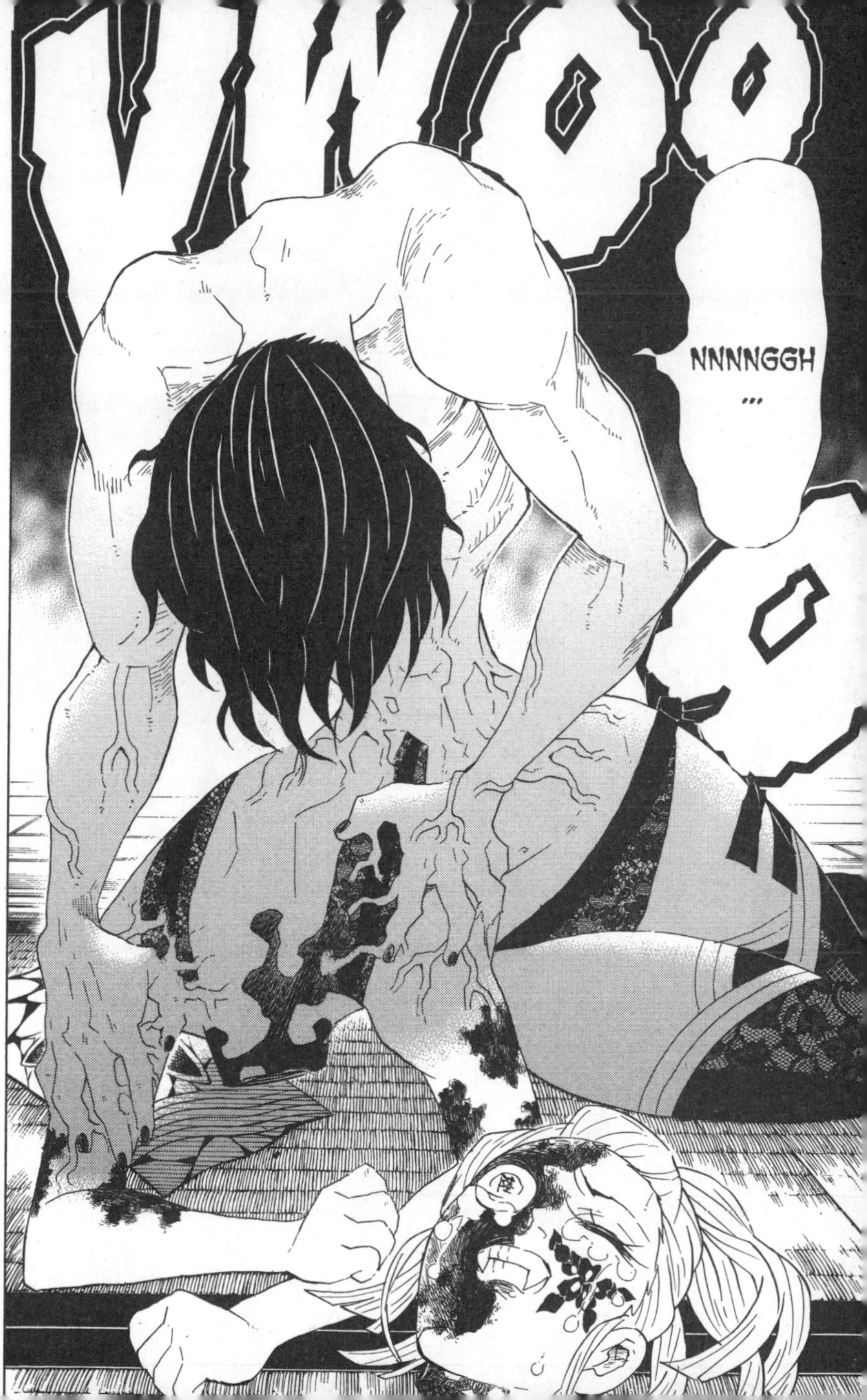
NNNNGGH ...

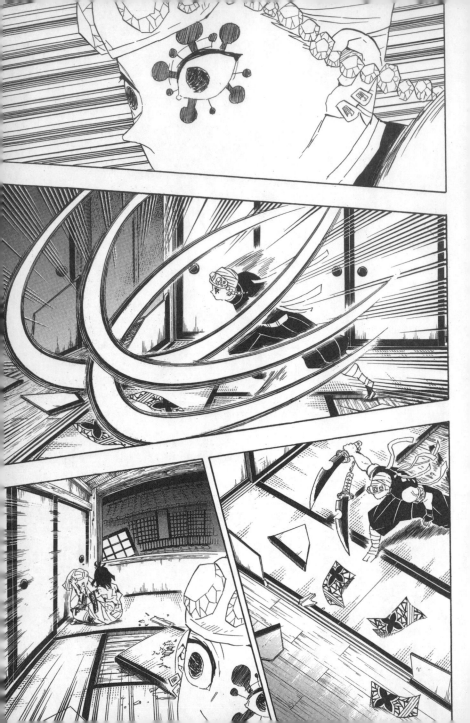

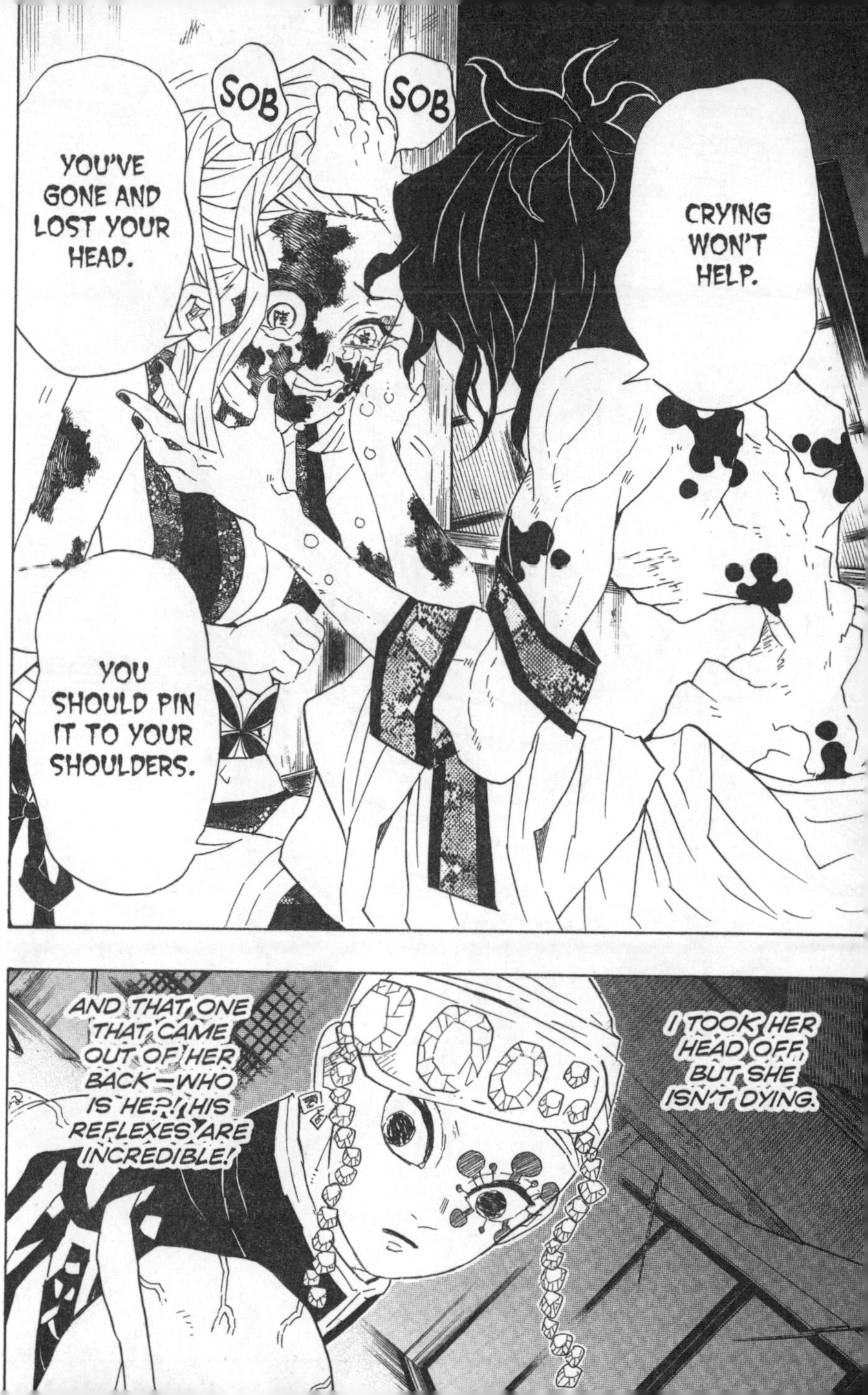
SOB
SOB
CRYING WON'T HELP.
YOU'VE GONE AND LOST YOUR HEAD.
YOU SHOULD PIN IT TO YOUR SHOULDERS.
I TOOK HER HEAD OFF, BUT SHE ISN'T DYING.
AND THAT ONE THAT CAME OUT OF HER BACK—WHO IS HE?! HIS REFLEXES ARE INCREDIBLE!

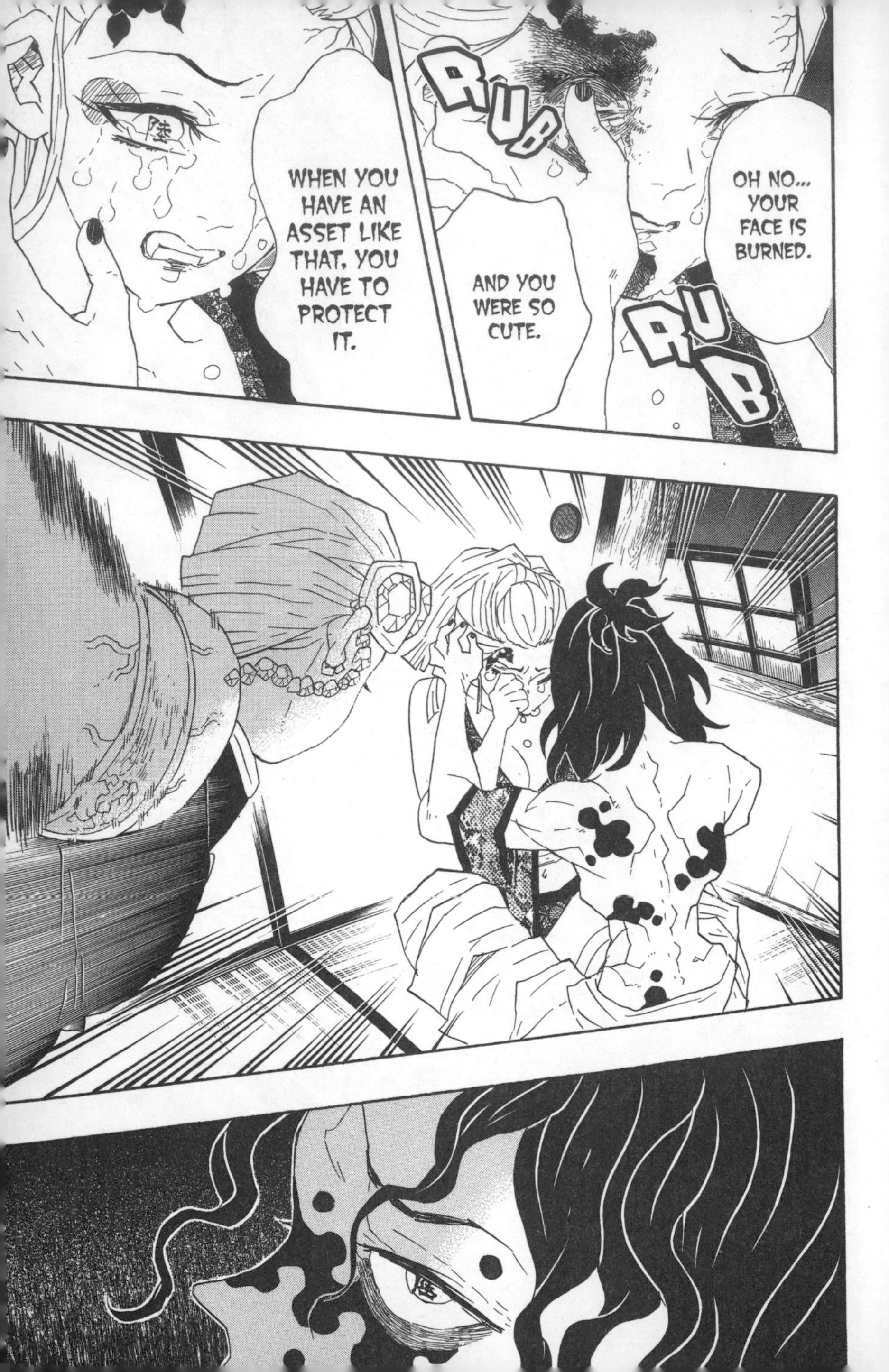
OH NO... YOUR FACE IS BURNED.
RUB
RUB
AND YOU WERE SO CUTE.
WHEN YOU HAVE AN ASSET LIKE THAT, YOU HAVE TO PROTECT IT.

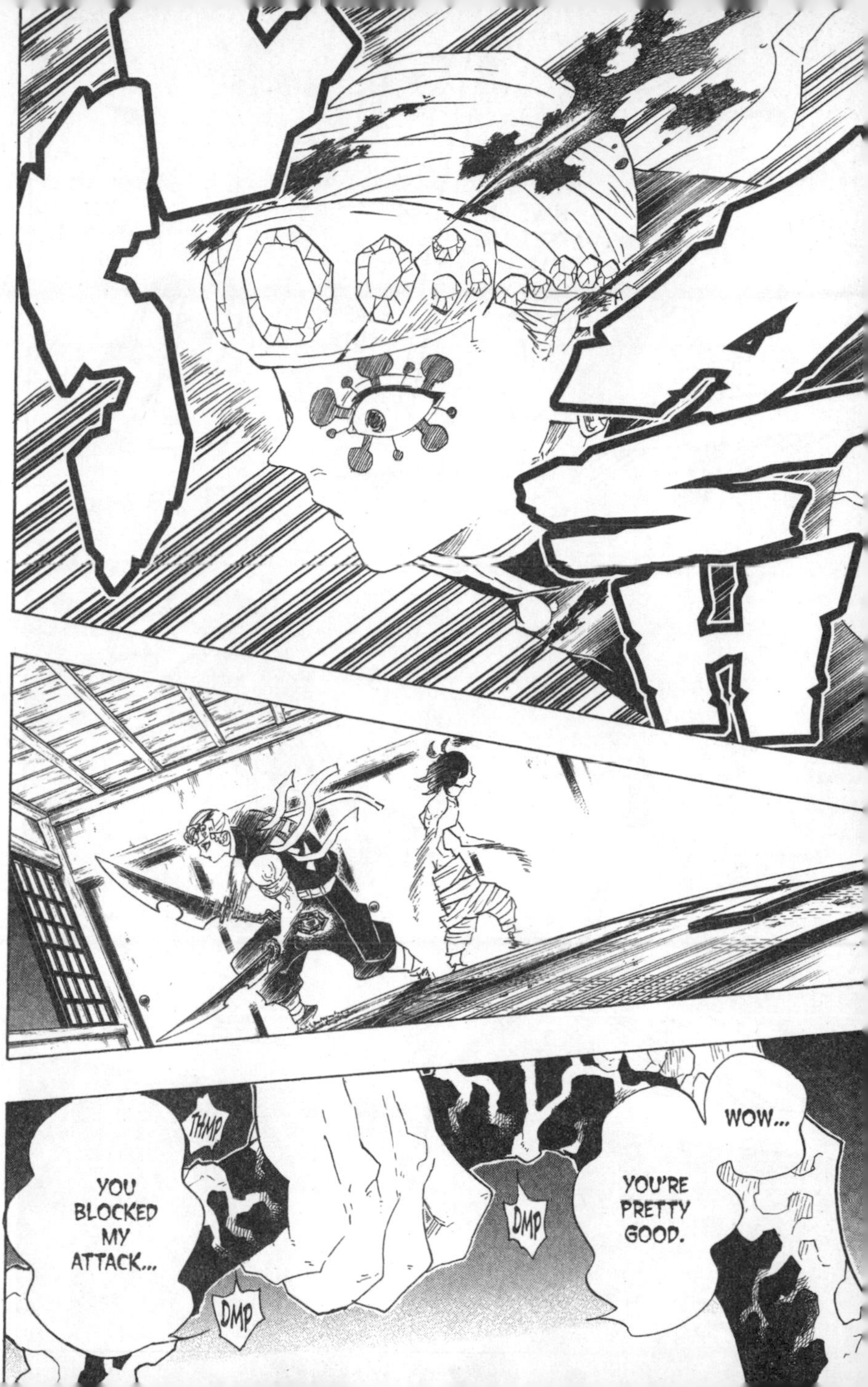
WOW...
YOU'RE PRETTY GOOD.
THMP
DMP
YOU BLOCKED MY ATTACK...
DMP

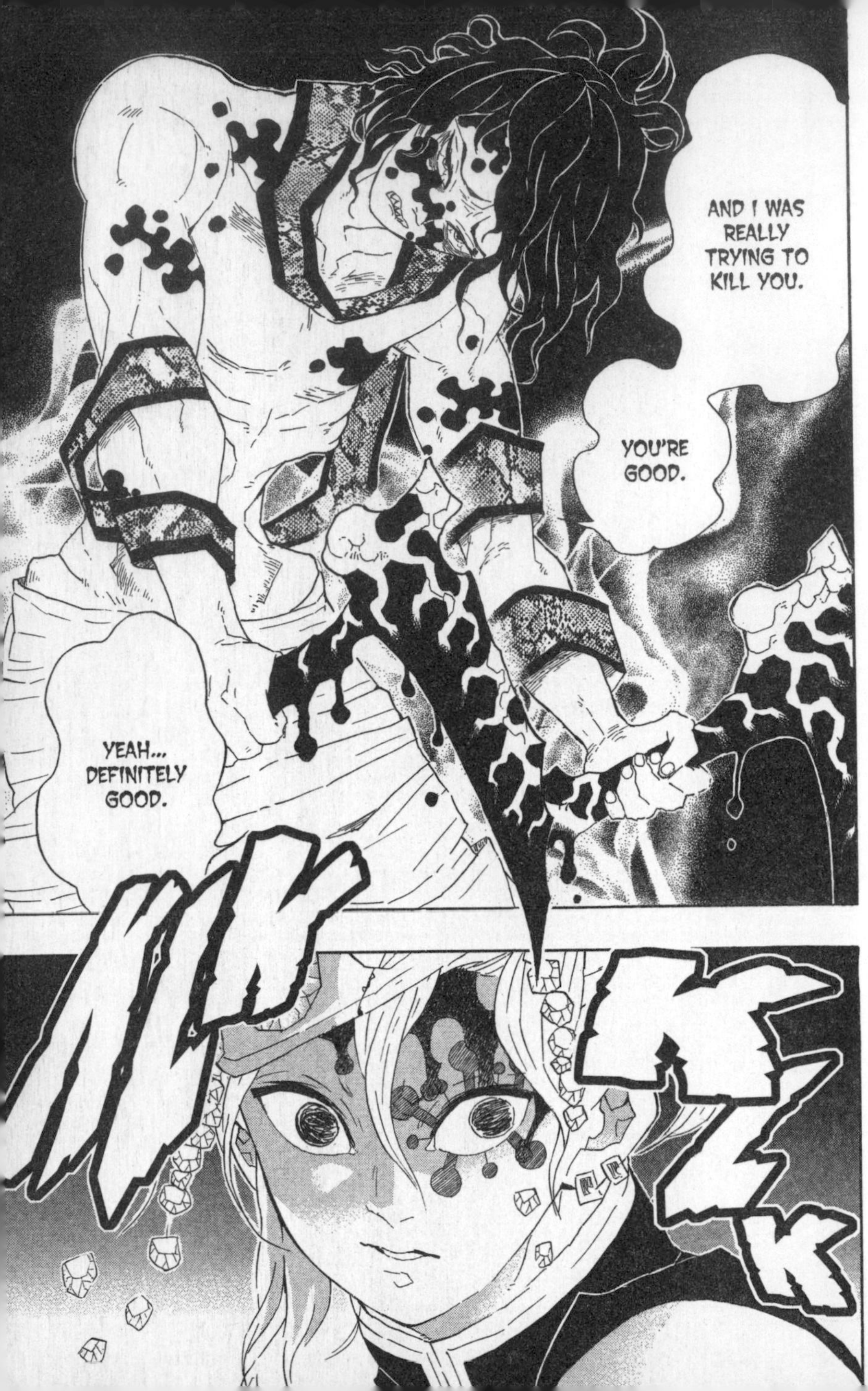
AND I WAS REALLY TRYING TO KILL YOU.
YOU'RE GOOD.
YEAH... DEFINITELY GOOD.

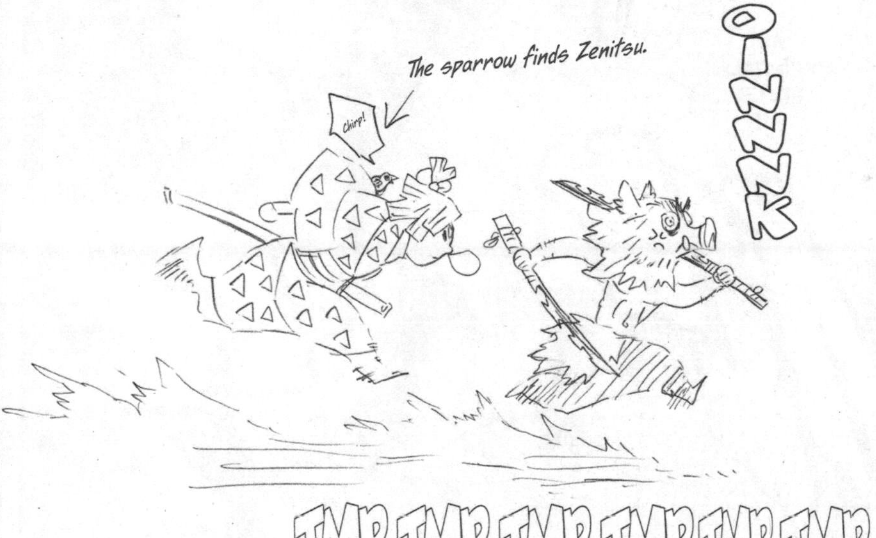
KZZZ!
The sparrow finds Zenitsu.
Chirp!
TMP TMP TMP TMP TMP TMP

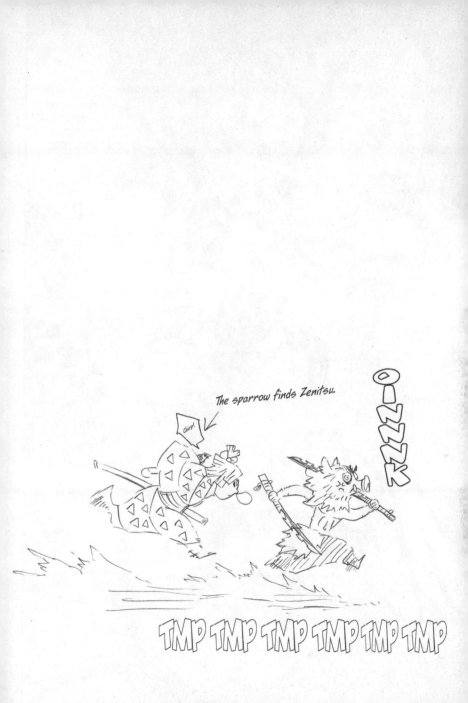

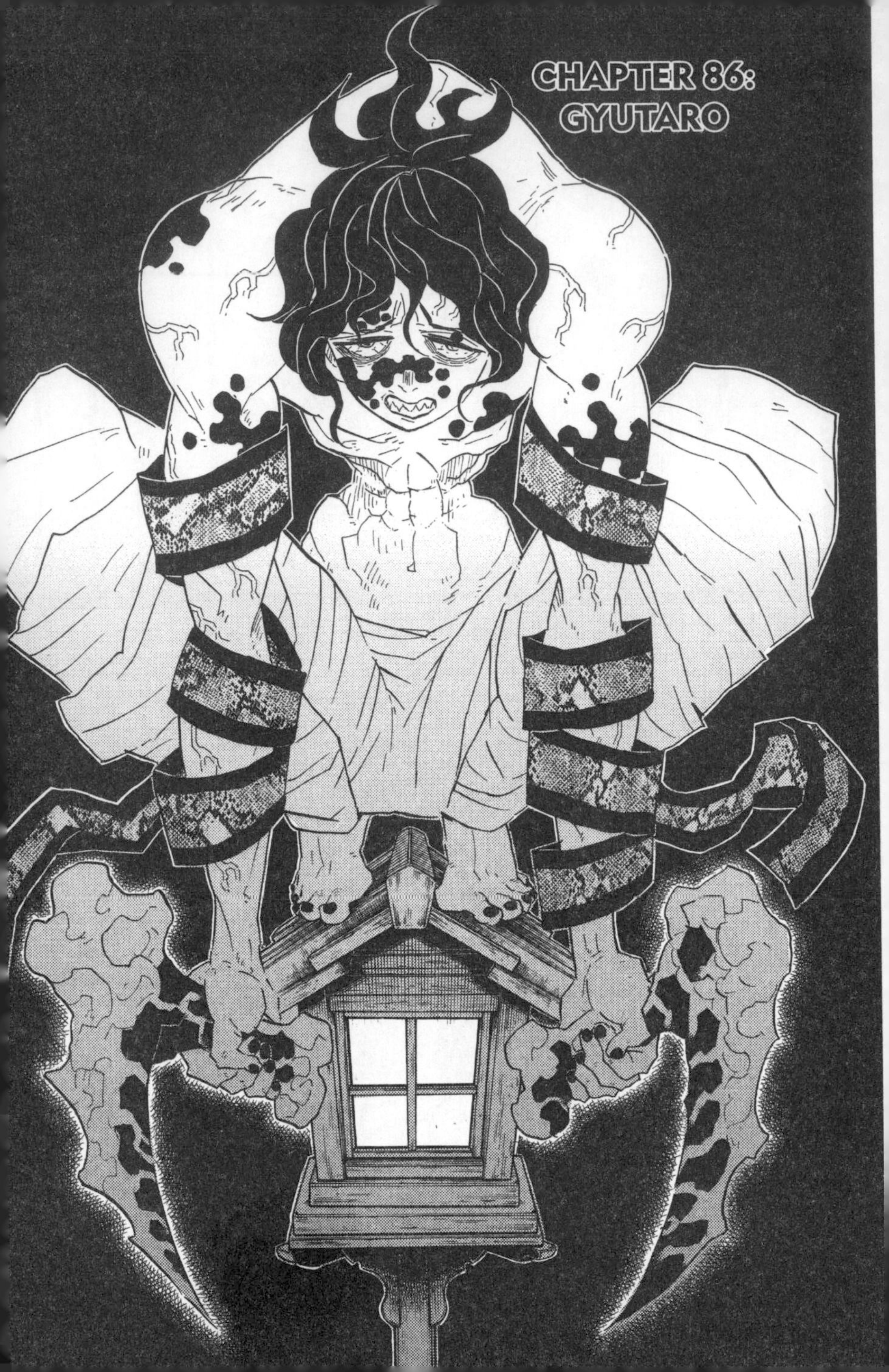
CHAPTER 86:
GYUTARO

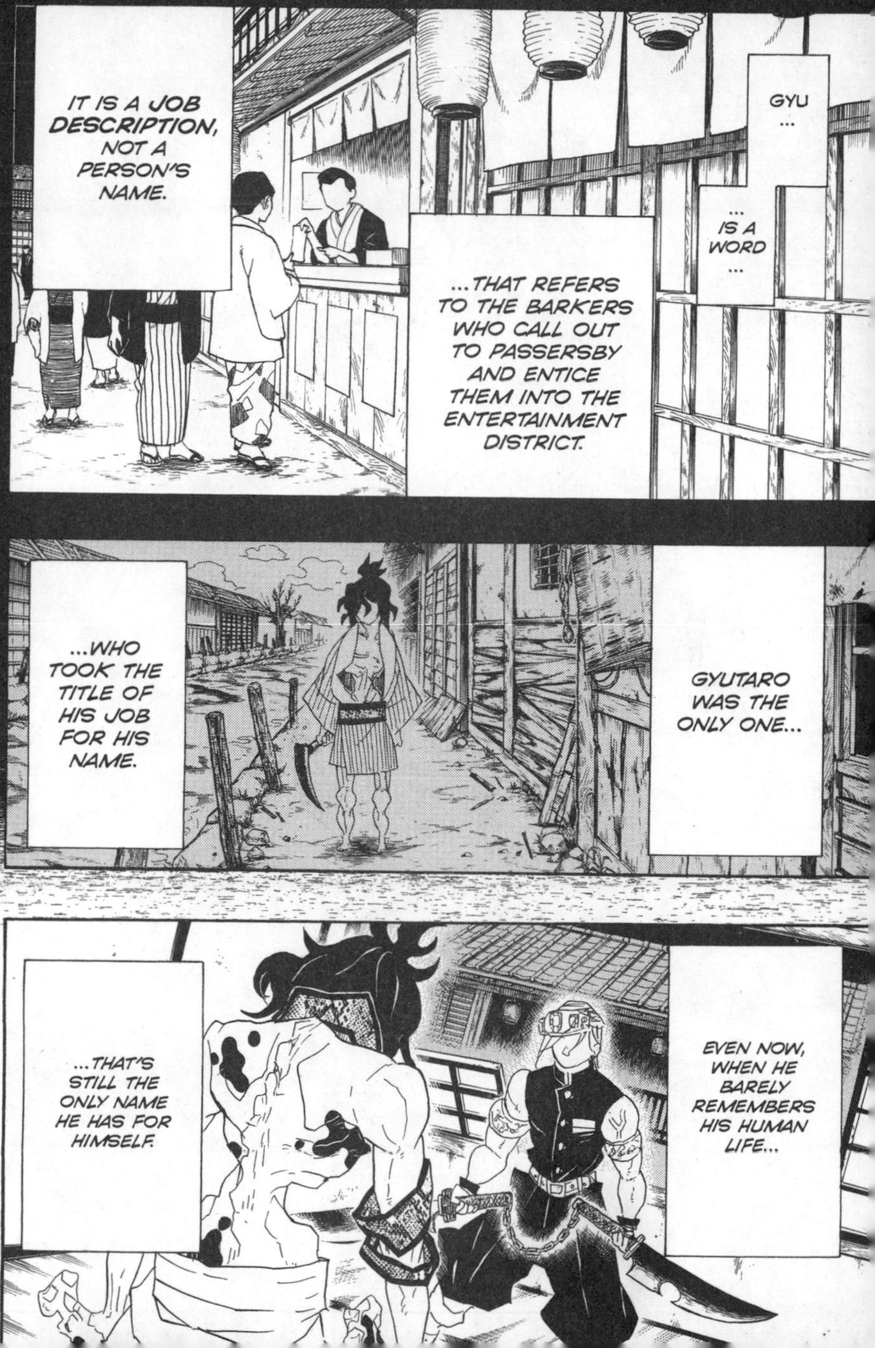
GYU ...
... IS A WORD ...
...THAT REFERS TO THE BARKERS WHO CALL OUT TO PASSERSBY AND ENTICE THEM INTO THE ENTERTAINMENT DISTRICT.
IT IS A JOB DESCRIPTION, NOT A PERSON'S NAME.
GYUTARO WAS THE ONLY ONE...
...WHO TOOK THE TITLE OF HIS JOB FOR HIS NAME.
EVEN NOW, WHEN HE BARELY REMEMBERS HIS HUMAN LIFE...
...THAT'S STILL THE ONLY NAME HE HAS FOR HIMSELF.

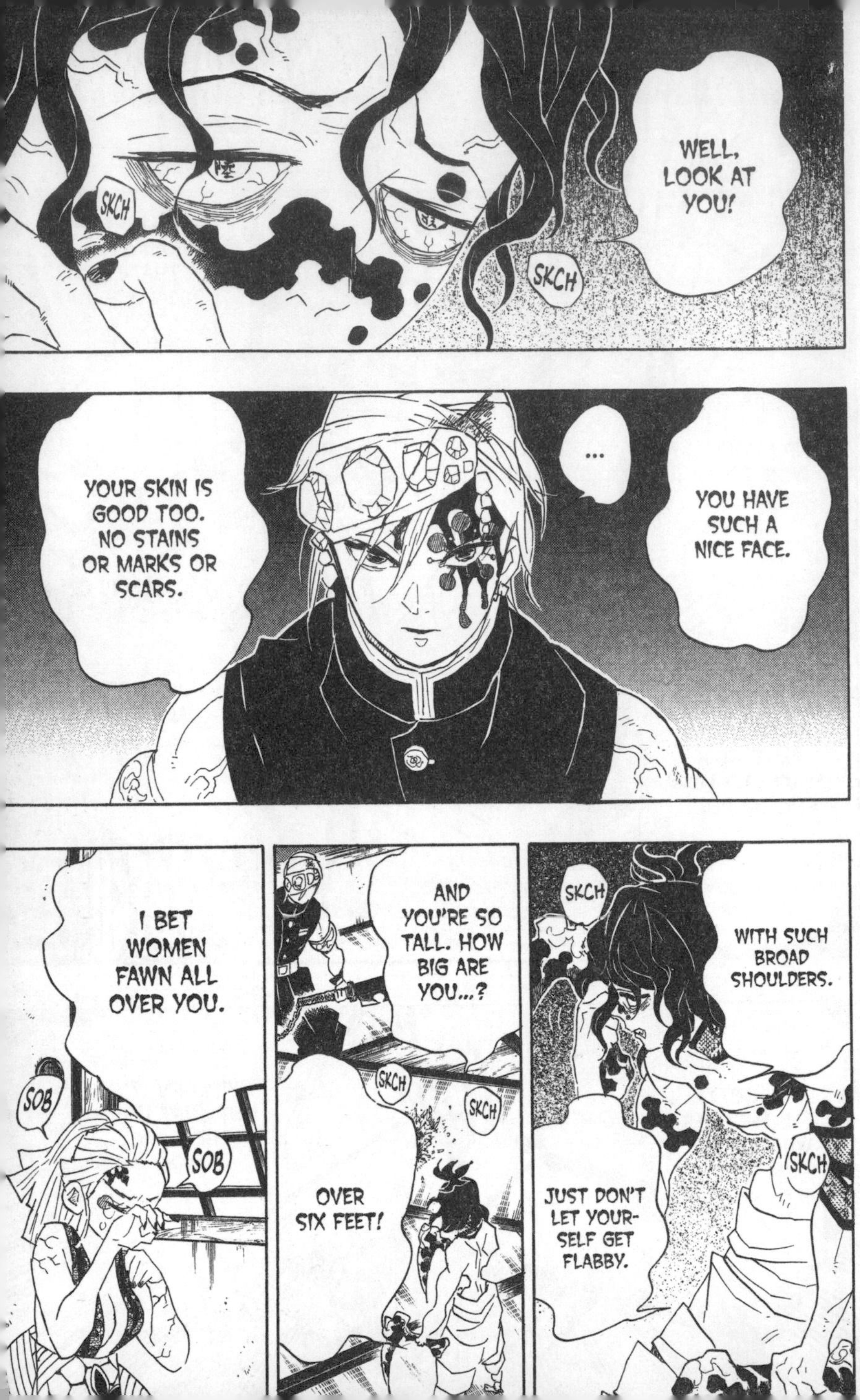
WELL, LOOK AT YOU!
SKCH
SKCH
YOU HAVE SUCH A NICE FACE.
...
YOUR SKIN IS GOOD TOO. NO STAINS OR MARKS OR SCARS.
WITH SUCH BROAD SHOULDERS.
SKCH
SKCH
JUST DON'T LET YOUR-SELF GET FLABBY.
AND YOU'RE SO TALL. HOW BIG ARE YOU...?
SKCH
SKCH
OVER SIX FEET!
I BET WOMEN FAWN ALL OVER YOU.
SOB
SOB

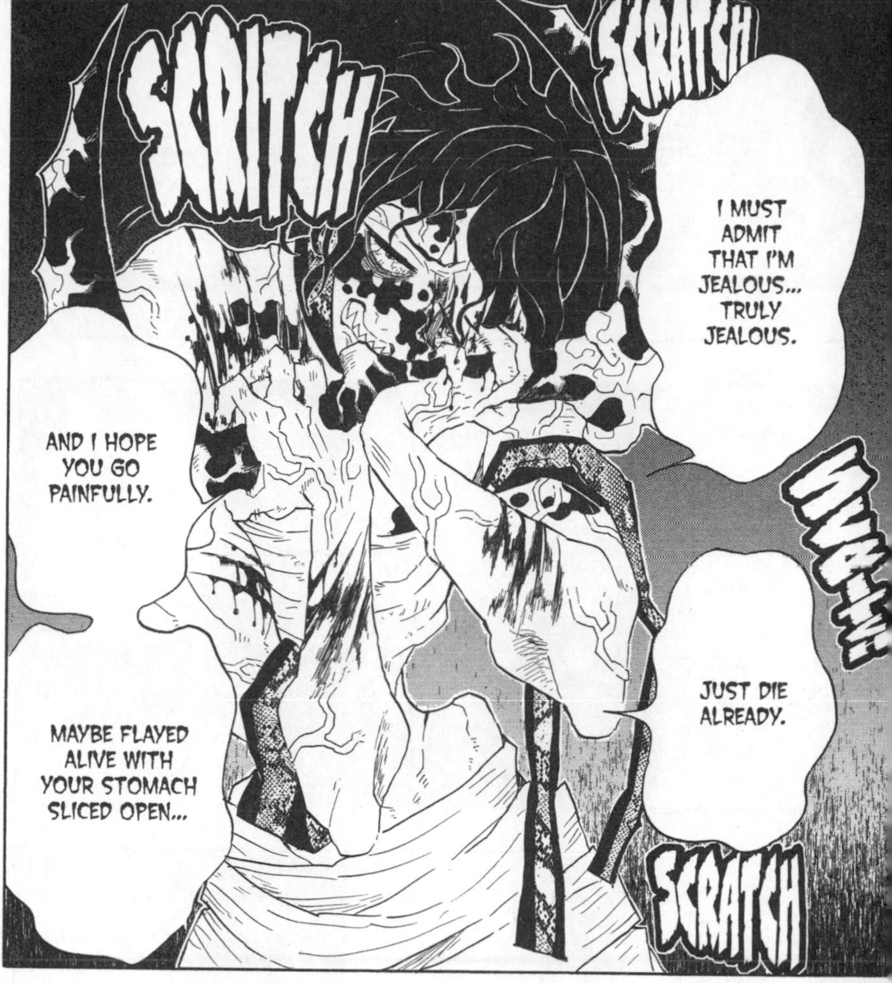
SCRATCH
I MUST ADMIT THAT I'M JEALOUS... TRULY JEALOUS.
SCRITCH
AND I HOPE YOU GO PAINFULLY.
JUST DIE ALREADY.
MAYBE FLAYED ALIVE WITH YOUR STOMACH SLICED OPEN...
SCRATCH

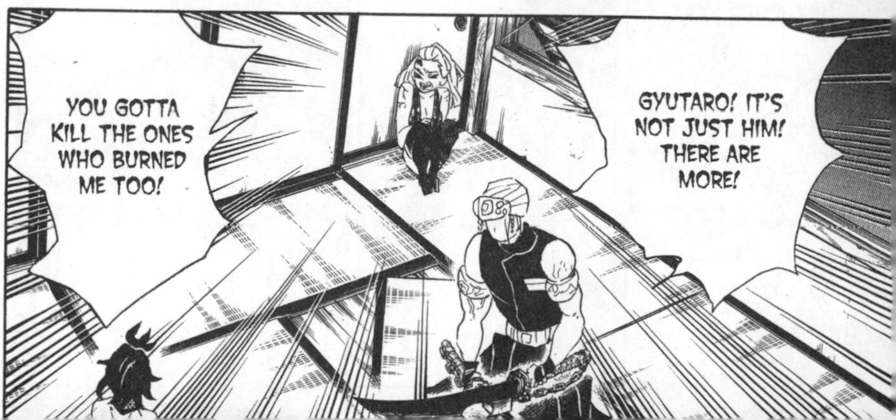
GYUTARO! IT'S NOT JUST HIM! THERE ARE MORE!
YOU GOTTA KILL THE ONES WHO BURNED ME TOO!

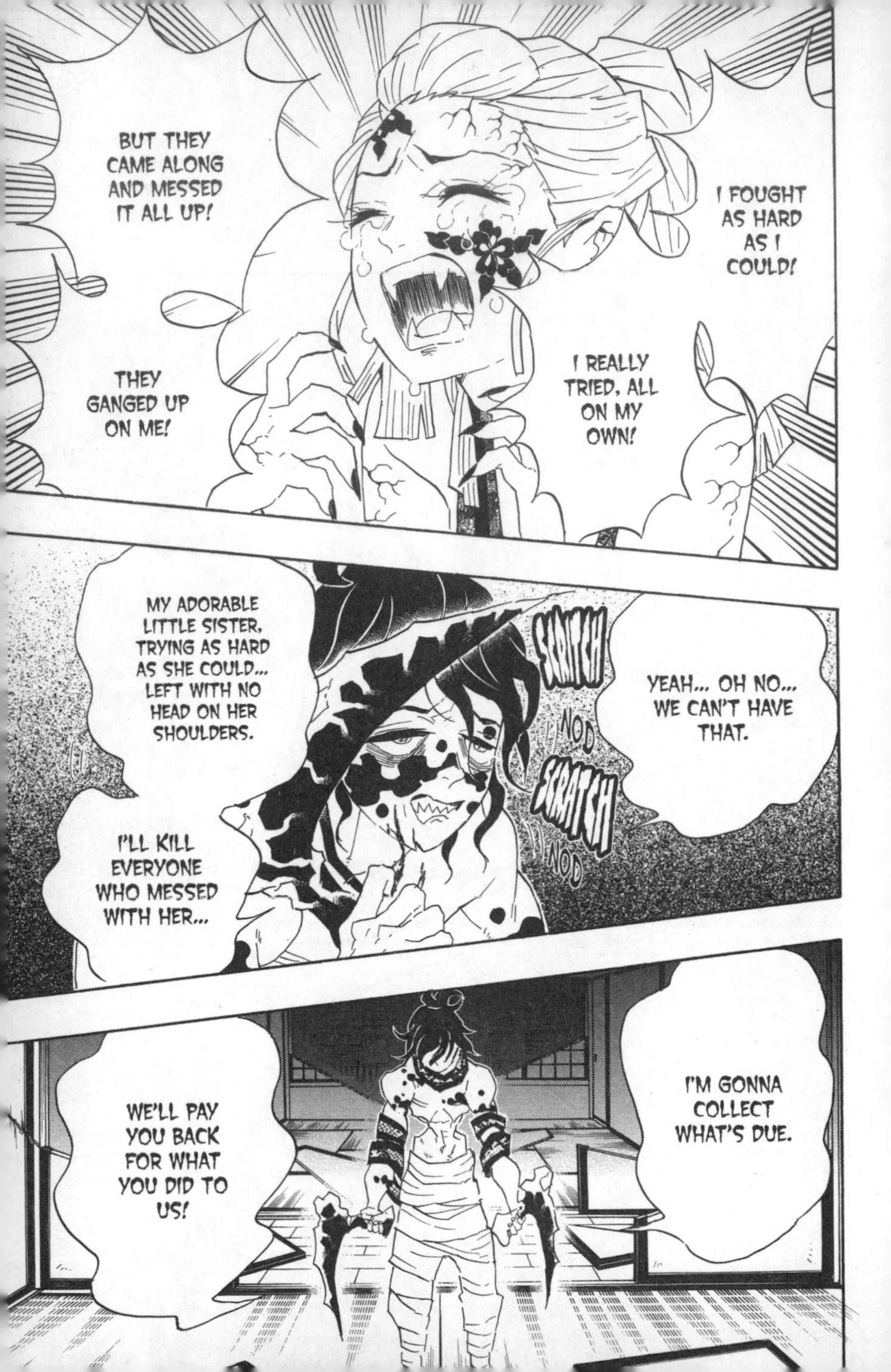
I FOUGHT AS HARD AS I COULD!
I REALLY TRIED, ALL ON MY OWN!
BUT THEY CAME ALONG AND MESSED IT ALL UP!
THEY GANGED UP ON ME!
YEAH... OH NO... WE CAN'T HAVE THAT.
SCRATCH
NOD
SCRATCH
NOD
MY ADORABLE LITTLE SISTER, TRYING AS HARD AS SHE COULD... LEFT WITH NO HEAD ON HER SHOULDERS.
I'LL KILL EVERYONE WHO MESSED WITH HER...
I'M GONNA COLLECT WHAT'S DUE.
WE'LL PAY YOU BACK FOR WHAT YOU DID TO US!

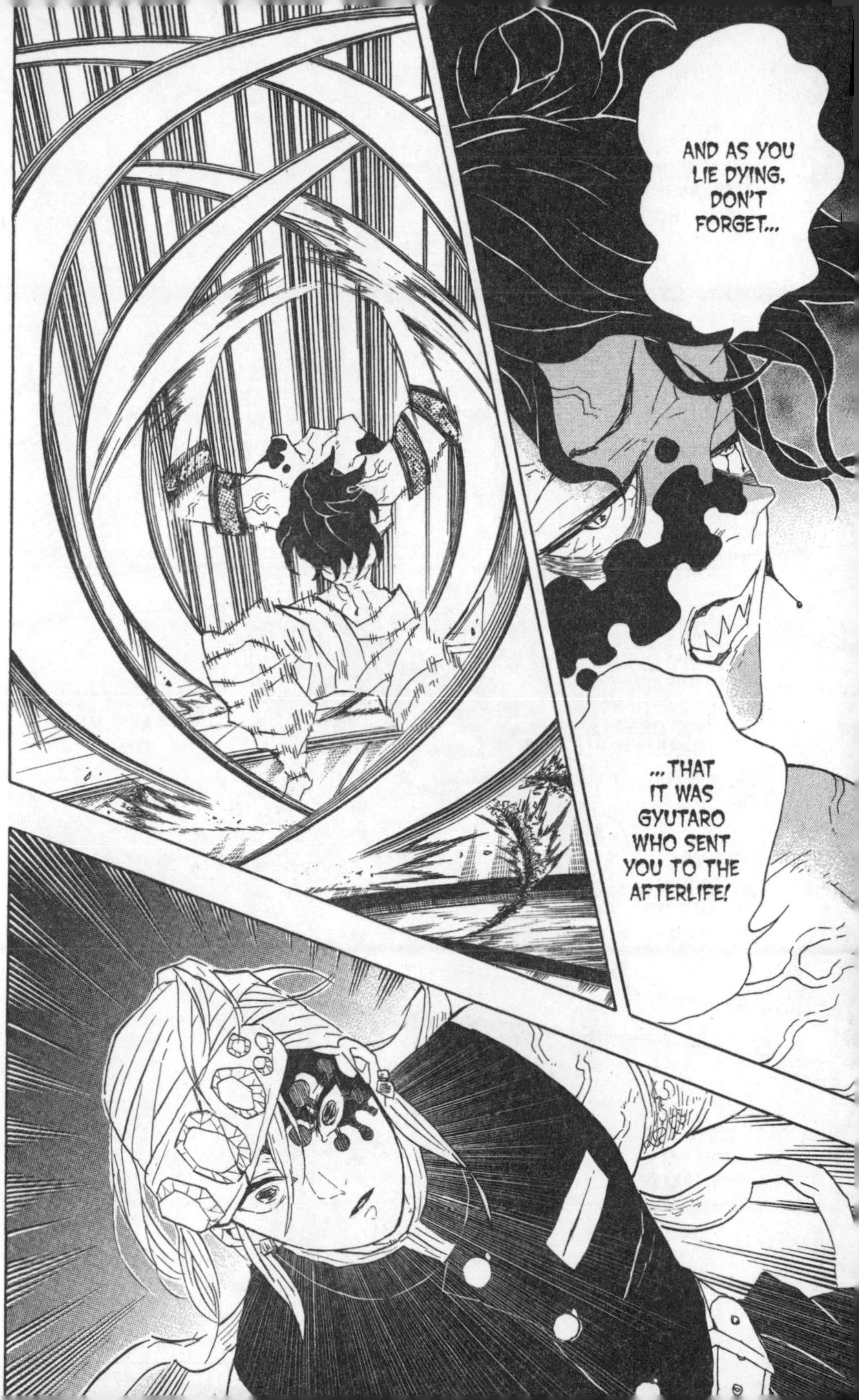
AND AS YOU LIE DYING, DON'T FORGET...
...THAT IT WAS GYUTARO WHO SENT YOU TO THE AFTERLIFE!

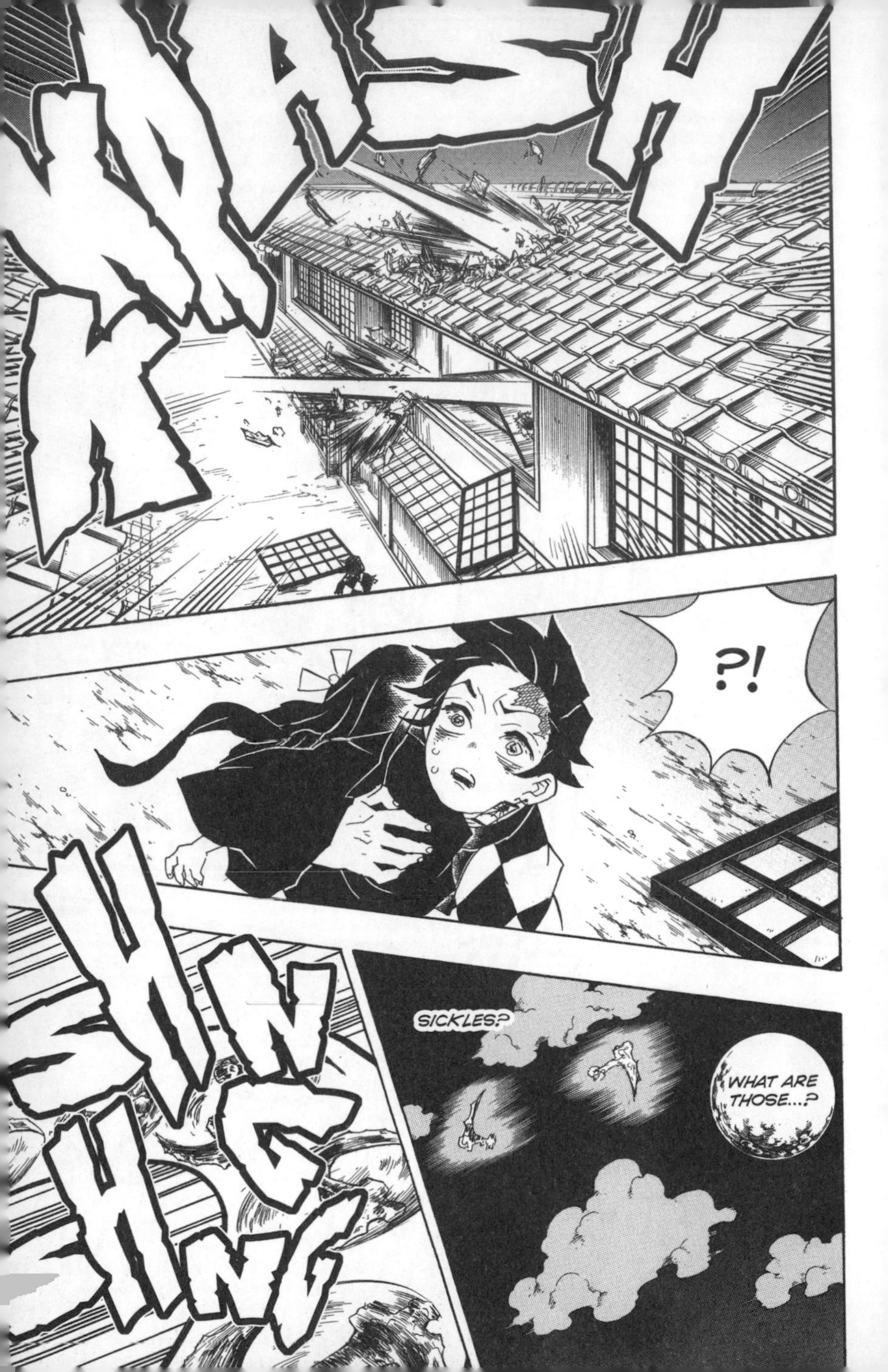
?!
SICKLES?
WHAT ARE THOSE...?

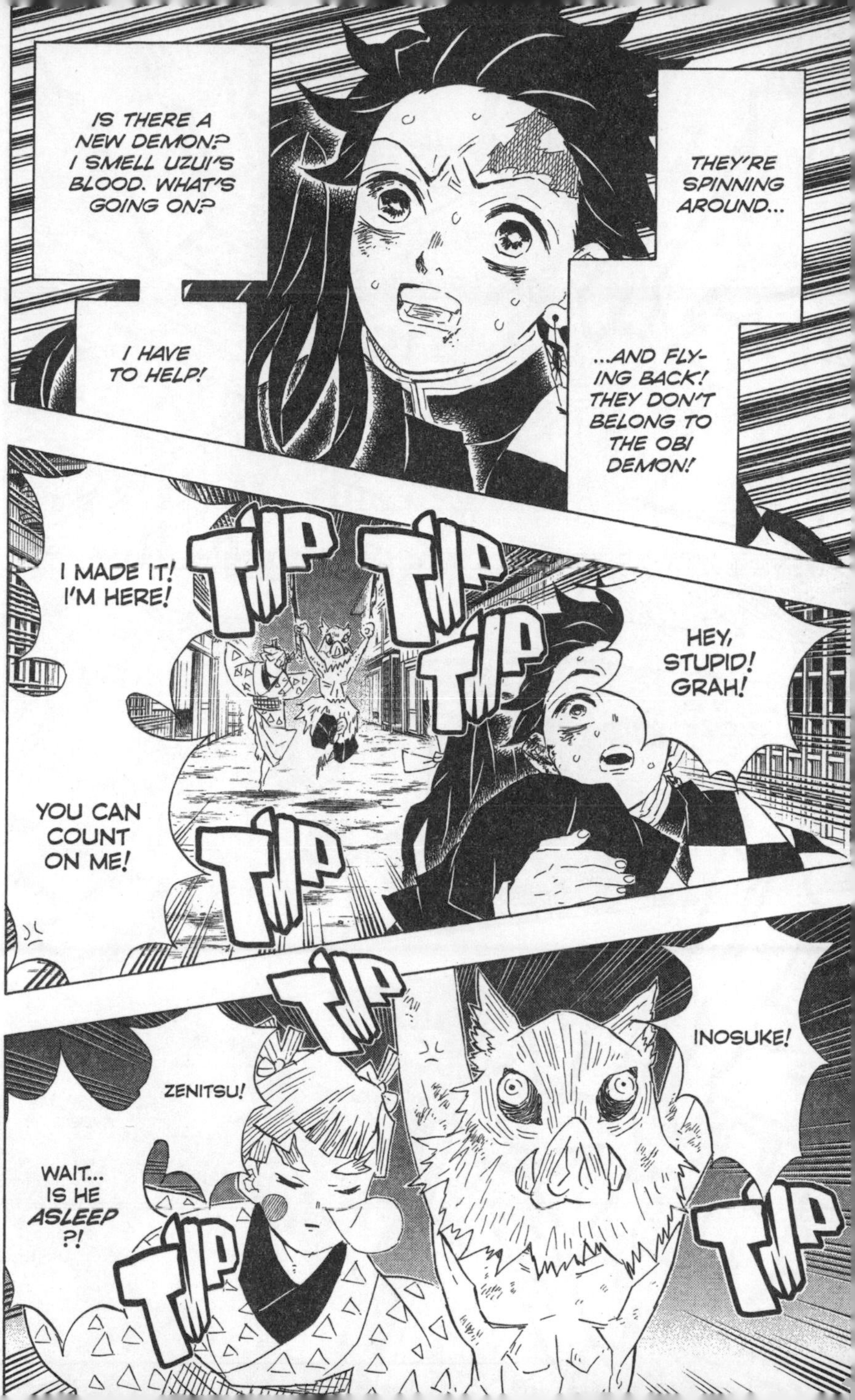
THEY'RE SPINNING AROUND...
...AND FLYING BACK! THEY DON'T BELONG TO THE OBI DEMON!
IS THERE A NEW DEMON? I SMELL UZUI'S BLOOD. WHAT'S GOING ON?
I HAVE TO HELP!
HEY, STUPID! GRAH!
TMP TMP TMP TMP
I MADE IT! I'M HERE!
YOU CAN COUNT ON ME!
INOSUKE!
TMP
ZENITSU!
WAIT... IS HE ASLEEP?!
TMP TMP

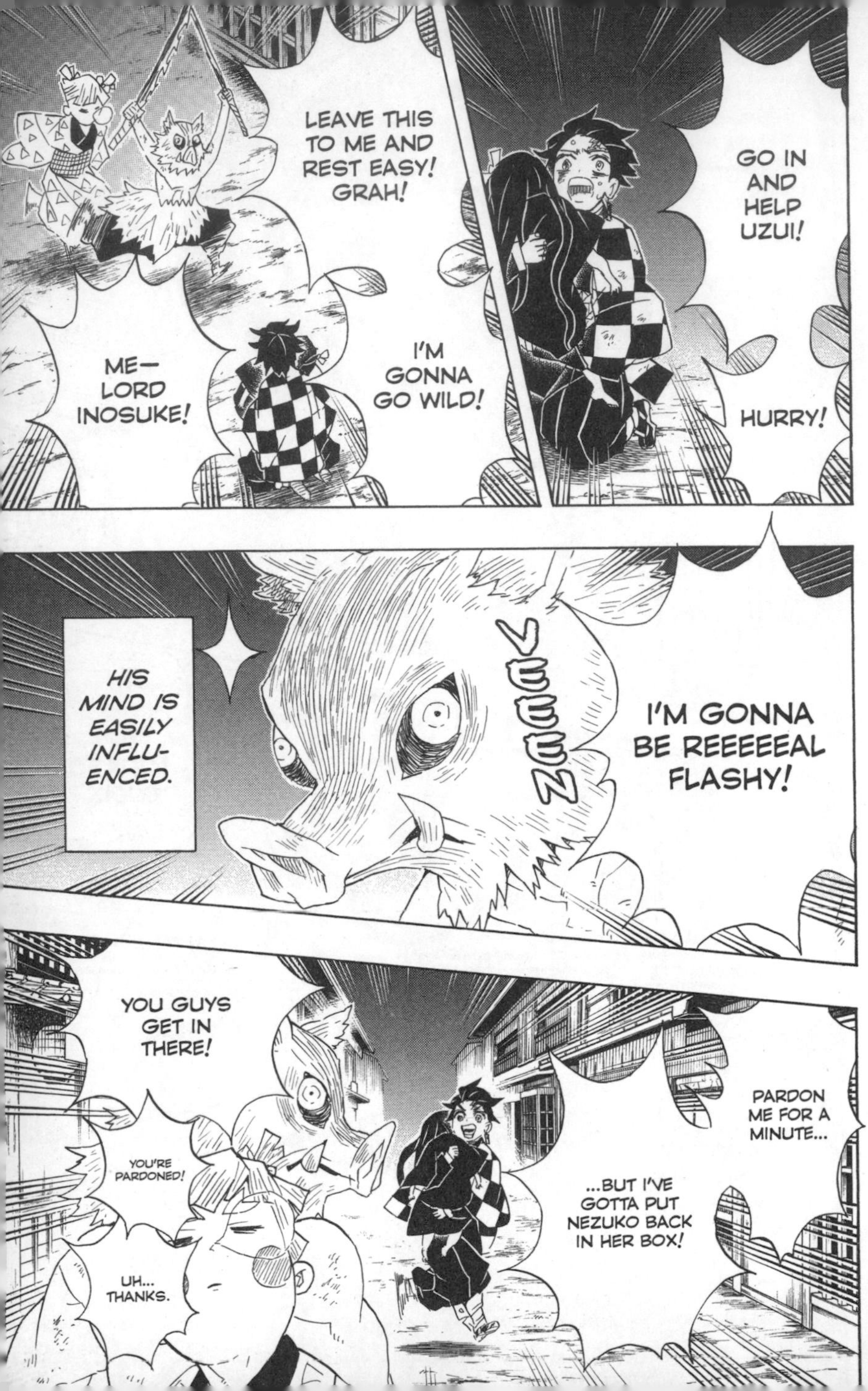
GO IN AND HELP UZUI!
HURRY!
LEAVE THIS TO ME AND REST EASY! GRAH!
I'M GONNA GO WILD!
ME— LORD INOSUKE!
I'M GONNA BE REEEEEAL FLASHY!
VEEEN
HIS MIND IS EASILY INFLU- ENCED.
PARDON ME FOR A MINUTE...
...BUT I'VE GOTTA PUT NEZUKO BACK IN HER BOX!
YOU GUYS GET IN THERE!
YOU'RE PARDONED!
UH... THANKS.

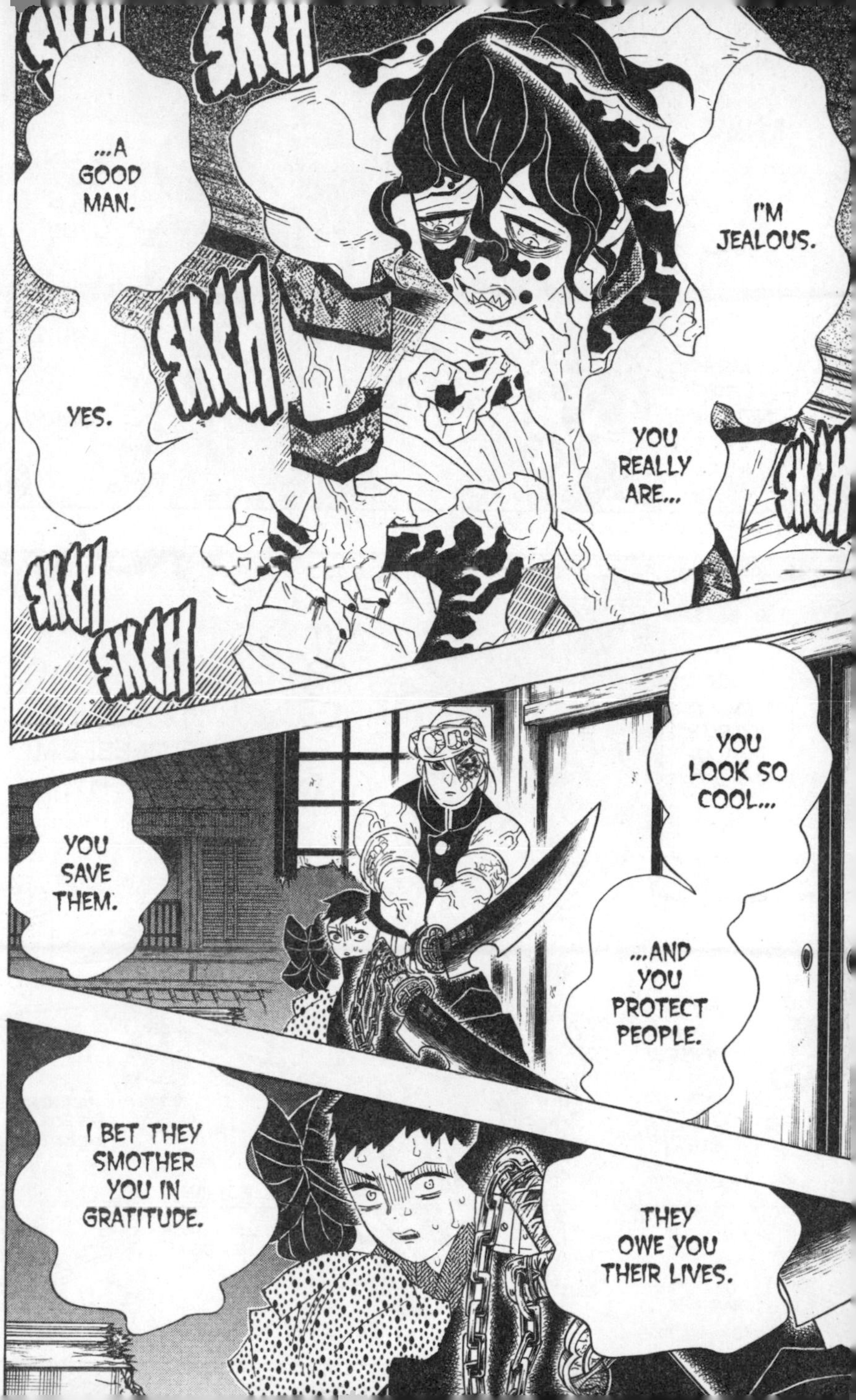
SKCH
I'M JEALOUS.
YOU REALLY ARE...
SKCH
...A GOOD MAN.
SKCH
YES.
SKCH
SKCH
YOU LOOK SO COOL...
...AND YOU PROTECT PEOPLE.
YOU SAVE THEM.
THEY OWE YOU THEIR LIVES.
I BET THEY SMOTHER YOU IN GRATITUDE.

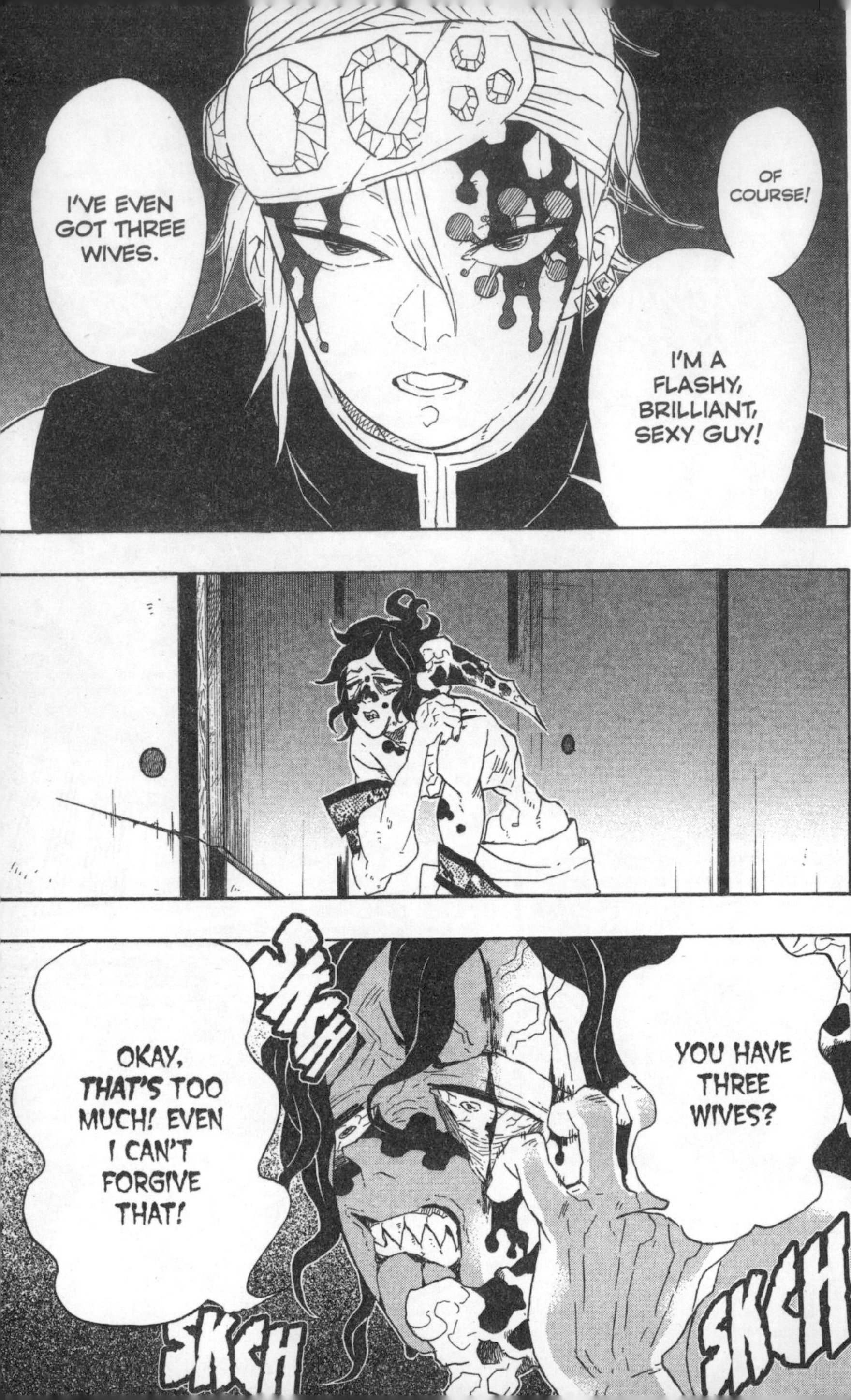
OF COURSE!
I'M A FLASHY, BRILLIANT, SEXY GUY!
I'VE EVEN GOT THREE WIVES.
YOU HAVE THREE WIVES?
SKCH
OKAY, THAT'S TOO MUCH! EVEN I CAN'T FORGIVE THAT!
SKCH
SKCH

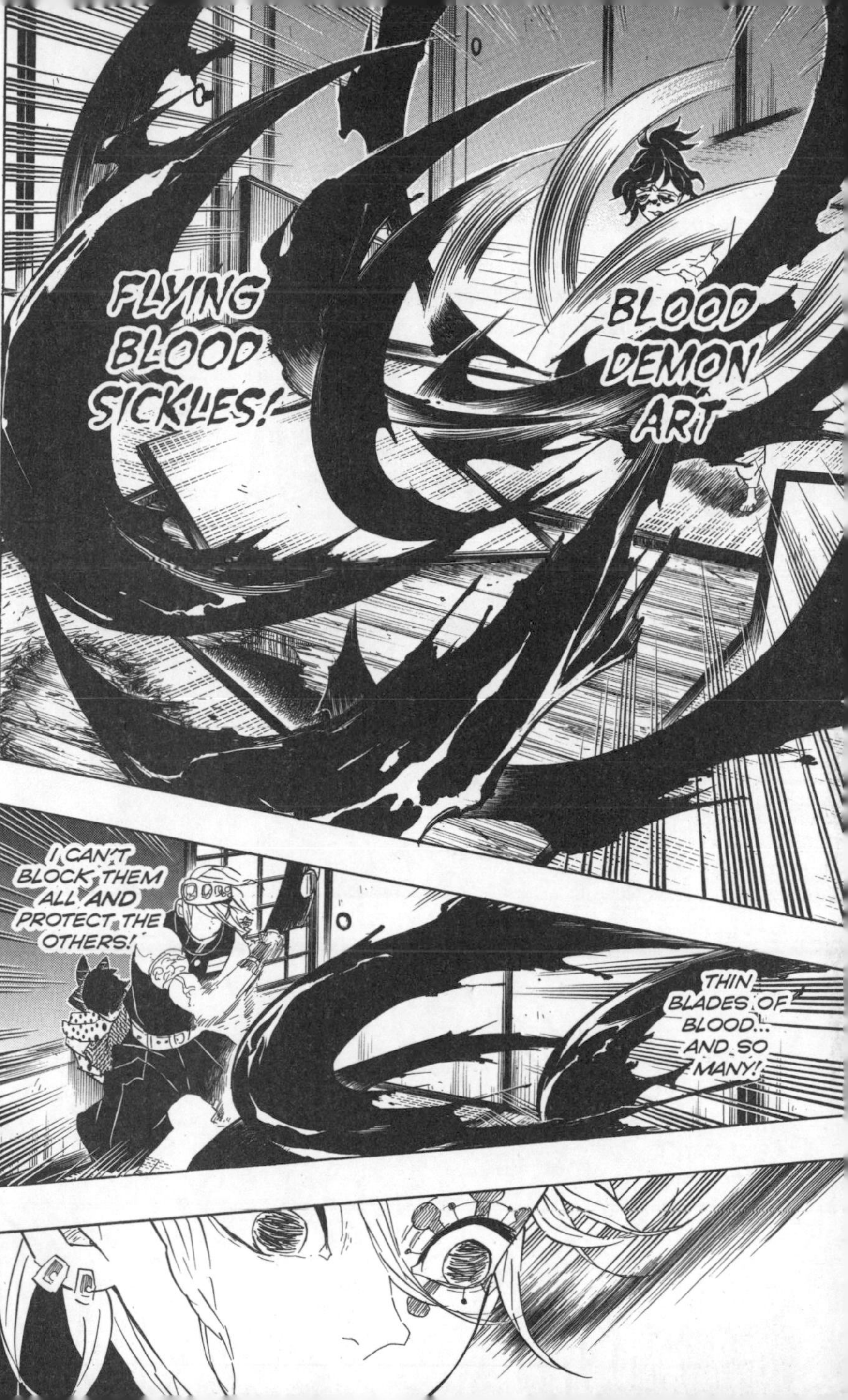
BLOOD DEMON ART
FLYING BLOOD SICKLES!
THIN BLADES OF BLOOD... AND SO MANY!
I CAN'T BLOCK THEM ALL AND PROTECT THE OTHERS!

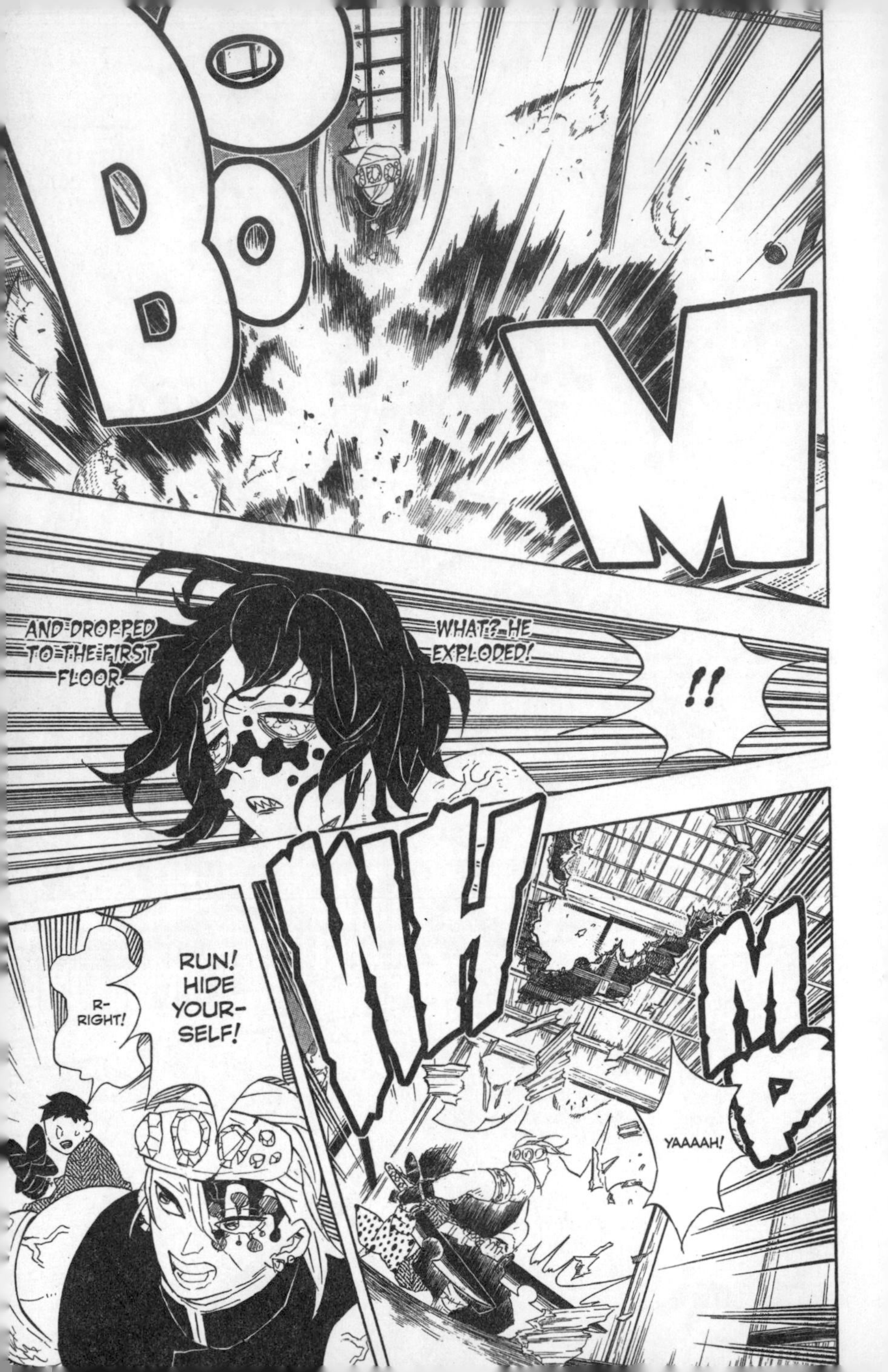
BOOM
!!
WHAT? HE EXPLODED!
AND DROPPED TO THE FIRST FLOOR.
WHUMP
YAAAAH!
RUN! HIDE YOURSELF!
R-RIGHT!

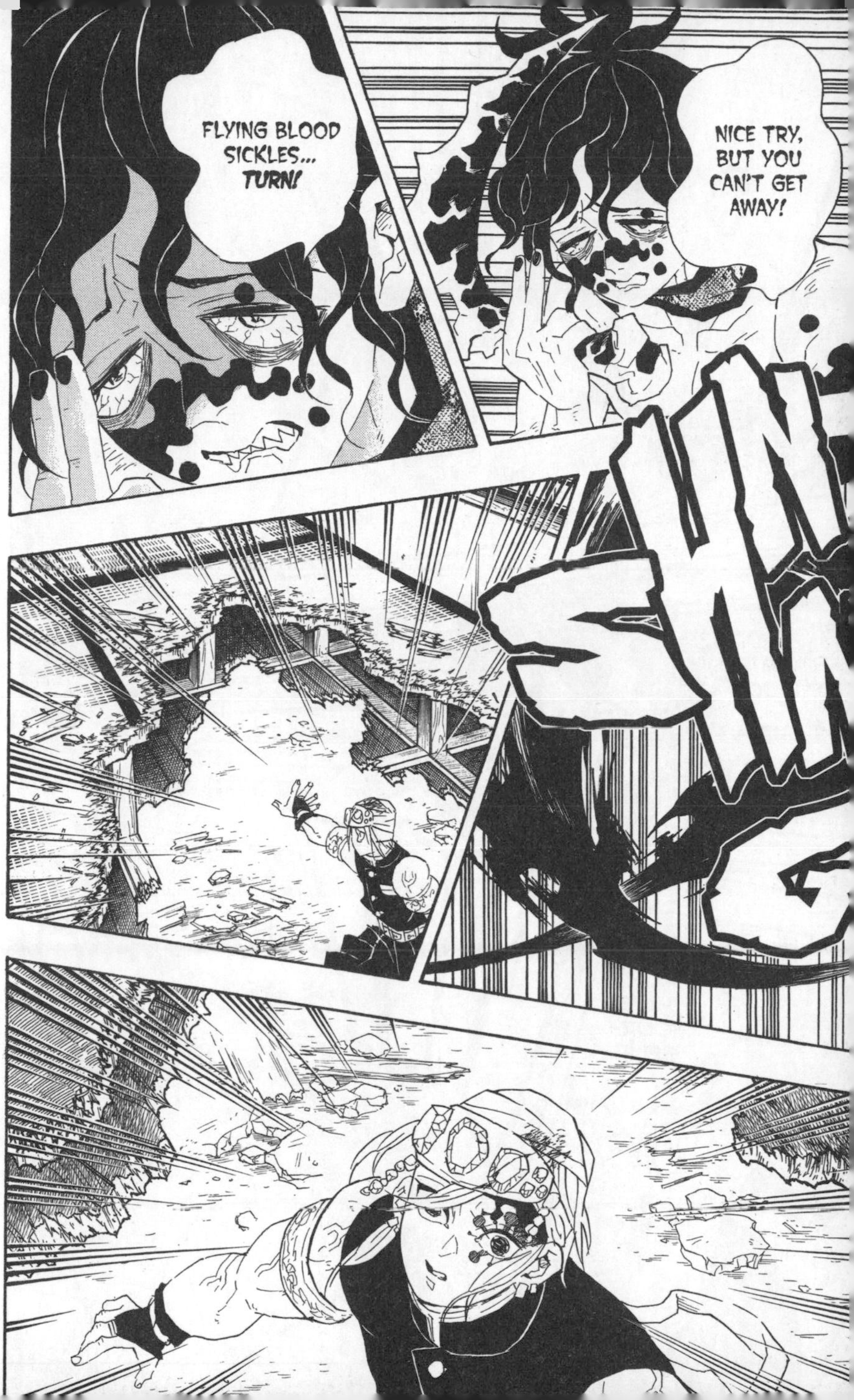
NICE TRY, BUT YOU CAN'T GET AWAY!
FLYING BLOOD SICKLES... *TURN!*

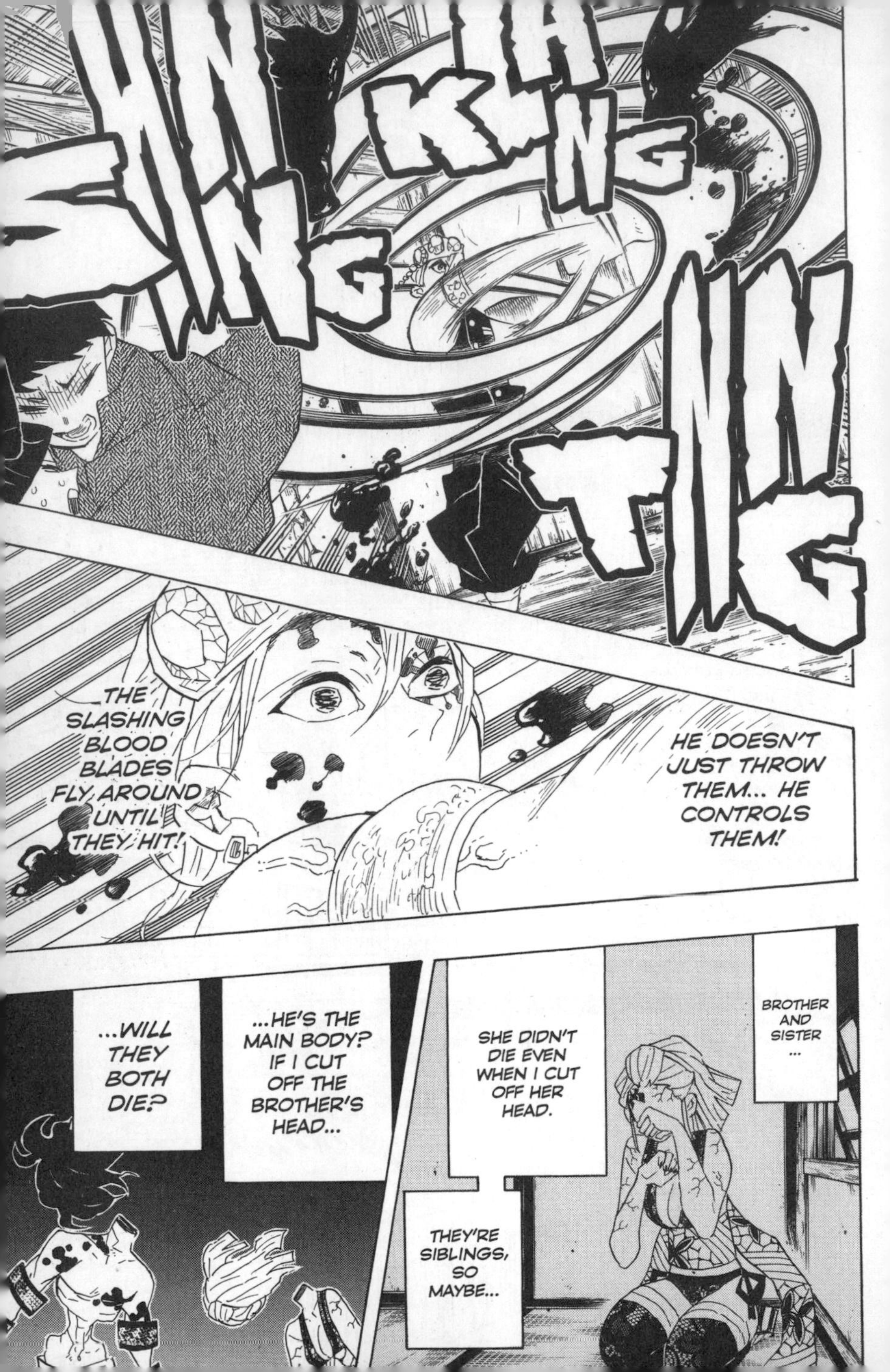
HE DOESN'T JUST THROW THEM... HE CONTROLS THEM!
THE SLASHING BLOOD BLADES FLY AROUND UNTIL THEY HIT!
BROTHER AND SISTER...
SHE DIDN'T DIE EVEN WHEN I CUT OFF HER HEAD.
THEY'RE SIBLINGS, SO MAYBE...
...HE'S THE MAIN BODY? IF I CUT OFF THE BROTHER'S HEAD...
...WILL THEY BOTH DIE?

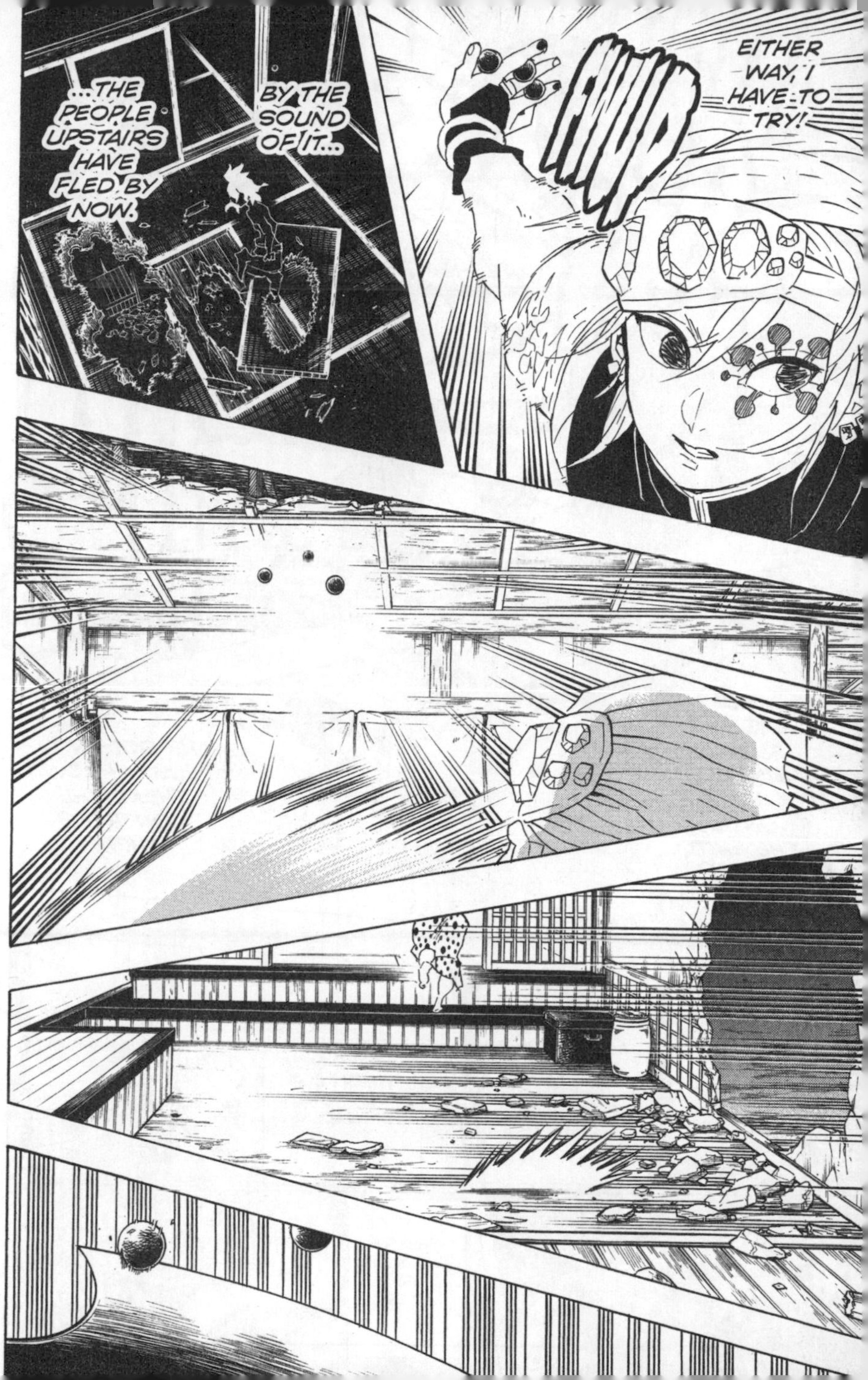
EITHER WAY, I HAVE TO TRY!
BY THE SOUND OF IT...
...THE PEOPLE UPSTAIRS HAVE FLED BY NOW.

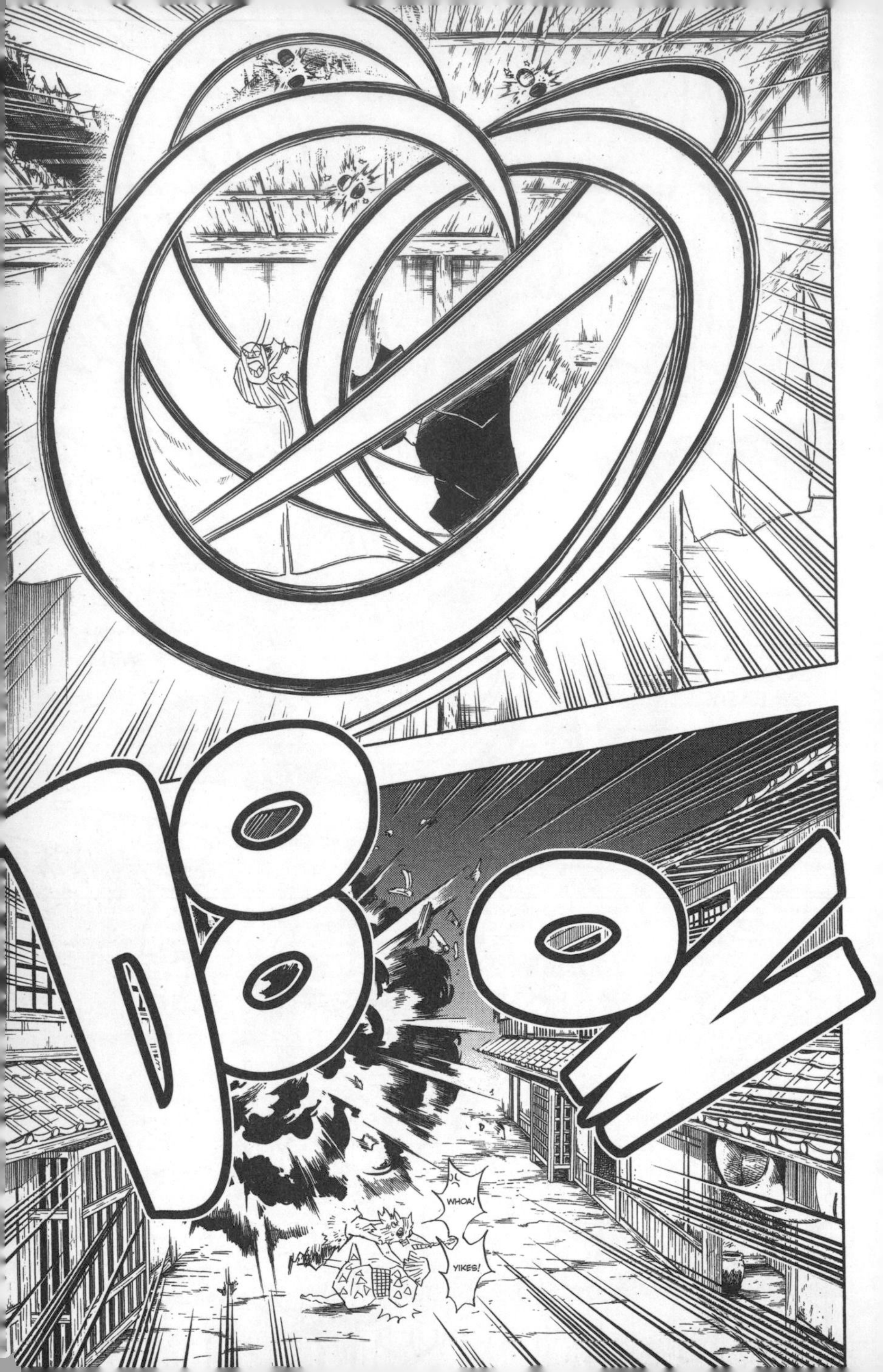
WHOA!
YIKES!

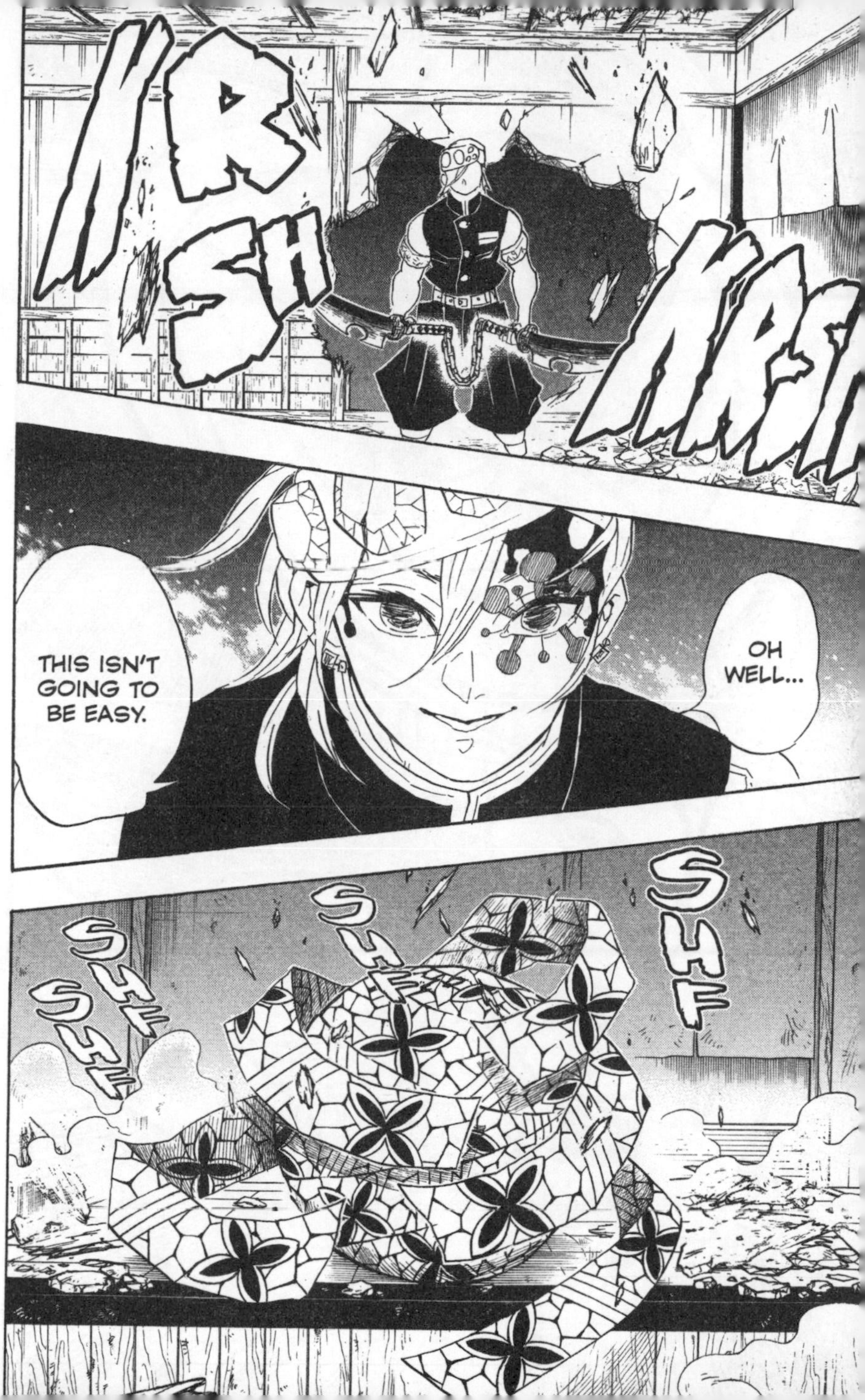
OH WELL...
THIS ISN'T GOING TO BE EASY.
SHF SHF
SHF SHF
SHF SHF

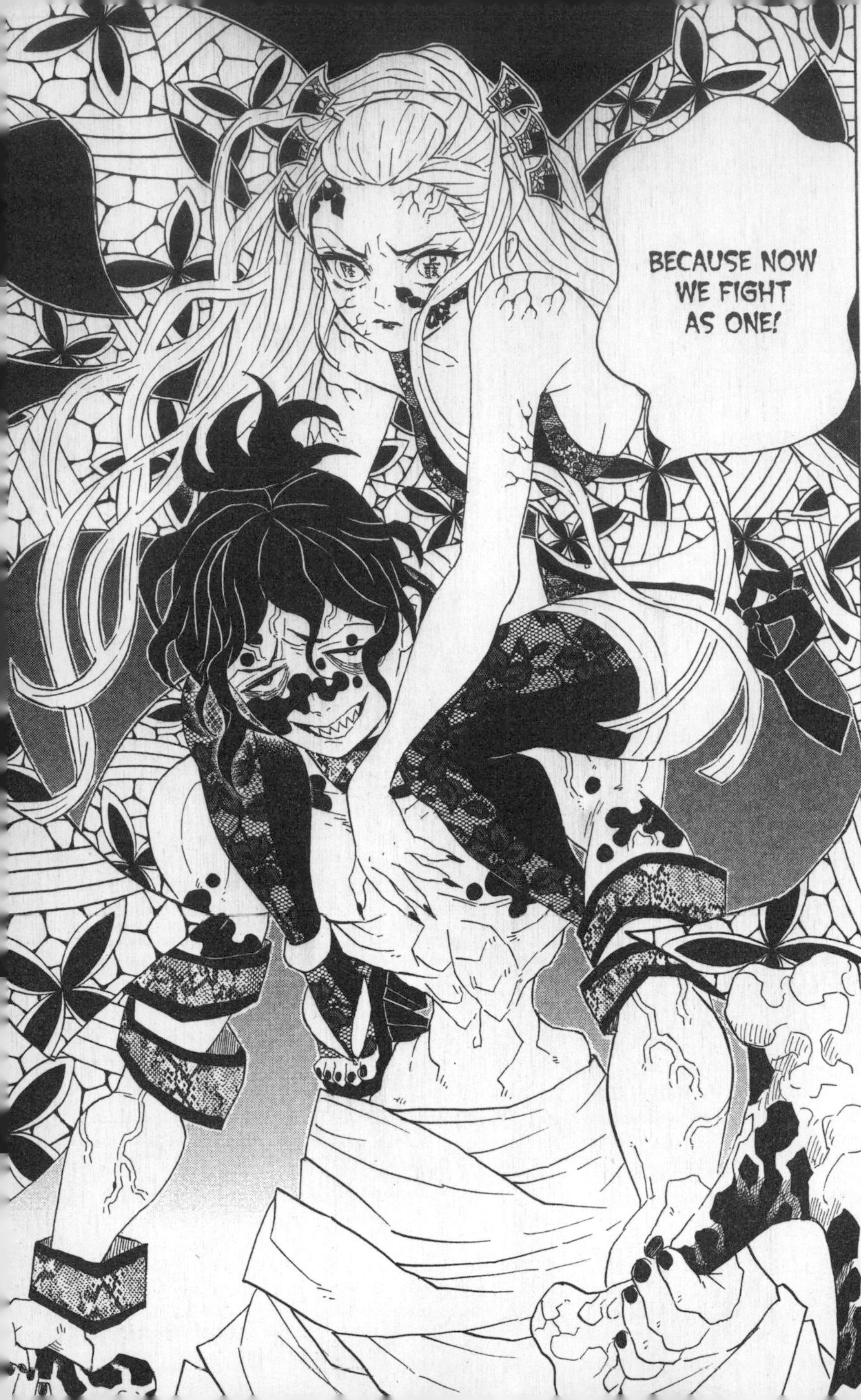
BECAUSE NOW WE FIGHT AS ONE!

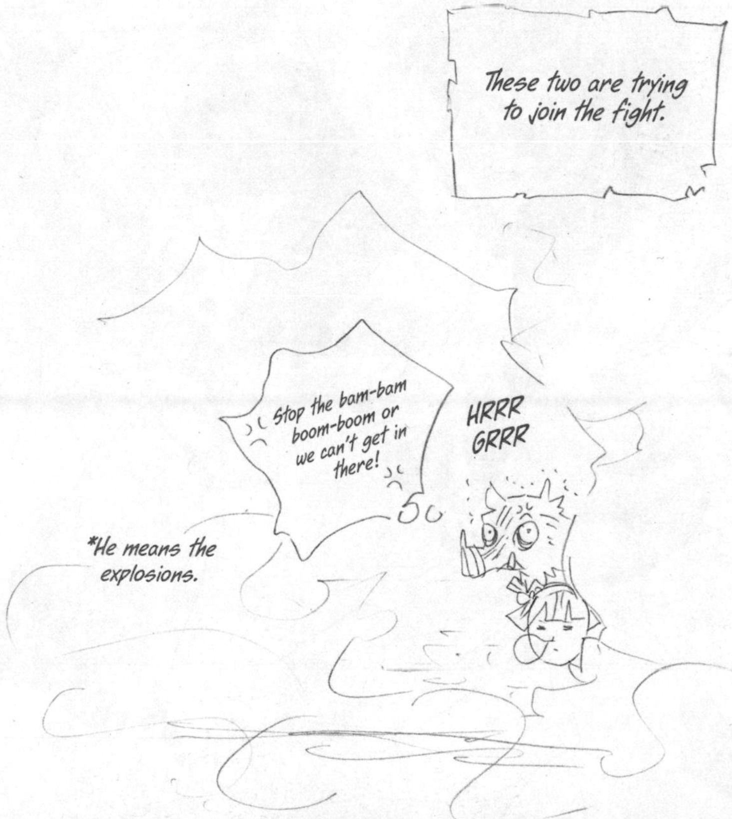
These two are trying to join the fight.
HRRR GRRR
Stop the bam-bam boom-boom or we can't get in there!
*He means the explosions.

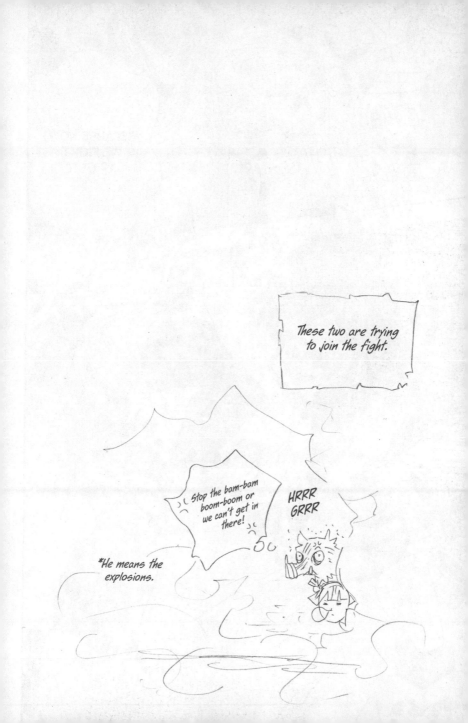

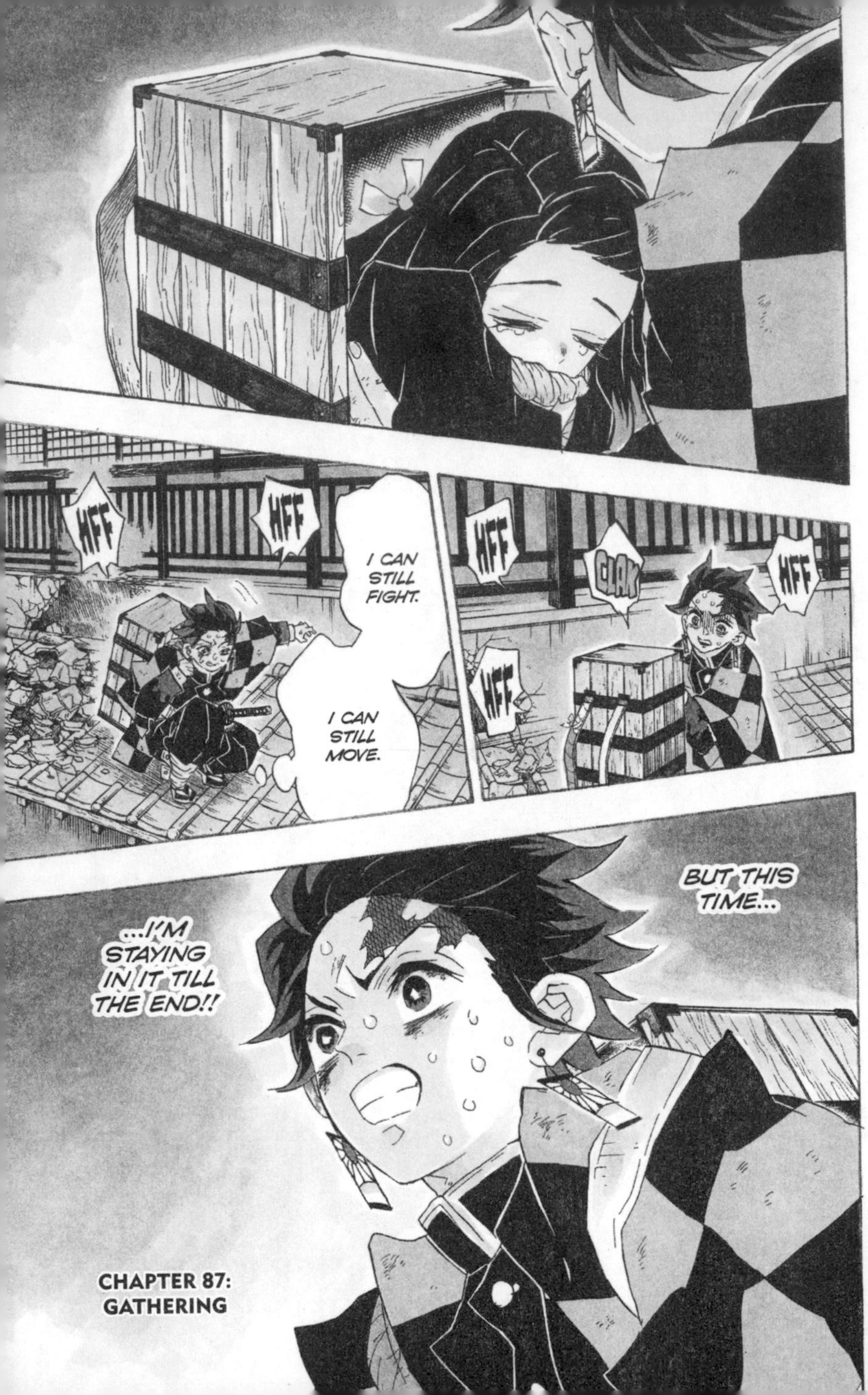
HFF
CLAK
HFF
HFF
HFF
HFF
I CAN STILL FIGHT.
I CAN STILL MOVE.
BUT THIS TIME...
...I'M STAYING IN IT TILL THE END!!
CHAPTER 87: GATHERING

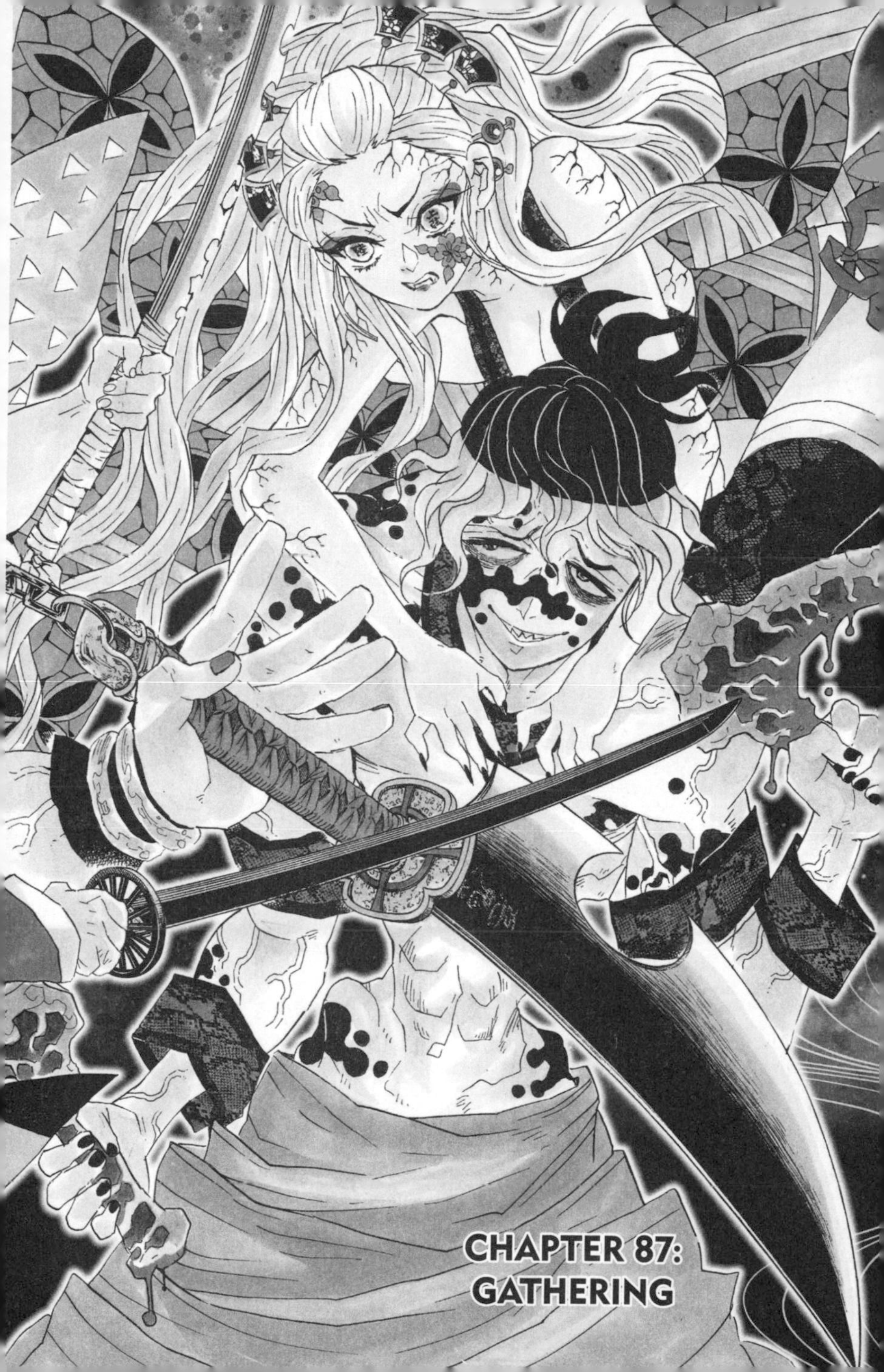

CHAPTER 87: GATHERING

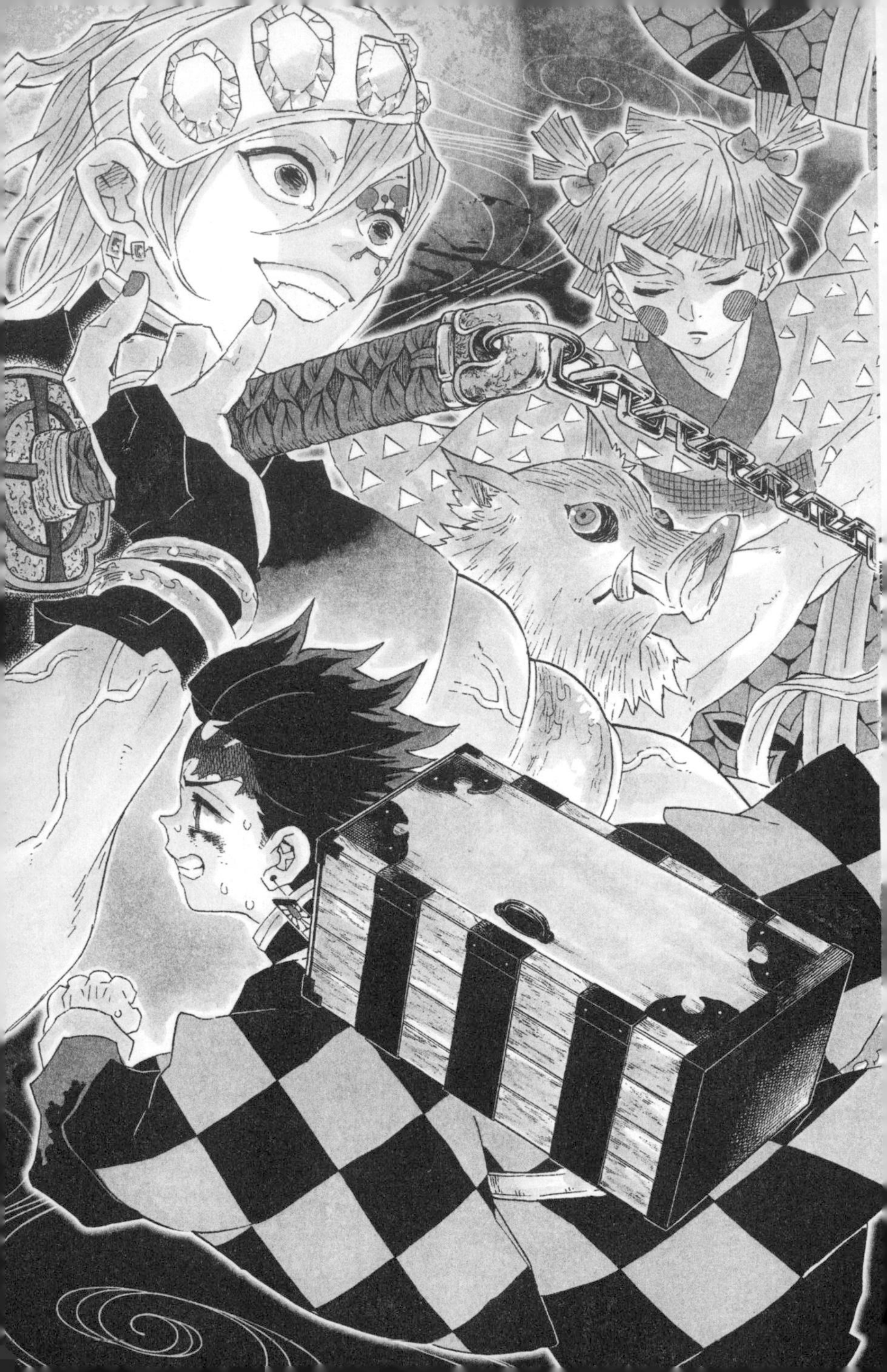

DEMON SLAYER

KIMETSU NO YAIBA

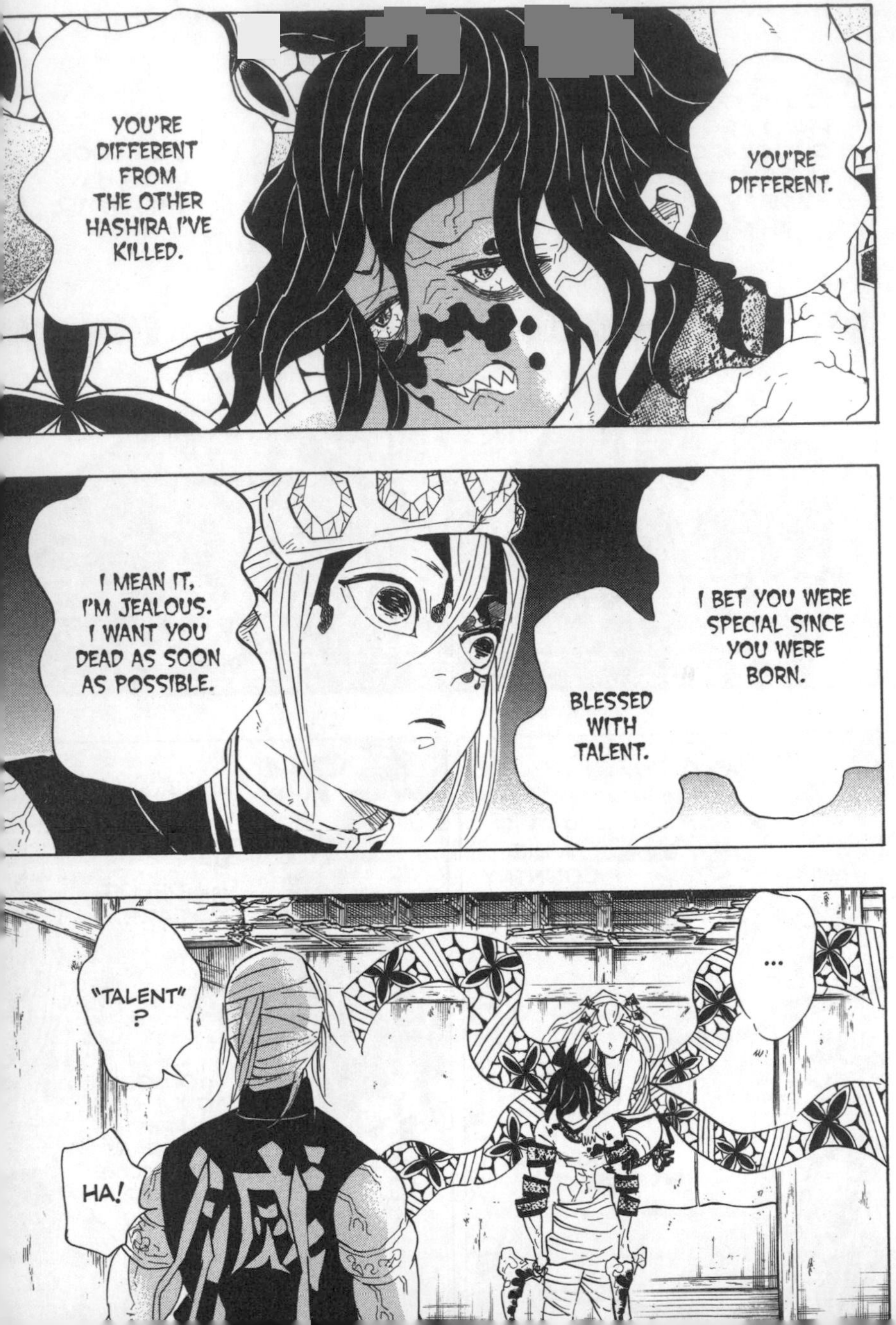
YOU'RE DIFFERENT.
YOU'RE DIFFERENT FROM THE OTHER HASHIRA I'VE KILLED.
I BET YOU WERE SPECIAL SINCE YOU WERE BORN.
BLESSED WITH TALENT.
I MEAN IT. I'M JEALOUS. I WANT YOU DEAD AS SOON AS POSSIBLE.
...
"TALENT"?
HA!

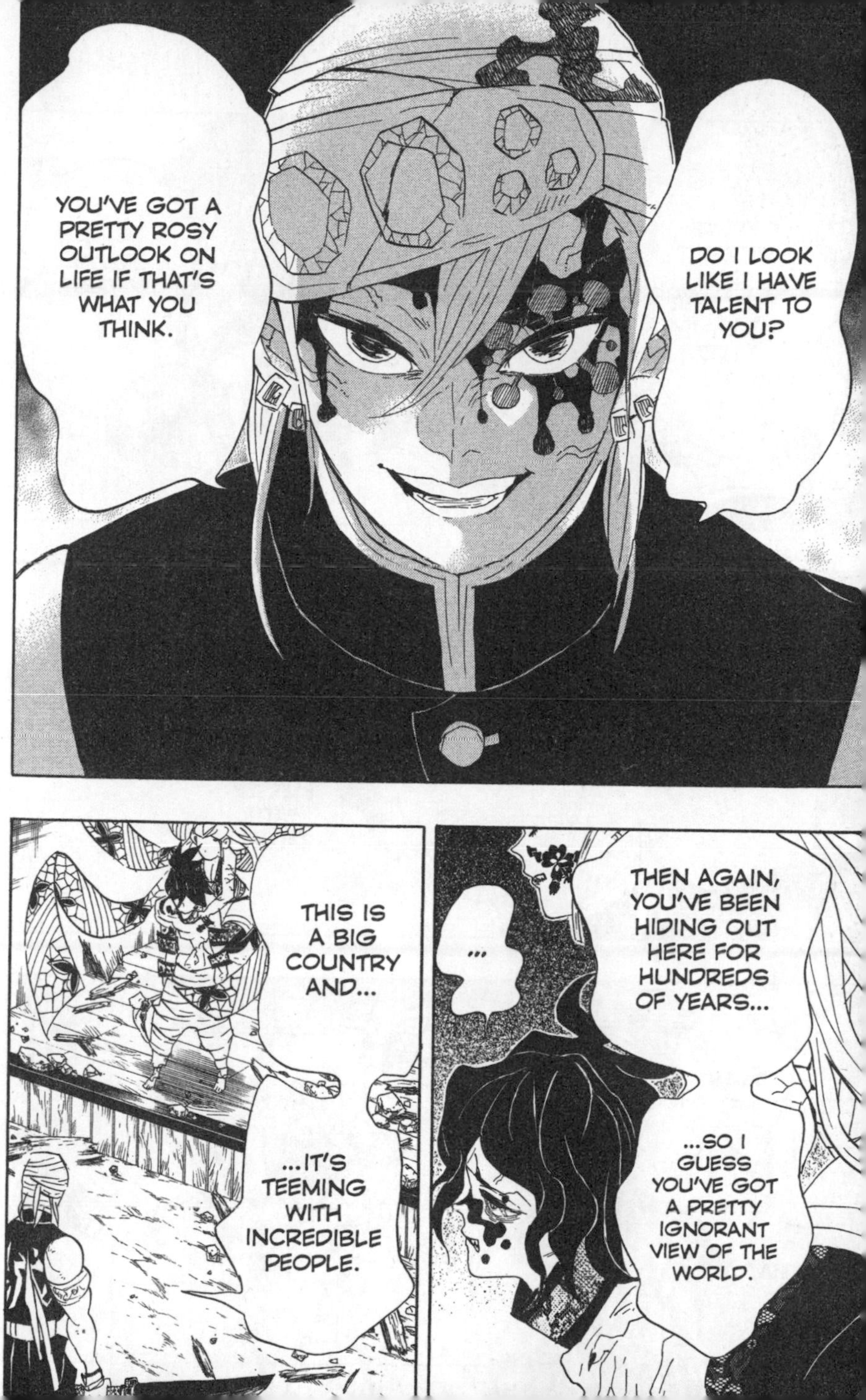
DO I LOOK LIKE I HAVE TALENT TO YOU?
YOU'VE GOT A PRETTY ROSY OUTLOOK ON LIFE IF THAT'S WHAT YOU THINK.
THEN AGAIN, YOU'VE BEEN HIDING OUT HERE FOR HUNDREDS OF YEARS...
...
...SO I GUESS YOU'VE GOT A PRETTY IGNORANT VIEW OF THE WORLD.
THIS IS A BIG COUNTRY AND...
...IT'S TEEMING WITH INCREDIBLE PEOPLE.

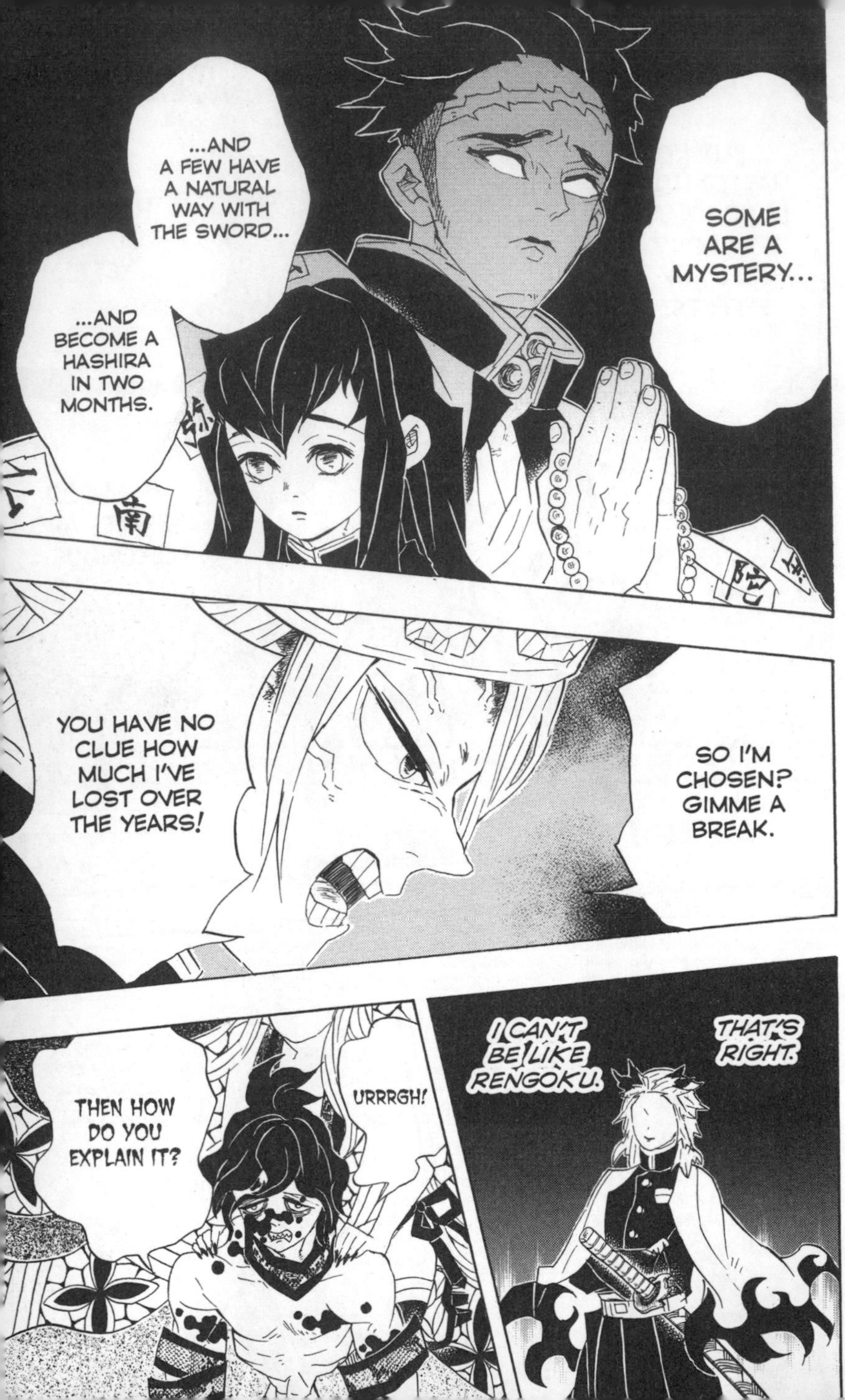
SOME ARE A MYSTERY...
...AND A FEW HAVE A NATURAL WAY WITH THE SWORD...
...AND BECOME A HASHIRA IN TWO MONTHS.
SO I'M CHOSEN? GIMME A BREAK.
YOU HAVE NO CLUE HOW MUCH I'VE LOST OVER THE YEARS!
THAT'S RIGHT.
I CAN'T BE LIKE RENGOKU.
URRRGH!
THEN HOW DO YOU EXPLAIN IT?

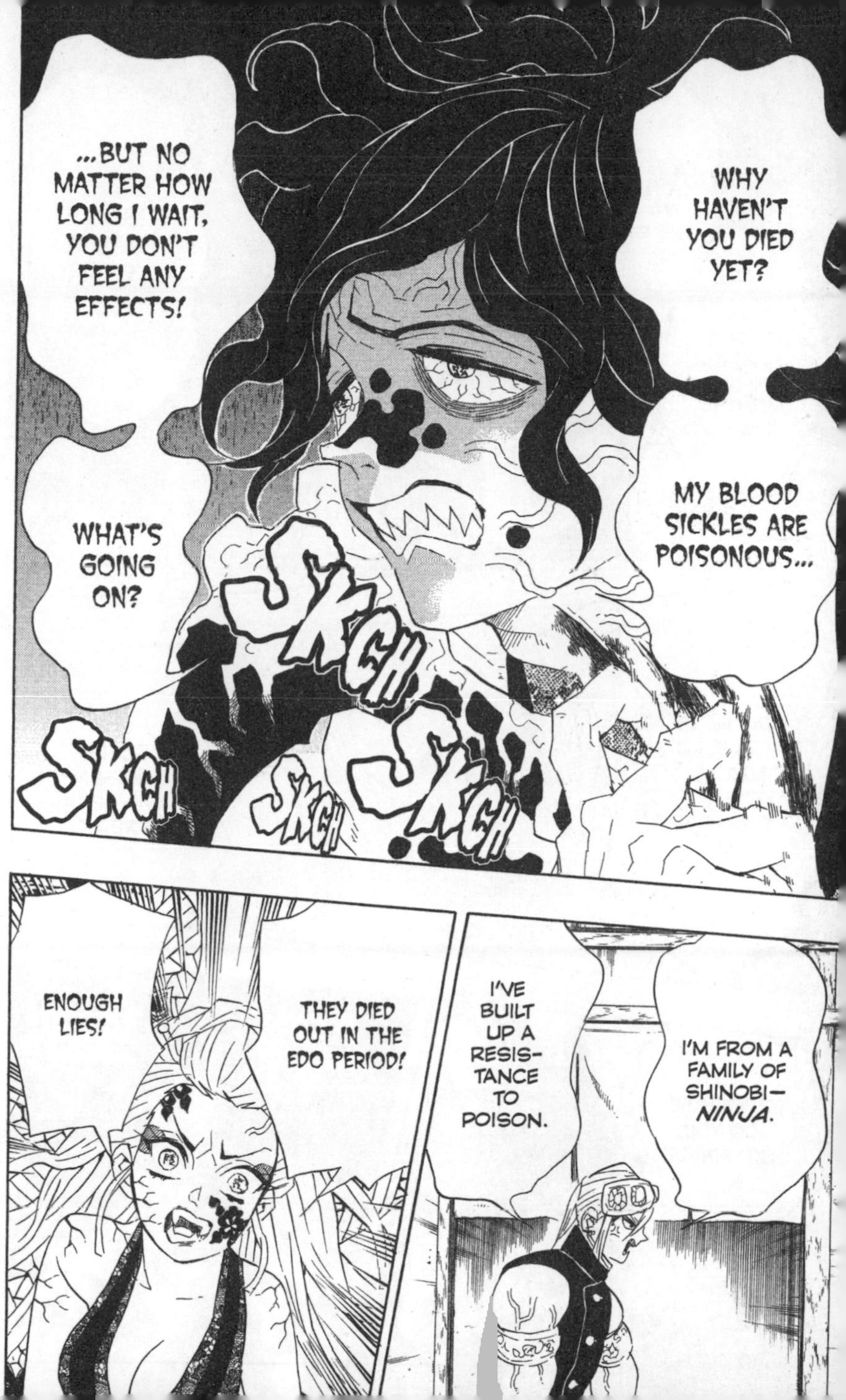
WHY HAVEN'T YOU DIED YET?
MY BLOOD SICKLES ARE POISONOUS...
...BUT NO MATTER HOW LONG I WAIT, YOU DON'T FEEL ANY EFFECTS!
WHAT'S GOING ON?
SKCH
SKCH
SKCH
SKCH
I'M FROM A FAMILY OF SHINOBI—*NINJA*.
I'VE BUILT UP A RESIS-TANCE TO POISON.
THEY DIED OUT IN THE EDO PERIOD!
ENOUGH LIES!

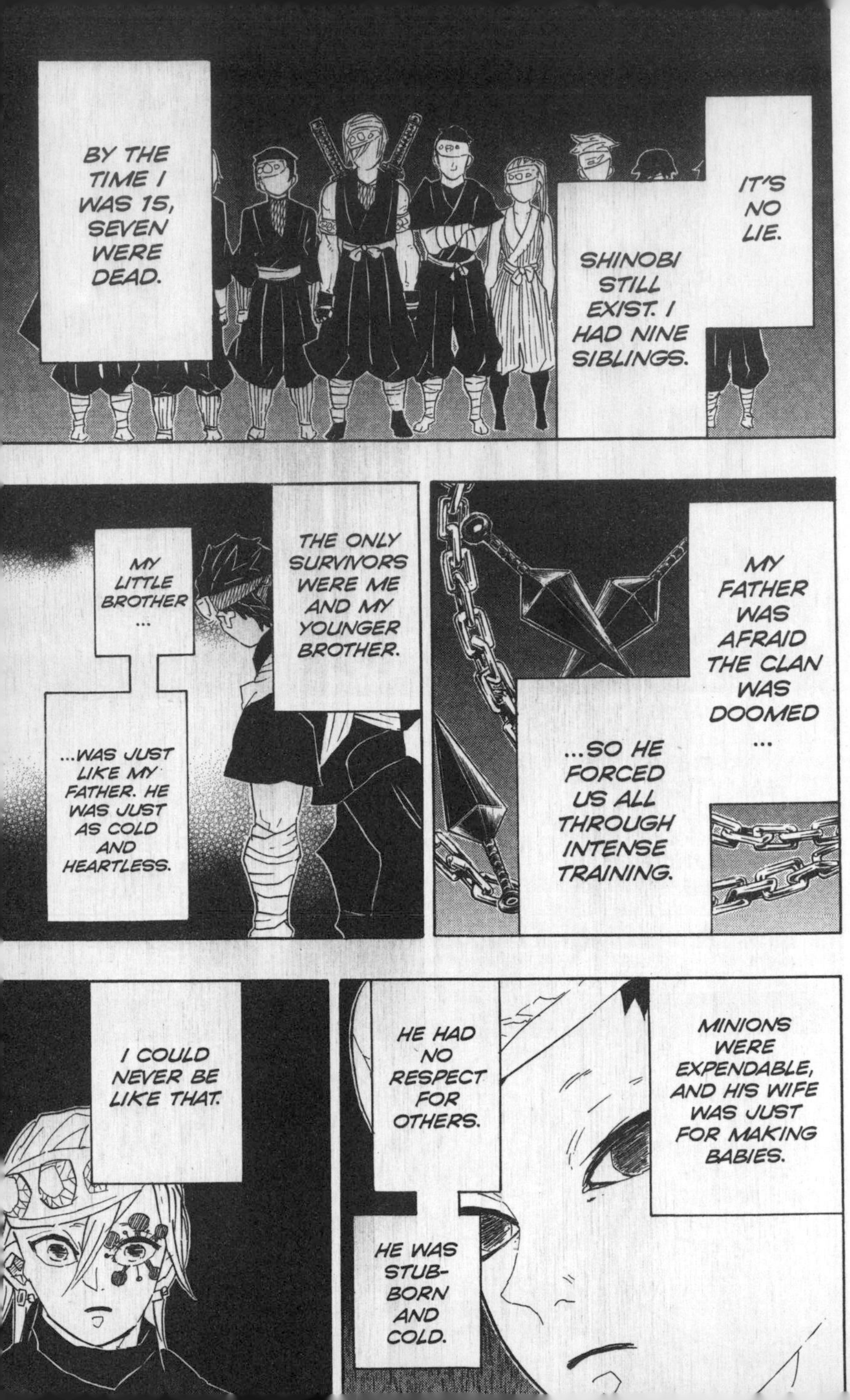
IT'S NO LIE.
SHINOBI STILL EXIST. I HAD NINE SIBLINGS.
BY THE TIME I WAS 15, SEVEN WERE DEAD.
MY FATHER WAS AFRAID THE CLAN WAS DOOMED...
...SO HE FORCED US ALL THROUGH INTENSE TRAINING.
THE ONLY SURVIVORS WERE ME AND MY YOUNGER BROTHER.
MY LITTLE BROTHER...
...WAS JUST LIKE MY FATHER. HE WAS JUST AS COLD AND HEARTLESS.
MINIONS WERE EXPENDABLE, AND HIS WIFE WAS JUST FOR MAKING BABIES.
HE HAD NO RESPECT FOR OTHERS.
HE WAS STUBBORN AND COLD.
I COULD NEVER BE LIKE THAT.

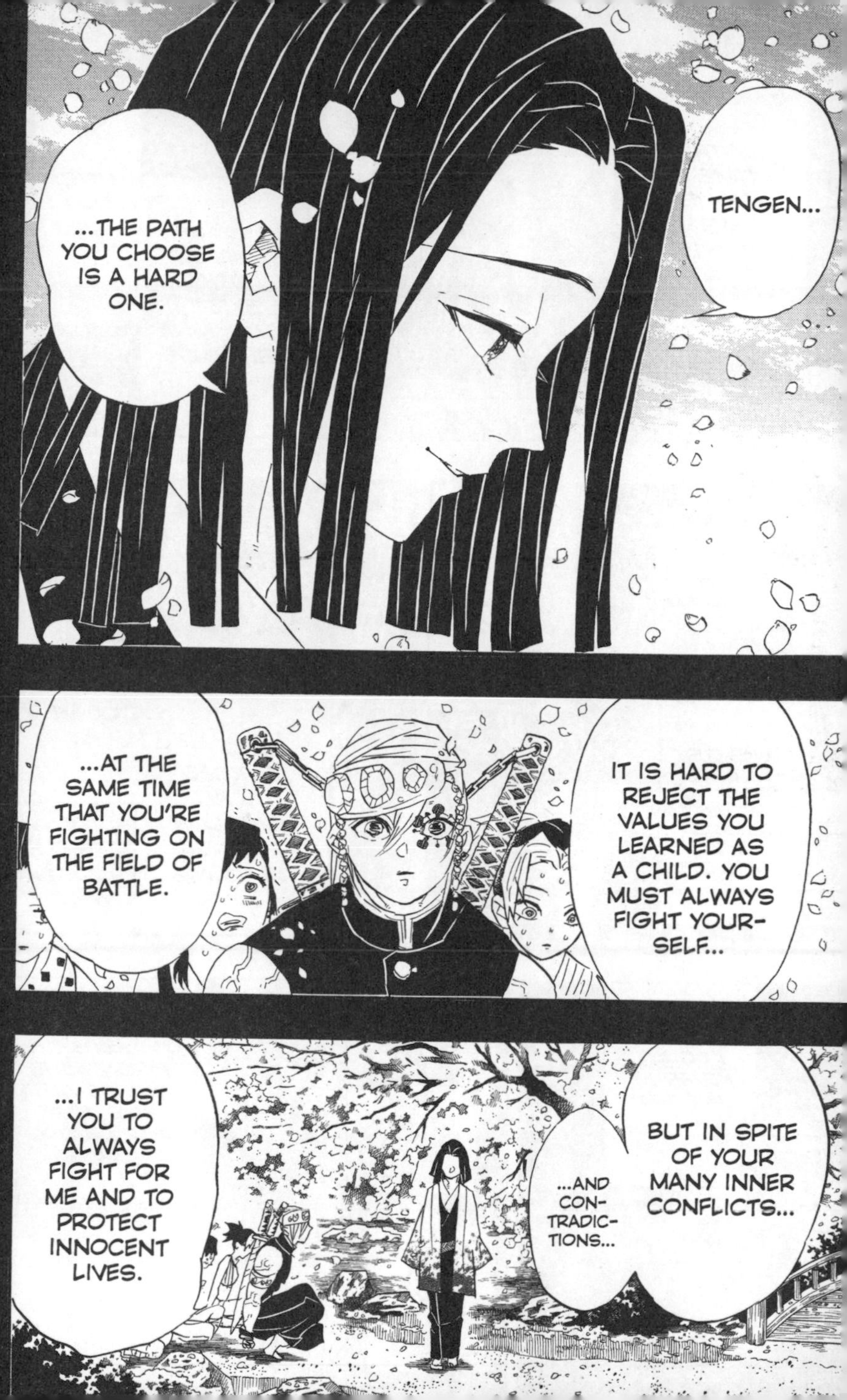
TENGEN...
...THE PATH YOU CHOOSE IS A HARD ONE.
IT IS HARD TO REJECT THE VALUES YOU LEARNED AS A CHILD. YOU MUST ALWAYS FIGHT YOUR-SELF...
...AT THE SAME TIME THAT YOU'RE FIGHTING ON THE FIELD OF BATTLE.
BUT IN SPITE OF YOUR MANY INNER CONFLICTS...
...AND CON-TRADIC-TIONS...
...I TRUST YOU TO ALWAYS FIGHT FOR ME AND TO PROTECT INNOCENT LIVES.

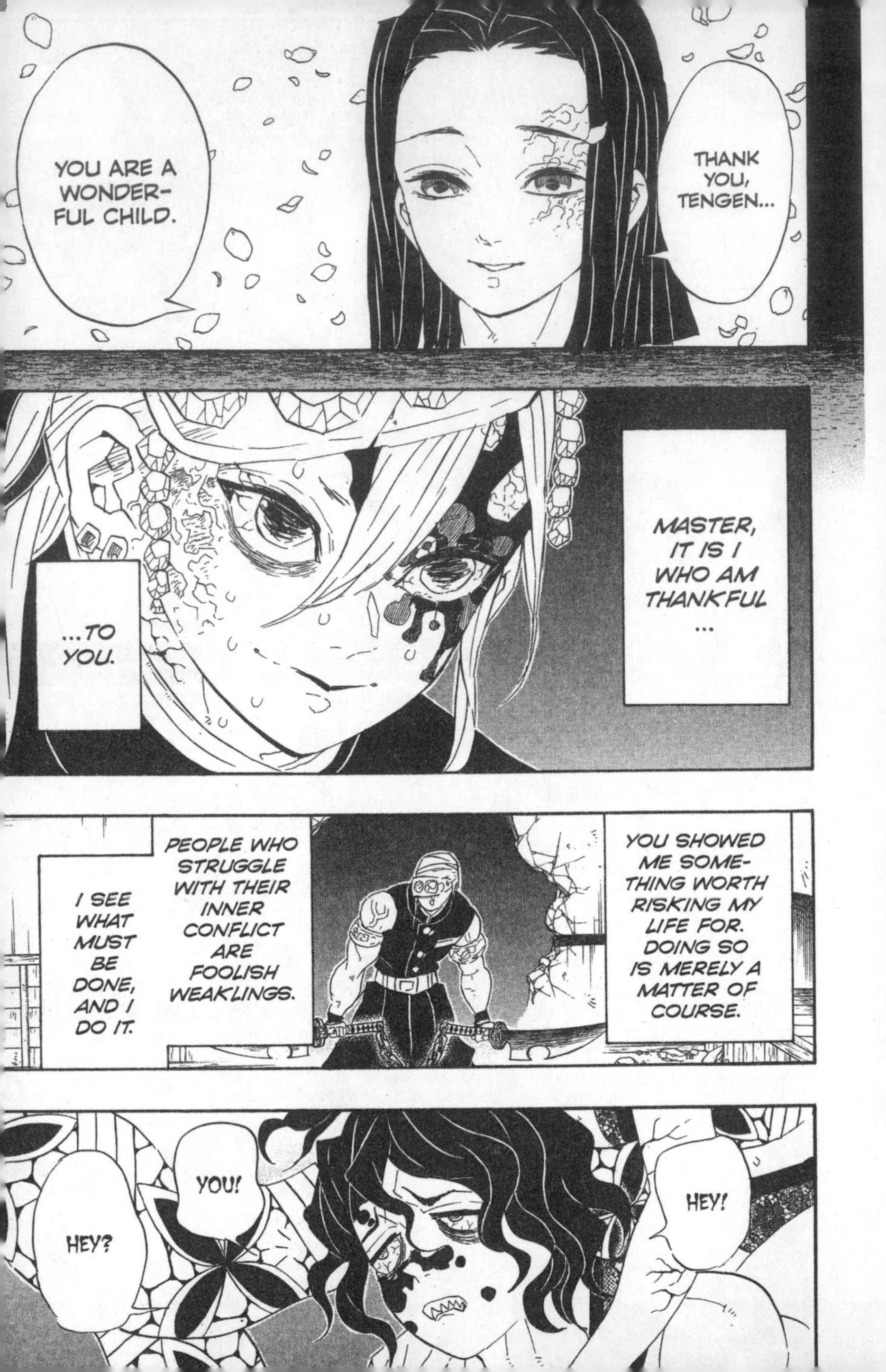
THANK YOU, TENGEN...
YOU ARE A WONDERFUL CHILD.
MASTER, IT IS I WHO AM THANKFUL ...
...TO YOU.
YOU SHOWED ME SOMETHING WORTH RISKING MY LIFE FOR. DOING SO IS MERELY A MATTER OF COURSE.
PEOPLE WHO STRUGGLE WITH THEIR INNER CONFLICT ARE FOOLISH WEAKLINGS.
I SEE WHAT MUST BE DONE, AND I DO IT.
HEY!
YOU!
HEY?

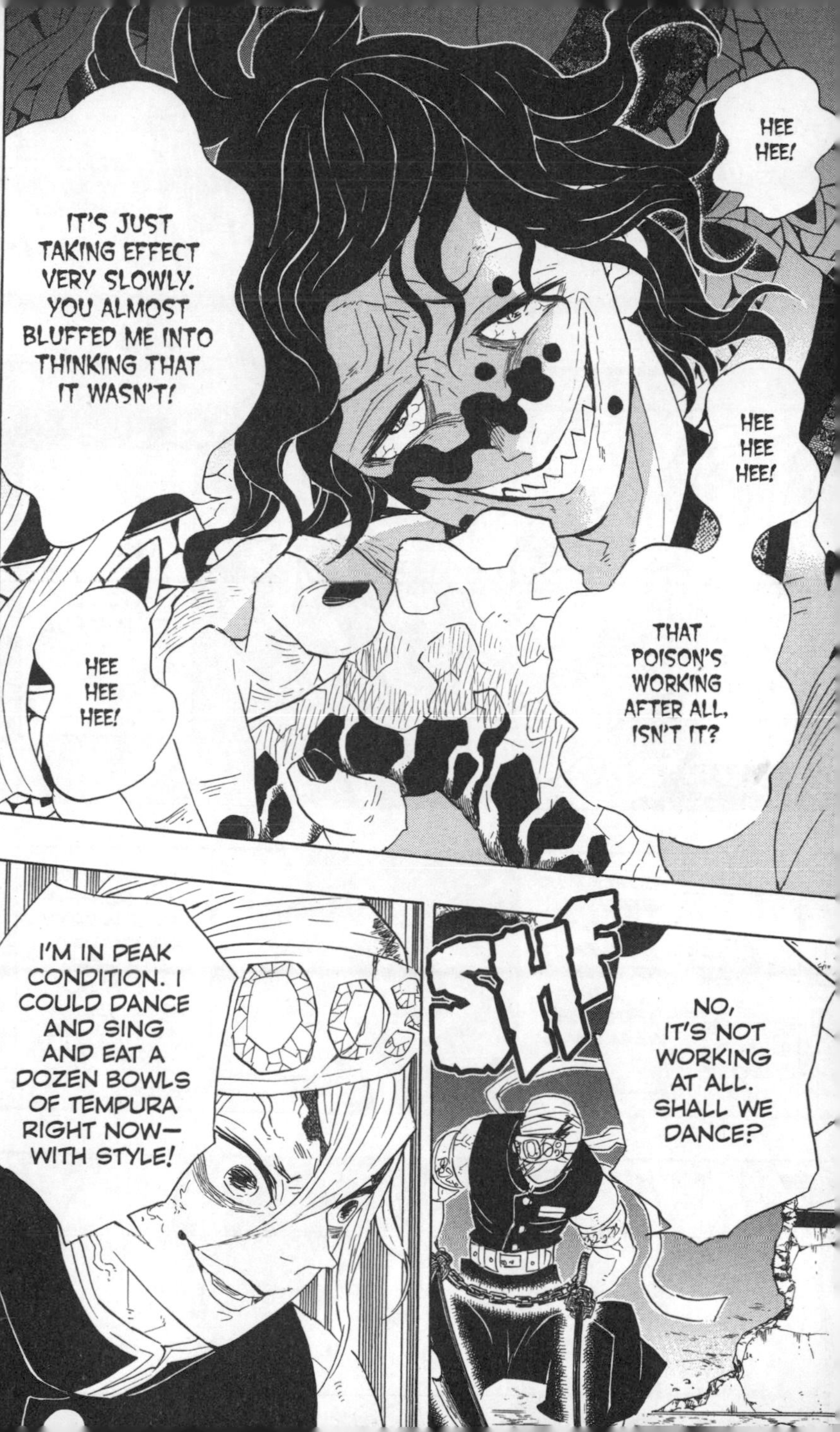
HEE HEE!
HEE HEE HEE!
THAT POISON'S WORKING AFTER ALL, ISN'T IT?
HEE HEE HEE!
IT'S JUST TAKING EFFECT VERY SLOWLY. YOU ALMOST BLUFFED ME INTO THINKING THAT IT WASN'T!
SHF
NO, IT'S NOT WORKING AT ALL. SHALL WE DANCE?
I'M IN PEAK CONDITION. I COULD DANCE AND SING AND EAT A DOZEN BOWLS OF TEMPURA RIGHT NOW—WITH STYLE!

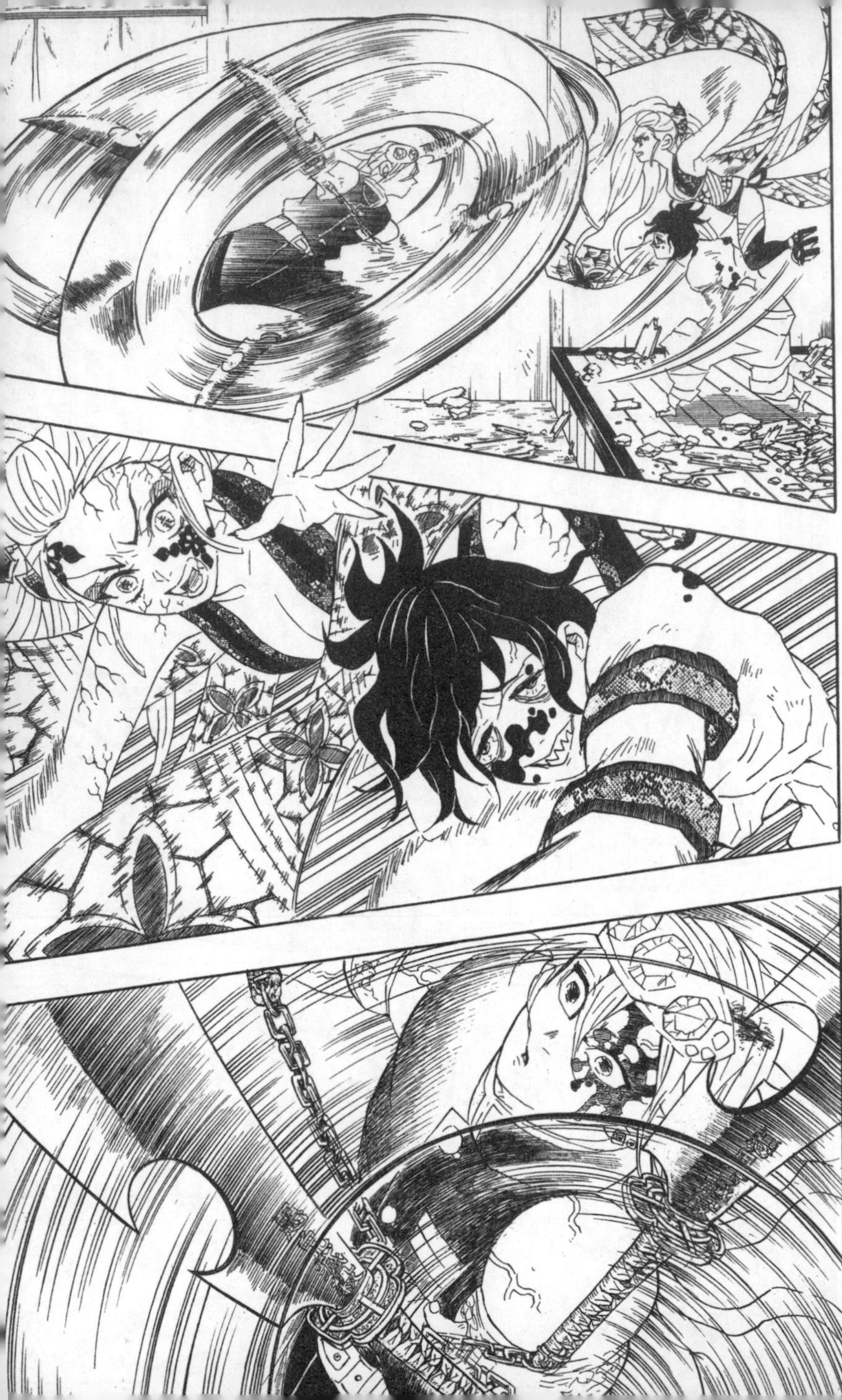

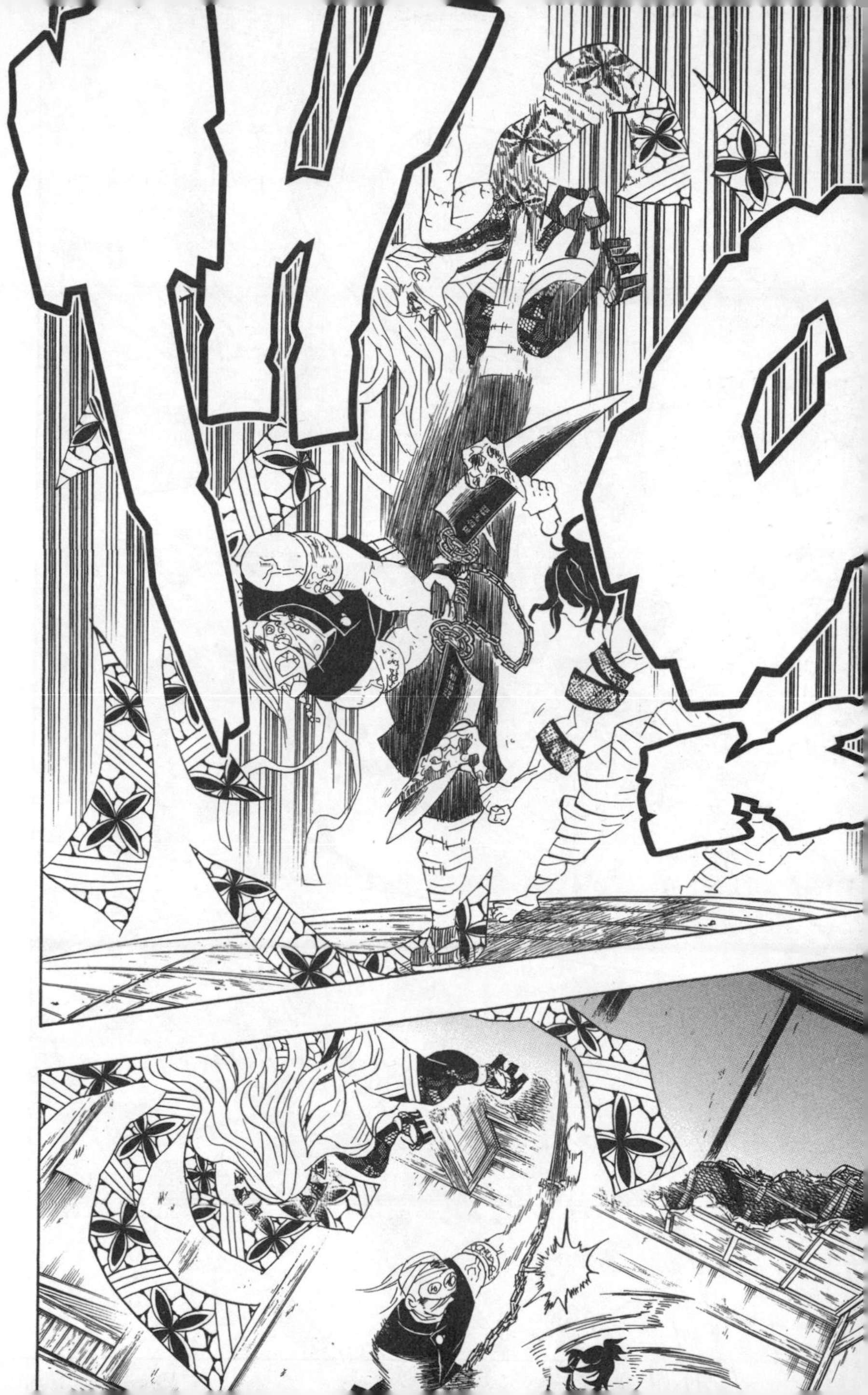

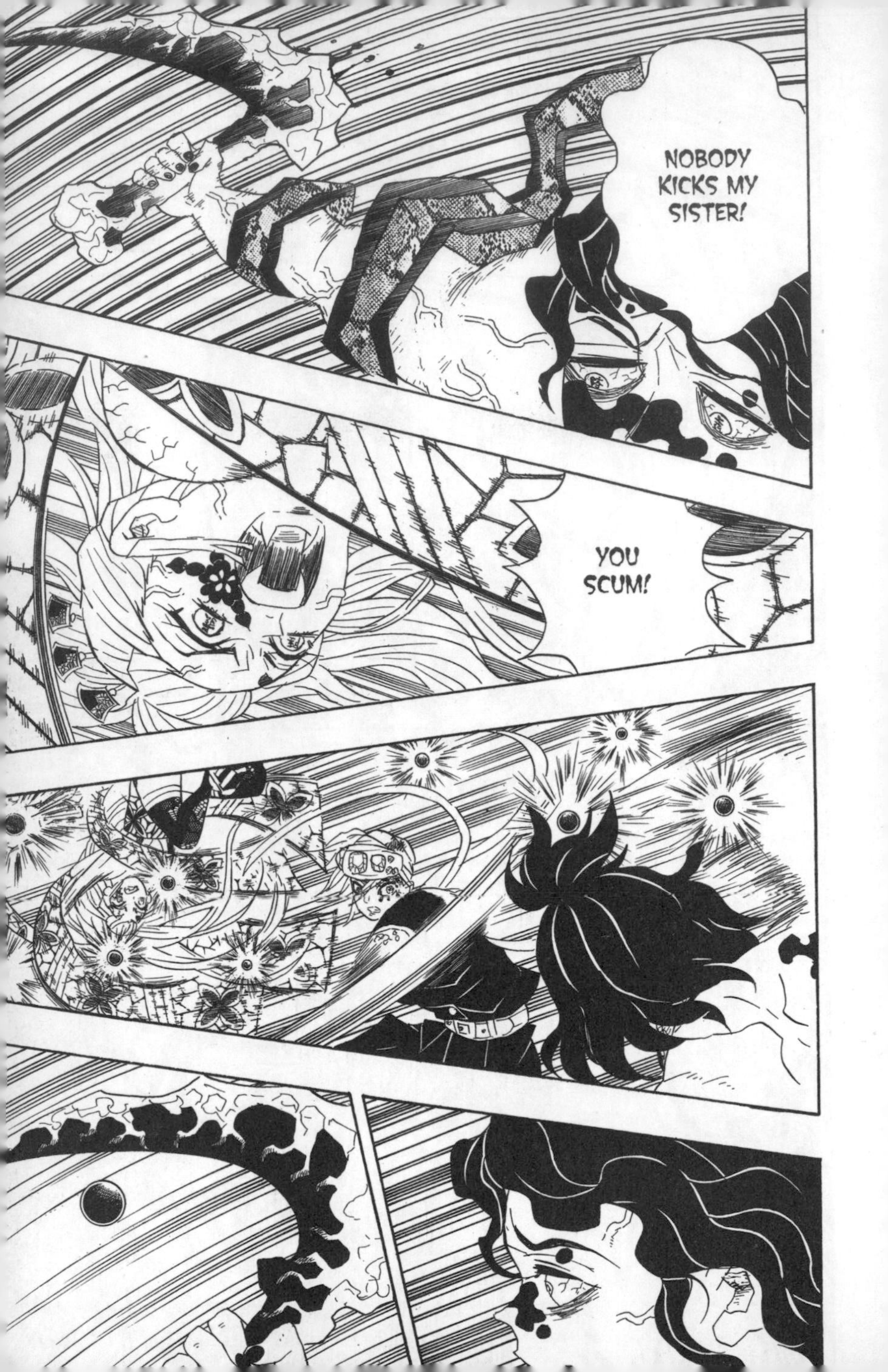
NOBODY KICKS MY SISTER!
YOU SCUM!

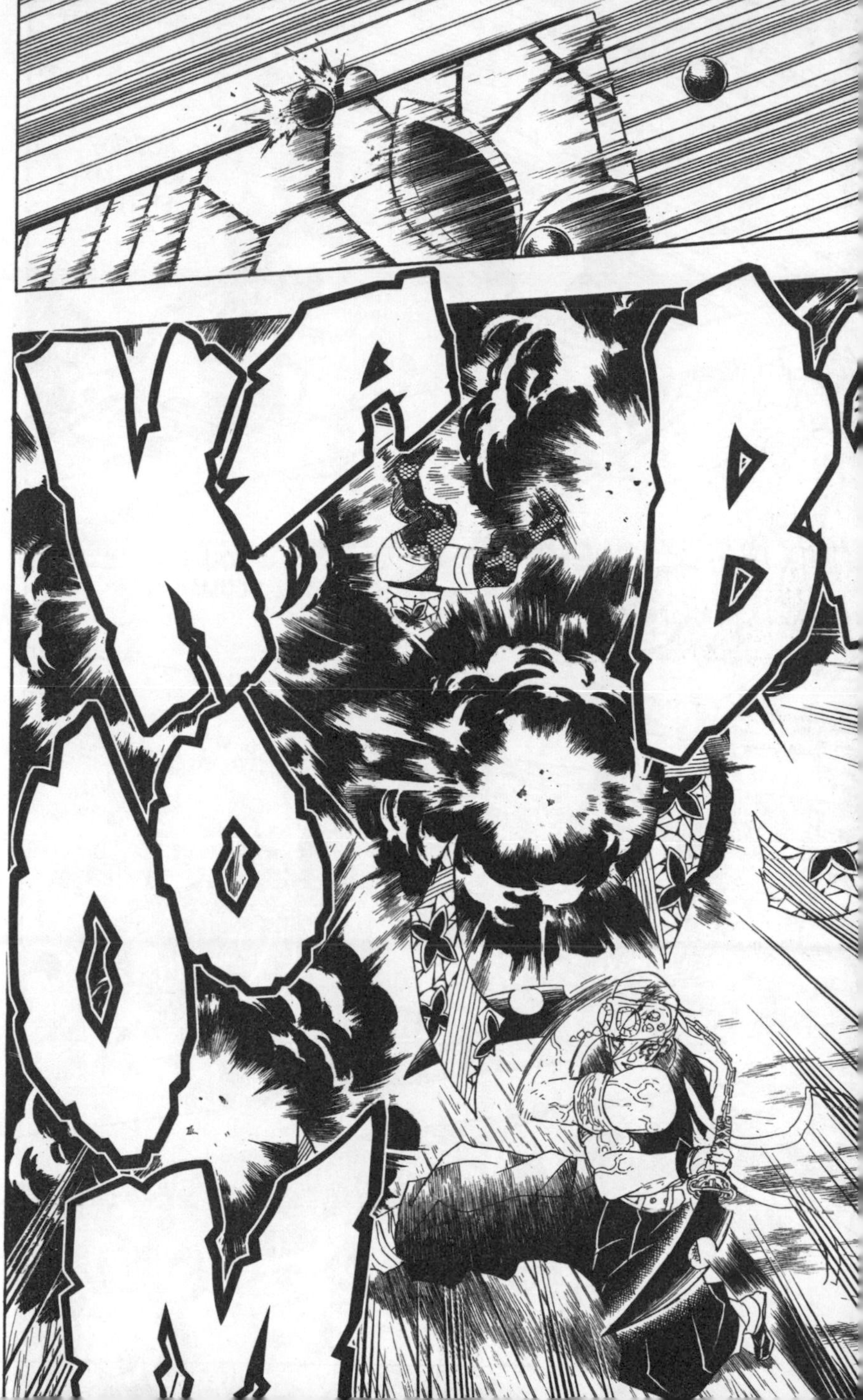

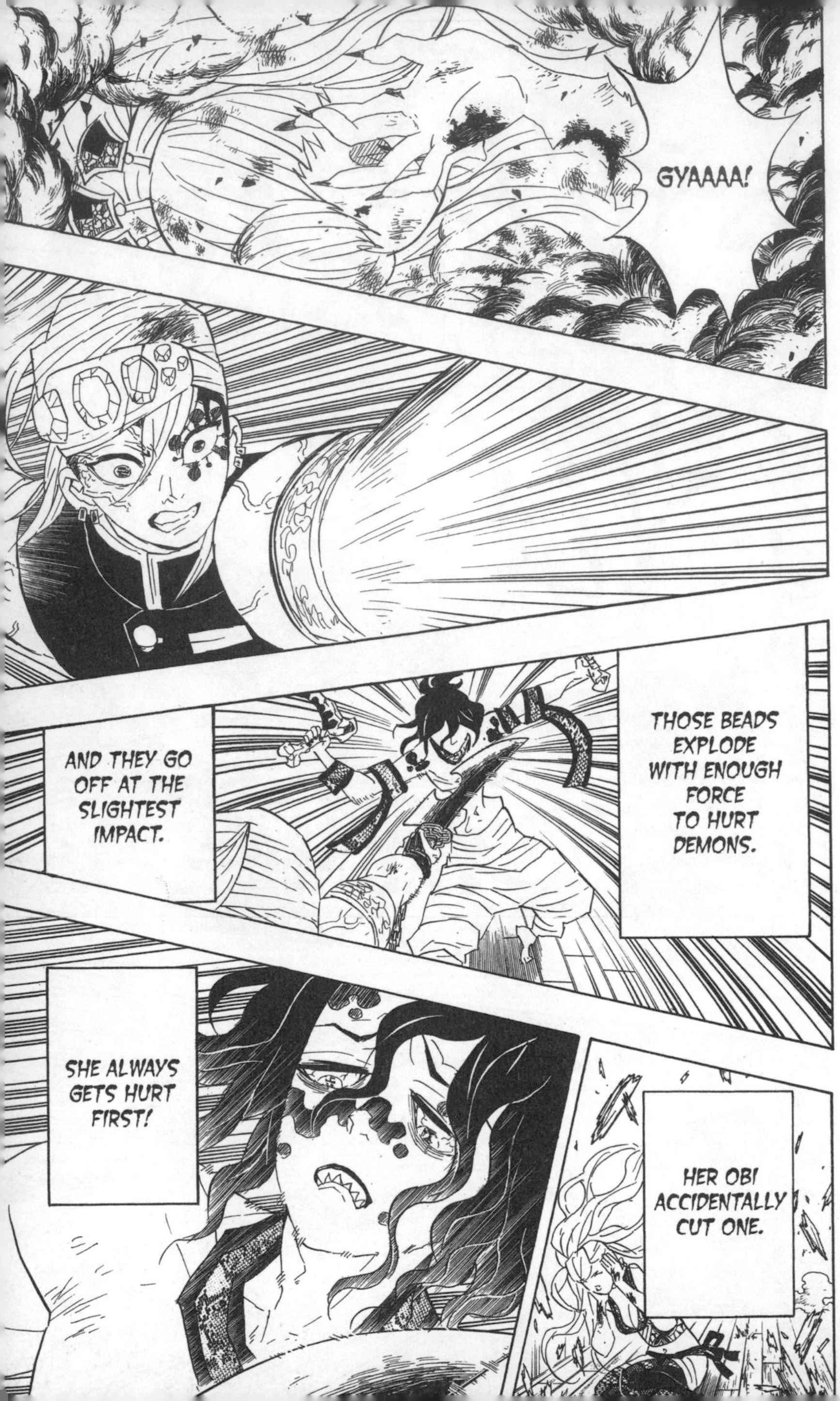
GYAAAA!
THOSE BEADS EXPLODE WITH ENOUGH FORCE TO HURT DEMONS.
AND THEY GO OFF AT THE SLIGHTEST IMPACT.
HER OBI ACCIDENTALLY CUT ONE.
SHE ALWAYS GETS HURT FIRST!

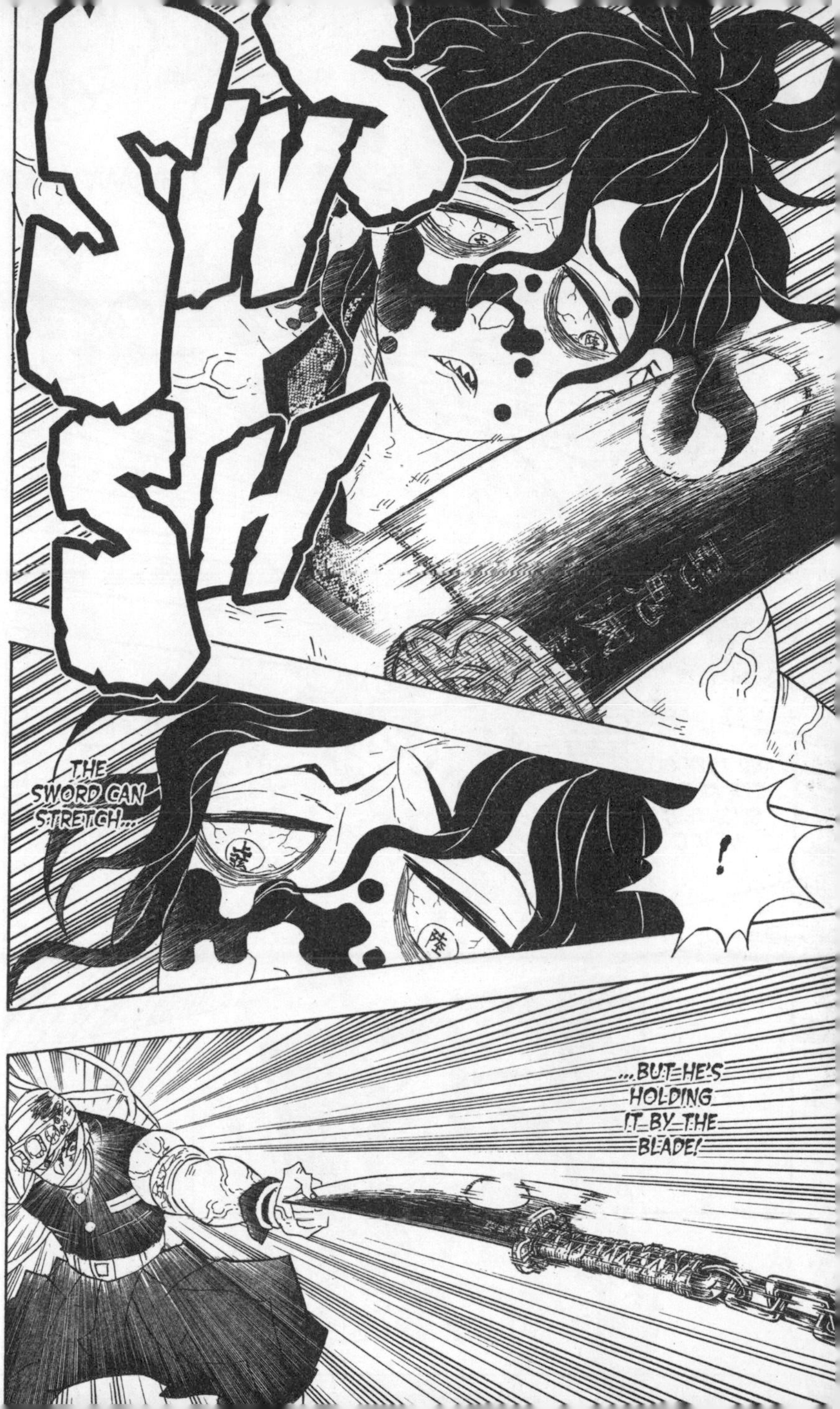
SWISH
!
THE SWORD CAN STRETCH...
...BUT HE'S HOLDING IT BY THE BLADE!

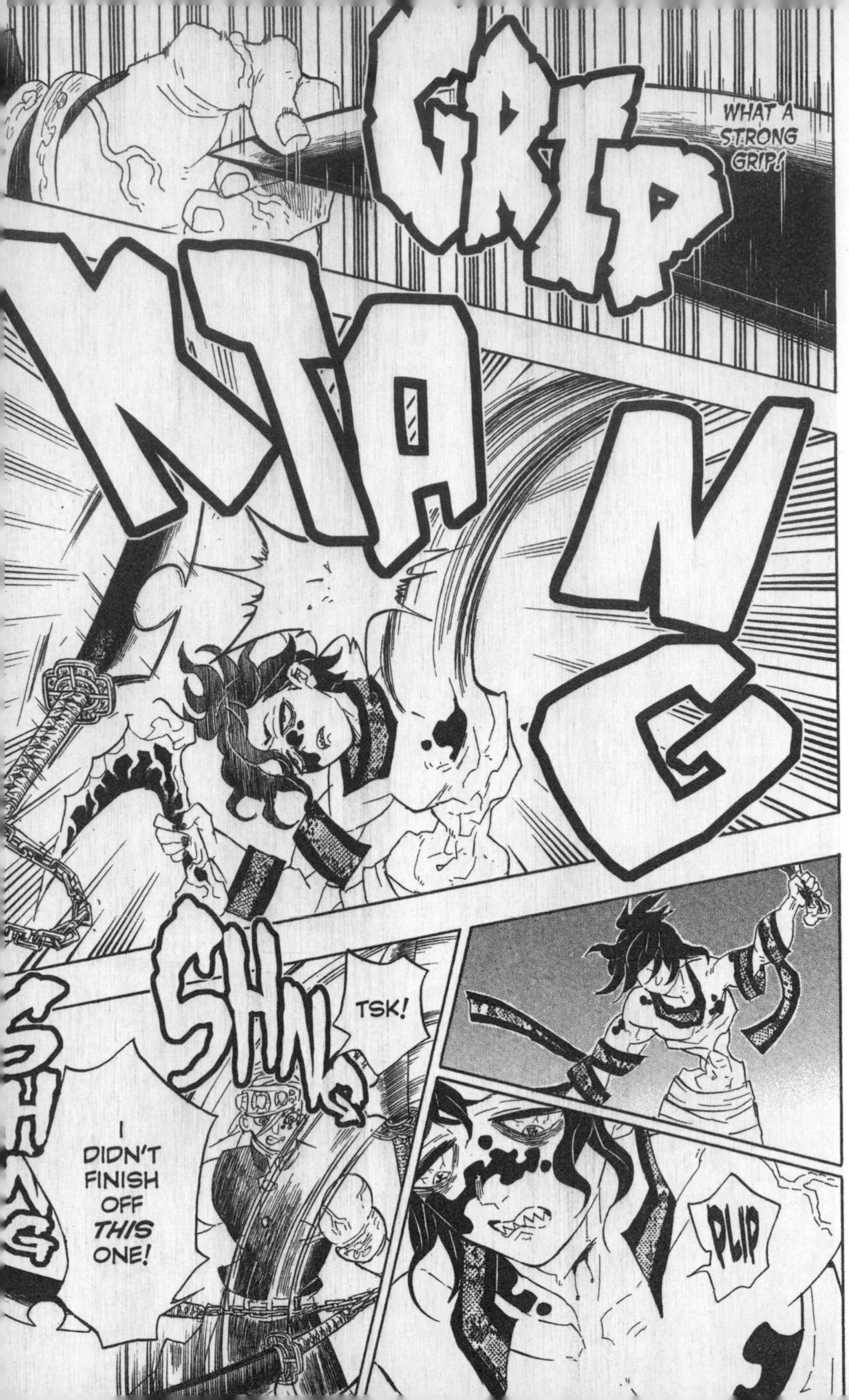
GRIP
WHAT A STRONG GRIP!
WHANG
PLIP
SHING
TSK!
I DIDN'T FINISH OFF THIS ONE!

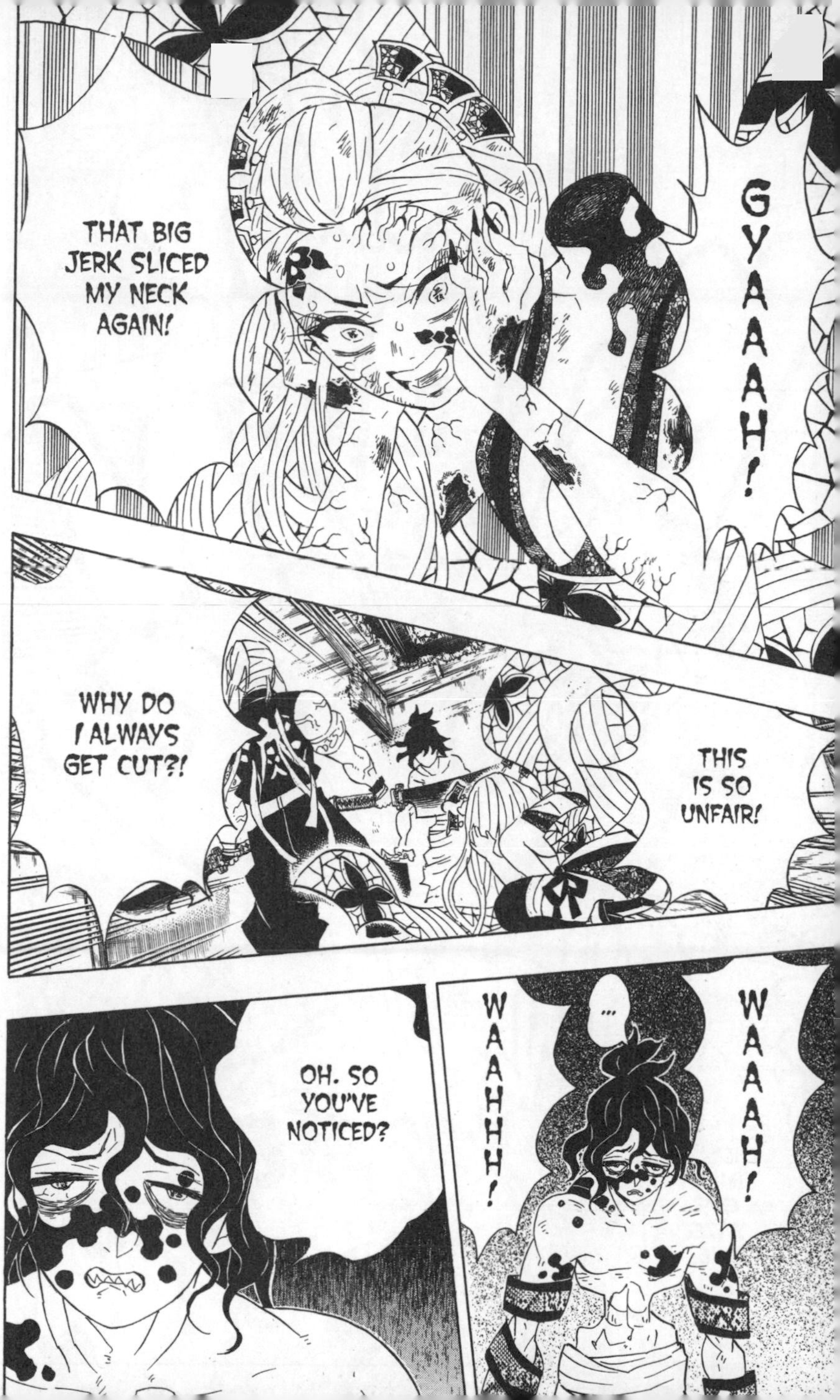
GYAAAH!
THAT BIG JERK SLICED MY NECK AGAIN!
THIS IS SO UNFAIR!
WHY DO I ALWAYS GET CUT?!
WAAAAH!
...
WAAHHH!
OH. SO YOU'VE NOTICED?

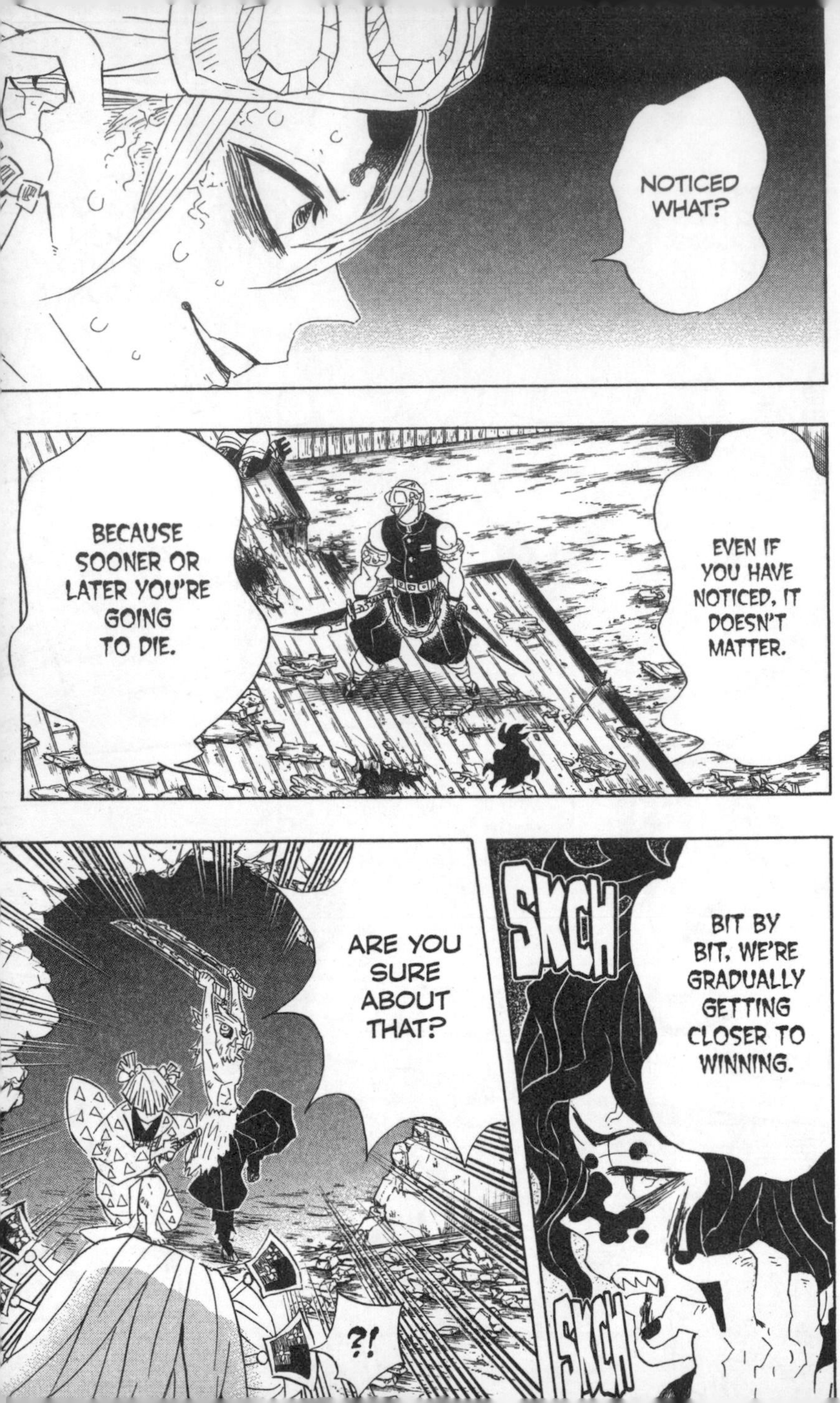
NOTICED WHAT?
EVEN IF YOU HAVE NOTICED, IT DOESN'T MATTER.
BECAUSE SOONER OR LATER YOU'RE GOING TO DIE.
SKCH
BIT BY BIT, WE'RE GRADUALLY GETTING CLOSER TO WINNING.
SKCH
ARE YOU SURE ABOUT THAT?
?!

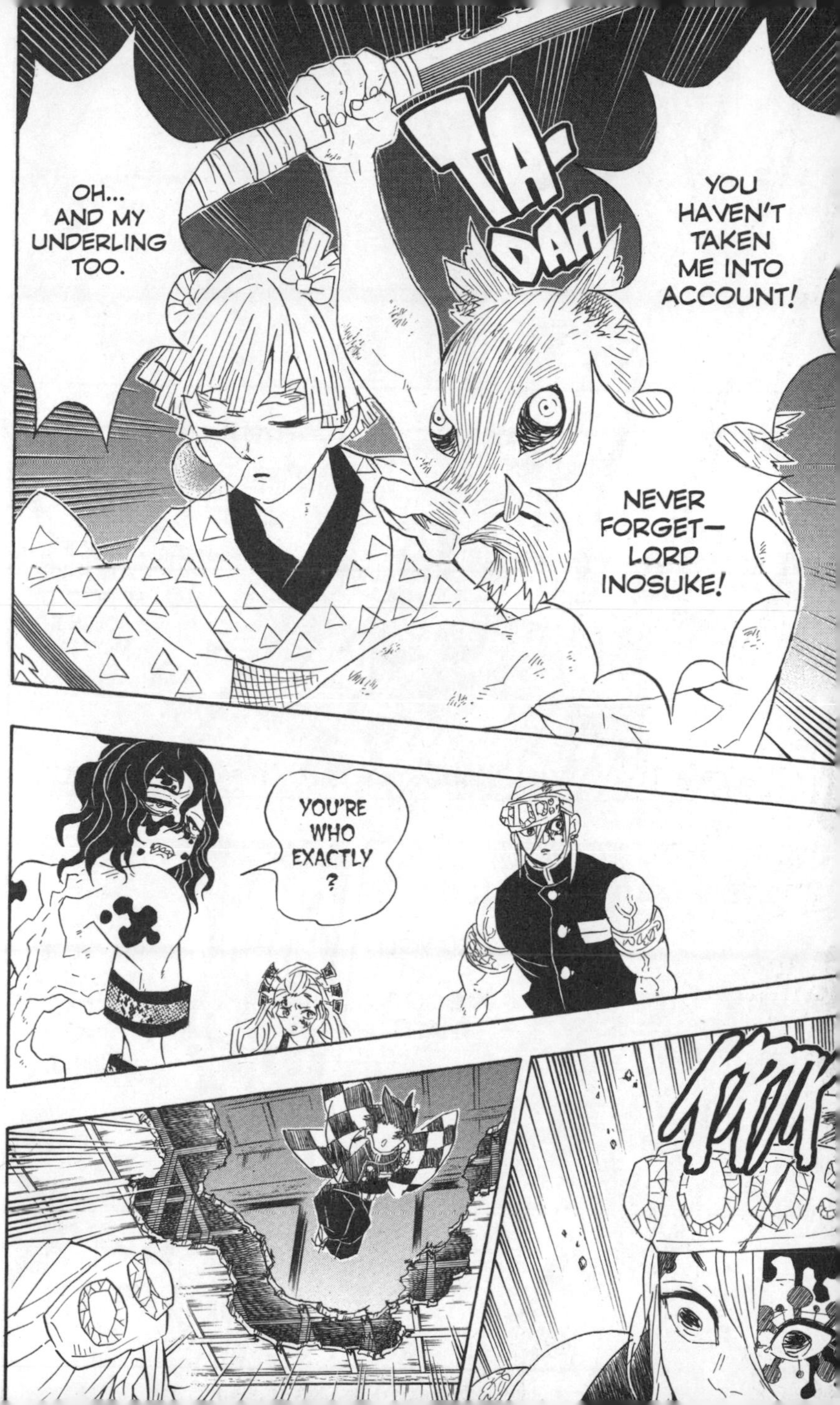
YOU HAVEN'T TAKEN ME INTO ACCOUNT!
TA-DAH
NEVER FORGET—LORD INOSUKE!
OH... AND MY UNDERLING TOO.
YOU'RE WHO EXACTLY ?

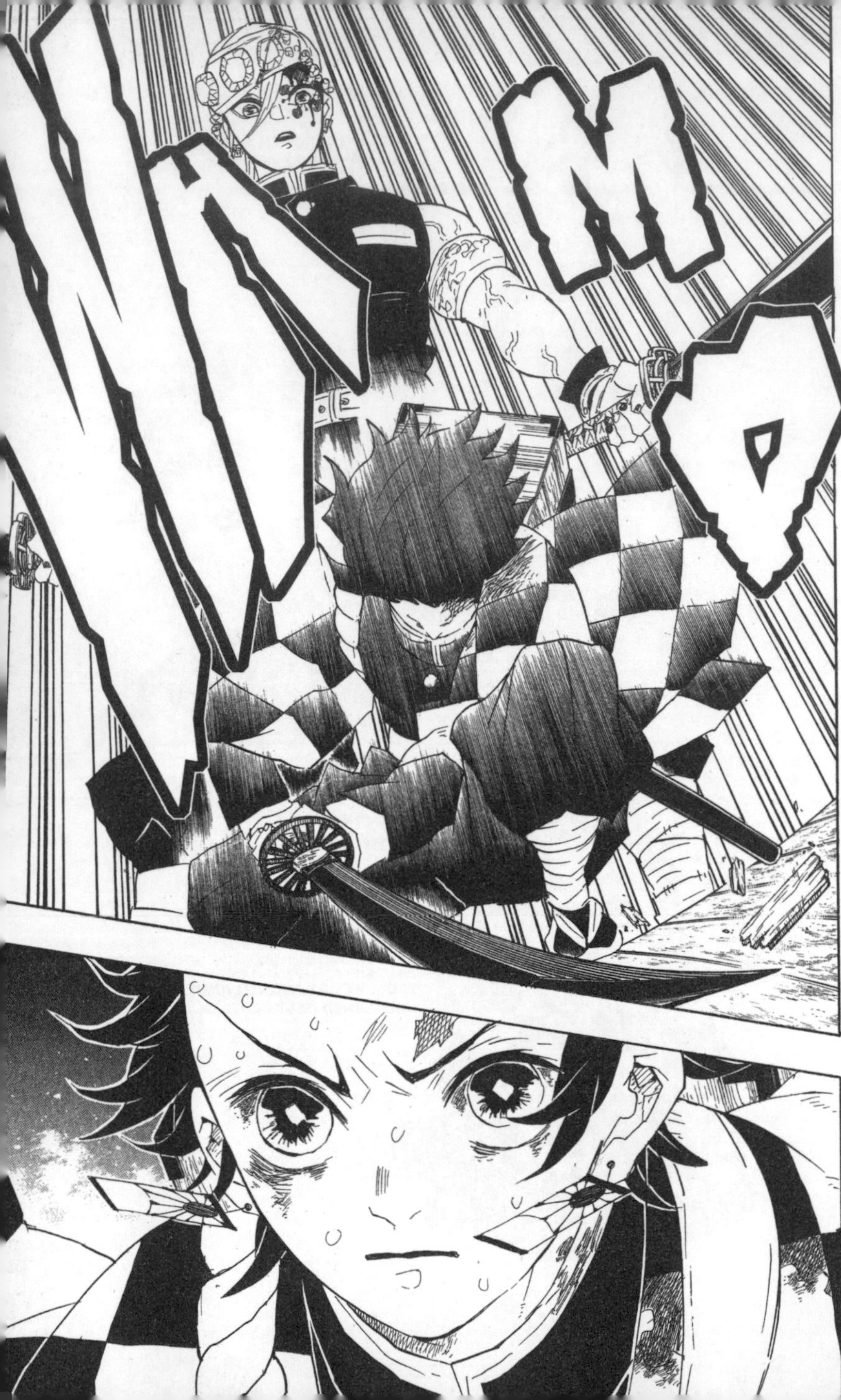
WMP

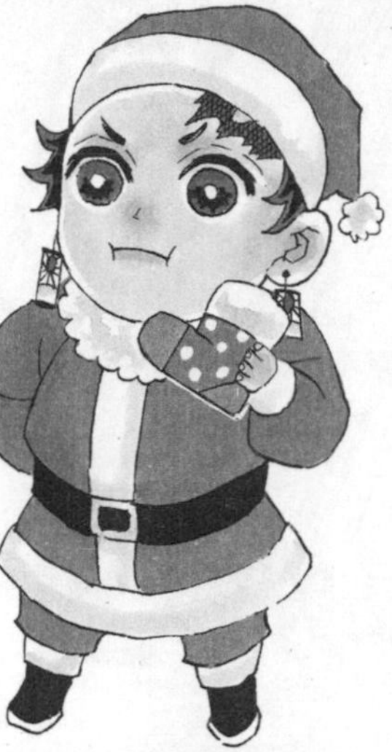

FROM *WEEKLY SHONEN JUMP*, COMBINED ISSUE 2/3, 2018.

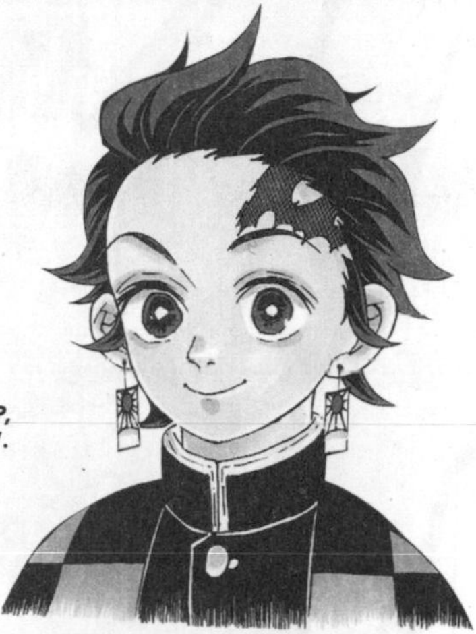

FROM *WEEKLY SHONEN JUMP*, COMBINED ISSUE 36/37, 2017.

DEMON SLAYER:
KIMETSU NO YAIBA
BY KOYOHARU GOTOUGE

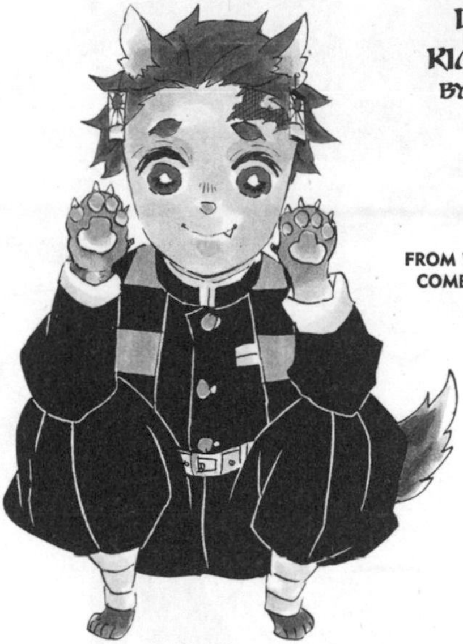

FROM *WEEKLY SHONEN JUMP*, COMBINED ISSUE 4/5, 2018.

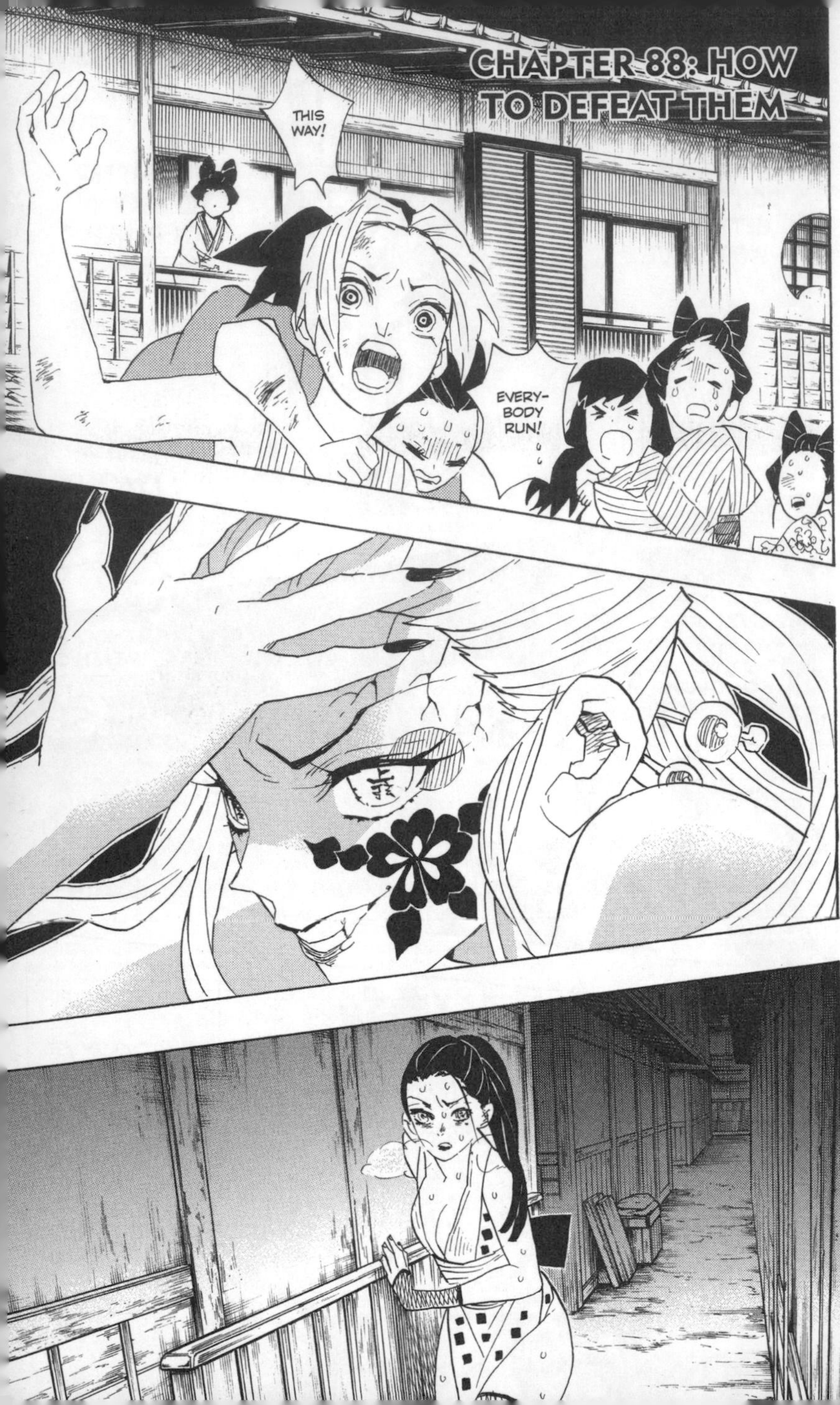
CHAPTER 88: HOW TO DEFEAT THEM
EVERYBODY RUN!
THIS WAY!

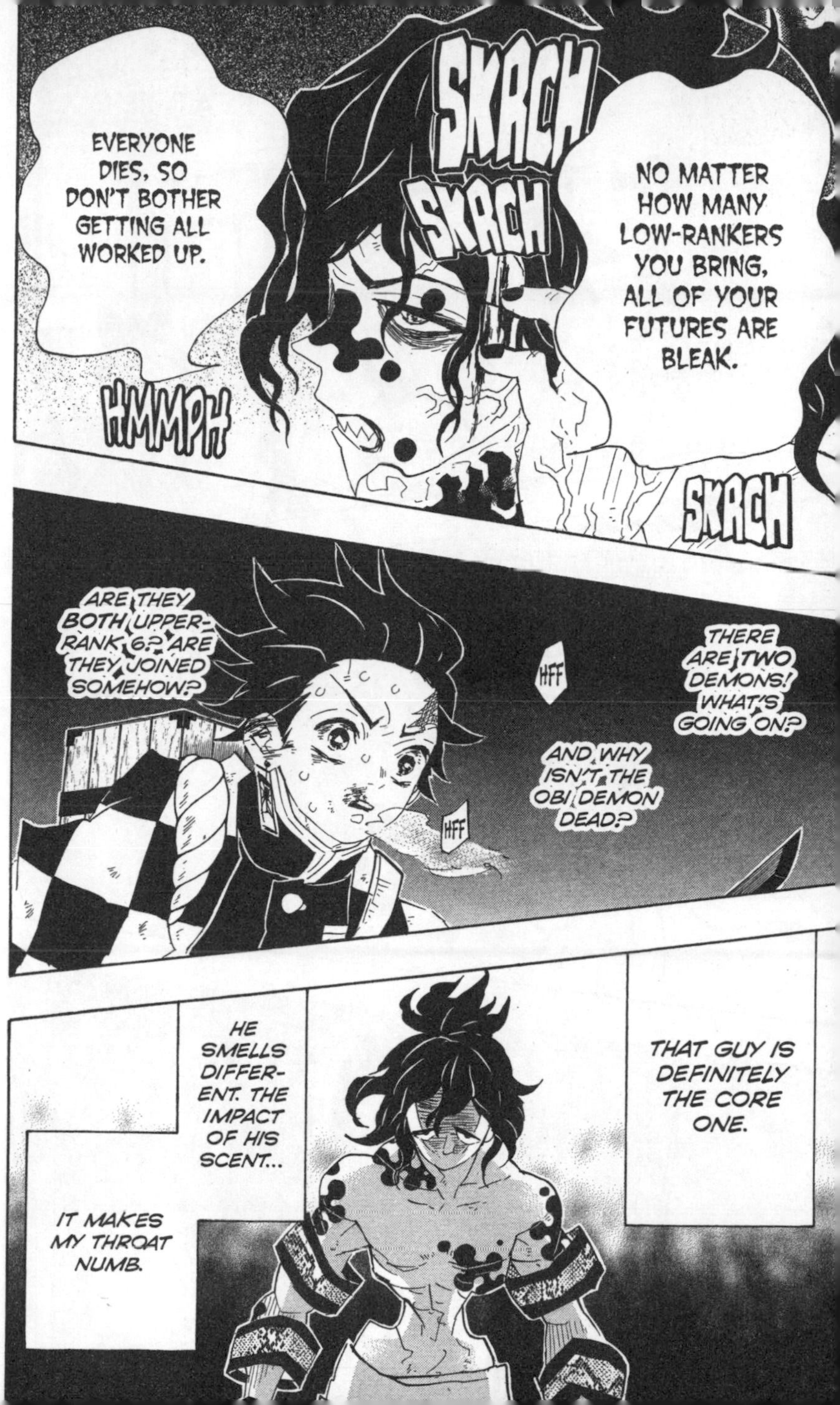
SKRCH
SKRCH
NO MATTER HOW MANY LOW-RANKERS YOU BRING, ALL OF YOUR FUTURES ARE BLEAK.
EVERYONE DIES, SO DON'T BOTHER GETTING ALL WORKED UP.
HMMPH
SKRCH
THERE ARE TWO DEMONS! WHAT'S GOING ON?
HFF
AND WHY ISN'T THE OBI DEMON DEAD?
HFF
ARE THEY BOTH UPPER-RANK 6? ARE THEY JOINED SOMEHOW?
THAT GUY IS DEFINITELY THE CORE ONE.
HE SMELLS DIFFER-ENT. THE IMPACT OF HIS SCENT...
IT MAKES MY THROAT NUMB.

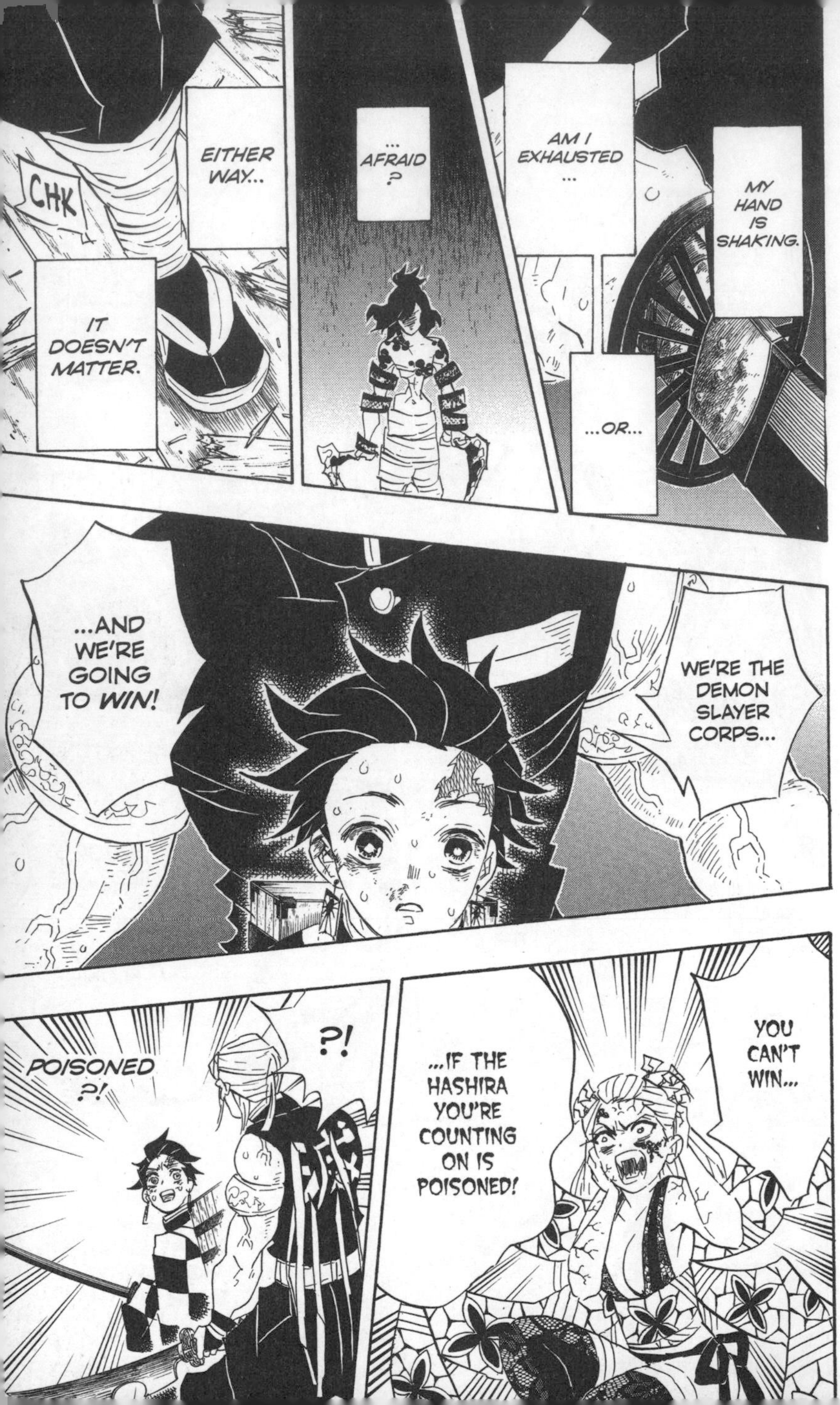
MY HAND IS SHAKING.
AM I EXHAUSTED ...
...OR...
... AFRAID ?
EITHER WAY...
IT DOESN'T MATTER.
CHK
WE'RE THE DEMON SLAYER CORPS...
...AND WE'RE GOING TO WIN!
YOU CAN'T WIN...
...IF THE HASHIRA YOU'RE COUNTING ON IS POISONED!
?!
POISONED ?!

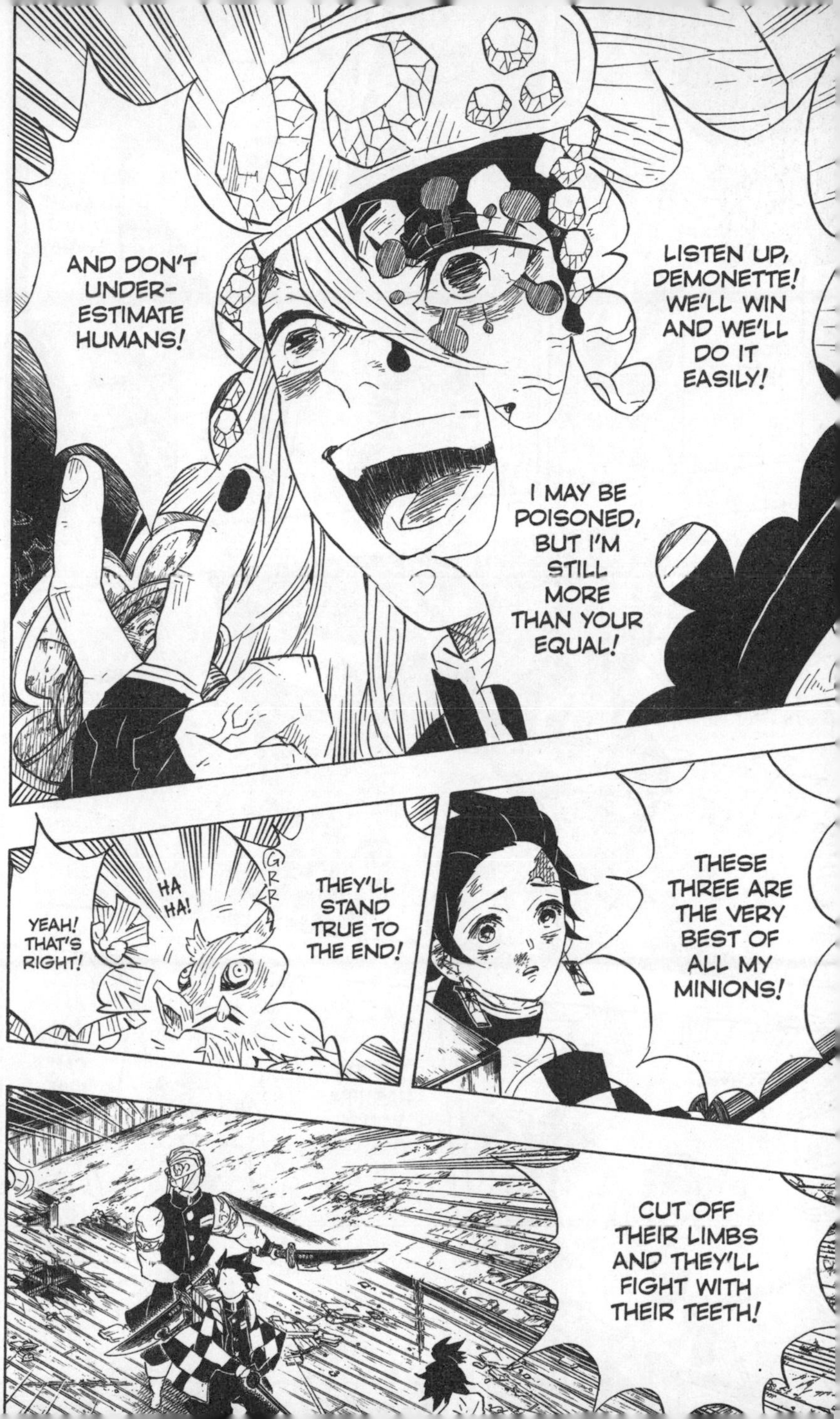
LISTEN UP, DEMONETTE! WE'LL WIN AND WE'LL DO IT EASILY!
I MAY BE POISONED, BUT I'M STILL MORE THAN YOUR EQUAL!
AND DON'T UNDER-ESTIMATE HUMANS!
THESE THREE ARE THE VERY BEST OF ALL MY MINIONS!
THEY'LL STAND TRUE TO THE END!
GRR
HA HA!
YEAH! THAT'S RIGHT!
CUT OFF THEIR LIMBS AND THEY'LL FIGHT WITH THEIR TEETH!

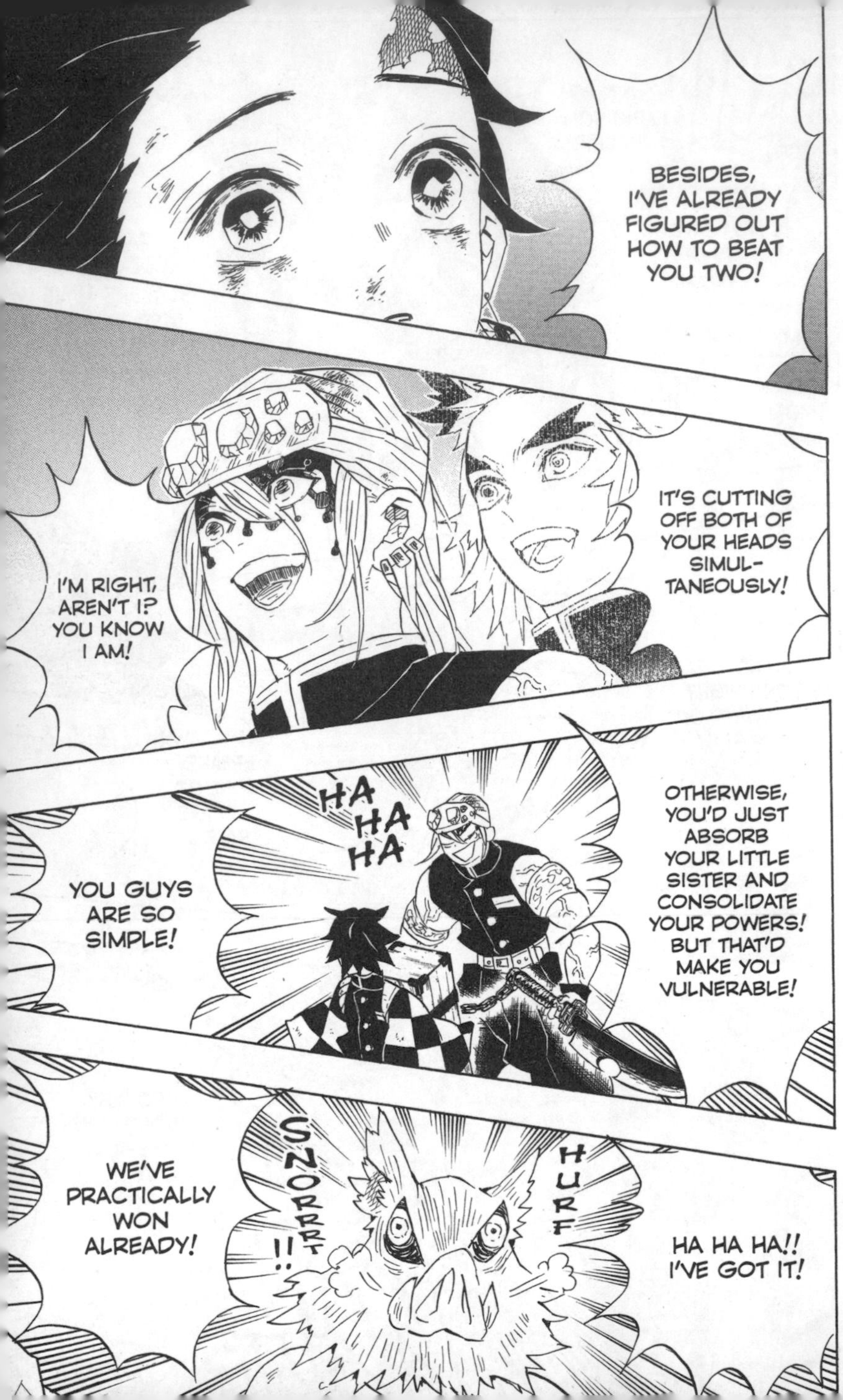
BESIDES, I'VE ALREADY FIGURED OUT HOW TO BEAT YOU TWO!
IT'S CUTTING OFF BOTH OF YOUR HEADS SIMUL-TANEOUSLY!
I'M RIGHT, AREN'T I? YOU KNOW I AM!
OTHERWISE, YOU'D JUST ABSORB YOUR LITTLE SISTER AND CONSOLIDATE YOUR POWERS! BUT THAT'D MAKE YOU VULNERABLE!
HA HA HA
YOU GUYS ARE SO SIMPLE!
HA HA HA!! I'VE GOT IT!
HURF
SNORRRT!!
WE'VE PRACTICALLY WON ALREADY!

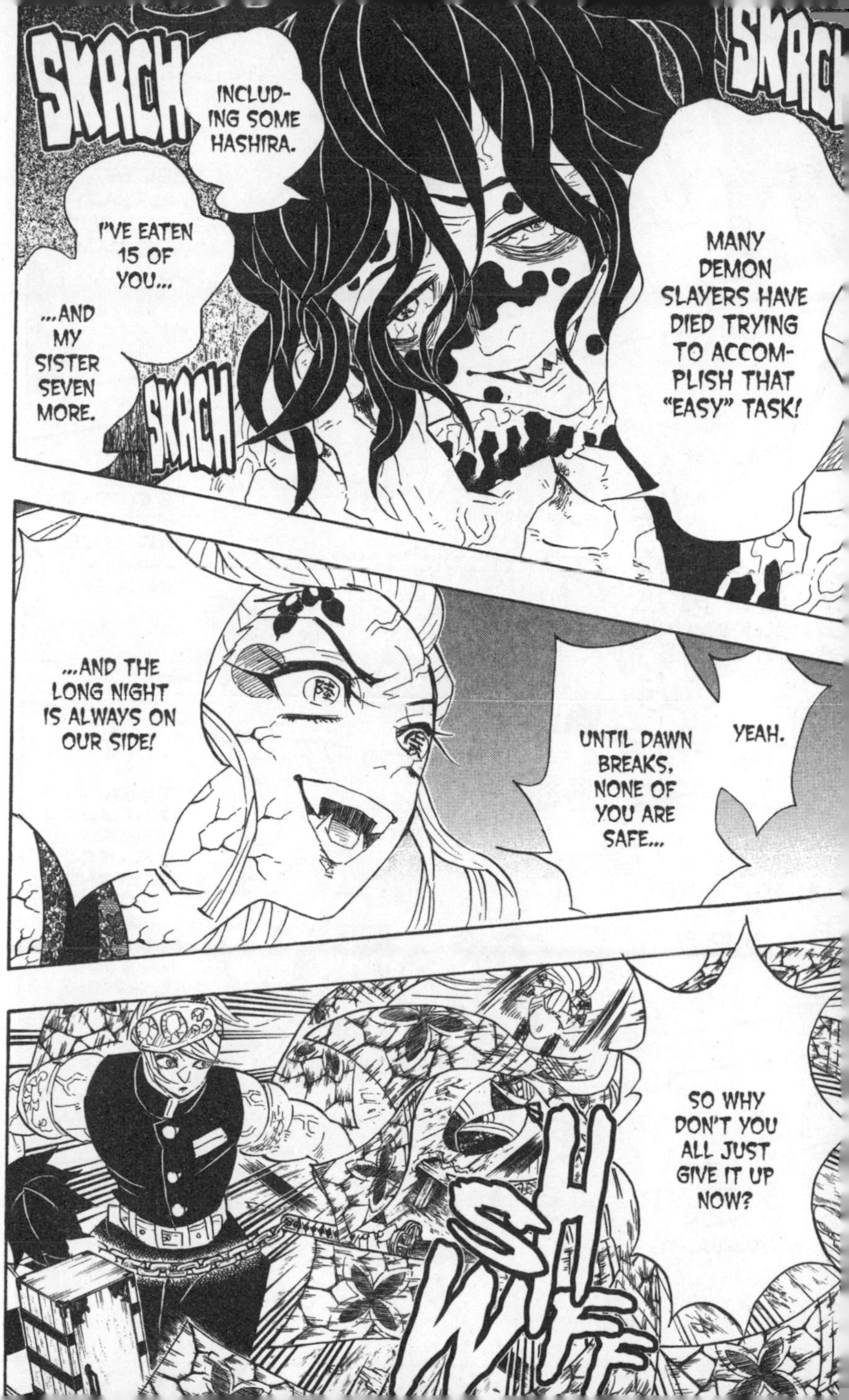
SKRCH
MANY DEMON SLAYERS HAVE DIED TRYING TO ACCOMPLISH THAT "EASY" TASK!
INCLUDING SOME HASHIRA.
SKRCH
I'VE EATEN 15 OF YOU...
...AND MY SISTER SEVEN MORE.
SKRCH
YEAH.
UNTIL DAWN BREAKS, NONE OF YOU ARE SAFE...
...AND THE LONG NIGHT IS ALWAYS ON OUR SIDE!
SO WHY DON'T YOU ALL JUST GIVE IT UP NOW?
SHWUF

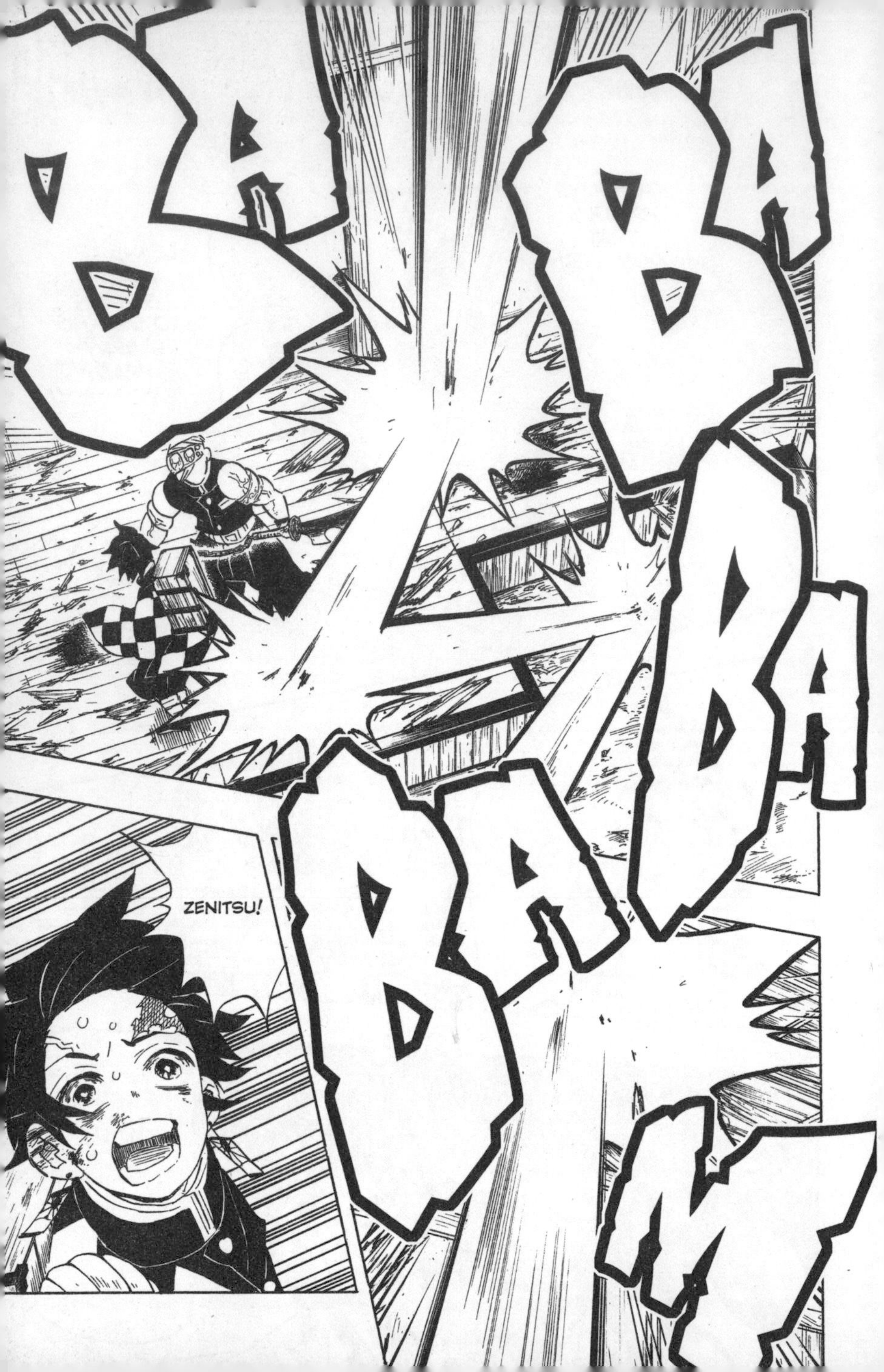
ZENITSU!

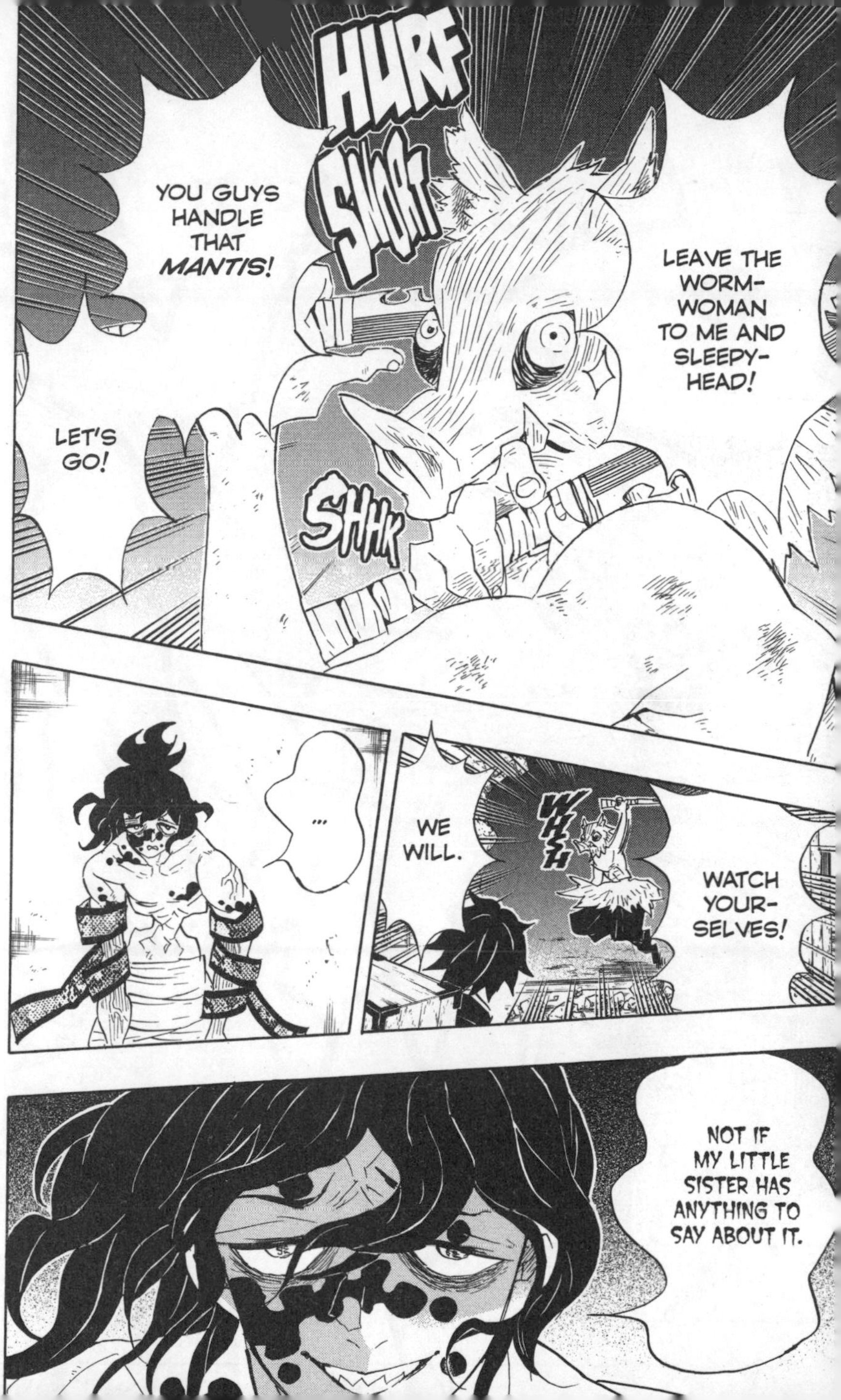
HURF
SNORT
LEAVE THE WORM-WOMAN TO ME AND SLEEPY-HEAD!
YOU GUYS HANDLE THAT *MANTIS*!
SHHK
LET'S GO!
WATCH YOUR-SELVES!
WHSH
WE WILL.
...
NOT IF MY LITTLE SISTER HAS ANYTHING TO SAY ABOUT IT.

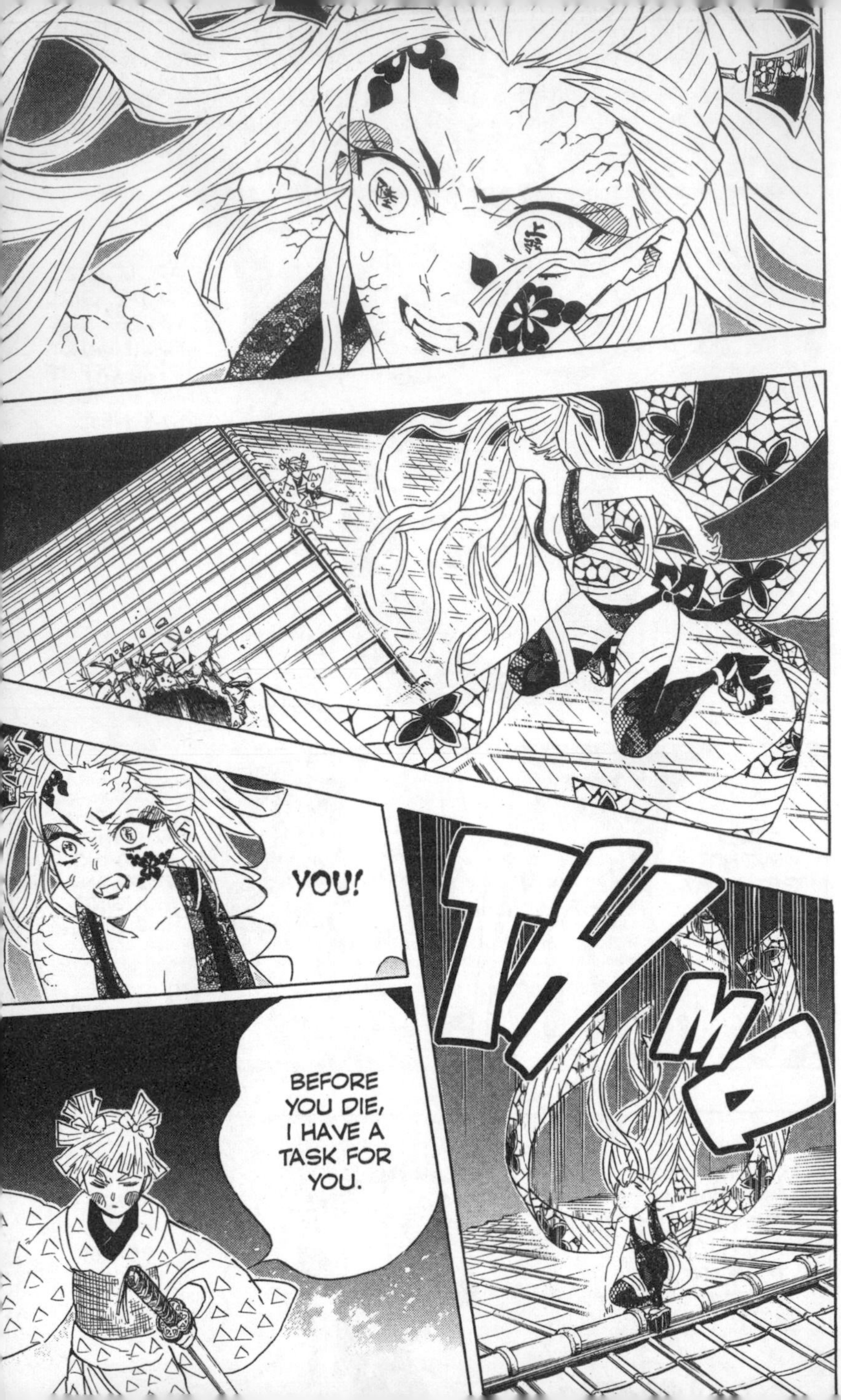
THMP
YOU!
BEFORE YOU DIE, I HAVE A TASK FOR YOU.

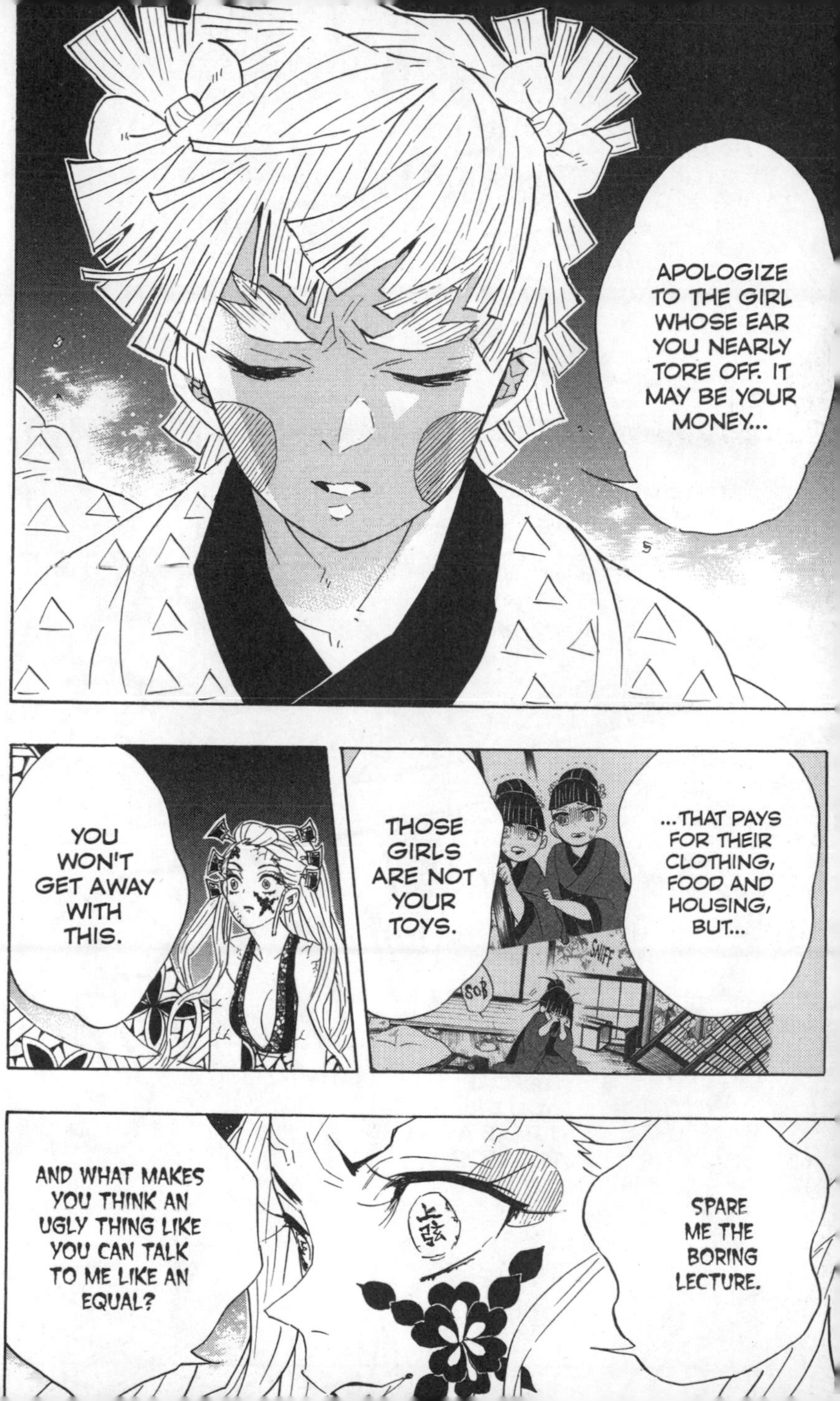
APOLOGIZE TO THE GIRL WHOSE EAR YOU NEARLY TORE OFF. IT MAY BE YOUR MONEY...
...THAT PAYS FOR THEIR CLOTHING, FOOD AND HOUSING, BUT...
SNIFF
SOB
THOSE GIRLS ARE NOT YOUR TOYS.
YOU WON'T GET AWAY WITH THIS.
SPARE ME THE BORING LECTURE.
上弦
AND WHAT MAKES YOU THINK AN UGLY THING LIKE YOU CAN TALK TO ME LIKE AN EQUAL?

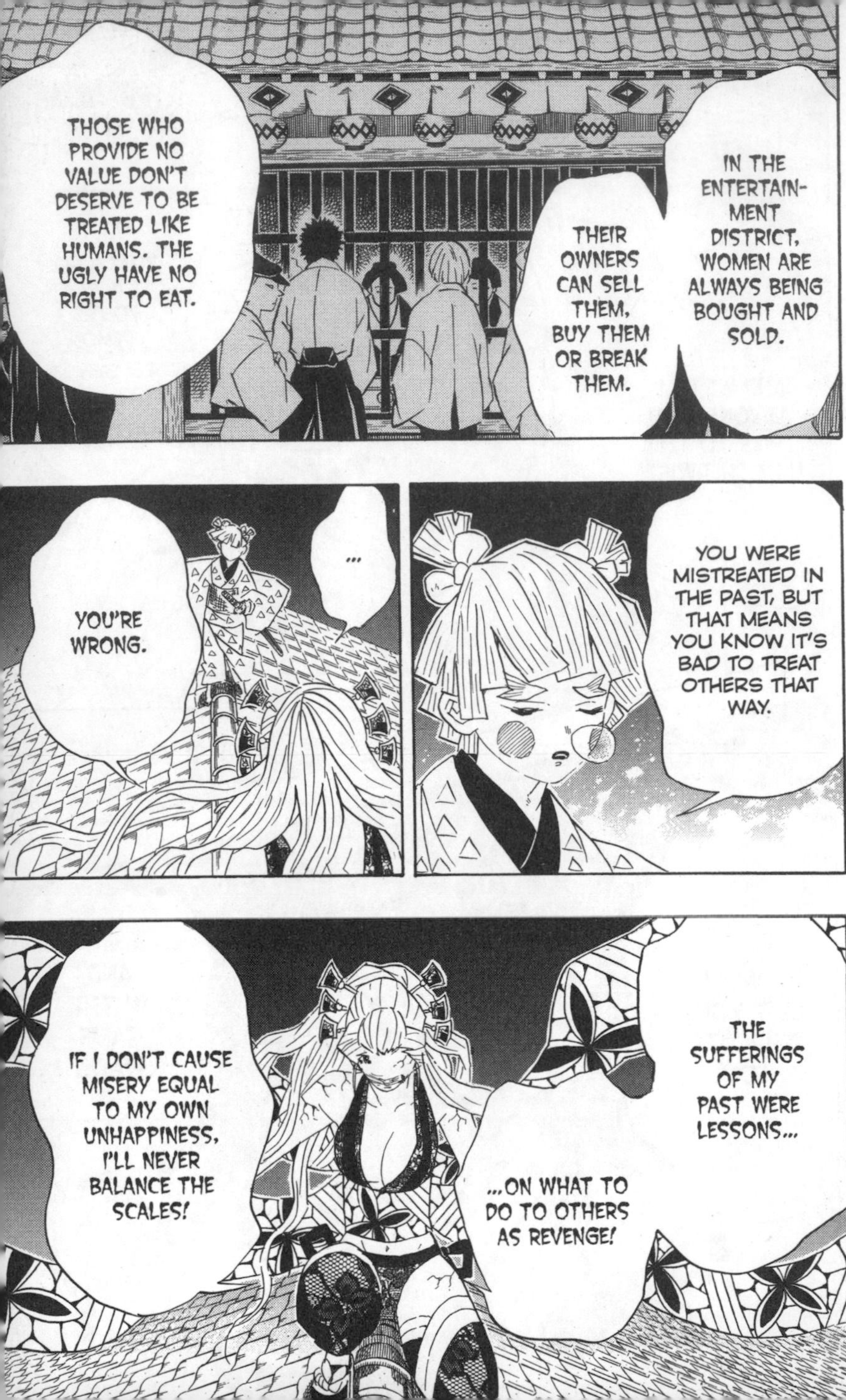
IN THE ENTERTAINMENT DISTRICT, WOMEN ARE ALWAYS BEING BOUGHT AND SOLD.
THEIR OWNERS CAN SELL THEM, BUY THEM OR BREAK THEM.
THOSE WHO PROVIDE NO VALUE DON'T DESERVE TO BE TREATED LIKE HUMANS. THE UGLY HAVE NO RIGHT TO EAT.
YOU WERE MISTREATED IN THE PAST, BUT THAT MEANS YOU KNOW IT'S BAD TO TREAT OTHERS THAT WAY.
...
YOU'RE WRONG.
THE SUFFERINGS OF MY PAST WERE LESSONS...
...ON WHAT TO DO TO OTHERS AS REVENGE!
IF I DON'T CAUSE MISERY EQUAL TO MY OWN UNHAPPINESS, I'LL NEVER BALANCE THE SCALES!

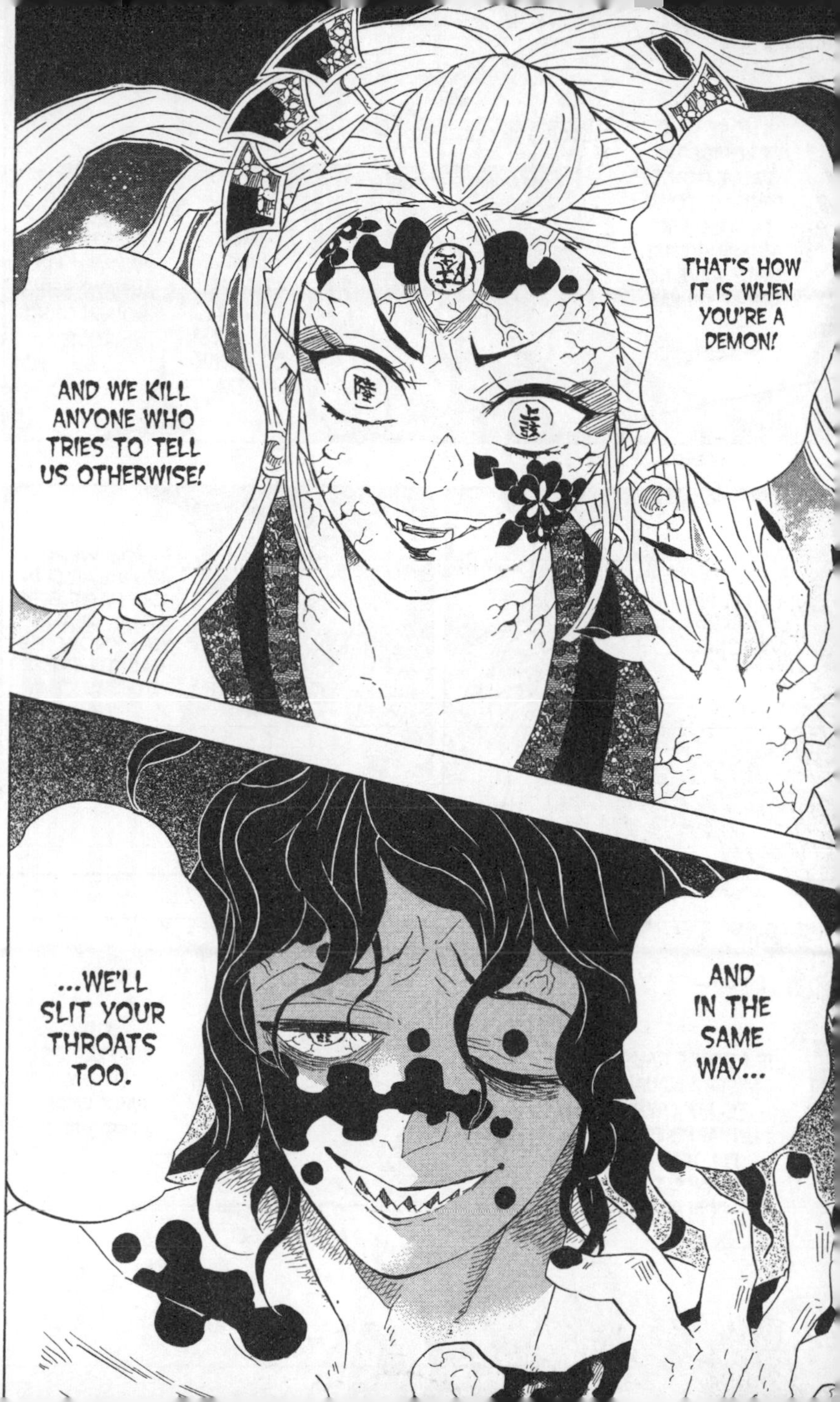
THAT'S HOW IT IS WHEN YOU'RE A DEMON!
AND WE KILL ANYONE WHO TRIES TO TELL US OTHERWISE!
AND IN THE SAME WAY...
...WE'LL SLIT YOUR THROATS TOO.

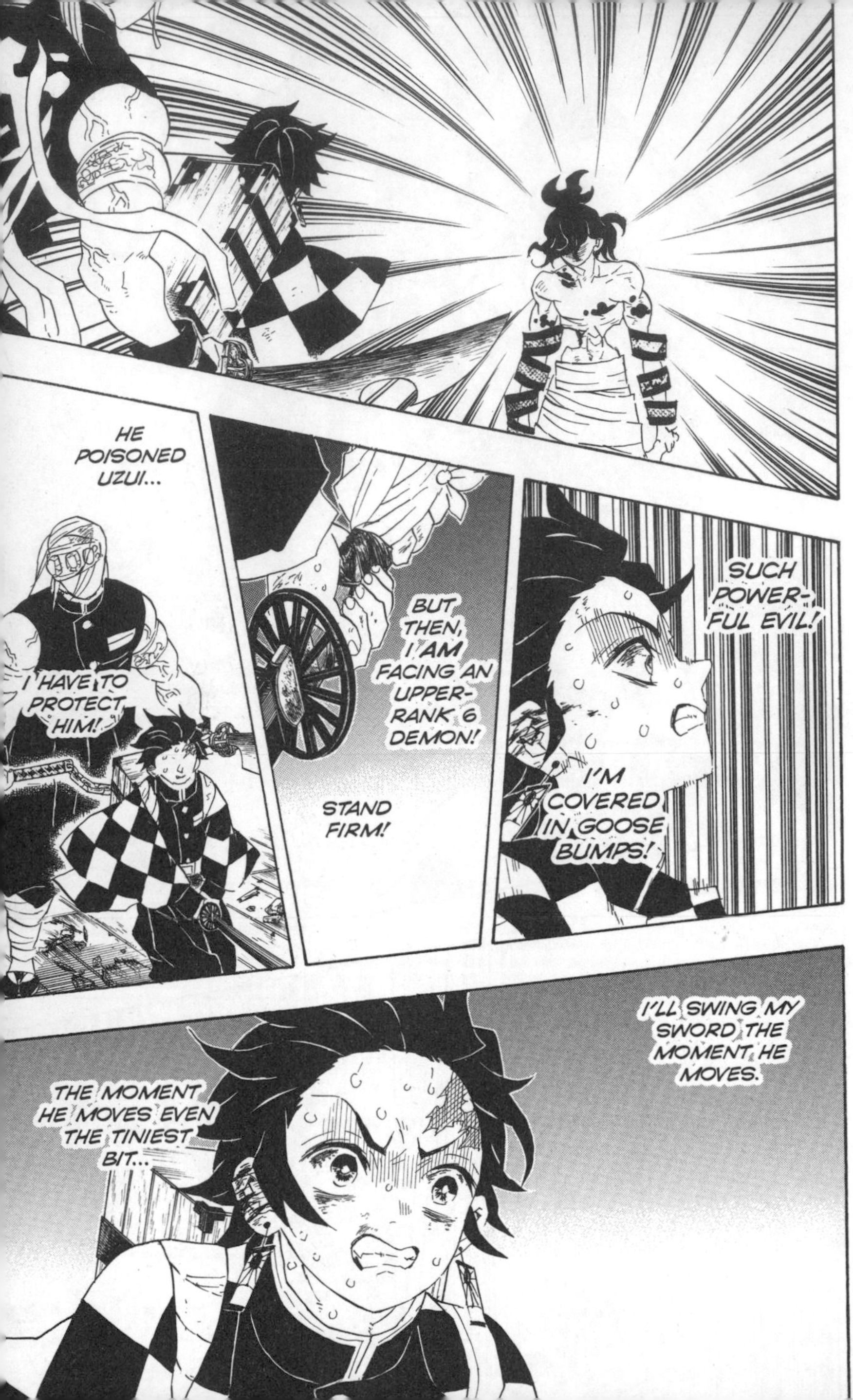
SUCH POWER-FUL EVIL!
I'M COVERED IN GOOSE BUMPS!
BUT THEN, I AM FACING AN UPPER-RANK 6 DEMON!
STAND FIRM!
HE POISONED UZUI...
I HAVE TO PROTECT HIM!
I'LL SWING MY SWORD THE MOMENT HE MOVES.
THE MOMENT HE MOVES EVEN THE TINIEST BIT...

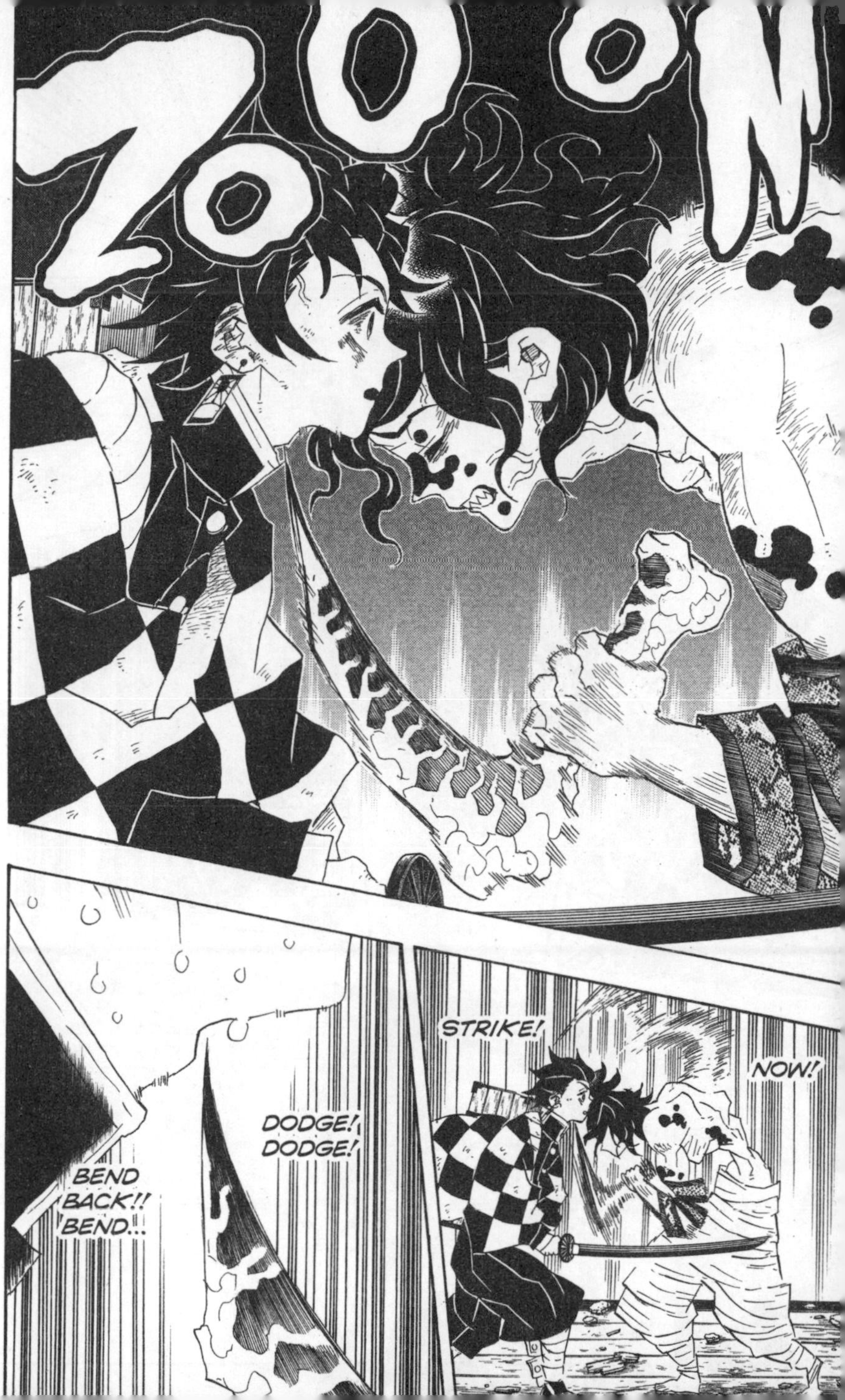
ZOOOM
NOW!
STRIKE!
DODGE! DODGE!
BEND BACK!! BEND...

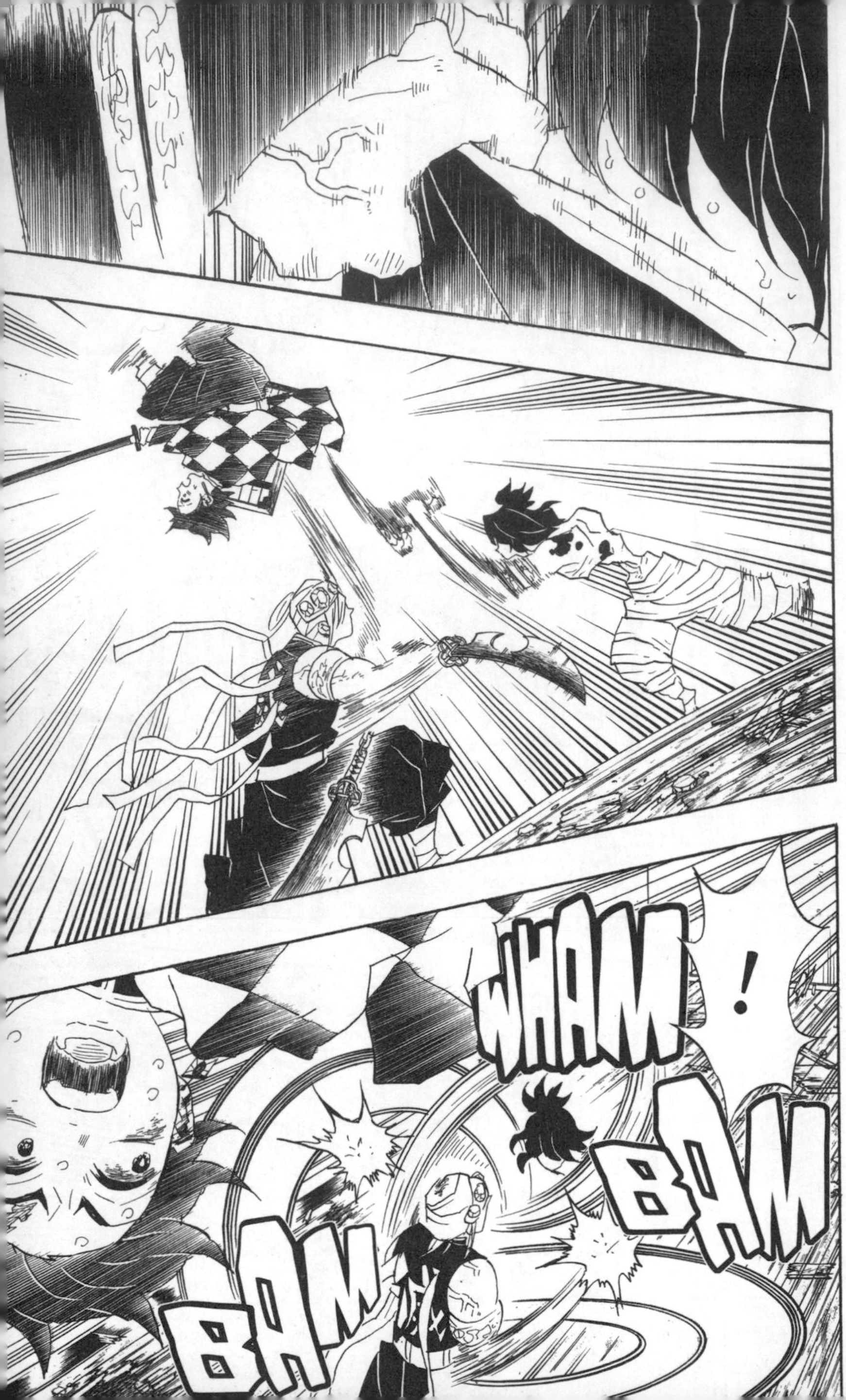
WHAM!
BAM
BAM

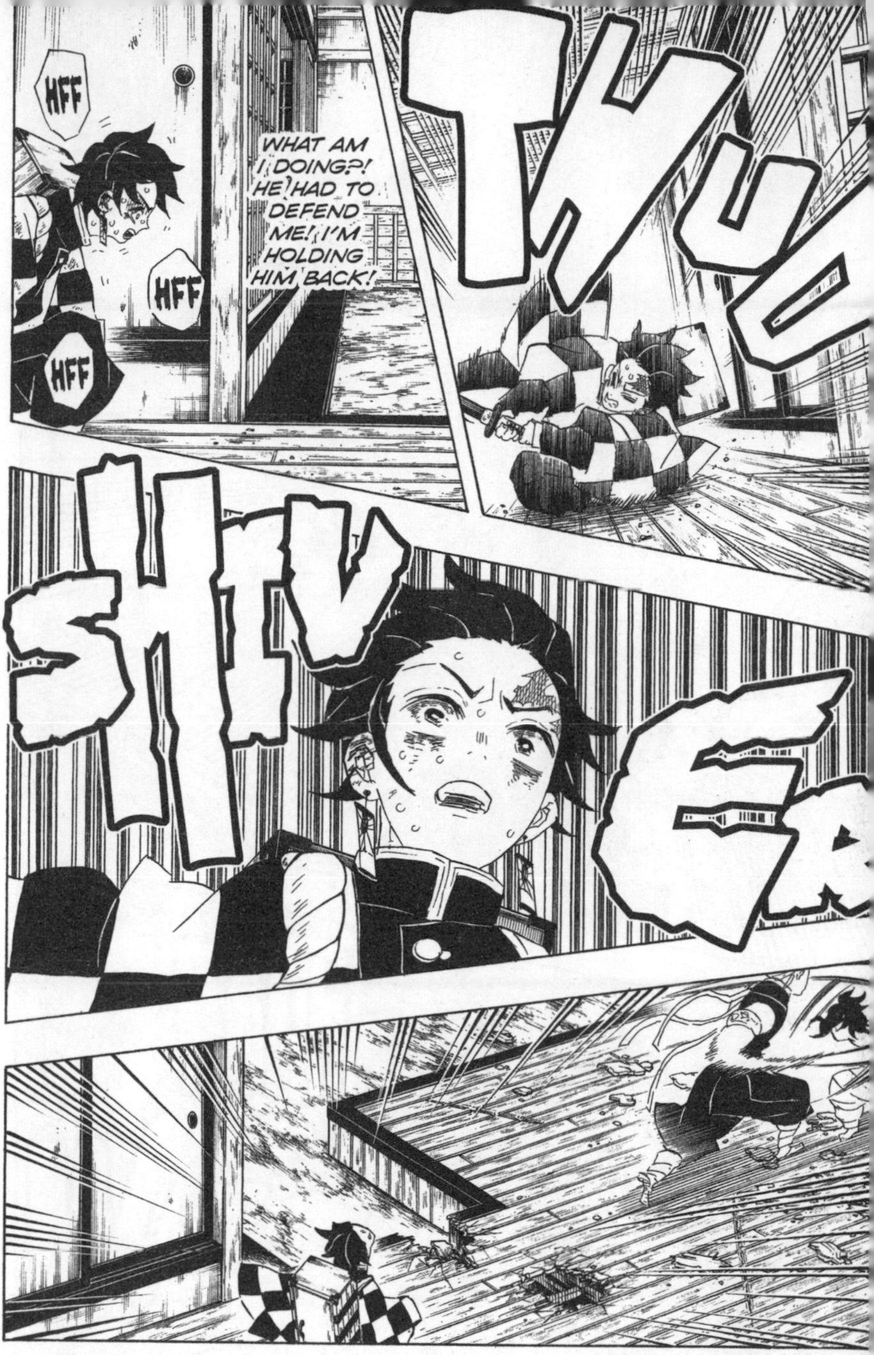
THU-
HFF
WHAT AM I DOING?! HE HAD TO DEFEND ME! I'M HOLDING HIM BACK!
HFF
HFF
SHIVER

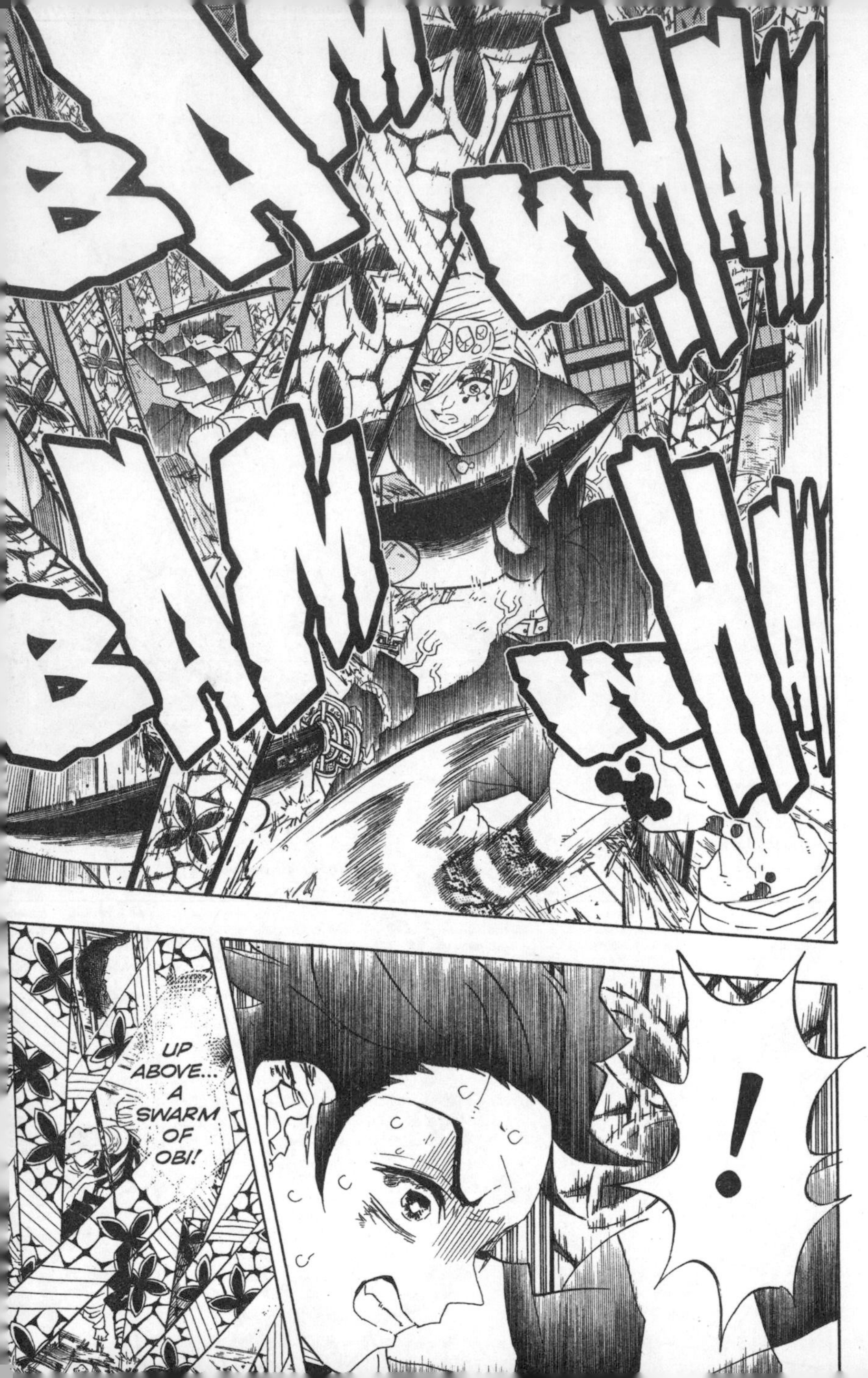
WHAM
BAM
WHAM
BAM
!
UP ABOVE... A SWARM OF OBI!

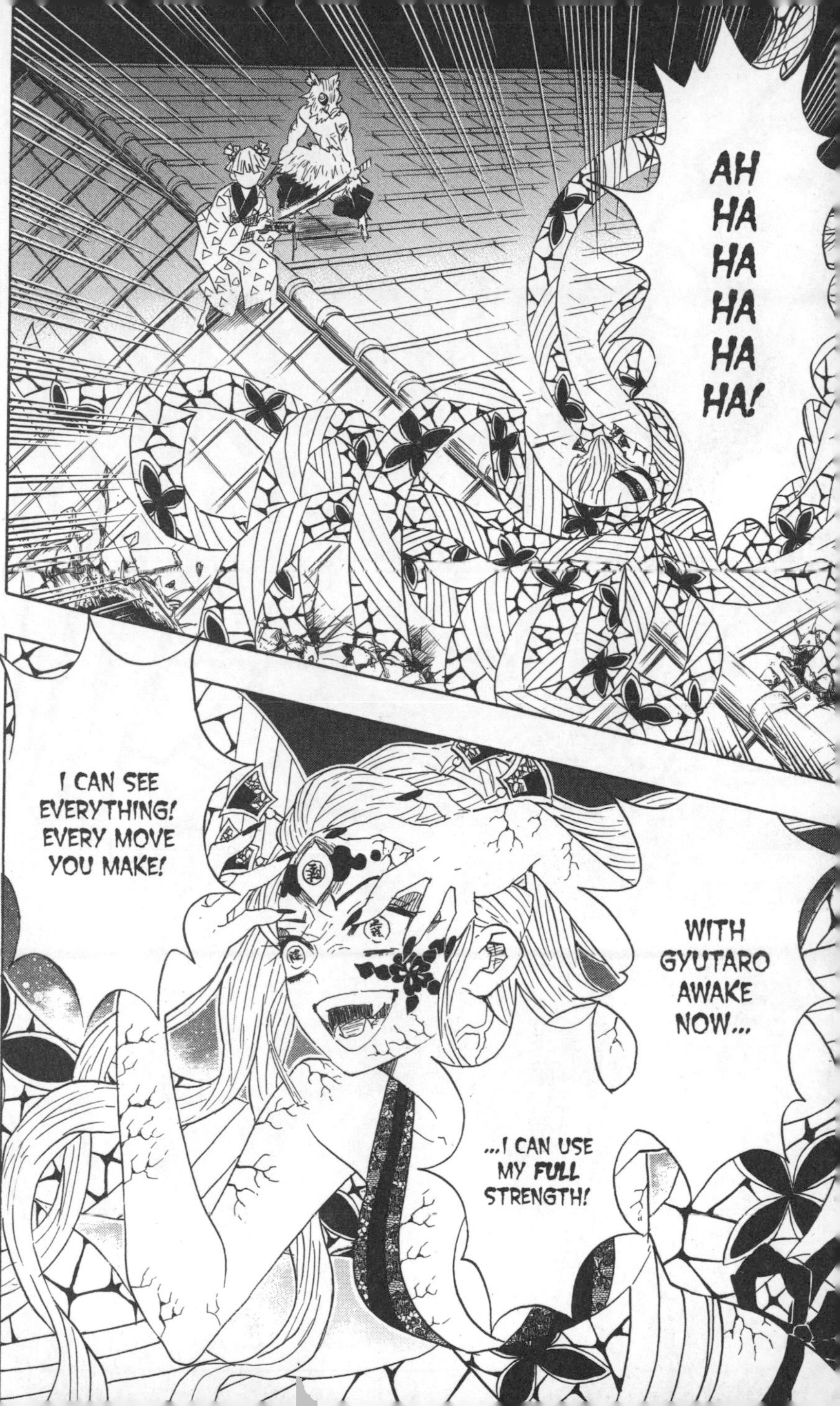
AH HA HA HA HA HA HA!
WITH GYUTARO AWAKE NOW...
I CAN SEE EVERYTHING! EVERY MOVE YOU MAKE!
...I CAN USE MY FULL STRENGTH!

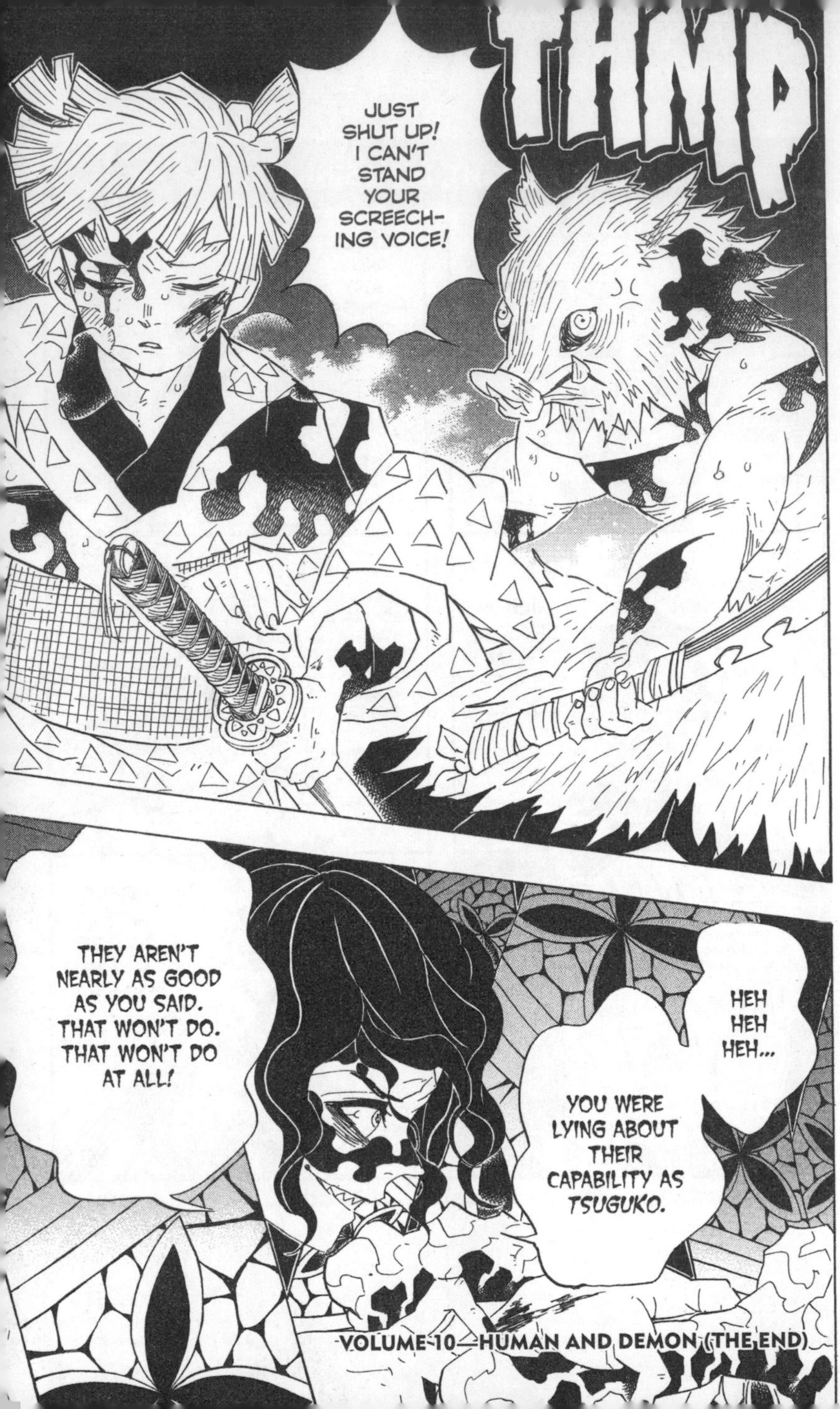
THMP
JUST SHUT UP! I CAN'T STAND YOUR SCREECH-ING VOICE!
HEH HEH HEH...
YOU WERE LYING ABOUT THEIR CAPABILITY AS *TSUGUKO*.
THEY AREN'T NEARLY AS GOOD AS YOU SAID. THAT WON'T DO. THAT WON'T DO AT ALL!

VOLUME 10—HUMAN AND DEMON (THE END)

ALL RIGHT, LET'S SING!

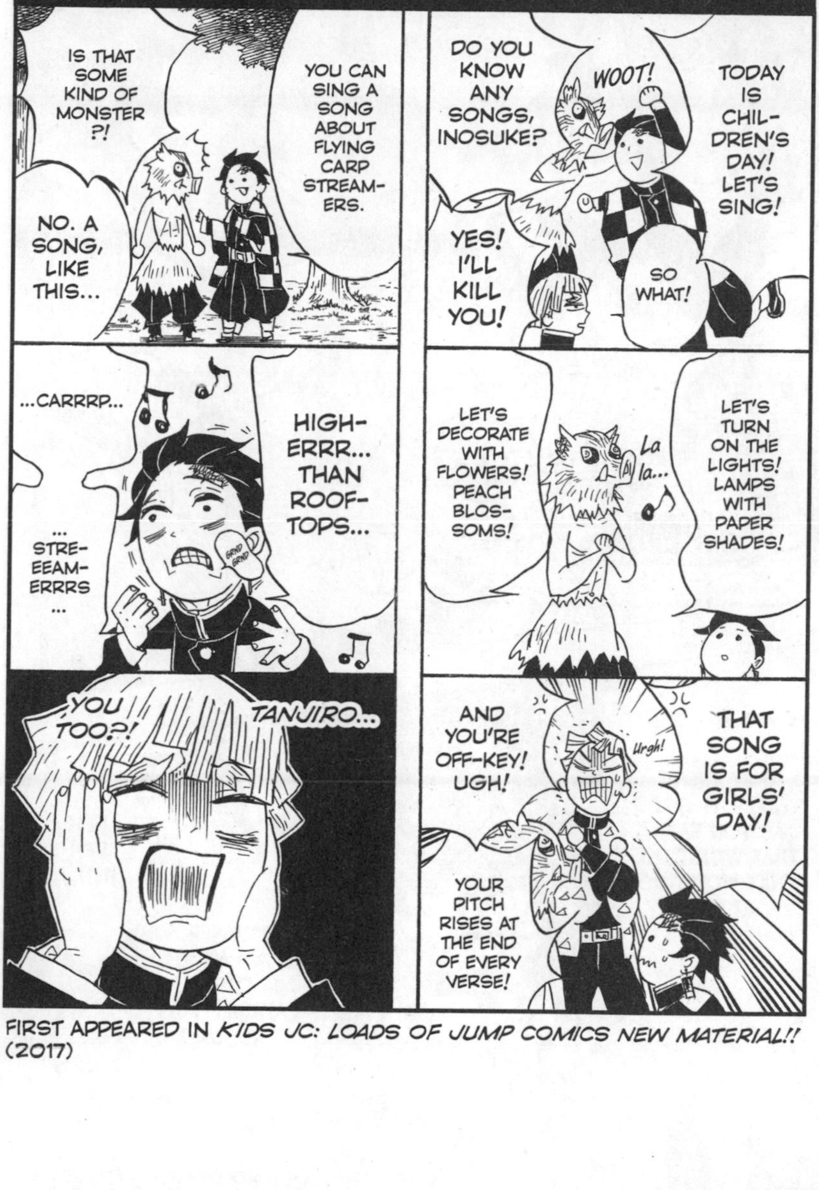
TODAY IS CHILDREN'S DAY! LET'S SING!
WOOT!
DO YOU KNOW ANY SONGS, INOSUKE?
SO WHAT!
YES! I'LL KILL YOU!
LET'S TURN ON THE LIGHTS! LAMPS WITH PAPER SHADES!
La la...
LET'S DECORATE WITH FLOWERS! PEACH BLOSSOMS!
THAT SONG IS FOR GIRLS' DAY!
Urgh!
AND YOU'RE OFF-KEY! UGH!
YOUR PITCH RISES AT THE END OF EVERY VERSE!
YOU CAN SING A SONG ABOUT FLYING CARP STREAMERS.
IS THAT SOME KIND OF MONSTER?!
NO. A SONG, LIKE THIS...
HIGHERRR... THAN ROOFTOPS...
GRND GRND
...CARRRP...
...STREEAMERRRS...
TANJIRO...
YOU TOO?!

FIRST APPEARED IN *KIDS JC: LOADS OF JUMP COMICS NEW MATERIAL!!* (2017)

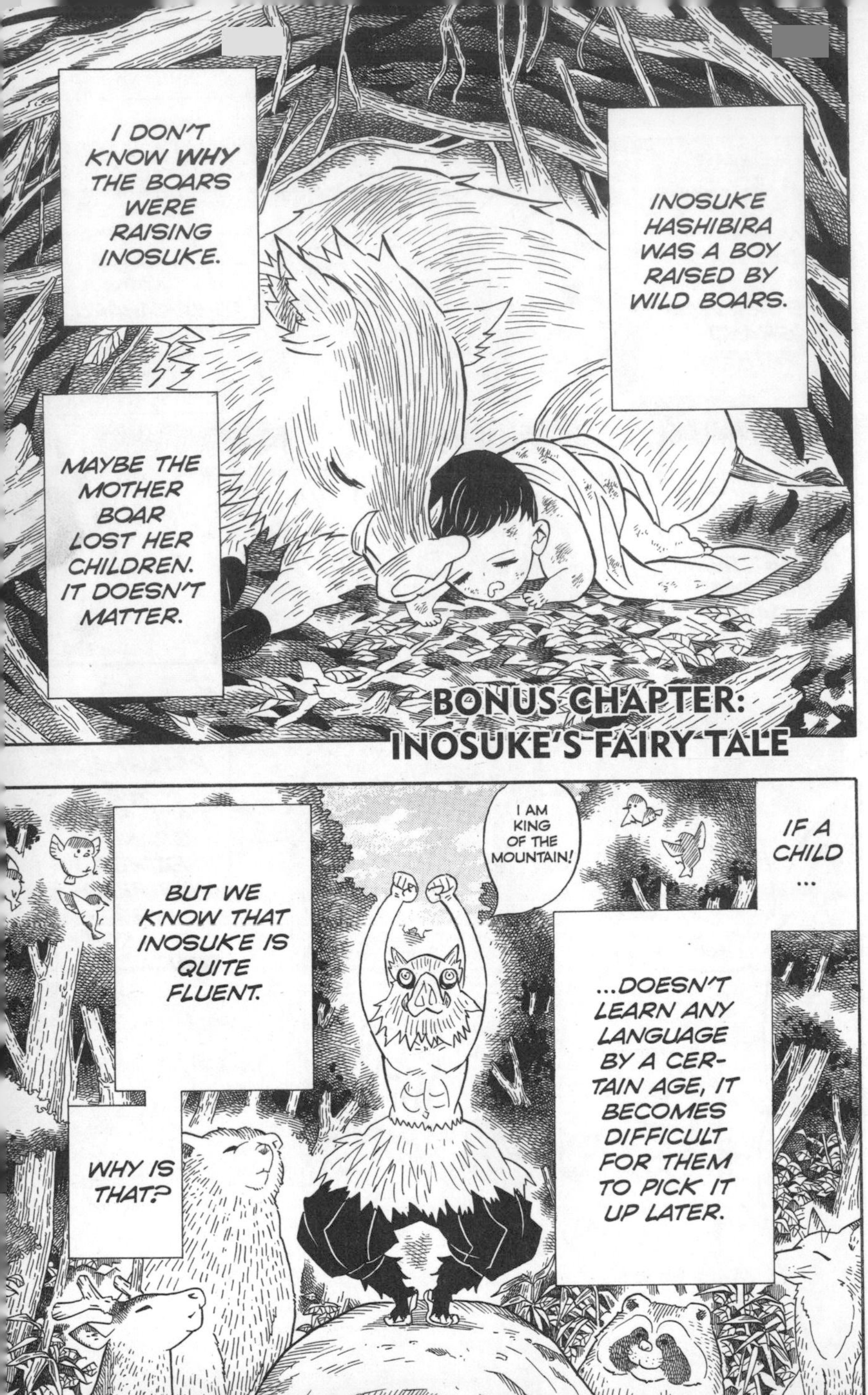
INOSUKE HASHIBIRA WAS A BOY RAISED BY WILD BOARS.
I DON'T KNOW WHY THE BOARS WERE RAISING INOSUKE.
MAYBE THE MOTHER BOAR LOST HER CHILDREN. IT DOESN'T MATTER.
BONUS CHAPTER: INOSUKE'S FAIRY TALE
IF A CHILD ...
...DOESN'T LEARN ANY LANGUAGE BY A CER-TAIN AGE, IT BECOMES DIFFICULT FOR THEM TO PICK IT UP LATER.
I AM KING OF THE MOUNTAIN!
BUT WE KNOW THAT INOSUKE IS QUITE FLUENT.
WHY IS THAT?

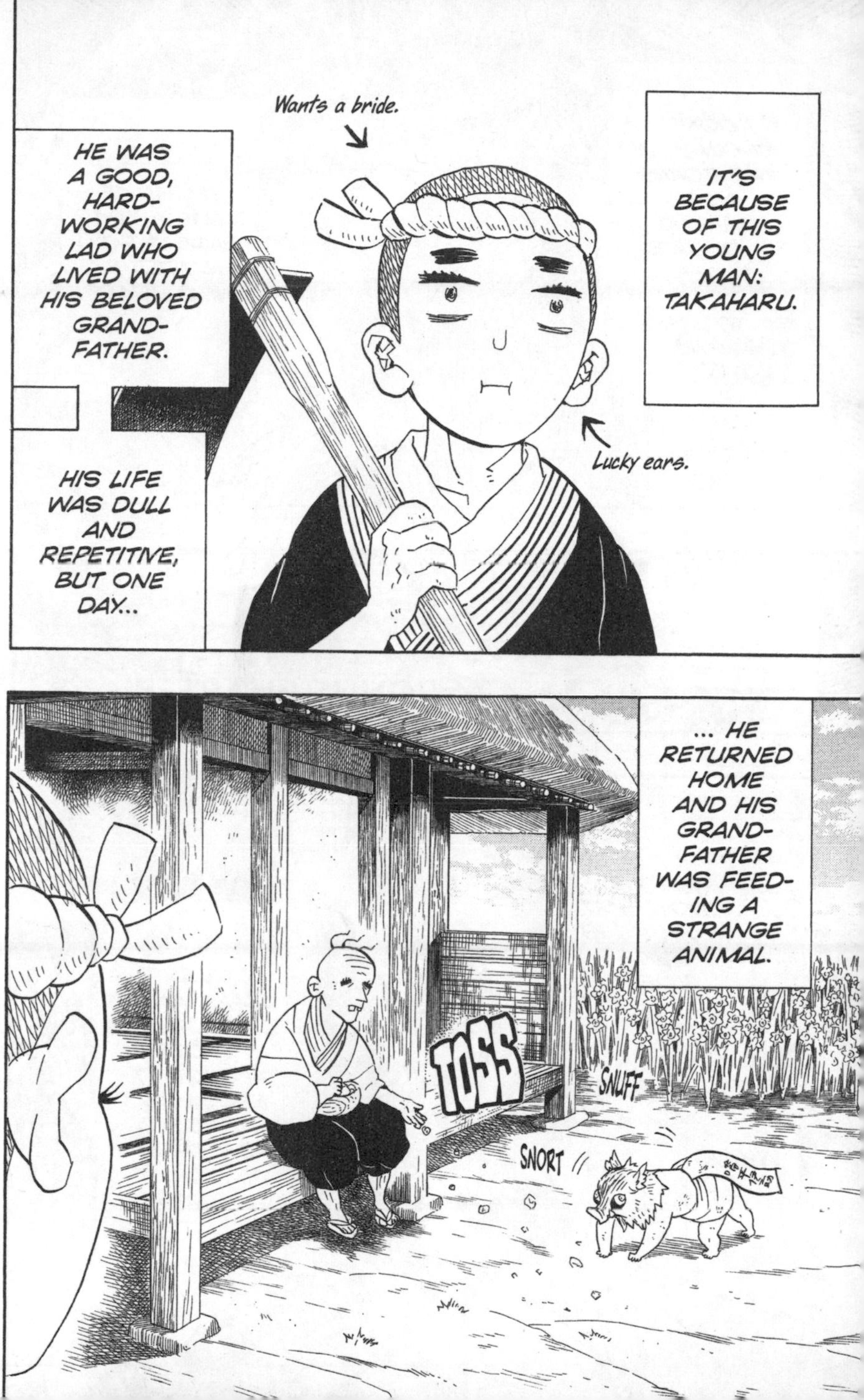
IT'S BECAUSE OF THIS YOUNG MAN: TAKAHARU.
Wants a bride.
Lucky ears.
HE WAS A GOOD, HARD-WORKING LAD WHO LIVED WITH HIS BELOVED GRAND-FATHER.
HIS LIFE WAS DULL AND REPETITIVE, BUT ONE DAY...
... HE RETURNED HOME AND HIS GRAND-FATHER WAS FEED-ING A STRANGE ANIMAL.
TOSS
SNUFF
SNORT

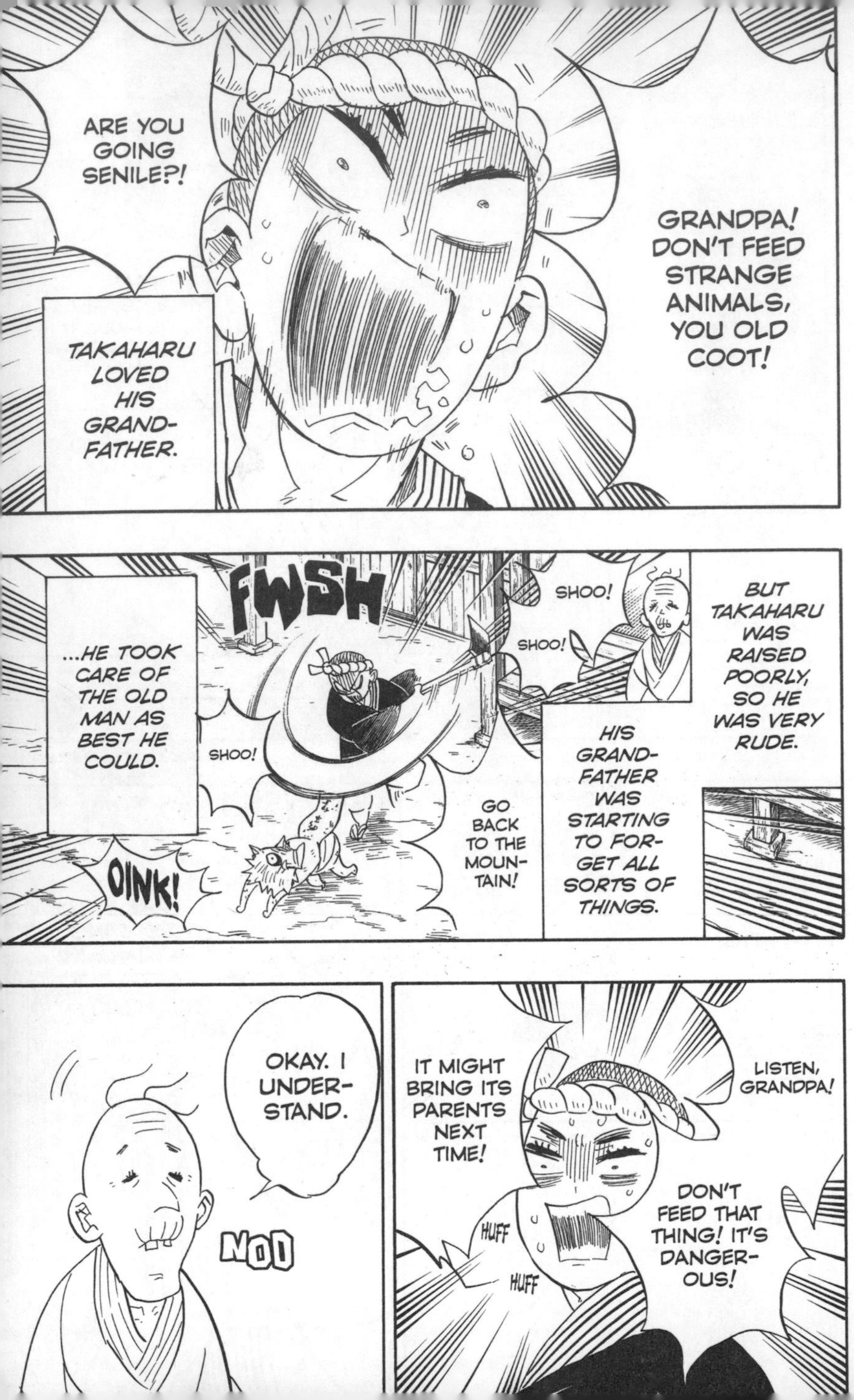
GRANDPA! DON'T FEED STRANGE ANIMALS, YOU OLD COOT!
ARE YOU GOING SENILE?!
TAKAHARU LOVED HIS GRAND-FATHER.
BUT TAKAHARU WAS RAISED POORLY, SO HE WAS VERY RUDE.
HIS GRAND-FATHER WAS STARTING TO FOR-GET ALL SORTS OF THINGS.
SHOO!
SHOO!
FWSH
...HE TOOK CARE OF THE OLD MAN AS BEST HE COULD.
SHOO!
GO BACK TO THE MOUN-TAIN!
OINK!
LISTEN, GRANDPA!
DON'T FEED THAT THING! IT'S DANGER-OUS!
IT MIGHT BRING ITS PARENTS NEXT TIME!
HUFF
HUFF
OKAY. I UNDER-STAND.
NOD

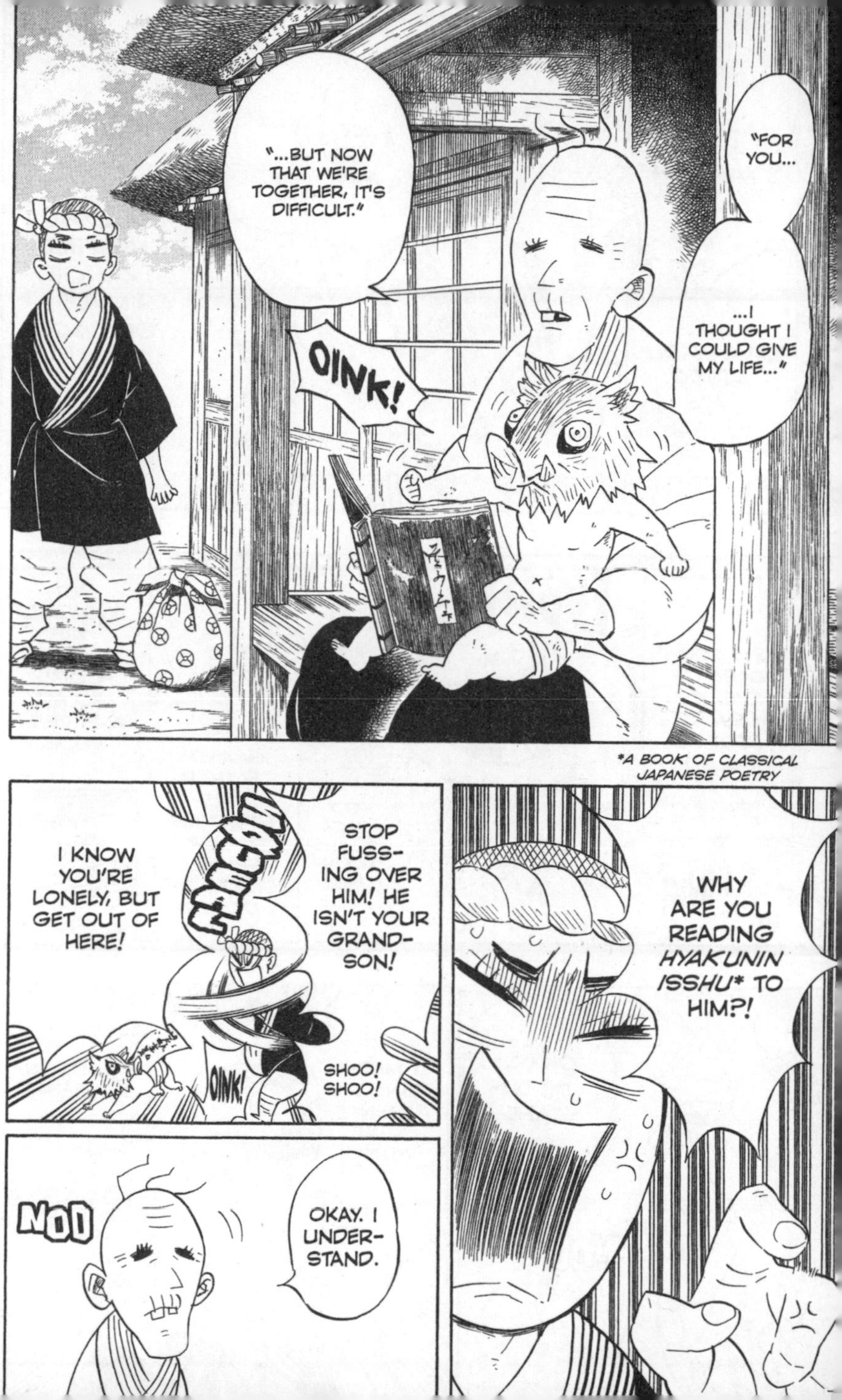
"FOR YOU...
...I THOUGHT I COULD GIVE MY LIFE..."
"...BUT NOW THAT WE'RE TOGETHER, IT'S DIFFICULT."
OINK!
WHY ARE YOU READING *HYAKUNIN ISSHU** TO HIM?!
STOP FUSSING OVER HIM! HE ISN'T YOUR GRANDSON!
I KNOW YOU'RE LONELY, BUT GET OUT OF HERE!
SHOO! SHOO!
OINK!
OKAY. I UNDERSTAND.
NOD

A BOOK OF CLASSICAL JAPANESE POETRY

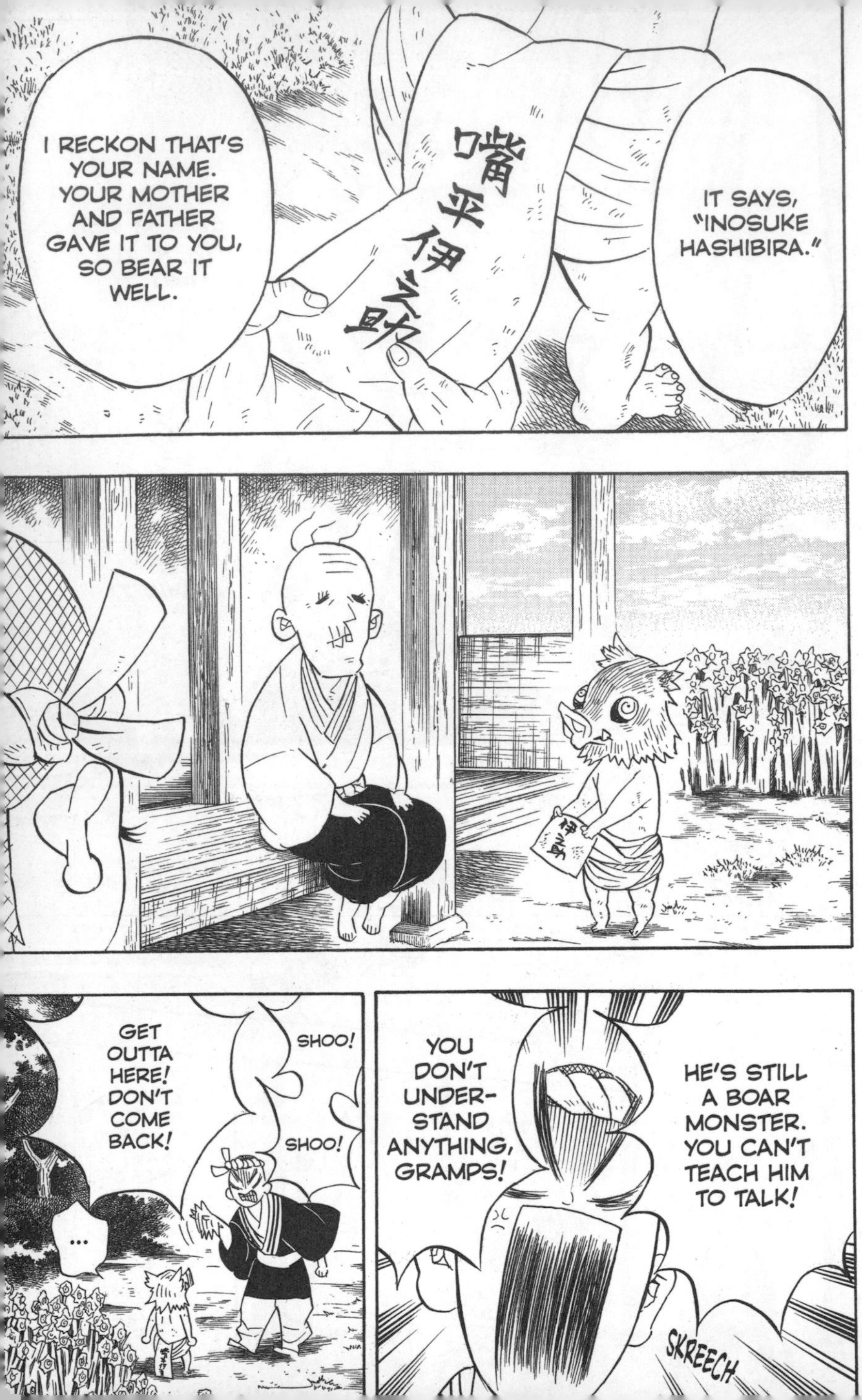
嘴平伊之助
IT SAYS, "INOSUKE HASHIBIRA."
I RECKON THAT'S YOUR NAME. YOUR MOTHER AND FATHER GAVE IT TO YOU, SO BEAR IT WELL.
HE'S STILL A BOAR MONSTER. YOU CAN'T TEACH HIM TO TALK!
YOU DON'T UNDER-STAND ANYTHING, GRAMPS!
SKREECH
SHOO!
SHOO!
GET OUTTA HERE! DON'T COME BACK!
...

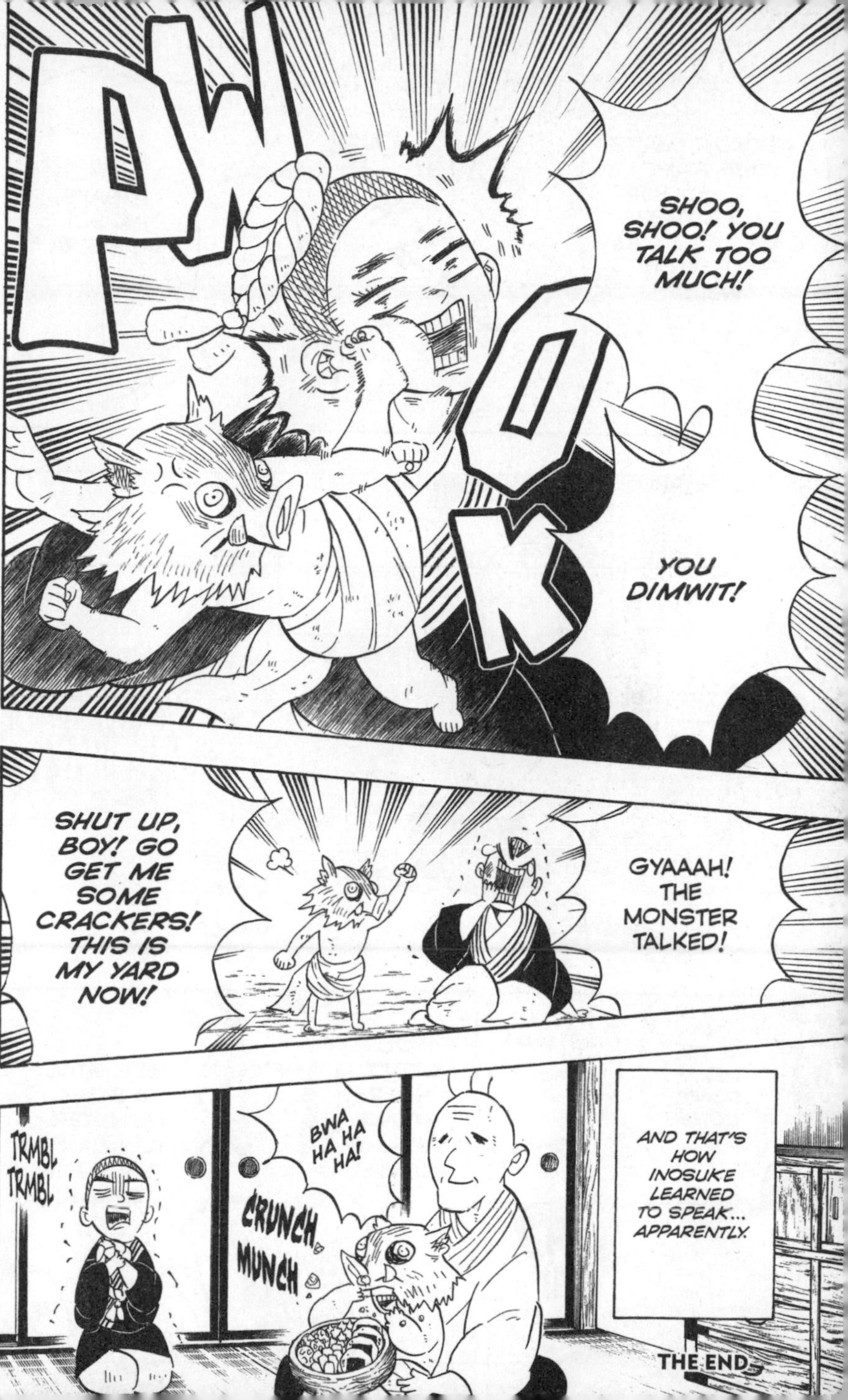
SHOO, SHOO! YOU TALK TOO MUCH!
YOU DIMWIT!
PWOK
GYAAAH! THE MONSTER TALKED!
SHUT UP, BOY! GO GET ME SOME CRACKERS! THIS IS MY YARD NOW!
AND THAT'S HOW INOSUKE LEARNED TO SPEAK... APPARENTLY.
BWA HA HA HA!
CRUNCH MUNCH
TRMBL TRMBL
THE END

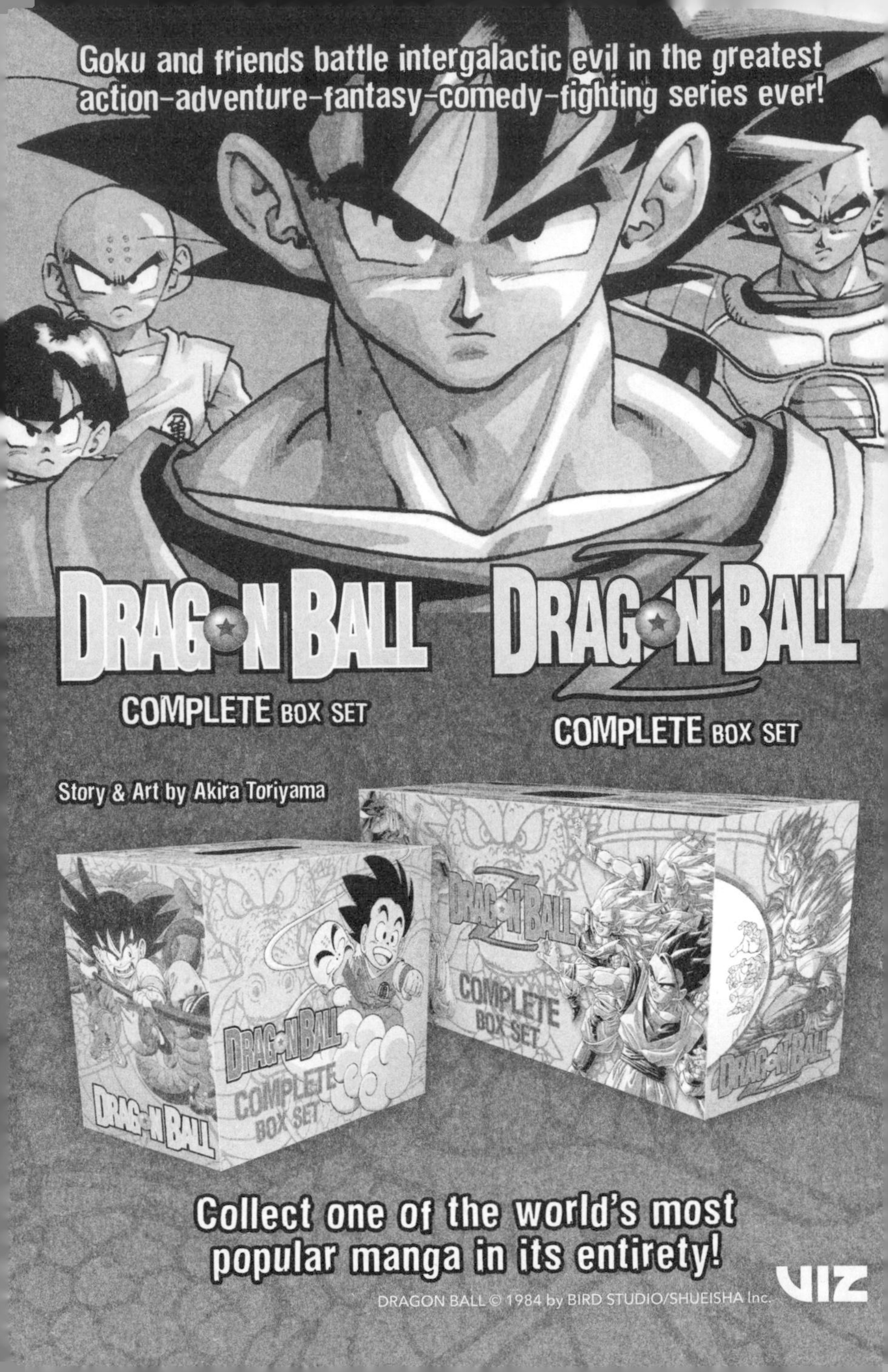
Goku and friends battle intergalactic evil in the greatest action-adventure-fantasy-comedy-fighting series ever!
DRAGON BALL
COMPLETE BOX SET
DRAGON BALL Z
COMPLETE BOX SET
Story & Art by Akira Toriyama
Collect one of the world's most popular manga in its entirety!
DRAGON BALL © 1984 by BIRD STUDIO/SHUEISHA Inc.
VIZ

Dr. STONE

STORY BY
RIICHIRO INAGAKI

ART BY
BOICHI

One fateful day, all of humanity turned to stone. Many millennia later, Taiju frees himself from petrification and finds himself surrounded by statues. The situation looks grim—until he runs into his science-loving friend Senku! Together they plan to restart civilization with the power of science!

YOU'RE READING THE
WRONG WAY!

DEMON SLAYER: KIMETSU NO YAIBA reads from right to left, starting in the upper-right corner. Japanese is read from right to left, meaning that action, sound effects and word-balloon order are completely reversed from English order.